Melville's Anatomies

Mark Milloff, *Queequeg Rescues Tashtego*, 1986. Pastel on paper, 48 × 48 in. Collection of Sandra and James Leitner.

Melville's Anatomies

Samuel Otter

UNIVERSITY OF CALIFORNIA PRESS
Berkeley · Los Angeles · London

The publisher gratefully acknowledges the generous contribution to this book provided by the General Endowment Fund of the Associates of the University of California Press.

University of California Press
Berkeley and Los Angeles, California

University of California Press, Ltd.
London, England

© 1999 by
The Regents of the University of California

Library of Congress Cataloging-in-Publication Data

Otter, Samuel, 1956–.
    Melville's anatomies / Samuel Otter.
        p.   cm.
    Includes bibliographic references and index.
    ISBN 0-520-20581-2 (cl : alk. paper).—
ISBN 0-520-20582-0 (pbk. : alk. paper)
        1. Melville, Herman, 1819–1891—
Knowledge—Anatomy.   2. Body, Human,
in literature   I. Title.
    PS2388.B57O88   1999
    813'.3—dc 21   97-50369

Printed in the United States of America

9 8 7 6 5 4 3 2 1

The paper used in this publication meets the minimum requirements of American National Standards
for Information Sciences—Permanence of Paper for
Printed Library Materials, ANSI Z39.48-1984.

For Caverlee

Give me a condor's quill! Give me Vesuvius' crater for an inkstand! Friends, hold my arms! For in the mere act of penning my thoughts of this Leviathan, they weary me, and make me faint with their outreaching comprehensiveness of sweep, as if to include the whole circle of the sciences, and all the generations of whales, and men, and mastodons, past, present, and to come, with all the revolving panoramas of empire on earth, and throughout the whole universe, not excluding its suburbs. Such, and so magnifying, is the virtue of a large and liberal theme! We expand to its bulk.

Herman Melville, Moby-Dick

Contents

Illustrations

Acknowledgments

In a famous 1851 letter to Hawthorne, Melville complains that he cannot attain "the silent grass-growing mood in which a man *ought* always
to compose." Instead he fears that he shall "at last be worn out and per-
ish, like an old nutmeg-grater, grated to pieces by the constant attrition
of the wood." The Berkeley English Department provided opportunities
for the grass to grow. I am grateful to the recent department chairs,
Anne Middleton, Frederick Crews, Ralph Rader, and Jeffrey Knapp, for
their confidence and support and especially for the time and space in
which this book was allowed to unfold. For respite from the nutmeg-
grater, in the form of fellowships and research funds, I am indebted to
the University of California, Berkeley, the Townsend Center for the Hu-
manities, and the Berkeley Committee on Research.

Dorothy Hale, Jeffrey Knapp, and Nancy Ruttenburg have been invaluable colleagues and the best of friends, and their intelligence and ca-
maraderie have made this book possible. Mitchell Breitwieser and Jenny
Franchot helped to shape this work through their trenchant responses,
as did the other four unnamed members of the Berkeley English department who evaluated my work at my fourth-year and tenure reviews.
Janadas Devan, Geraldine Heng, Suvir Kaul, and Martin Wechselblatt
have been paramount in my intellectual and personal life over the past
years, as have Gretta Anderson, Phillip Barrish, Paul Bay, Judy Frank,
Rosemary Kegl, David and Ellen Knudsen, James Lance, Christopher
Newfield, and Kathy Smits.

I am grateful for the support of the Editorial Committee of the University of California Press. In an act of extraordinary generosity, David Leverenz, one of the readers for California, wrote the most detailed, encouraging, and discerning reviewer's report any writer could wish. The following pages have benefited also from the scrupulous attention of other readers for California and other presses, including Robert S. Levine and Priscilla Wald, and from the suggestions of William Murphy, my original editor at California. William bolstered the manuscript and its author, as did his successor, Linda Norton. Erika Büky and Jan Johnson skillfully oversaw the production of the book. As copyeditor, Mandy Woods sharpened its lines. Sean Goudie, Joe Jeon, Ann-Marie Karlsson, Julie Ruiz, and Lynette Ubois helped with research and manuscript preparation. I have been lucky at Berkeley to work with a spectacularly talented group of graduate students. I learned most of what I know about nineteenth-century American literature from Michael J. Colacurcio, Henry Louis Gates, Jr., and Mark Seltzer, all of whom assisted with this project in its early stages. William Paul taught me the pleasures of close reading. Louise DeSalvo, Dorothy Mermin, and James Ransom sustained me at crucial stages of my career.

Parts of chapters 1 and 2 were first published in *The Cambridge Companion to Herman Melville,* edited by Robert S. Levine (New York: Cambridge University Press, 1998). Parts of chapter 4 were first published in *American Literature* 66 (1994): 55–81 and in *Melville's Ever-moving Dawn: Centennial Essays,* edited by John Bryant and Robert Milder (Kent, Ohio: Kent State University Press, 1997). The Art Institute of Chicago, the Bancroft Library, the Bernice P. Bishop Museum Press, the Brown University Library, the Metropolitan Museum of Art, and the National Gallery of London granted permission to reproduce the illustrations in this book. Mark Milloff and Sandra and James Leitner graciously allowed me to use *Queequeg Rescues Tashtego* as the frontispiece. The following professional organizations provided venues in which I was able to present and test my ideas: the Modern Language Association, the American Studies Association, the American Literature Association, the Melville Society, Interdisciplinary Nineteenth-Century Studies, and the International Association of Word and Image Studies. My debt to individual scholars will be clear in the following pages.

Sometimes perplexed but always encouraging, many family members watched as this book developed, especially Marjorie Otter, Nelson Otter, Ruth and Philip Rubinstein, and William and Marion Sherry. Much credit must be given to Jeanne and Robert Otter, who did not live to see this publication, and to Sara and Sturges Cary, my other parents. Neither I nor this book would be here today if it were not for the humanity and skill of Robert Meister and others at the National Cancer Institute. As my dedication implies, for her intellectual companionship, her patience, her humor, and her love, I would like to thank, most of all, Caverlee Cary.

Introduction

Intimate Excess

In *Queequeg Rescues Tashtego*, reproduced as the frontispiece of this book, Mark Milloff goes where no illustrator of *Moby-Dick* has gone before: inside the sperm whale's head. Improvising on the chapter "Cistern and Buckets," Milloff shows the Polynesian harpooneer diving into the "secret inner chamber and sanctum sanctorum of the whale" to save the Native American Tashtego, who has fallen in the head while emptying its precious contents.[1] Queequeg plunges toward the viewer, his muscular arm grasping Tashtego's hair as he prepares to use his boarding-sword to extricate him. Tashtego's head at the lower left and Queequeg's lustrous skull at the center are balanced at the upper right by a shark's head, pierced by a harpoon, its jaws locked open. Inside the whale are not only other heads and arms and jaws, but also eyes. Above Tashtego, embedded in the flesh, a lidless pupil and iris stare at Queequeg's limbs. Other eyes gaze out at the viewer: a small, pale eye above the harpooneer's raised hand, the bloodshot eye of the shark, the eye-like wheels in the torn line of tackle, and especially Queequeg's glistening orb. Only the apparently unconscious Tashtego's eyes remain closed. Ropes, blubber hook, and cables curl around the Polynesian in the murky interior. The bubbles rising to the right of the shark's mouth, too large to be the product of its own gasps, suggest that the huge severed head itself is breathing—is alive.

In Melville's chapter, Queequeg slices open the whale's head, reaches in, and pulls out Tashtego. Translating reach into dive, Milloff emphasizes

the force of the efforts to gain access to the whale's interior that are catalogued in the cetological chapters that precede and follow "Cistern and
Buckets." In the book, Queequeg's skin is a "dark, purplish, yellow
color" (21), checkered with tattoos. In smoothing Queequeg's skin, the
artist draws attention to the surface of his body amid the chaos of forms,
as characters in several of Melville's early books will look to the colors,
shapes, and textures of the body for meaning and order. Rather than literally illustrating scenes from the book, Milloff provides visual analogues for the topics and textures of Melville's prose. With a keen eye
and ear, he conveys the bold gestures toward the reader; the corporeal
immersions; the visceral, viscous desires; the strange incorporations and
animations; the twisting of lines and turning of tropes; and the piercing,
unsettling scrutiny. Like Melville's prose, Milloff's picture represents the
quest for depth through overwrought surface. The excess first drew me
to Melville. That excess—revealing, intricate, funny—will be the obsession of this book.[2]

At the center of Melville's texts in the first phase of his career is the
human body, tangled in lines of knowledge and desire. In *Typee* (1846),
a sailor hiding in a valley on one of the Marquesan islands is troubled
by the tattoos on the bodies of his hosts. He violently recoils at the
prospect of having his own face marked. In *White-Jacket* (1850), a sailor
serving on a regimented naval vessel wears a white cloak that becomes
unendurably scarred and burdensome. He slices himself out of his own
skin. In *Moby-Dick* (1851), all eyes focus on the massive corpus of the
whale. Associating cetology with ethnology, Ishmael details the epic
quest for the secrets of the body, and especially of the head, which en-
grosses narrator, characters, and writer. In *Pierre* (1852), the narrator
links the exterior landscape of the nation to the interior landscape of his
young American heir. This narrator holds out his character's heart to his
readers, and crushes it.

In the chapters that follow, I read these texts and these scenes in the
contexts of contemporary discourses of racial encounter (South Pacific
narratives, seamen's narratives, slaves' narratives) and racial ethnology
(the "American school" of Samuel George Morton, Josiah Nott, and
George Gliddon); aesthetic treatises, gift books, and landscape paintings
(particularly works by Thomas Cole, Nathaniel Parker Willis, and Susan Cooper); and essays and novels of sentiment by antebellum women
and men (such as Fanny Fern and Donald Grant Mitchell). Some of
these texts are documented sources for Melville; others share formal and

figural concerns. While benefiting from the invaluable work of Melville scholars, I also extend the notion of sources to include patterns of representation in which Melville participates, even if we have not been able to demonstrate that he owned or read particular volumes. I press the relationship between Melville and his sources as Melville himself does, treating them not as informational ballast or dross to be transmuted into literary gold, but as revealing structures that show how nineteenth-century Americans articulated their world.

In the first three chapters, I argue that the corporeal fascinations in *Typee, White-Jacket,* and *Moby-Dick* are charged by nineteenth-century efforts to know the racial body. In these texts, Melville examines how the parts of the body—face, skin, and head—became invested with world historical meanings. In the last two chapters, I argue that in *Pierre* Melville explores the operations of ideology, in the visual education of the early chapters and in the narrator's scrutiny of his protagonist's heart and mind over the course of the book. Melville restages crucial scenes in antebellum United States culture, exposing and analyzing their characters, properties, scripts, and motivations. He brings exorbitant pressure to bear on the fraught figures of antebellum discourse. In *Typee,* the key figure is the sacred symbol of the Caucasian face, whose impeccable features secure identity; in *White-Jacket,* it is the analogy with slavery, the pivot upon which antebellum debate about individual rights turns; in *Moby-Dick,* it is the synecdoche of the head, seen as the key to politics, aesthetics, and history; in *Pierre,* it is the catachresis of the eloquent heart, the organ which comes to have a voice and to assume material form on the surface of the printed page.

In my arguments, the corporeal obsessions of Melville, Hawthorne, Poe, Whitman, and Dickinson are illuminated by the ardor of ethnologists and by the ethnological critiques of Frederick Douglass, William Wells Brown, and William Apess. Herman Melville and Lydia Maria Child are joined as acute explorers of ethnology and intersubjectivity. Donald Grant Mitchell, Herman Melville, and Fanny Fern participate in a shared project of sentimental exposure. While my chapters may seem to digress in that monstrous or magnificent (depending on one's taste) Melvillean way, I seek to detail the rich discursive terrain in which Melville positions himself. In his extended fiction, Melville incorporates a vast amount of material, painstakingly attends to detail, and shows that conventional forms are not empty but, rather, are full of meaning. To read Melville closely is to read deeply and widely. The interpretations of passages in the following chapters are formal, contextual, historical, and ideological. In searching for sources of Melville's excess, we will travel far.

I discuss the attractions but resist the formulations of Melville as outcast, the "isolato" striving for original expression against the constraints of conventional antebellum America (the traditional critical view of Melville), and of Melville as the product of circumstance (the newer "historical" view). I argue for a Melville fascinated with the rhetorical structures and ideological functions of antebellum discourse. Melville offers neither a transcendent critique nor a symptomatic recapitulation, but an inside sense of the power of ideology, its satisfactions and its incarcerations. Thus I argue for a notion of verbal doubleness in Melville that is different from the deus ex machina of irony often used to redeem him from the taint of his culture or from the too-easy ambivalence used to describe an author said to see "both sides." Melville is critical but does not claim, or rather realizes that he cannot sustain, an outsider's privilege. Instead of dismissing contemporary beliefs about race, nation, and self, he acknowledges their appeal and probes their sources and sway.[3]

I offer the term "anatomy" to invoke the literary genre whose forms and gestures Melville drew upon, to describe Melville's concern with ideology, and to emphasize his examination of the body and its parts. The first Melville critic to use the term "anatomy" was Fitz-James O'Brien, who, in a sympathetic but exasperated review in 1857, laments that Melville had demonstrated that he was capable of writing "good, strong, sweet, clear English" but persists in "distorting the images of his mind, and in deodorizing the flowers of his fancy; a man born to create, who resolves to anatomize; a man born to see, who insists upon speculating." O'Brien argues that Melville's works register "the conflict between resolute nature and stubborn cultivation," with nature calling for an unobtrusive representation of "the realities of life and man" and cultivation responding "No! you shall dissect and divide; you shall cauterize and confound; you shall amaze and electrify; you shall be as grotesquely terrible as Callot, as subtly profound as Balzac, as formidably satirical as Rabelais." O'Brien's insights about Melville's conflicted impulses and formal mixtures will be developed by twentieth-century critics. He suggests a restless dissecting consciousness that will be the focus of this book.[4]

Ever since Northrop Frye revived scholarly interest in the genre of the anatomy in *Anatomy of Criticism* (1957) and identified *Moby-Dick* as part anatomy and part romance, critics have placed Melville's texts in the tradition of Lucian, Petronius, Erasmus, Rabelais, Burton, Bayle, Swift, Voltaire, and Sterne. I am less concerned here with the history of genre than with the functions of form in the antebellum United States. My claims about Melville have been shaped by theoretical accounts of the anatomy provided by Frye and by Mikhail Bakhtin: the heterogeneous, omnivorous, encyclopedic, rhetorically experimental, stylistically dense form, in which linguistic features—diction, syntax, metaphor—become the vehicle for intellectual inquiry. According to Bakhtin, these features express orientations toward society, time, nation, and tradition that are laid bare in the literary anatomy.[5]

I use the term "anatomy" to describe the material analyses of consciousness conducted by Melville in the first phase of his career. From *Typee* through *Pierre,* Melville attempts to provide what Antonio Gramsci has called an "inventory" of the verbal contents of consciousness. The relentless borrowings and turnings in Melville's prose give heft to thought: the incorporated passages, incessant allusions, layered symbols, and eerie personifications. The excess in Melville's anatomies derives, in part, from the scope and reach of this task. Melville analyzes what Raymond Williams has called "structures of feeling," the complex dynamics through which form and response shape meaning and value. Such an effort elicits the remarkable intimacies of Melville's first phase—the theatrical confessions, exuberant embrace of readers, pressing of boundaries, and bodily exposures. "Race" is a key epistemological category for Melville, as it was for his culture and continues to be for our own. In his meticulous anatomies, Melville insists that readers acknowledge "race" not as the abstract property of others but as the grammar book of graded meanings that United States culture has assigned to the features of human bodies. He details what Foucault has called "the nomination of the visible." Melville shows how a world of definition, coherence, and difference became located in the skin and in the skull.[6]

In his anatomies, Melville combines the encyclopedic form and extravagant rhetoric of the literary anatomy with nineteenth-century ideology critique. Anatomies have been part of the American tradition in literature dating back to Cotton Mather's *Magnalia Christi Americana* (1701). Melville's books are part of a renaissance of anatomy in the decades before the Civil War. Theorists have advanced the idea that there have been national occasions for the literary anatomy, periods of interpretive crisis that renew interest in its mixed forms and discursive

inquiries. I suggest several circumstances that helped to incite the antebellum anatomy: the obsession with slavery; the intellectual and rhetorical passions of racial scientists; American encounters with South Pacific
cultures; the struggles for territorial possession; and the expanding literary market. Terry Eagleton argues that the term "ideology" arose in
late-eighteenth-century bourgeois Europe, "at the historical point where
systems of ideas first became aware of their own partiality; and this
came about when those ideas were forced to encounter alien or alternative forms of discourse." Much of the textual production of the
antebellum United States is marked by such a sense of partiality and self-
consciousness, fractured by alien encounters.[7]

Melville performs anatomies of anatomies. He tests the limits of
analysis and critique. In inhabiting the structures of antebellum discourse, Melville comes to occupy an increasingly precarious position.
He is not a transcendent but an immanent manipulator, subject to en-
tanglement and complicity. Melville's closest attention is not directed
toward the form or features of another. The face whose contours he outlines, the skin whose substance he examines, the head whose contents
he inventories, and the heart whose motions he traces are his own. Lay-
ing himself open, he exposes shared structures of feeling and belief.
Across the chapters, I trace Melville's development, climax, and retreat
from his anatomy project.

Although I discuss other works by Melville, I focus on *Typee, White-
Jacket, Moby-Dick,* and *Pierre* because of the remarkable ways in which
these texts conjoin corporeal, discursive, and ideological inquiry. *Mardi*
(1849) would seem to be a likely candidate for inclusion, given its pro-
lixity and its concern with the definitions and deformations of human
bodies. Yet *Mardi* treats its bodies thematically rather than substantially.
In Volume Two, Melville represents the tropes and twisted bodies of
Manifest Destiny. Yet in *Mardi* the rhetoric and the history are separate
rather than fused. The corporeal conceits and political allegory are located in different chapters. Melville juxtaposes the reduced and divided
bodies of the island inhabitants with the inflated oratory of Manifest
Destiny, thus suggesting the double operation of American expansion-
ism. Yet he does not provide the kind of sustained performative critique
found in his most telling anatomies. Often the verbosity in *Mardi* serves
merely as self-display or pedantry or excess for the sake of excess, rather
than also serving as the object of analysis. Melville tends to flex his
rhetorical muscles more than he dissects them. Although there is nothing wrong with writerly exhibitionism (as any Melville devotee must

concede), the shapelessness of *Mardi* renders it a less revealing work. More literary than literal anatomy, steeped in Melville's encounter with Rabelais, Browne, and Burton, *Mardi* seems to have energized his rhetoric and intellect and enabled the palpable achievements of *Moby-Dick* and *Pierre*.[8]

One of the oldest gestures in twentieth-century Melville criticism is to invoke a passage from the famous letter Melville wrote to Hawthorne in May or early June 1851 in order to construct a tragic Melville and ratify a set of defining oppositions: "What I feel most moved to write, that is banned,—it will not pay. Yet, altogether, write the *other* way I cannot. So the product is a final hash, and all my books are botches." Written by Melville on his farm in Pittsfield, Massachusetts, while he struggled to finish *Moby-Dick,* this passage has assumed an almost incantatory quality for Melville critics. The lines have been used to summon a series of biographical images: the Thwarted Melville, the Torn Melville, the Botched Melville—a Melville pulled apart by the urge for self-expression and the need to cater to the constricting expectations of a mid-nineteenth-century readership. "What I feel most moved to write" is set against "the other way," the impulses of the first-person male author are set against the demands of the "mass audience" or "the common reader" (often figured as female), creator is set against consumer, elite against popular, pure against contaminated, freedom against necessity, depth against surface. Undoubtedly, Melville felt confined by his real and imagined audiences. In the summer of 1851, he was writing under severe financial and domestic pressures. Yet the "other way" model does not begin to articulate the tangled relationships among its terms or between Melville's texts and the world of texts that surrounds them. The passage is often abstracted from the letter, in which Melville offers several self-representations to the successful Hawthorne. Over the course of this book, I will open up these critical conventions and offer a different Melville—a Melville who analyzes the forces that move him to feel, who examines the ties between his way and the ways of others, and whose botches are the product of his effort to anatomize nineteenth-century American features and figures.[9]

To read Melville closely is a pleasure and a risk. In his reflexive textual surfaces, we may see our own assumptions. We may find our own approaches tested.[10] This book both analyzes and embodies Melville's intimate excess. Somewhat obsessively, I attempt to get inside Melville's voluminous effort to get inside his compatriots' heads. I hope this enterprise will reveal, rather than confine. In the "Epilogue" to *Moby-Dick,*

Melville describes Ishmael's position, which is also the position of writer and readers:

> So, floating on the margin of the ensuing scene, and in full sight of it, when the half-spent suction of the sunk ship reached me, I was then, but slowly, drawn towards the closing vortex. When I reached it, it had subsided to a creamy pool. Round and round, then, and ever contracting towards the button-like black bubble at the axis of that slowly wheeling circle, like another Ixion I did revolve. Till, gaining that vital centre, the black bubble upward burst. (573)

These are the rhetorical and ideological movements of Melville's anatomies: pulling viewers from the margin to the center, turning them around, drawing them into and behind the eye.

CHAPTER I

Losing Face in *Typee*

"A white man decomposing is a ghastly sight," writes D. H. Lawrence, in an influential attempt to answer one of the oldest questions in criticism of Melville's first book, *Typee: A Peep at Polynesian Life* (1846): Why does the narrator and protagonist Tommo violently flee the South Sea "paradise" he encounters on the island of Nukuheva? According to Lawrence, he flees because he perceives the danger that this "soft hell" poses to his conscious, strenuous, progressive Western sense of self. "If you prostitute your psyche by returning to the savages," explains Lawrence, "you gradually go to pieces." The Pacific is the realm of sleep and unconsciousness, containing fragments of the Stone Age surviving in the modern world, "a vast vacuum." While burying his explicit concern with race, the traditional line of twentieth-century *Typee* criticism follows Lawrence, retaining the racialist emphasis on the spiritual dangers faced by the Western sojourner in the Pacific islands. When a Westerner arrives in the valley of the Typee, it is argued, an evolutionary psychodrama is played out in which an advanced stage of consciousness confronts an earlier stage. The sojourner is attracted to the apparent simplicity and ease of life in the northwest Marquesas, but ultimately recoils from it, recognizing its emptiness and violence and choosing a frustrated, anxious Western identity over no identity at all.[1]

Despite the recent turn in criticism that has emphasized Melville's ironic manipulation of point of view in order to critique the narrator Tommo's perspective, Lawrence is right. While Melville does not share

Lawrence's stark evolutionary sense of the gap separating the Pacific and the Atlantic, in *Typee* he was absorbed by the linked concerns of race, masculinity, and disintegration, that come together in the ghastly sight of a white man decomposing. Melville identifies two Marquesan practices that specifically threaten the narrator's identity and impel his flight: cannibalism and tattooing. The narrative foregrounds these two practices, but it does so in different ways and with different results.

Although many critics have fixed upon cannibalism as the "dark refrain" that haunts the text and "the horror that exists not far beneath the placid surface" of the Typee valley, for Melville cannibalism is not the universally recognized sign of savage difference. Tommo might be eaten on the island of Nukuheva, and such an event would be unfortunate, but far more troubling to Melville is the prospect that Tommo will be incorporated in native systems in a more enduring sense: not through metabolism but through inscription.[2] The violations of cannibalism and tattooing are twinned in the pages of *Typee*. Male identity is threatened by violent assault, directed most forcefully and fearsomely at the face and head—the crucial, vulnerable surfaces of human identity. In a pattern of representation repeated in *White-Jacket* (1850) and *Moby-Dick* (1851), the most penetrating assault envisions the body not as meat to be sliced and devoured but as a text to be engraved and read.[3]

To specify the geography in which this action takes place and to detail the processes of Tommo's aesthetic and psychic decomposition, I interpret Melville's representations of cannibalism and tattooing in two related contexts: first, in late-eighteenth- and nineteenth-century narratives of Pacific and particularly Marquesan encounter, many of which Melville used as sources in writing *Typee;* and second, in late-eighteenth- and nineteenth-century racial ethnology.[4] In the shift from cannibalism to tattooing as the keen threat to identity faced by the Western sojourner on Nukuheva, Melville discloses anxieties about racial identity and particularly about the assumptions and procedures of the influential antebellum "American school" of ethnology. The "American school" sought to divide the human body into significant features and to engrave character on its surface. The key sites of attention were the face, the head, and the skin. Melville's uneasiness about tattooing reflects with a vengeance American obsessions with making the surface of the body speak eloquently of inherent human difference. In the graphic consequences of Marquesan tattooing as represented in *Typee,* the procedures of this "American school" are rendered vivid and disturbing. Tommo is threatened with disintegration when the Marquesan tattooist Karky turns from his work to confront the Western observer and, in a striking reversal, Tommo—and especially his *face*—becomes the object of this kind of devouring, inditing knowledge.

OF CANNIBALISM: EATING THE BODY IN COOK, KRUSENSTERN, AND PORTER

Part autobiography, part anthropology, part travelogue, part adventure story, part social criticism, *Typee* is the account of an American sailor's four-month stay among a group of islanders on Nukuheva in the east-central Pacific Ocean. The narrator, who calls himself Tom and is later dubbed "Tommo" by the islanders, is a crew member on the American whaleship *Dolly*. Along with his friend Toby, he breaks his contract to serve because he feels that the captain has wrongly permitted abuses to flourish on board ship. Coming to the Marquesas with a set of expectations about the "civilized" and the "savage," the narrator is transfixed by the question of cannibalism. Has he landed in the valley of the ferocious Typee or in that of the friendly Happar? This question is posed over and over again during the first part of the narrative.[5]

Typee or Happar? The anxious refrain echoes the founding European trope of colonial encounter in the Caribbean: Carib or Arawak? Fierce cannibal or noble savage? Yet from the start of *Typee*, the refrain echoes with a difference. Both Typee and Happar are cannibals. The choice, as the narrator points out, is no longer the clear one (at least in Western eyes) between flesh eater and noble savage; instead, it is the less reassuring alternative posed by two varieties of cannibal. This unsettling of terms is the first of many gestures in *Typee* that question the naming of "savages." After situating a narrative of Typee ferocity in the context of American military atrocity, Melville concludes: "Thus it is that they whom we denominate 'savages' are made to deserve the title" (26). Refuting the growing consensus among mid-nineteenth-century ethnologists, Melville argues that savagery is not innate but is a product of the "fatal embrace" of islander and European (26).[6]

By the time of *Typee*—the middle of the nineteenth century—horror stories of cannibalism had become a staple in narratives of South Sea encounter. The various accounts of Cook's voyages published in the late eighteenth century were significant texts in this genre. Despite doubts about the existence and prevalence of anthropophagy, and in the face of tenuous evidence, such stories took on a life of their own. The "facts" of cannibalism were amplified and filled with meaning by

Euro-American observers. As William Arens sharply puts it, the idea of cannibalism was "able to gain and retain the aura of essential truth through telling and retelling." I do not mean here to "formalize" cannibalism, to deny its occurrence or assert wholesale European literary invention. Observers did report instances of anthropophagy in the South Pacific. Yet the enormity of these reports in European interpretations and evaluations of South Pacific cultures was out of proportion to the indigenous significance of the practice. In *Typee,* Melville uses this disproportion to forge narrative suspense, and he interrogates the content of its forms.[7]

Certain stories seem to have captured the public imagination in the late eighteenth and early nineteenth centuries. On board Captain Cook's ship *Resolution,* it is reported, New Zealanders consumed a steak sliced from a human head. Captain Brown, of the whaleship *Catherine,* we are told, was lured on shore by the ferocious Typees "to gratify their cannibal appetites," and was forced to watch the ovens being prepared for his own roasting. He barely escaped his fate, with the assistance of a Spanish boy who had been adopted by another Nukuhevan tribe. Firsthand experience of anthropophagism is rare. Stories feed upon stories. In *Typee,* Melville offers a version of the Captain Brown story, substituting for the Spanish boy a young native girl, a Pocahontas-like intermediary who risks her life to save that of the captain (25). This alteration seems to be a joke about redemptive native interpositions in narratives of colonial captivity in general and about the emblematic and immensely popular John Smith narrative in particular: Melville's gesture evokes Smith's placement of Pocahontas between his head and the clubs of the Algonquian warriors in the 1624 version of his captivity. Melville's gesture also prefigures his own insistently artificial insertion of the beautiful Fayaway.[8]

The story of the events on board Cook's *Resolution* offers a resonant example of the conventions and conundrums of the cannibal narrative. In November 1773, during Cook's second voyage, the *Resolution* was anchored in Queen Charlotte Sound in New Zealand. Some of the officers went ashore, where they discovered the head of a man, viscera strewn on the ground, and a heart stuck on a spear and tied to the prow of a canoe; cannibalism is thus shown to tear out and expose the insides. One of the officers traded a New Zealander two nails for the severed head, which he then proceeded to take on board the ship. To the horror of some, the indignation of others, and the laughter of still others, the natives on board the ship cut pieces of flesh from the head and then broiled and avidly ate them.

In stories of cannibalism, the human head is portrayed as the particular target of native violence. William Wales, the *Resolution*'s astronomer, elongates the details of corporeal discovery on shore in his version of the story. He describes the finding of the body parts one by one, thereby distending the horror.

James Burney, another Cook seaman, also masterfully draws out the lurid details in his telling of a related cannibal narrative—that of the December 1773 "Massacre at Grass Cove."[9] Burney extends over several pages the discovery of grisly evidence on a beach in Queen Charlotte Sound. The sailors find shoes that belong to one of Cook's midshipmen, a piece of fresh meat, baskets full of roasted flesh, more shoes, and finally the pièce de résistance: the severed hand of one of their shipmates, identified by his tattooed initials. In this account, tattooing discloses identity. Such betrayals become the crosscultural obsession of *Typee*. In Burney, the few strokes that compose the sailor's initials confirm the identity of his severed hand and the loss of his devoured body. In Melville, the profuse lines in Marquesan tattooing threaten to unfix Tommo's face and to dissolve his constitution. In Burney's story, the sailors are reluctant to acknowledge the presence of cannibalism until they come upon a sight that is unrepresentable in its violation of civilized standards: "I then searched all along at the back of the beach to see if the Cutter was there—we found no boat—but instead of her—Such a shocking scene of Carnage & Barbarity as can never be mentioned or thought of, but with horror.—whilst we remained almost stupefied on this spot Mr. Fannin call'd to us that he heard the Savages gathering together in the Valley" (*Journals of Captain Cook*, 2: 751). Many cannibal narratives employ these gestures—the search for evidence, the slow disclosure that strains belief, the mounting unease, the oblique yet petrifying revelation.[10]

For most cannibal narrators, the sight of human flesh being eaten is too disturbing to be represented. They shield their readers' eyes (and their own). In *Adventures in the Pacific* (1845), published the year before *Typee*, John Coulter describes the aftermath of a Marquesan battle, in which bodies were gathered and those of enemies were separated from those of allies and prepared for cooking. The vanquished bodies were cut apart, rolled in packages of leaves, and placed in pit ovens. For Coulter, as for Burney, the eyes must be averted from the next scene: "I must throw a veil over the feast of the following day, as I had only one look at the beginning of it, and left the arena sick to loathing: went off to the house, and did not leave it until this horrid scene was ended. Thus terminated the Marquesan battle, and its consummation" (232). Such a "peep" at Polynesian life is enough to nauseate. A longer look might blind, or, as implied in several narrators' descriptions of cannibalism as an "addiction," it might tempt. Cannibalism is the indescribable, unrestrained consummation of savage life.[11]

Cannibal accounts interrupt many narratives of colonial encounter, as writers pause before the horrifying prospect. In *Journal of a Cruise* (1815), one of Melville's sources for *Typee,* Captain David Porter digresses from a story of warfare between two Nukuhevan groups, explaining that he felt compelled to determine conclusively whether the natives were cannibals. As he explains, he was "Desirous of clearing up in [his] own mind a fact which so nearly concerned the character of a whole people" (2: 45). Assuming the tone of a concerned and disciplining father, Porter decides that the circumstantial evidence does not support a finding of cannibalism and that an inadequate understanding of Polynesian languages may have led to European misinterpretation. In *Voyages and Travels* (1813), which Melville drew upon extensively, G. H. von Langsdorff inaugurates his discussion of Marquesan cannibalism with a long digression on anthropophagy in general, declaring: "it appears to me a matter of sufficient importance to be investigated somewhat minutely" (1: 141). Recounting a series of lurid secondary accounts, Langsdorff examines the motives (revenge, want of food, unruly and inordinate desires, mistaken belief that consuming one's relatives will preserve their power) and locations (Mexico, South America, Africa, ancient Europe) of the "unnatural practice." For Porter, Langsdorff, and many others, cannibalism is the ultimate sign of the unnatural and the uncivilized. Cannibal interruptions register the writer's ambivalence toward "savage" cultures. These passages are about the reading of cultural signs, the interpretation of performance, and the desire for and fear of discovery.

Cook's version of the flesh-eating on board the *Resolution* conveys the desires and anxieties that shaped many stories of cannibalism:

> I now saw the mangled head or rather the remains of it for the under jaw, lip &c were wanting, the scul was broke on the left side just above the temple, the face had all the appearence of a youth about fourteen or fifteen, a peice of the flesh had been broiled and eat by one of the Natives in the presince of most of the officers. The sight of the head and the relation of the circum-

stances just mentioned struck me with horor and filled my mind with indignation against these Canibals, but when I considered that any resentment I
could shew would avail but little and being desireous of being an eye wittness
to a fact which many people had their doubts about, I concealed my indignation and ordered a piece of the flesh to be broiled and brought on the quarter deck where one of these Canibals eat it with a seeming good relish before
the whole ships Company which had such effect on some of them as to cause
them to vomit. [Oediddee] was [so] struck with horor at the sight that [he]
wept and scolded by turns, before this happened he was very intimate with
these people but now he neither would come near them or suffer them to
touch him. (2: 293)

Here again we have the stupefying power of cannibalism. According to
his modern editor Beaglehole, Cook heavily revised this passage to
perfect its dramatic effect. In the revised version, the Raiatean islander
Oediddee "was so affected with the sight as to become perfectly mo-
tionless and seemed as if metamorphosed into the Statue of horror: it is,
utterly impossible for Art to depict that passion with half the force that
it appeared in his Countenance when roused from this state by some of
us" (2: 293). Neither cannibalism nor the response to cannibalism is capable of being fully represented. The horror can only be intimated. Cannibalism is imagined as the most disturbing act that can be performed
on the human body. In *Voyage round the World* (1813), Krusenstern's
disgust with cannibalism also focuses on violence directed at the head.
He offers a sensational second-hand account of a ferocious cannibal
feast on Nukuheva: "These Europeans described, as eye-witnesses, the
barbarous scenes that are acted . . . the desperate rage with which they
fall upon their victims; immediately tear off their head, and sip their
blood out of the skull, with the most disgusting greediness, completing
in this manner their horrible repast" (1:180). The most vulnerable part
of the body is the head, whose contents are the particular target of savage thirst.[12]

Yet while Oediddee is petrified and silenced by what he sees, Cook
has no difficulty describing his own response to the act of cannibalism,
an act which he himself has choreographed. As represented by Cook,
the cannibalism that takes place on the decks of the *Resolution* is of a
peculiar sort: "I concealed my indignation and ordered a piece of the
flesh to be broiled and brought on the quarter deck where one of these
Canibals eat it" (2: 293). Cook desires to be an eye-witness as well as an
ear-witness to the much-disputed practice. He seeks evidence more compelling than the mere fact of the severed head and the mere hearing of
stories. With ardent curiosity, he orders the broiling and consumption of

flesh. This is cannibalism as command performance. The proof is in the performance. This kind of European mediation of Polynesian cultural practice, of course, has been responsible for complicating the historical recovery of the "facts" of cannibalism.[13]

Cannibal performance—that is, the eating of human flesh as a ferocious spectacle staged for Euro-American eyes—was not only scripted by captains. Edward Belcher, a British captain and defender of the Marquesans, describes how the Teii, a Nukuhevan tribe, rehearsed their cannibalism so as to maximize their own viewing pleasure at the discomfort of their Western audience:

> In the case of the captain and mate of a whaler, not many years since cut off by the natives in Comptroller's Bay, the Teii, said to be the most ferocious on the island, seldom communicating with their neighbours, and never with foreigners,—how did they act? They amused themselves by exciting their fears. Having made a fire sufficiently large to bake them, a hog was substituted, which, when cooked, they were invited to partake of. They were afterwards ransomed. On no other island would their lives have been saved.[14]

However seldom the Teiis communicated with outsiders, assuming that this story is true, they seem to have had a sufficient awareness of the customary cannibal plots to deliciously manipulate audience expectations. Casting their audience in the role of anxious participants, the Teii climaxed their exhibition with a narrative twist. This is a cannibal joke, with a vengeance.

In *Typee*, Melville is conscious of the theatricality of "cannibalism." He understands that some acts of cannibalism have resulted from command performances and that, with the passage of time, cannibal stories have become intensely conventionalized, composed of a set of gestures that produce certain familiar and disturbing effects. Cannibalism is not the ultimate sign of difference in Melville's narrative, as it is in Krusenstern, Langsdorff, Porter, and, to some extent, Cook. Melville trots out the specter of cannibalism as a stage prop with which to frighten his audience and build narrative suspense. Like Belcher's whalers, Tommo and Toby watch the islanders prepare a large fire, increasingly worried that they will become the main dish. Finally, to their great relief, they are invited to partake in a feast of pig flesh (93–95).

Melville provides a condensed and parodic version of cannibal narratives: "According to the popular fictions, the crews of vessels, shipwrecked on some barbarous coast, are eaten alive like so many dainty joints by the uncivil inhabitants; and unfortunate voyagers are lured into smiling and treacherous bays; knocked on the head with outlandish war-clubs; and served up without any preliminary dressing" (205). Here the narrator pointedly refers to the popular distortions and the inventions of cannibal narratives. Using fastidious adjectives ("dainty," "uncivil," "unfortunate," "outlandish") to satirize his audience's eager squeamishness, Melville reduces the civilized victims to items on a Polynesian menu served without the proper condiments, and he objects not so much to the savage appetites of the natives as to their unfortunate culinary habits.[15]

The force of the cannibal representations that climax *Typee* is blunted by Melville's interpolated critiques of colonialism, several of which focus on Western obsessions with savage anthropophagy. In chapter 17, the narrator, in the style of Montaigne, juxtaposes savage cannibalism with civilized barbarity and suggests that the savage version might be preferable, or at least that it should be judged in a framework that is not centered in European assumptions. That these passages did interfere with conventional readerly expectations of the South Pacific narrative seems to be confirmed by the fact that they were excised from the second American edition, published in July 1846, as the result of negotiations between Melville and his publisher, John Wiley. Remaining in the revised edition, however, is Melville's paragraph in chapter 27 describing cannibalism, in the fashion of Cook, as a Polynesian rite practiced in some cases on the bodies of enemies killed in battle—a judicious appraisal that rejects the exaggerations of most travelers' accounts.

The conventions of the cannibal narrative are used most intensely in *Typee* in the chapters that follow these passages of cultural critique. In chapter 32, Tommo returns unexpectedly to the dwelling of Marheyo, where he has been housed during his stay. He finds his companions examining three "mysterious packages" wrapped in tappa cloth, which had been suspended over his sleeping place and had often excited his curiosity (232). The "mysterious packages" function as both device and joke in *Typee*. They are suspended not only over Tommo's bed but also over the course of the narrative. They are bundles that incite Tommo's curiosity and provoke his horror, and they also represent the looming specter of cannibalism that quickens reader interest and creates tension: cannibalism as stage property. Before the Marquesans can conceal the contents of the packages, Tommo glimpses inside them three preserved human heads, two Marquesan and one "white." Fearing that the white head belongs to his lost friend Toby, he is terrified that he himself will be devoured and his own head preserved as a souvenir. A week later, after a battle between the Typee and the Happar, Tommo sees four Typee

men return with three long, narrow, red-stained bundles. He is removed
from the scene by Kory-Kory, his man Friday. The next day, the suspicious Tommo is kept away from the Ti, the ceremonial building, by
Kory-Kory and Fayaway, although he can hear the ominous sound of
ceremonial drums. Wandering around the temple precincts the next af-
ternoon, Tommo lifts the lid on a curiously carved vessel, and he and the
reader are greeted by a "horrid revelation":

> As the vessel had been placed in its present position since my last visit, I at
> once concluded that it must have some connection with the recent festival;
> and, prompted by a curiosity I could not repress, in passing it I raised one end
> of the cover; at the same moment the chiefs, perceiving my design, loudly
> ejaculated, "Taboo! taboo!" But the slight glimpse sufficed; my eyes fell upon
> the disordered members of a human skeleton, the bones still fresh with mois-
> ture, and with particles of flesh clinging to them here and there! (238)

Once again, the glimpse of cannibalism terrifies the observer and inter-
rupts the narrative of South Pacific encounter. Once again, too, Western
curiosity effects the revelation of native savagery and confirms the observer's suspicion of irredeemable difference. After this moment, Tommo
can think of nothing but escape.[16]

But there is something wrong with this picture and with this narrative. If the book's opening flirtation with the cannibal question—Typee
or Happar?—is qualified and analyzed by the cultural critique in chapters 17 and 27, in the middle of the book, then what are we to make of
the apparently crucial use of anthropophagy toward the end? One answer might be to say that the preceding critique undermines and renders
ironic the climactic conventions. This is true, to some extent; that is, the
fear of cannibalism should be mitigated if we have attended to both
chapters analyzing Western obsessions, or even only to the passage from
chapter 27 that survived the 1846 revisions. Yet this ironic reading
clashes with the narrator's deep apprehension and with the violence
against the Typees, justified by the narrative, that closes the book. The
cannibal conventions still seem to have a life of their own, so vital are
they to Euro-American defenses of civilization against savagery.

We might read the cannibal climax as augmented rather than diminished by the critique. The return to convention could be seen as an instance of Melville's enduring anxieties about the threatening difference
represented by Marquesan culture. In such a reading, these anxieties
would overwhelm Melville's conscious criticism. Or we could offer the
antebellum marketplace reading: Melville wanted to have his cake and
eat it, too. He wanted both critique and capitulation. He wanted to sat-

isfy both audiences—the enlightened comparative culturalist and the benighted popular reader.

None of these readings seems satisfactory, though. They all focus on literal cannibalism as the defining term and on the glimpse of the remains of a cannibal feast as the turning point. In one sense, the narrative structurally reinforces this notion, since the cannibal revelations in chapter 32 precede the final two chapters of the book, in which Tommo manages to escape. Yet the fears about loss of identity in chapter 32 seem redundant, given the severe threat to the integrity of the body and the existence of the soul described two chapters earlier. Tommo's glimpse of flesh and bones is a much diminished moment when compared with the intimations of cannibalism in other South Pacific narratives. In *Typee,* the nauseating and indescribable scenes of Burney and Coulter are reduced to a stagy peep into a flesh pot. The emphasis on cannibalism at the end of *Typee* diverts attention from the deeper threat—that of the facial and racial vulnerability revealed in the scene of tattooing.

In *Typee,* Melville translates anxieties about corporeal disintegration from cannibalism to tattooing. The gut fear is not that the insides will be torn out and that flesh will be devoured; rather, it is that the insides will be made visible and vulnerable on the surface of the body and that flesh will be inscribed. Then, because the specter of inscription is so unsettling, the narrative turns to cannibalism once again. In *Typee,* tattooing, not anthropophagy, becomes the horror from which the writer must avert his eyes. Faced with such a threat to identity, Tommo returns to the conventional danger from which he can flee to civilization and to his own kind. Cannibalism functions not only as an object of cultural analysis in *Typee,* nor only as a theatrical device; it is also a refuge. Cannibalism offers escape from the indelible disfigurement of tattooing. In *Typee,* to be eaten would be a relief. Though torn, the flesh would still preserve its immaculateness; though digested, it would be out of sight and beyond inditement. The text is preoccupied by the search for conspicuous signs of tattooing, not for the absent signs of cannibalism. Rather than being characterized as beyond artistic representation, tattooing is depicted as being the product of it. Rather than turning the observer into a "Statue of horror," tattooing dispels the observer's fantasy of his own statuesque state. In *Typee,* the threat of literally being eaten is less disturbing than the risk that the body will be consumed by the lines of the tattooist and the eyes of observers.

At the end of chapter 27, the narrator Tommo trenchantly and rationally dispenses with Western fixations on cannibalism. Yes, the Typees practice cannibalism, he explains to his readers, but "to a certain moderate extent" and "upon the bodies of slain enemies alone"—and, he implies, there are worse practices in the West (205). In the next two chapters, he describes the idyllic Typee life and his adoption of Marquesan culture. Tommo does as the Typee do: He eats their food; he wears their clothes. In these chapters, the gesture of reversing reader expectations about the civilized and the savage reaches its peak. The savage Typee have come to occupy the position of the noble Happar, the tribe of Nukuhevans Tommo had hoped to encounter. Polynesia is described as more humane than Europe or America. At the height of admiration for and participation in Typee society, Tommo describes the health, the justice, and the nobility of the islanders. This idyll is ruptured at the start of chapter 30, when he realizes that the Typee have designs on him—or, to be more precise, that they have designs for his white skin.

OF TATTOOING: READING THE BODY
IN LANGSDORFF AND MELVILLE

Strolling with his companion Kory-Kory, Tommo stumbles upon a scene of plein-air tattooing, in which the Marquesan artist Karky is repairing the designs on an old man's skin:

> I beheld a man extended flat upon his back on the ground, and, despite the forced composure of his countenance, it was evident that he was suffering agony. His tormentor bent over him, working away for all the world like a stone-cutter with mallet and chisel. In one hand he held a short slender stick, pointed with a shark's tooth, on the upright end of which he tapped with a small hammer-like piece of wood, thus puncturing the skin, and charging it with the coloring matter in which the instrument was dipped. (217)

Melville here emphasizes the violence of tattooing. (The word "tattoo" itself derives from Marquesan and Tahitian verbs meaning "to strike.") The body is compared to a sculptor's blank, composed not of marble but of a soft and sensitive material subjected to the blows of a hammer. For many nineteenth-century tattooed Europeans and Americans, the ability to endure the extended and painful procedure was a sign of masculine fortitude. In *A Residence of Eleven Years in New Holland and the Caroline Islands* (1836), James F. O'Connell describes how he withstood the punctures, which he compares to thorns being driven into his flesh, while his weak companion George swore and railed (112–17). In

Adventures in the Pacific (1845), John Coulter describes the incessant hammering at his skin, comparing the rapidity and force of the blows to those of a trunk-maker driving in his nails (211). In *Typee,* too, the narrator connects masculinity and the ability to endure tattooing. Shortly after Tommo's escape from Karky, with the threat of forced tattooing still looming, his famous phallic leg begins to throb anew, a malady which, Tommo explains, "nearly unmanned" him (232).[17]

Yet the violence in *Typee* is of a different order from that in O'Connell or Coulter. For Melville, the most exquisite instrument of torture is not the thorn or the hammer and nails or the mallet and chisel, but the short slender stick. Tommo is less afraid of the blunt physical blow that would rend large pieces of flesh than he is of the delicate inscription that penetrates and contaminates the interior. Thus the artistic analogy that Melville uses to define the tattooing process more sharply is printing rather than sculpture: the body is a surface to be cut and inked. Melville gives an accurate account of tattooing techniques, drawing heavily from Langsdorff's *Voyages and Travels* (1813): the skin is punctured and coloring matter is injected into a deeper layer. This is the layer of human skin that early nineteenth-century ethnologists called the rete mucosum, the stratum where color resides, lying below the epidermis and above the cutis vera, or "true skin," which the ethnologists claimed was universally "white." [18]

Melville draws out the analogy between tattooing and intaglio printing. Karky's instruments are described as being like the graduated tools of the etcher or engraver:

> Beside the savage, and spread out upon a piece of soiled tappa, were a great number of curious black-looking little implements of bone and wood, used in the various divisions of his art. A few terminated in a single fine point, and, like very delicate pencils, were employed in giving the finishing touches, or in operating on the more sensitive portions of the body, as was the case in the present instance. Others presented several points distributed in a line, somewhat resembling the teeth of a saw. These were employed in the coarser parts of the work, and particularly in pricking straight marks. Some presented their points disposed in small figures, and being placed upon the body, were, by a single blow of the hammer, made to leave their indelible impression. I observed a few of the handles of which were mysteriously curved, as if intended to be introduced into the orifice of the ear, with a view perhaps of beating the tattoo upon the tympanum. (217–18)

In Melville's account, the procedures for writing on the skin are not only violent but also alarmingly intrusive. This passage figures a literal and intimate "earmarking." Among the many instruments used to perform the operation, Melville imagines one that is designed to beat a tattoo upon the tympanum, to reach inside the body to the middle ear and mark it—to, in Melville's pun, strike and stroke the eardrum.

The violence that Tommo witnesses at the start of chapter 30 is rendered somewhat comically. Karky's victim shudders under the artistic attention being paid to his eyelids: "In spite of all the efforts of the poor old man, sundry twitchings and screwings of the muscles of the face denoted the exquisite sensibility of these shutters to the windows of his soul, which he was now having repainted" (218). Literalizing the cliché of ocular casements, Melville converts eyelids to shutters and translates the pain of punctured lids into the inconvenience of domestic refurbishing. This is exterior decoration rather than the unsettling interior decoration threatened by Karky's small curved implement.

Melville's tone changes abruptly, however, when Tommo's gaze is returned and the positions of observer and observed are reversed. Karky the tattoo artist seizes Tommo and threatens him with his tools:

> grasping his implements, he flourished them about in fearful vicinity to my face, going through an imaginary performance of his art, and every moment bursting into some admiring exclamation at the beauty of his designs.
>
> Horrified at the bare thought of being rendered hideous for life if the wretch were to execute his purpose upon me, I struggled to get away from him. (218)

Here tattooing is represented as attack. To be tattooed is to be the object of "execution." At the core of Tommo's "bare thought" is the fear of being covered, of being "rendered hideous for life" by indelible and invidious marks, the stark fear of having his bare skin written upon for all to read. Karky's designs are seen as disfiguring. In order to understand the sources of Tommo's dread and the consequences of facial assault in mid-nineteenth-century America, it is necessary to consider first the links between Western narratives of voyage to the Marquesas and the quest for knowledge of the racial body.

From Figueroa's history of Mendaña's Pacific voyages (1613) to Melville's *Typee* (1846), the attention of travel narrators had been drawn to the "European" features and the light skin of the Marquesans. Yet the fascination had not been one of mere similarity. Marquesan skin seems to have served as an uncanny screen upon which European and American observers projected their desires and anxieties. Although Charles Anderson speculates that Melville relied so heavily on previous visitors' descriptions in order to extend the material he collected during his brief stay and to compensate for his own inexperience as a writer, the repetition of images and scenes is a feature of many Marquesan narratives. Writers engaged in an unfolding debate about the nature and appearance of the Marquesans and about the racial relations between Westerners and Polynesians. Melville not only participates in this debate but articulates its agitated, self-conscious climax.[19]

In *Voyages and Travels* (1813), G. H. von Langsdorff, a German naturalist attached to the expedition of A. J. von Krusenstern, offers high praise of the Marquesan form and a striking aesthetic equation:

> I am inclined to think that the people of the Marquesas and Washington Islands excel in beauty and grandeur of form, in regularity of features, and in colour, all the other South-Sea islanders. . . . We did not see a single crippled or deformed person, but such general beauty and regularity of form, that it greatly excited our astonishment. Many of them might very well have been placed by the side of the most celebrated chef-d'oeuvres of antiquity, and they would have lost nothing by the comparison. . . . A certain Mau-ka-u, or Mufau Taputakava, particularly attracted our attention from his extraordinary height, the vast strength of his body, and the admirable proportion of his limbs and muscles. . . . Counsellor Tilesius [the chief naturalist on the Krusenstern expedition], who unites the eye of a connoisseur and an artist, said, he never saw any one so perfectly proportioned. He took the trouble of measuring every part of this man with the utmost exactness, and after our return to Europe imparted his observations to Counsellor Blumenbach, of Gottingen, who has studied so assiduously the natural history of man. This latter compared these proportions with the Apollo of Belvedere, and found that those of that master-piece of the finest ages of Grecian art, in which is combined every possible integer in the composition of manly beauty, corresponded exactly with our Mufau, an inhabitant of the island of Nukahiwa. [There follow in Langsdorff's text thirty-two lines detailing the exact measurements of Mufau.] (1: 108–09)

Expecting that the journey away from Europe would also be a deviation from the prime meridian of human beauty, Langsdorff is astonished at the European-type beauty of the Marquesans. His aesthetic appreciation is genuine, but it is inseparable from the pleasure experienced at discovering similarity instead of divergence; it is inseparable, too, from the implied comparisons with the less pleasing forms of other South Sea islanders. According to Langsdorff, Counsellor Tilesius took measurements and forwarded them to Johann Friedrich Blumenbach (1753–1840), the German physiologist and comparative anatomist who helped to establish modern European ethnology. From empirical observation, Blumenbach had divided humankind into five races (American, Ethiopian, Mongolian, Malayan, and Caucasian) and argued that the Caucasians were the most beautiful race. After evaluating the shapes of different human heads, Blumenbach concluded that the Caucasian cranium was aesthetically superior by virtue of its symmetry. Thus, he concluded, it must have been the original type of head created by God. Blumenbach pronounces Mufau's body an exact fit with the dimensions of the *Apollo Belvedere,* the enormously popular Roman copy of the Greek statue, which was viewed by eighteenth- and nineteenth-century Europeans and Americans as the paragon of classic beauty. Langsdorff has sailed from Europe to the south Atlantic and around Cape Horn to a remote island in the east-central Pacific Ocean to discover . . . the *Apollo Belvedere.* Several other travelers also compared male Marquesan bodies to classical sculptures, as though the journey to the Marquesas traced a path to the heart of whiteness, where the observer confronted models of pristine Caucasian beauty. Counsellor Tilesius is one in a long line of nineteenth-century connoisseurs of the human form, Blumenbach among them. These ethnologists, amateur and professional, measure with keen eyes and render judgments on the meanings of the human body. This taste for human flesh is conspicuously on display in Western encounters with the inhabitants of the Marquesas.[20]

Part of the attraction of Marquesan skin for European and American observers must have been that there was so much of it to see. Melville mentions the prevalence and allure of female skin. Describing his first encounter with the Marquesans in Nukuheva Bay, Tommo envisions enticing "mermaids" who board and "capture" the ship: "What a sight for us bachelor sailors! how avoid so dire a temptation?" (15). The spectacle of Marquesan women dancing in the moonlight is "almost too much for a quiet, sober-minded, modest young man" (152).[21] The skin of the beautiful Fayaway tantalizes with a revelation of similarity: "Her complexion was a rich and mantling olive, and when watching the glow upon her cheeks, I could almost swear that beneath the transparent medium there lurked the blushes of a faint vermillion" (85). Fayaway's skin is imagined as transparent, offering access to the inside. Her cheeks disclose—almost—the sign of the blush, the crucial revelation of Caucasian female interiority. As the comparative anatomist Charles White rhetorically asked at the end of his 1799 *Account of the Regular Gradation in Man,* "In what other quarter of the globe shall we find the blush that overspreads the soft features of the beautiful women of Europe, that emblem of modesty, of delicate feelings, and of sense?"[22] The tantalizing prospect offered by Fayaway is that just beneath this Polynesian surface there lurks a girl like the girls Tommo left back home. A blush is the natural and temporary register of discomfort with public exposure. It conveys the reassurance of female propriety, a consciousness of the gap between the profane world of social encounter and sacred private space. White skin reddens to warn of transgression; when the danger has passed, the color recedes.

Yet Tommo only imagines that he detects the trace of a blush in Fayaway's olive skin, and the verb "lurks" indicates that danger, as well as opportunity, awaits in Fayaway's "free pliant figure" (85). The next item catalogued in her series of charms is her mouth, whose metaphors are extended and literalized until the organ becomes a menacing vagina dentata: "Her full lips, when parted with a smile, disclosed teeth of a dazzling whiteness; and when her rosy mouth opened with a burst of merriment, they looked like the milk-white seeds of the 'arta,' a fruit of the valley, which, when cleft in twain, shows them reposing in rows in either side, imbedded in the red and juicy pulp" (85). In this revealing image, the transparent becomes opaque and blushes turn to blood. Fayaway's mouth suggests an appetite that knows no limits. One way of reading the bizarre image in chapter 18 of Fayaway volunteering to serve as the mast and spars of a canoe is as a reaction to the threat posed by her freedom and pliancy. Tommo claims he convinced Mehevi, the chief of the village, to suspend the taboo on women riding in canoes so that he and Fayaway can take a pleasure excursion on the lake. (Adding to the unreality of this passage is the fact that, as Anderson points out, there were no lakes in the Typee valley.) While on the water, Fayaway springs up, removes her robe of tappa cloth, spreads it out like a sail, and stands erect with upraised arms in the head of the canoe. Clearly a fabrication, this sentimental interlude in the middle of a nonexistent lake is one of the most artificial episodes in the book. Melville weirdly transposes a stock middle-class scene of leisure from the Catskills to the Typee valley and transforms it into a scene of bondage and exposure.

Yet the narrative interest of *Typee* is only momentarily beguiled by women's bodies and only briefly concerned with the delectations and dangers of female license. It is male skin rather than female skin on which Tommo fixates: the skin of the Marquesan men he meets and his own skin. As early travelers and later anthropologists all reported, the Marquesan practice was for only men to have their bodies heavily tattooed. If unmarked female skin is the object of fantasy, and the incitement for moments of fear, in the narrative, then male skin covered with tattoos is the stuff of nightmare. The beautiful skin of Typee men is displayed and disfigured. In the narrator's response to this skin, aesthetics, sexuality, and race converge.

The vivid evidence of difference inscribed on Marquesan skin complicated Western travelers' classical vision of the inhabitants. Before
Western eyes, a fascinating drama of transformation was enacted. Visitors offered meticulous accounts of the procedures by which the light
skin of the Marquesan women was made paler and the light skin of Marquesan men was colored. And the operative term here is color. Travelers
remarked upon the range of colors, natural and artificial, they encountered on the skins of the Marquesans. In *Voyages and Travels,* Langsdorff describes the skin of the people he saw as "almost as white as that
of Europeans" (1:113). In *A Visit to the South Seas* (1831), Stewart details the skin-lightening performed daily by many Marquesan women,
who anointed themselves with the juice of the papa vine (1:256). Langsdorff depicts a Marquesan method of bleaching tanned skin in a few
days. The whole body is rubbed with sap from the leaves of three plants
and then the individual is confined to her home. The liquid turns her
skin entirely black for five or six days, after which time she washes herself with fresh water, "which takes off the black sap, and leaves the skin
its natural, nearly white, colour" (1:113–14). In *Narrative of a Whaling Voyage* (1840), Bennett reports that Marquesan women and male
chiefs maintained a fair complexion by smearing their skin with a lotion
prepared from turmeric root mixed with the adhesive juice of the keku
tree. This preparation adhered to the skin, "staining" it yellow, Bennett
explains, but since the dye was not fast it often rubbed off and was
"communicated from their persons to surrounding objects" (1:308–
09). Coulter describes the variegated aspect of Marquesan dancers:
"then you see neither a black nor a white man, but (from the turmeric)
a golden yellow one, perfectly naked, in all the wildness and the frenzy
of the heathen dance" (169). In *Voyage round the World* (1813),
Krusenstern observes that the black of the tattooing dye ages into
a "bluish tinge" (1:155). Ellis concurs in his *Polynesian Researches*
(1831), explaining how the tattooing dye in male Marquesans passed
through their "thin transparent skin" and imparted to the surface of
their bodies a "tinge of blue" (1:208). Langsdorff graphically describes
the tattooing operation: designs are sketched upon the body, the skin is
punctured along these lines, blood and lymph ooze through the wounds,
thick dye is rubbed in, the skin inflames, heals, forms a crust, and after
several days the crust falls off and blackish-blue figures appear (1:118).

Travelers envisioned the end product of these male experiments in
color as the transformation to black. They commented on the extensive
tattooing in the Marquesas, comparing the designs to articles of cloth-

ing and suggesting a racial conversion from Caucasian to Negro. Stewart describes a tattooed Marquesan named Piaroro: "though it is apparent that naturally his complexion was as fair as most of his countrymen, his whole face and head, chest and shoulders are, from this cause [tattooing], as black as ever an Othello is ever pictured to be" (1:228). Krusenstern describes the "black appearance" of tattooed bodies (1:152). Bennett writes that some of the men he saw were "literally blackened from head to foot: the tattooed figures being so inextricably blended, as to destroy the ornamental effect which a more moderate display of this art decidedly confers" (1:306). These men have become decomposed. Their tattooing is associated with excess, mixture, and essence. Ellis remarks upon the ingenious ways in which Marquesan tattooing designs sometimes "covered the body so as nearly to conceal the original colour of the skin" (1:207). He reprints a section from the new colonial code of laws prohibiting tattoos, which threatens to destroy the designs of repeated offenders by "blacking them over" (1:142–43). To be punished is to be rendered black. In his notes to one of the engravings of tattooed Marquesans in *Voyages and Travels,* Langsdorff writes: "The portrait here delineated is of a man about thirty years of age, a period at which the figures formed by the punctures appear the most distinctly. In later years, one figure is made over another, till the whole becomes confused, and the body assumes a Negro-like appearance" (1:xiv). According to Langsdorff, the symmetry and clarity of Marquesan designs disintegrate over time into a "Negro-like" disarray. Whenever Europeans and Americans encountered other races, the impulse not only to compare but also to rank seems to have operated, and always the two poles of the spectrum, the terms of evaluation, are black and white.[23]

To Western eyes, the Marquesas offered a chromatic laboratory. On these islands, almost-white skin became yellow. Yellow color communicated itself from hand to object. Almost-white skin became tanned and then black and then almost white again. Almost-white skin became black and then blue. And, most enthralling of all, "white" skin became "black." In these early-nineteenth-century experiments performed before their eyes and to some extent by their eyes, observers watched as the color of Marquesan skin approached and then diverged from their own. Early-nineteenth-century observers responded to the intricate tattooing designs on male Marquesan bodies, to the transformational possibilities of light-colored skin, with a complex mixture of astonishment, appreciation, and anxiety.

The illustrations in Langsdorff's *Voyages and Travels* (1813), Melville's most important source for the tattooing chapters in *Typee,* make vivid the prospect of Marquesan tattooing. During his ten-day stay on Nukuheva in May 1804, Langsdorff was fascinated by tattooing methods and the appearance of tattooed male bodies. In referring to the process as "punctuation" (1:116), he nicely combines the senses of tattooing as both piercing the body and writing upon it. He lavishes detail on the tattooed men encountered on Nukuheva, including in his text a series of engravings produced from drawings made at the scene.[24]

The first figure represented in the engravings of tattooed bodies is actually not a Marquesan but a Frenchman, Jean Baptiste Cabri (see figure 1). Cabri was exhibited upon the stage at Moscow and St. Petersburg to great interest. He was one of several tattooed Europeans and Americans on display in the first half of the nineteenth century; others included John Rutherford in England (1828) and James O'Connell in America (1840). The public interest in tattooed white men was a product of both visual and narrative fascinations. Audiences seem to have been fascinated by seeing white men who had been colored by their encounter with South Pacific islanders and by hearing them tell their usually fabricated tales of being marked against their will. According to contemporary reports, O'Connell's delineated body was so disturbing that women and children screamed in horror on the streets when they met him. Ministers warned that unborn children would bear his marks if pregnant women viewed them. Fears about legibility, indelibility, and contagion seem to have been at the core of audience captivation with O'Connell's tattooed body.[25]

Antebellum audiences also flocked to see South Pacific cannibals on exhibit. The appeal of such scenes is puzzling. While the difference signified by tattoos on a white man is visible and immediate, the difference implied by the practice of cannibalism is internal and antecedent. The possibility that the object of attention might begin to consume human flesh before one's eyes (and that the observer might be regarded with appetite) may have charged the viewing experience. The crucial issues of "evidence" may have been a part of the transaction as well. In what senses was seeing believing? With the "knowledge" that these islanders had been cannibals, could the viewer detect telltale signs in their aspect or movements? William Arens claims that the idea of cannibalism exists prior to and thus independent of any evidence, and that it functions to define the cultural boundary between civilization and sav-

Figure 1. *Portrait of Jean Baptiste Cabri,* engraving by R. Cooper, from
Voyages and Travels, vol. 1, by G. H. von Langsdorff (1813). Courtesy of
the Bancroft Library, University of California, Berkeley.

agery. This claim seems to be enacted in the spectacle of antebellum
Americans gasping at the tableau of South Pacific "cannibals" on domestic display.[26]

The evidence of difference is clear in the case of tattooed white men.
The antebellum concern with involuntary color transformation can be

compared to the earlier interest in "white Negroes," African Americans whose albinism produced skin that was both black and white. These figures were the subjects of scientific study and public exhibition in the late eighteenth and early nineteenth centuries. The American physician Benjamin Rush examined the famous Henry Moss, whose black skin seemed to be disappearing under the spread of white blotches. Rush hoped that Moss would support his theory that dark skin color was a disease, a potentially curable form of leprosy. In an address before the American Philosophical Society, Rush worried that black skin might be slightly infectious, adducing the unsettling instance of two white women whose skin had darkened as a result of their living with black husbands. In the cases of both tattooed white sailors and black albinos, the skin is viewed as a dynamic surface of patches and zones. Yet there is a striking shift in visual interest from the late eighteenth to the mid-nineteenth century: from the spectacle of blacks naturally turning white, which was greeted as a positive development by Enlightenment scientists, to the antebellum specter of whites being coerced into indelible color.[27] In the early-nineteenth-century depiction of Cabri in Langsdorff's *Voyages and Travels,* there is not the sense of coercion and revulsion that we find in audience reactions to O'Connell or in Tommo's reaction to Karky's artistry in *Typee.* Cabri's tattoos are decorative, rather than defining. Cabri is represented as a European who is playing native. His hair is swept up and disheveled. His arms and chest have been tattooed with stripes and circles, forming an arc of design. Cabri is a light-colored man whose body has been embellished. Yet in the upper part of his countenance, with its white and black quadrants, there is the hint of an about-face: the possibility that black, rather than white, might serve as ground.

In plate 6 of *Voyages and Travels,* entitled *An Inhabitant of the Island of Nukahiwa*—this is a man without a proper name—the intricate tattooing is almost like a new skin (see figure 2). The body is heavily marked, filled with points, lines, circles, squares, and bands. (In plate 8, Langsdorff provides a guide to some of these emblems, reproducing the shapes and describing their meanings.) The forehead of the *Inhabitant* looks like a map, traversed with chart lines. The designs on this head resemble the lines and arcs that give character to the heads in nineteenth-century phrenology manuals. Both the head of Langsdorff's *Inhabitant* and the exemplary heads in the Fowler brothers' phrenology manuals display a surface to be navigated. In the Fowlers' *Grouping of Organs,* the head is divided into significant, inscribed regions (see

Figure 2.   *An Inhabitant of the Island of Nukahiwa,* engraving by J. Storer, from *Voyages and Travels,* vol. 1, by G. H. von Langsdorff (1813). Courtesy of the Bancroft Library, University of California, Berkeley.

figure 3). In the *Symbolical Head,* scenes epitomizing mental faculties are marked on the cranium (see figure 4). The Fowlers' popular series of *Self-Instructors* in phrenology announced "a chart of the character" on the title page, in addition to the do-it-yourself manual and one hundred illustrative engravings. Melville literalizes the conjunction between

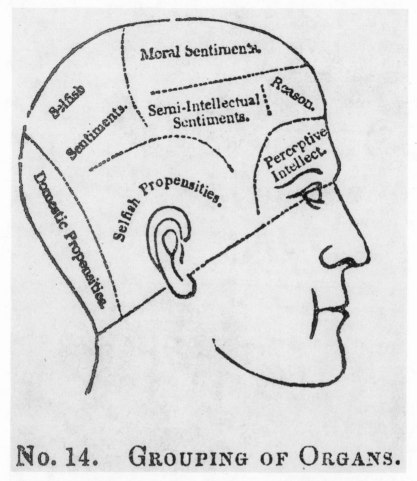

No. 14.   GROUPING OF ORGANS.

Figure 3. *Grouping of Organs,* from *The Illustrated Self-Instructor in Phrenology and Physiology,* by O. S. Fowler and L. N. Fowler (1852).

cartography and craniology in chapter 44 of *Moby-Dick,* "The Chart." While Ahab sits in his cabin plotting new courses on his yellowing maps, the heavy pewter lamp rocks with the motion of the ship and casts shadows on his brow, "till it almost seemed that while he himself was marking out lines and courses on the wrinkled charts, some invisible pencil was also tracing lines and courses upon the deeply marked chart of his forehead." In *Typee,* the deep marks are cut by the instruments of the tattoo artist and by the "invisible pencil" of the ethnologist.[28]

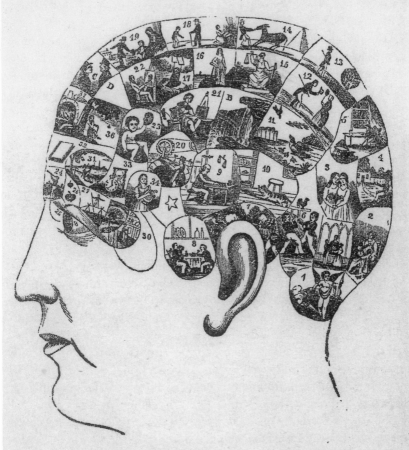

NUMBERING AND DEFINITION OF THE ORGANS.

1. AMATIVENESS, Sexual and connubial love.
2. PHILOPROGENITIVENESS, Parental love.
3. ADHESIVENESS, Friendship—sociability.
4. UNION FOR LIFE, Love of one only.
5. INHABITIVENESS, Love of home.
6. CONTINUITY, One thing at a time.
7. COMBATIVENESS, Resistance—defence.
8. DESTRUCTIVENESS, Executiveness—force.
9. ALIMENTIVENESS, Appetite, hunger.
10. ACQUISITIVENESS, Accumulation.
11. SECRETIVENESS, Policy—management.
12. CAUTIOUSNESS, Prudence, provision.
13. APPROBATIVENESS, Ambition—display.
14. SELF-ESTEEM, Self-respect—dignity.
15. FIRMNESS, Decision—perseverance.
16. CONSCIENTIOUSNESS, Justice—equity
17. HOPE, Expectation—enterprise
18. SPIRITUALITY, Intuition—spiritual revery.
19. VENERATION, Devotion—respect.
20. BENEVOLENCE, Kindness—goodness.
21. CONSTRUCTIVENESS Mechanical ingenuity

21. IDEALITY, Refinement—taste—purity.
B. SUBLIMITY, Love of grandeur.
22. IMITATION, Copying—patterning.
23. MIRTHFULNESS, Jocoseness—wit—fun.
24. INDIVIDUALITY, Observation.
25. FORM, Recollection of shape.
26. SIZE, Measuring by the eye.
27. WEIGHT, Balancing—climbing.
28. COLOR, Judgment of colors.
29. ORDER, Method—system—arrangement
30. CALCULATION, Mental arithmetic.
31. LOCALITY Recollection of places.
32. EVENTUALITY, Memory of facts.
33. TIME, Cognizance of duration.
34. TUNE, MUSIC—melody by ear.
35. LANGUAGE, Expression of ideas.
36. CAUSALITY, Applying causes to effects
37. COMPARISON, inductive reasoning.
C. HUMAN NATURE, perception of motives
D. AGREEABLENESS, Pleasantness—suavity.

Figure 4. *Symbolical Head,* from *The Illustrated Self-Instructor in Phrenology and Physiology,* by O. S. Fowler and L. N. Fowler (1852).

The invisible pencil traces lines on the human body over the course
of the late eighteenth and early nineteenth centuries, beginning with Enlightenment European and American investigations of human anatomical differences and climaxing in the efforts of the antebellum "American
school" of ethnology. We can see the invisible pencil trace its lines
and inscribe its message of separation and hierarchy in the graduated
facial angles of the Dutch anatomist Petrus Camper; in the physiognomic grids of the Swiss pastor Johann Lavater; in the phrenological di-
agrams of Orson and Lorenzo Fowler; in the craniometrical plates of the
premier American ethnologist, Samuel George Morton; and in the dia-
grams of comparative anatomy in the leading antebellum American ethnology textbook, Josiah Nott and George Gliddon's *Types of Mankind*
(1854).[29]

American scientists hailed the United States as the preeminent arena
for the study of human racial differences, since at least three of the five
major racial groups lived in close proximity there. The archaeologist
and ethnologist Ephraim George Squier announced in 1849 that "Ethnology is not only the science of the age, but also . . . it is, and must continue to be, to a prevailing extent, an *American science.*" Aligned with
the justifications for African American slavery and Native American
"removal," American ethnology transformed scientific thinking and political and popular culture. By the 1850s, the claim that American racial
groups were inherently unequal, the result of separate and hierarchical
divine creations, was approaching the status of "fact." [30]

To draw ethnological lines on the human body was to interpret them.
The angle formed by the forehead and the jaw; the distance between
hairline, eyebrow, and nosetip; the cranial swells and depressions—to
mark these lines on the face and head and to imagine them as measures
of an interior state was to make visible a new kind of knowledge. These
lines were not neutral. In the words of the English anatomist Charles
White, they traced "accounts of the regular gradation in man." In nineteenth-century racial theory and aesthetics, there was a standard for the
angles, inches, and contour lines. Camper arranged his skulls in ascending order, *From Ape to Apollo Belvedere,* and he determined the geo-
metrical equations by which the angle of the face increased in direct proportion to the civilized characteristics of its wearer. The Fowlers ranked
the shapes of the heads and foreheads of the three major racial groups
in America, declaring that the Caucasian was visibly superior in reasoning power and moral elevation. Morton demonstrated the permanence
of racial inequalities through his painstaking appraisal of the cranial ca-

pacities of the five different races. Features of the body were identified, isolated, and abstracted, and then lines were drawn on and across these features. Lines were drawn first with the eyes and then with fingers, calipers, and scalpels. These lines were filled with meaning. Knowledge was conceived in visual and spatial terms and the linear was seen as giving access to the depth of human character and human difference. Color, texture, contour, line—these are the elements of visual representation and also the strategies of ethnological investigation of the face, the skin, and the head. The racial body was known and owned through reading the lines engraved on its surface.[31]

The invisible pencil of antebellum ethnology is itself made visible in one of the frontispiece engravings to *An Examination of Phrenology* (1837), the published lectures of the anatomist and physiologist Thomas Sewall (see figure 5). Sewall describes this "craniometer" as "the instrument principally in use" to ascertain the volumes of the brain. The craniometer measured the size of a phrenological organ by determining its distance from the ear. Although the tips of the craniometer rest on the external ear, from the perspective of the frontal view in the engraving the spikes seem to have been inserted into the orifice with a view of inscribing the middle ear or, we might say with Melville, of beating a tattoo upon the tympanum. In the engraving, the contents of the cranium appear to be drawn into the spikes, up the quadrant arms of the craniometer, and down through the ruler to its tip, which has inscribed the elaborate tattoo of zones and numbers on the surface of the head. These marks appear to have been made through the natural workings of the craniometer, without the intervention of a human hand. In making visible knowledge about the head, the craniometer empties its contents. Karky's curved aural implement is unsettling because it threatens an interior decoration that is also an interior evacuation. From a phrenological perspective, the eyes are not windows to the soul. There is no need to peer into the eyes when character is inscribed on the surface of the face and head. Here, phrenology is not exactly learning to draw-by-numbers; rather, it is learning to know by the numbers. Phrenology teaches the observer to abstract, delineate, and enumerate features of the head and to read these features as eloquent markers of interior state.[32]

The desire to read the surface of another's skull and body is intensely registered in Langsdorff's plate 7, *A young Nukahiwan not completely Tattooed* (see figure 6). The buttocks seem marked with bull's-eyes. This body is a work in progress. Its figures are tantalizingly incomplete, awaiting the penetrations of a viewer. The *young Nukahiwan* is

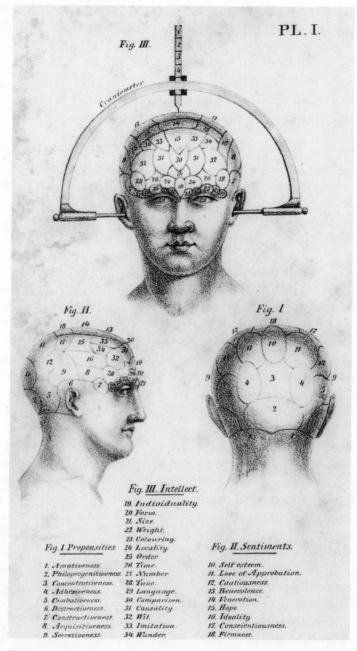

PL. I.

Fig. III.

Craniometer

Fig. II.

Fig. I.

Fig. III. Intellect.
19. *Individuality.*
20. *Form.*
21. *Size.*
22. *Weight.*
23. *Colouring.*
24. *Locality.*
25. *Order.*
26. *Time.*
27. *Number.*
28. *Tune.*
29. *Language.*
30. *Comparison.*
31. *Causality.*
32. *Wit.*
33. *Imitation.*
34. *Wonder.*

Fig. I. Propensities.
1. *Amativeness.*
2. *Philoprogenitiveness.*
3. *Concentrativeness.*
4. *Adhesiveness.*
5. *Combativeness.*
6. *Destructiveness.*
7. *Constructiveness.*
8. *Acquisitiveness.*
9. *Secretiveness.*

Fig. II. Sentiments.
10. *Self esteem.*
11. *Love of Approbation.*
12. *Cautiousness.*
13. *Benevolence.*
14. *Veneration.*
15. *Hope.*
16. *Ideality*
17. *Conscientiousness.*
18. *Firmness.*

Figure 5. *Craniometer*, from *An Examination of Phrenology*, by Thomas Sewall (1837). Brown University Library.

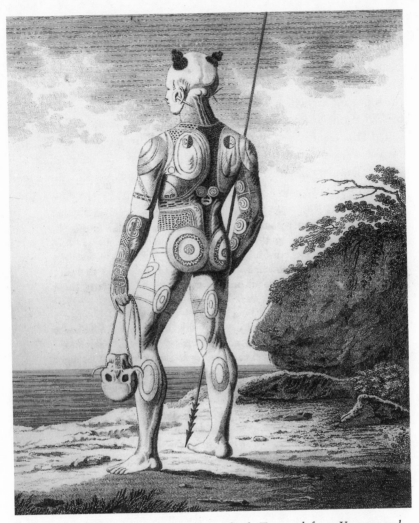

Figure 6. *A young Nukahiwan not completely Tattooed*, from *Voyages and Travels*, vol. 1, by G. H. von Langsdorff (1813). Courtesy of the Bancroft Library, University of California, Berkeley.

positioned so that the viewer can see but not be seen and so that curiosity is incited. While the *young Nukahiwan* carries the skull of an enemy, possessing its power, the observer dominates the Marquesan figure. There is a triangulation of visual power here, a trajectory that extends from the inverted sockets of the decapitated skull to the averted eyes of the *young Nukahiwan* to the viewer's gaze. Even with the viewer in the commanding position, there is an unsettling quality to the visual transaction: the sockets of the skull, while apparently empty, still stare back.[33]

In *Polynesian Researches* (1831), William Ellis captures and condemns the erotic aspect of tattoos when he retells a Polynesian myth about their origin. According to Ellis, after repeated acts of "visual intercourse," in which the male god Taaroa and his female progeny looked at one another and produced a series of children, a female child called Hinaereeremonoi was born. In an effort to preserve her chastity, she was kept in an enclosure and constantly attended by her mother. Her brothers, intent on seducing her, invented tattooing and punctured their flesh with a figure called Taomaro. Attracted by the marks and wishing herself to be ornamented, Hinaereeremonoi left her refuge, was tattooed, "and became also the victim to the designs of her brothers" (1:205–06). Ellis describes an impregnating gaze and he puns on the word "designs." The literal tattoo designs are contrived as part of a plot to seduce and ensnare the viewer. Ellis's account evokes the aura of Langsdorff's *young Nukahiwan*: the invitation to look, the power to mark the object, the risk of being drawn into the picture—the pleasures and dangers of visual exchange.

In *Typee*, the fascination turns to revulsion. If Langsdorff emphasizes the appeal of reading others' bodies, Melville in *Typee* fixates on the anxieties of having one's own body marked and read. Bodily designs, even on native bodies, repel the narrator. Only the tatooing of the wanderer Marnoo elicits the narrator's praise because of its symmetry and its confinement below the neck:

> his face was free from the least blemish of tattooing, although the rest of his body was drawn all over with fanciful figures, which—unlike the unconnected sketching usual among these natives—appeared to have been executed in conformity with some general design.
> The tattooing on his back in particular attracted my attention. The artist employed must indeed have excelled in his profession. Traced along the course of the spine was accurately delineated the slender, tapering, and diamond-checkered shaft of the beautiful "artu" tree. Branching from the stem on either side, and disposed alternately, were the graceful branches drooping with leaves all correctly drawn, and elaborately finished. Indeed, this piece of tattooing was the best specimen of the Fine Arts I had yet seen in Typee. . . . Upon his breast, arms, and legs, were exhibited an infinite variety of figures; every one of which, however, appeared to have reference to the general effect sought to be produced. (136)

On Marnoo's body, the various shapes are unified in a recognizable pattern. The central figure depicts the shaft of the "artu" tree, whose authentically rendered branches extend from the spine across the back, giving it support and coherence. Tommo approves of the representational, rather than abstract, quality of the figure, its balance and its secure bodily coordinates. Marnoo's tattoos highlight and articulate his statuesque body, "one of the most striking specimens of humanity that [Tommo] ever beheld" (135). In the familiar aesthetic analogy of travelers to the Marquesas, Tommo suggests that Marnoo could stand as a model for "the Polynesian Apollo" (135).[34]

Yet Marnoo's tattooing, rooted to the spine and composed according to principles of mimesis, hierarchy, and proportion, is, like Marnoo himself, an anomaly among the Typees. When a boy, Marnoo had been forced into service on a trading vessel and spent three years at sea and in Australia. This "intercourse with the white men" (140) seems to have left its mark not only on his quick mind and accomplished speech (he has a partial knowledge of English) but also in the aesthetically pleasing lines on his body.

Tommo describes the tattoos of other Nukuhevans with dread or disgust. Mehevi's tattooing "stains" the lids of his eyes (78). The vertical stripes on Kory-Kory's face are compared to "the grated bars of a prison window" (83). Fayaway's "beauteous form" is not "altogether free from the hideous blemish" and the "desecrating work" of tattooing (86, 87). Age and tattooing combined "have obliterated every trace of humanity" in a group of old men Tommo encounters: "Owing to the continued operation of this latter process, which only terminates among the warriors of the island after all the figures sketched upon their limbs in youth have been blended together . . . the bodies of these men were of a uniform dull green color—the hue which the tattooing gradually assumes as the individual advances in age. Their skin had a frightful scaly appearance, which, united with its singular color, made their limbs not a little resemble dusty specimens of verde-antique" (92). These men are not Apollos composed of polished marble but decrepit organic creatures. Tattooing here is associated with the burden of time and the blot of history. Tattooing has bequeathed to these men not simply a different skin, but the skin of a different species.[35]

In *Typee,* the Western observer of Marquesan bodies does not remain at a privileged vantage point. Karky does not passively let Tommo watch him perform his art. Tommo's stumbling upon a tattooing session in the open air is Melville's invention—as Anderson points out, in reality, the operation was always performed indoors, in a tabooed dwelling.[36] By placing this scene outdoors, Melville allows Tommo to be a voyeur and contrives the sudden reversal of his position. Karky turns toward Tommo, seizes hold of him, and brandishes his tattoo implements, "going through an imaginary performance of his art" (218). And what part of Tommo's body does Karky specifically threaten? His *face*:

> The idea of engrafting his tattooing upon my white skin filled him with all a painter's enthusiasm: again and again he gazed into my countenance, and every fresh glimpse seemed to add to the vehemence of his ambition. Not knowing to what extremities he might proceed, and shuddering at the ruin he might inflict upon my figure-head, I now endeavored to draw off his attention from it, and holding out my arm in a fit of desperation, signed to him to commence operations. But he rejected the compromise indignantly, and still continued his attack on my face, as though nothing short of that would satisfy him. When his fore-finger swept across my features, in laying out the borders of those parallel bands which were to encircle my countenance, the flesh fairly crawled upon my bones. . . . This incident opened my eyes to a new danger; and I now felt convinced that in some luckless hour I should be disfigured in such a manner as never more to have the *face* to return to my countrymen, even should an opportunity offer. (219)

The flesh "crawls" on Tommo's bones at the prospect of having his white skin marked by tattoos. Tattooing is described as "encircling" the countenance, like a noose. Tommo explains to the reader that his resistance to being tattooed hardened when he learned the fact that the Typees regarded tattooing as a badge of religious identity. Yet this "fact" is nowhere corroborated, either in Melville's sources or in twentieth-century anthropological accounts, which emphasize the ornamental functions of the designs. The religious fear seems to be an artful dodge. Tommo is afraid not of theological conversion but of racial conversion. Tattoos are "engrafted upon white skin"—as though the operation involved a translation of living tissue from Polynesian to American.[37]

Tommo's face is under "attack." The piercing anxiety here registers the literal and figurative importance of the head and the face, as Melville makes explicit in his pun: "I now felt convinced that in some luckless hour I should be disfigured in such a manner as never more to have the *face* to return to my countrymen." Here "face" means both the sense of dignity and, literally, the surface of the front part of the head. Tommo's sense of dignity and his reputation—his identity—are bound up with his unmarked face. His figure, as Melville suggests, is in his head. The face is the conspicuous surface of contact between the individual inside and the social outside, the only such surface, with the exception of the hands, regularly exposed in Western fashion. It is the " 'face divine' " exalted by poets, as Tommo reminds his readers (220). The face is the site of the expressive features, the eloquent features targeted by antebellum ethnologists and saturated with aesthetic and racial meanings: the chin, the mouth, the nose, the brow—not windows to the interior as much as signatures of the interior. Confronted by Karky, Tommo is in danger of losing his face. This vital surface will be imprinted permanently with degrading lines of difference for his countrymen to see and to read. No longer will he have a face that permits him to move undetected through American society. He will be a marked man.[38] Take my arm, he offers Karky, tattoo my arm—but leave me my *face*. Yet Karky is not "satisfied" with the limb. The more he looks into Tommo's face, the more his appetite and his ambition increase. Karky displays an artist's hunger to delineate the body, a "painter's enthusiasm." In *Typee,* as in the cannibal narratives of Cook and Krusenstern, the native assault is directed at the head. Yet in Melville's text the contents of the head are figuratively drawn out rather than literally devoured.

The dread of facial marking is present in several other mid-nineteenth-century accounts of Polynesian encounter. Coulter (1845) explains that he agreed to being tattooed, as long as his hands and face were not touched—that is, as long as the punctures were made on his body in places that could be concealed by his Western clothing (208). In the frontispiece of William Torrey's *Life and Adventures* (1848), Torrey is represented from the waist up, looking at the viewer, with his two tastefully tattooed hands resting at the bottom of the picture. Torrey, at least, has the face to return to his countrymen. In Melville's *Omoo* (1847), the sequel to *Typee,* the narrator describes the "feeling akin to horror" with which he and his fellow sailors gazed upon the renegade sailor Lem Hardy, who had voluntarily submitted to having the middle of his face tattooed with horizontal blue lines and his forehead tattooed with a blue shark.[39]

The parallel bands that Karky desires to draw across Tommo's countenance threaten to mark a face that had been unmarked—or, to be more precise, to etch lines of deviation on a face that had been imagined as composed of standard lines, to color a face that had been imagined as uncolored. A tattoo is not a blush, not a temporary shading that confirms the decorous distance between inside and outside. In *Typee,* the punctures seem to rupture the cutaneous border and fill the surface with intimate meanings.

The scene of tattooing in *Typee,* I have been suggesting, draws upon Euro-American representations of Marquesan encounter and is entwined with a scientific racialism on the American continent that came to a head in the 1840s. The Marquesan scene of tattooing is projected on a screen of skin: Marquesan, European, and American. The clear skin of female Marquesans, visible, available, and strangely familiar, entices Western sailors and incites the censure of missionaries. The inscribed skin of male Marquesans offers the spectacle of voluntary racial transformation from light to dark and intrigues the eyes of such travellers as Langsdorff. The tattooed white skin of Euro-American sailors is exhibited on stage before fascinated American eyes. The drama in these scenes of tattooing shifts in emphasis and meaning as the nineteenth century progresses. By mid-century in *Typee,* with the intervention of elaborate scholarly efforts to delineate the signs of inherent, hierarchical difference on the surface of human bodies and the popular dissemination of these views, the lines on Marquesan skin speak eloquently and disturbingly to Tommo. The ellipses on Langsdorff's *young Nukahiwan* have been filled with indelible meaning by anatomists, phrenologists, and craniometrists.

Tommo's "flesh fairly crawled upon [his] bones" (219). In Melville's hands, this idiom emerges from the rind of cliché and conveys the revulsion of many antebellum observers at the thought of contagion across racial lines and the animation imparted to the flesh by ethnologists.[40] Tommo's flesh crawls at the proximity of Karky's probing forefinger. Tommo's flesh crawls at the thought of having degraded meanings fastened to his body. Confronted with such a nightmare of corporeal limits, the protagonist of Melville's *White-Jacket* (1850) liberates himself through excoriation (chapter 92, "The last of the Jacket"). The designs of the Typee seem eerily reminiscent of nineteenth-century ethnological engravings on the skin, face, and head. These ethnological lines chart departures from the human norm and, in so doing, they establish and reinforce the norm. They are lines that fulfill the ethnological vision of a body whose surface is legible—of a face with character, a skin that is revealing.

In *Polynesian Researches* (1831), Ellis confesses that he has "frequently thought the tattooing on a man's person might serve as an index to his disposition and his character" (1:208).[41] Karky's sweeping finger offers such an index. In an illuminating moment in *Typee,* Tommo dismisses his doubts about the royal paternity of a boy he sees—doubts based on the child's not having inherited the triangular facial tattoo of his apparent father, the chief Mehevi: "but on second thoughts, tattooing is not hereditary" (190). The narrator's first thought is, naturally, to expect to see the marks of the father upon the son. His second thoughts are deleted from the revised American edition of *Typee* published in July 1846. Someone—either Melville or his American editors, or both— had second thoughts about these second thoughts. In the revised edition, the joke about the permanency of tattooing through generations remains unqualified: "a noble boy about a year old, who bore a marvellous resemblance to Mehevi, whom I should certainly have believed to have been the father, were it not that the little fellow had no triangle on his face" (190). These lines suggest ancestry not artistry.

When Karky sweeps his index finger across Tommo's features and when he brandishes his tattooing instruments, the invisible pencil of antebellum ethnology is made palpable and ominous. In Karky's tattooing, Melville represents the shared assumptions and procedures of the artist and the scientist: the desire to visualize knowledge, which Melville characterizes in *Typee* as a "painter's enthusiasm" (219) and which Hawthorne, in his *Scarlet Letter* portrait of Roger Chillingworth, calls a "physician's ecstasy"; the reliance on the technology of color, contour, and line; the attachment to symmetry, proportion, and balance and the charting of deviation from these orders; the investment in the intaglio process, whereby designs incised below the surface are made visible and reproducible; the belief that lines on the surface of the human body will give access to the depth and difference of human character.[42] Both Karky and Samuel George Morton unite the eye of the connoisseur, the eye of the artist, and the eye of the scientist. In chapter 30 of *Typee*, tattooing looks like the line cuts of the "American school" of ethnology.

Yet these lines also look different, drawn by Karky's hand. Karky is an artist and a scientist performing his operations on the human body, but he is a Marquesan artist and scientist. It is as a result of his multiple, overlapping figurations that he is such an unsettling figure for Tommo. On the island of Nukuheva, Tommo is confronted with the deformed visages of classically featured Marquesans. In the parallel bands that encircle the faces of Karky's victims, Tommo sees a reflection of the Marquesan fate of his own statuesque face. The anthropologist W. C. Handy's illustrations of tattoo face patterns for men convey the extent of Marquesan facial marking (see figure 7).[43] The patterns are eerily reminiscent of the division of the body's surface into specific, densely inscribed areas in racial ethnology. Yet in contrast to the lines and angles, the latitudes and longitudes, of physiognomy and phrenology, which construct the Caucasian face in a firm grid of proportioned

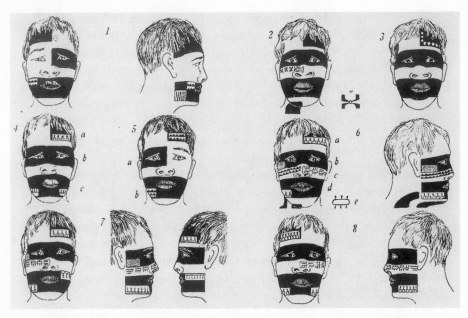

Figure 7. *Face Patterns for Men,* from *Tattooing in the Marquesas,* by
Willowdean C. Handy (1922). Bishop Museum Press, Honolulu, Hawai'i.

features, these designs threaten to unfix the face. The zoning here divides
the face into interchangeable parts and colors. Unlike the numbered
phrenological faculties in the Fowlers' charts, which signify permanent
locations, the denotations in Handy correspond to design motifs, which
are transposable. The positions and colors of these facial features appear
arbitrary; the relationship among features seems unstable, the foundation for the color uncertain. The artistry and the artifice in the composition of these faces are apparent. Tommo is not only threatened with
having his face indelibly marked and "rendered hideous for life" (218),
he is threatened with the dissolution of the face as he knows it.

In Marquesan tattooing, the ethnologist's dream of definitive facial
geometry decomposes into an illegible nightmare: the prospect of designs without spines. This incoherence is much more unsettling than the
confusion that is described by Langsdorff and Bennett as characteristic
of immoderate or aged tattooing designs and that is associated with a
"Negro-like appearance." While visually disordered, such an appearance is cognitively precise, conveying the stable imperfections of blackness. Marquesan faces, on the other hand, are unpredictable. Marquesan tattoos sever the link forged by antebellum ethnology between

individual and collective character. While the markings on individual Marquesan faces are permanent, the location and arrangement of these marks do not persist from face to face. The ethnological guarantee that the individual recapitulates the race is invalidated. Marquesan faces offer the horrifying prospect of indelibility *and* insecurity. On Marquesan faces, it becomes impossible to chart the regular gradations in man.

Marquesan tattooing is so disturbing because, in the mid-nineteenth-century imagination of *Typee*, it represents a native artistic retribution for the Western science of racial ethnology. Karky wants to decorate Tommo's body, and Tommo goes to pieces. Tattooing is at the same time ethnology and anti-ethnology—or ethnology as revenge. The ethnologist sought to trace lines on the body in order to read racial character and separate and rank human types. In *Typee,* in a case of measure for measure, the Polynesian tattooist turns to the American observer, seizes him, flourishes his instruments—not the scalpel and the calipers, but the shark's tooth and the small wooden hammer—and threatens to return the gesture. And Karky's lines *are* lines. They are not the figurative tracings on Camper's faces or on the Fowlers' heads. Karky threatens to literalize the lines drawn by ethnologists and to carve them on the body of the observer. Whatever ornamental or social functions these lines served in Polynesian culture, for many American observers of the time, they indicated lines of denigration. Not only is the invisible pencil of ethnology made visible in Karky's operations, it draws with abandon: Marquesan tattooing threatens to hatch and crosshatch the observer's body with so many lines that they will alter and confound his complexion.

The emphasis on bodily peril in the scene of tattooing in *Typee* is extreme, even in the context of the repeated links in Polynesian travel narratives between tattooing and violence, color and pain. Karky's assault materializes and turns back the ethnologist's cognitive violence. This is the scene that is foregrounded in *Typee*, not the late-eighteenth- or early-nineteenth-century exhibition holding out the hopeful prospect of black skin maturing into white; not the exotic prospect of illuminated male bodies outlined by Langsdorff; not the ethnological calibration of faces; not the mid-nineteenth-century display of tattooed European and American sailors who claimed that they were marked against their will. Such scenes preserve the distance between observer and observed. In the crucial chapter 30 of *Typee*, "A Professor of the Fine Arts—His Persecutions," the insulating distance is traversed by the tattoo artist Karky, who, with enthusiasm and vehemence, threatens to impart color to the colorless Tommo. It is a scene that threatens transformative penetration and graphic rape. The reversal, the invasiveness, the excess, the arbitrariness, and the indelibility all disturb in this scene and ultimately provoke the violent counterattack that climaxes the book.[44]

The tattooing scene in *Typee* raises the specter of racial revenge and suggests a revolution in perspective. Tommo, "unmanned" (232), runs away. Melville, too, seems to flee. That is, the distance between narrator and writer seems slight. Tommo's response is validated by the subsequent account of escape and culminating fury, when he delivers the ultimate retort to Karky's facial assault by hurling a boat hook at the throat of a pursuing Marquesan chief. The tattooing scene has not been staged so that the reader perceives the limits of Tommo's cultural horizons and racial perceptions. Instead, the scene as written and positioned invites the reader to share those limits. In the end, the narrative descends into scenes of contrived sentiment (old Marheyo commands Kory-Kory to assist Tommo in his escape and grants him a parting benediction consisting of the only two English words Tommo claims he has taught him, "Home" and "Mother") and spurious adventure (the final violent heroism could have been lifted from O'Connell or Torrey). Yet before these final protective gestures, the reader is given a glimpse of profound cultural encounter—profound, if not in its critical transcendence or dramatic irony, then in its revelation of the depth and the sources of American anxiety. Karky's assault on Tommo is a raw and vibrant textual moment.[45]

Although Tommo resists Karky's approach, Melville's own literary practice bears a conspicuous resemblance to the excessive inscriptions of the Marquesan artist. In the overdetermined lines of the long fiction from *Typee* (1846) to *Pierre* (1852), Melville illuminates—renders strangely material—the ideological designs of his culture. He inhabits and manipulates crucial figures, probing the structures and functions of antebellum discourse on race, nationalism, gender, and the sentiments. With increasing artistry, Melville anatomizes the ways in which antebellum features—faces, heads, skin, eyes, hearts, and minds—have been inscribed.

In this first book, Melville demonstrates an intimate knowledge of the shaping obsessions of antebellum racial discourse and the ways in which the scientist and the artist operated on the human body. He offers a telling scene of reversal in which the observer's body is threatened with being scarred by the object of study. Yet the detail and the force of the representations do not indicate a critical distance from the observer's anxieties about having his own body invidiously marked or from the observer's distress at being dislodged from his privileged position. For all the compelling comparative anthropology, the domestications of canni- balism, the reversal of expectations about civilization and savagery, and the perspectival shifts achieved through juxtaposing American and Poly- nesian cultures, Melville wishes to save his face. Relativism has its limits.

Yet these are revealing limits. *Typee* is a text structured by reversals. In a minor reversal, the ferocious Typee and the gentle Happar change positions. In the major double reversal of the book, the islanders switch places with the civilized Europeans and Americans, and then switch again, as native practice is revealed to be savage indeed at its core and the narrator seeks to escape to "Home" and "Mother." Yet these rever- sals conceal a fundamental similarity between the two spheres and a recognition that there is no escape, a recognition whose full acknowl- edgment is postponed until the lacerating incarcerations of *White-Jacket* (1850). The savagery of the Typee is artistic, and the conjunction be- tween Marquesan artistry and Western science suggests that in both Marquesan and American cultures there is no refuge from inscription, no safe haven for whiteness. The "ghastly" aspect of "whiteness," to use Melville's language from "The Whiteness of the Whale" in *Moby-Dick* (189), lies in its failure to live up to its pristine promise. Imagined as the visible absence of color, white at the same time is "the concrete of all colors" (195)—not blank, but fraught with meaning.

Melville writes *Typee* in the tradition of judicious crosscultural criti- cism, practiced most famously by Montaigne in Europe in the late six- teenth century (discoursing, secondhand, "Of Cannibals" in Brazil) and continued in the North American colonies by Roger Williams in the middle of the seventeenth century (describing his encounter with the Narragansett Indians in *A Key into the Language of America*) and in the United States after the Civil War by Lydia Maria Child (protesting cultural extermination in *An Appeal for the Indians*). Like his predeces- sors, Melville questions Western claims about "savage" behavior by comparing the practices of native peoples understood in context with the unchristian acts of "civilized" men. Like Montaigne, Melville at- tempts to demystify the practice of cannibalism and to defuse Western obsessions with cannibalism as the crucial sign of savagery. Like both Montaigne and Child, Melville in *Typee* offers a defamiliarizing cata- logue of cultured brutality:

> But it will be urged that these shocking unprincipled wretches are cannibals. Very true; and a rather bad trait in their character it must be allowed. But they are such only when they seek to gratify the passion of revenge upon their

enemies; and I ask whether the mere eating of human flesh so very far exceeds
in barbarity that custom which only a few years since was practised in enlightened England:—a convicted traitor, perhaps a man found guilty of hon-
esty, patriotism, and suchlike heinous crimes, had his head lopped off with a
huge axe, his bowels dragged out and thrown into a fire; while his body,
carved into four quarters, was with his head exposed upon pikes, and permitted to rot and fester among the public haunts of men! (125)

For Melville, as for Montaigne, the savage practice of cannibalism,
moderate and in proportion to the martial circumstances, pales when set
against the civilized slicing and tearing of human flesh as punishment for
breaches of conscience. Yet for Melville, the most appalling spectacle is
not carving the body into quarters (such surgery is the stuff of humor in
White-Jacket) or lopping off the head and exposing it on a pike (such a
sight is more the object of curiosity than fear for the narrator at the end
of "Benito Cereno"). The deepest horror in *Typee* is maiming the body
by writing upon it—not the severed head upon a pike, but the head still
attached to the body, the face and skull punctuated with conspicuous
lines of difference for all to read. This punishment is a particularly post-
Enlightenment torture, a nineteenth-century version of Montaigne's
"lacerating the body of a man still full of feeling" ("a deschirer par tour-
mans et par geines un corps encore plein de sentiment"), executed by the
"American school." [46]

Typee begins as Melville's "Of Cannibalism" and, despite the anxious reversion to anthropophagy, ends as his "Of Tattooing." In the shift
from literal to figurative decomposition as the primal fear of the Western sojourner in the Pacific, we see the conventional anxieties about loss
of identity transformed by the assumptions and procedures of nineteenth-century ethnology and refocused on the body's surface, rather
than viscera. While the scene of cannibalism is emptied, a new nineteenth-century scene is filled with dread. In the shift from anthropophagy to tattooing, from the contents of the body being devoured to
the character of the individual being made visible in the skin, the risk becomes deeper, rather than superficial. Confined in the skin, identity becomes more vulnerable.

In the northwest Marquesas, Melville's Tommo flees the abusive society on board the American whaleship *Dolly,* but realizes that he is unable to survive in the island mountains. Descending to a valley, he hopes
to sojourn with the nobly savage Happar, but finds himself among the
ferocious Typee, who turn out to be noble cannibals but savage tat-
tooists. At the end of the book, Tommo escapes in search of civilization

once more. Yet embedded in the crucial twist of the narrative—the revelation of tattooing in the Karky scene—is a deeply unsettling insight. Rather than confronting his likeness in the unblemished marble of an *Apollo Belvedere*, Tommo sees himself in the stippled flesh of Karky's subjects. On the island of Nukuheva, Tommo has discovered civilization, and its mark—whether in the nineteenth-century Marquesas or in nineteenth-century America—is the tattoo.

CHAPTER 2

Jumping out of One's Skin in *White-Jacket*

Melville's *White-Jacket* (1850) is a book about the extension of black slavery to the decks of United States naval frigates and to the backs of white sailors. As Melville indicates in his subtitle, "The World in a Man-of-War," his book takes as its subject an entire set of analogies that links ship to shore. These analogical ambitions are the ambitions of the genre in which *White-Jacket* was written, the popular antebellum seaman's narrative. The seaman's narrative detailed the structures of order, the varieties of labor, and the social relations in ship and state. It was a subgenre in a wider cultural effort to anatomize the political and social constitution of the United States during the decades of crisis before the Civil War. This effort included slave narratives by Frederick Douglass, James Pennington, and Solomon Northup, political oratory such as the triumvirate of speeches by Clay, Calhoun, and Webster delivered during the debates over the Compromise of 1850, and the polemical comparisons between Southern and Northern society made by slavery defenders such as George Fitzhugh. In *White-Jacket,* Melville takes the seaman's genre as the synecdoche for this effort to analyze America, and he probes to the core of the genre. At the core, he discovers a crucial analogy, that between the white and the black "slave." He locates a defining scene: the scene of flogging, in which the similarities and the differences between the bodies of white and black men are exposed. In both sailor and slave narratives, flogging is represented in explicitly theatrical terms, with actors, victims, audiences, and intricate spatial arrangements. The flogger is represented as having the power to define and convert human skin. These scenes display the textures, properties, and limits of different skins. Melville represents the scene of flogging four times, the first three as tragedy and the last as fantasy. On the decks of the United States frigate *Neversink,* Melville shows how the national drama of freedom and slavery is enacted on and in the skins of black and white slaves.[1]

The analogy with slavery was at the center of antebellum political debate. Northern labor radicals, slavery apologists, women's rights advocates, military reformers, and nationalists all used the analogy to clarify their positions. The presence of chattel slavery shaped antebellum political discourse. Yet the analogy, while pervasive, was not self-evident. What did it mean to be "like a slave"? What was a slave? A laborer? A man? A sailor? A woman? In what senses do these positions intersect? In what senses do they diverge? Is analogy identity?

In *White-Jacket,* Melville focuses on the figure of the sailor, the emblem of vulnerability for many mid-nineteenth-century reformers, and scrutinizes the analogy between sailor and slave. He embodies this analogy in the characters on board his man-of-war and repeatedly dramatizes the defining scene of flogging. He presses the analogy to its limits, revealing its terms and relations. Melville tells the story of the analogy in antebellum culture: a story of white attraction, bondage, and release, in which the resemblances between white sailor and black slave become too intimate and unruly. It is a story of an analogy that gets out of hand, that threatens to confound the distinctions between terms and to mark its user, and that then must be disciplined.

In *White-Jacket,* Melville locates the structure of the United States in a man-of-war and shows the uniform of that society to be a white jacket. How we get from nation to man-of-war to white jacket is the American story of Melville's book. At the pivot of this story is the lash. Describing the flogging of African American slaves, Frederick Douglass tells a British audience in his 1846 "Reception Speech" at Finsbury Chapel: "I am afraid you do not understand the awful character of these lashes. You must bring it before your mind."[2] For Melville and for Douglass, although in different ways for the two men, as we shall see, the awful character of the lash—its power to expose, to inscribe, and to liberate character—enforces a split American identity. *White-Jacket* begins with a searing analysis of shipboard order and climaxes in the anatomy of the title character, who, breathtakingly, slices himself out of his own white skin.

THE ANATOMICAL IMPULSE: SHIP, STATE, AND BODY

White-Jacket is a book about a ship and a jacket. Melville's narrator White-Jacket recounts his experience on board the United States frigate *Neversink,* drawing, in part, upon Melville's own stint as a seaman on the first-class frigate *United States* from August 1843 to October 1844. White-Jacket is not interested in conventional character and plot. He does not report on the thoughts and feelings of human figures and the effects of their actions. Instead, he describes the "interior life of a man-of-war" (304) and he tracks the birth, life, and death (rather we should say murder) of a handmade naval coat.

To say that textual detail is lavished on a ship and a jacket is not to argue that the book lacks animation but to observe that Melville reserves his most vivid personifications for these inanimate features. The narrator is certainly a "person," but he is bound to his jacket. Until the end of the book, when he removes himself from his white jacket in an astounding act of liberating evisceration, he is defined in its terms, literally named by it.

Other characters are given varying degrees of specificity. The narrator's idol, the literary Jack Chase, captain of the maintop, is presented in a glowing but monotoned halo of esteem. Most of the other characters appear and disappear according to their use in clarifying the dynamics of shipboard life. In this category would fall Nord and Williams, the thoughtful misanthrope and the laughing philosopher, the narrator's "friends" who are introduced in chapter 13, hardly ever to be mentioned again; also included would be the old Ushant, who retains his beard despite Captain Claret's shaving edict, stoically receives his lashes at the gangway, and endures as a symbol of manly defiance.

The ship and the jacket, on the other hand, are given meticulous, impassioned regard. Forty-one of the ninety-three chapter titles describe aspects of a man-of-war's character. Both ship and jacket are invigorated through figurative links, especially through the circuit of analogies between ship and state, sea and land. The *Neversink* is "a bit of terra firma cut off from the main" (23), "like life in a large manufactory" (35), "a lofty, walled, and garrisoned town" (75), and "a sort of State Prison afloat" (175). The narrator's eponymous white jacket is a marker of his class status, an emblem of Melville's textual production, the fabric of ideology, and, most resonantly, the surface of human skin. The jacket protects, defines, differentiates, exposes, constricts, and liberates. Both ship and jacket overflow with meaning.

In *White-Jacket,* ship and jacket are personified for the purpose of anatomy. That is, Melville analyzes antebellum American society and individual identity through the figures of the ship and the jacket. Melville's materialist perspective may account for the relative absence of conventional human "character" on board the *Neversink.* Like his contemporary Marx, Melville details how individual consciousness is shaped in the relations of economic production and in "the incurable antagonism of interests" between classes, which White-Jacket describes as "the height of the perfection of Navy discipline" (208).[3] In chapter 12, "The Good or Bad Temper of Men-of-war's men," Melville hyperbolically describes the ways in which the sailors' personalities are tempered by their naval stations and duties. Gunners become cross and quarrelsome as the result of spending so much time among the ordnance. The bodies of those who oversee the gunners become altered, as their authority stiffens their upper lips and aristocratically cuts their noses. Those who work in the cellars and caves below the berth-decks become gloomy; those who work in the open air and sunshine of the forecastle become charitable. Those sailors who work in the exalted maintop, like the narrator, become exuberant and objective, as White-Jacket explains:

> And I feel persuaded in my inmost soul, that it is to the fact of my having been a main-top-man; and especially my particular post being on the loftiest yard of the frigate, the main-royal-yard; that I am now enabled to give such a free, broad, off-hand, bird's-eye, and, more than all, impartial account of our man-of-war world; withholding nothing; inventing nothing; nor flattering, nor scandalizing any; but meting out to all—commodore and messenger-boy alike—their precise descriptions and deserts. (47)

The paradox of position is clear here. In a chapter exposing the conditioned characters of the sailors on board the *Neversink,* the narrator proclaims his elevated stance and insists that he alone is "impartial." White-Jacket's impartiality will be challenged over the course of the book. His position in shipboard society will be relegated to the margins after repeated acts of ostracism by his fellow crew members. His status as observer will be reversed when he is arraigned at the mast to be flogged in front of the assembled crew. White-Jacket's claim for authorial power—the power to deliver to commodores and messenger-boys alike their just descriptions and deserts—will be superseded by Melville's authority to mete out punishment. At the end of the book, White-Jacket loses his lofty perch. His insistence on impartiality shown again and again to be the mark and mystification of his status as a maintop man, White-Jacket is pushed by Melville from the yardarm.[4]

White-Jacket's fall is a complicated joke not only about the narrator's claims of transcendence but also about the author's critical position. Although White-Jacket affirms that he invents nothing in his account of his man-of-war world, Charles Anderson has shown that Melville invented key scenes and elaborated on his many sources for this narrative of fact. Although White-Jacket proclaims that he neither flatters nor scandalizes, Melville did both in his diatribe against flogging in *White-Jacket*. He flattered those reformers who were on the verge of gaining passage of an anti-flogging law in the United States Congress and scandalized those navy men who rose to defend in print the system of corporal punishment.[5] White-Jacket's partial impartiality and his confession of privilege seem Melville's own, and the character's punishment seems a self-inflicted blow. Yet the illusion of transcendence is not Melville's. Throughout the book he conveys his awareness that he stands inside the man-of-war world he evaluates. This awareness is partly registered in the strange narrative tone. White-Jacket's maintop point of view persists throughout the narrative and inflects the unrelenting account of the disciplined and regulated shipboard society. *White-Jacket* offers a buoyant critique of a brutal system. This formal situation intensifies the critique, as the reader is given a precise analysis of the operations of a brutal society by a narrator whose claims of detachment from that society become increasingly less plausible as the narrative progresses. The narrator's detachment seems an effect of, rather than an antidote to, the system described.

Melville's anatomy of antebellum American society is excruciating. *White-Jacket* describes how order is established and regulated in a U.S. man-of-war. In chapter after chapter, Melville analyzes the techniques through which discipline is maintained: the duration and rotation of deck watches (chapter 21); the allocation and withholding of alcohol (chapters 14 and 43); the beneficences of shore leave (chapter 54); the obsession with neatness and unobstructedness on the three decks (chapter 22); the omnipresence of punishment for the slightest infraction and the spectacle of flogging (chapters 33–36); the monthly muster around the capstan and ritual reading of the Articles of War (chapter 70); the mock-tragic "Massacre of the Beards," according to army standards by which sailors' facial hair was to be "accurately laid out and surveyed" (356; chapters 85–87). While mock, these scenes are still tragic, showing how military authority extends to the most personal spaces.[6]

White-Jacket dissects "The Social State in a Man-of-War": the "checks and balances," the "system of cruel cogs and wheels," the "endless ramifications of rank and station," the "immutable ceremonies and iron etiquette," the "spiked barriers separating the various grades of rank," the "delegated absolutism of authority on all hands," and the "impossibility of appeal," all of which shape and regulate the "domestic interior" of a man-of-war (373–75). These are "organic evils" of naval life, concludes White-Jacket, "incurable, except when they dissolve with the body they live in" (375). The perfect product of this man-of-war world is a sailor named Landless, or "Happy Jack," a foretopman who is always smiling despite the grid of welts on his back, always obedient, satisfied with his tobacco and his rum, all exterior—no shame, no soul (383–85). Shakings, a minor acquaintance of White-Jacket, approvingly compares life on board a man-of-war to imprisonment, evoking the allure of discipline and the comfort of dependence. On the decks of the *Neversink* is made material Jeremy Bentham's vision of a disciplinary society. Melville details what Michel Foucault will term a "carceral" existence.[7]

The intimate, regulated brutality on the *Neversink* cannot be explained away by critical insistence on the separate realms of sea and land. Melville's analogies between the two spheres are too frequent and too raveled to be so cleanly separated. Nor should the confinement be caricatured. There are avenues of resistance to authority, ranging from tactics of loitering to the mutinous moment when the sailors perform and witness scenes of their own oppression in a Fourth-of-July theatrical on the boards of the *Neversink*. Naval discipline is reasserted by a timely call to order to protect the ship against an approaching storm (chapter 23). Shakings may be intoxicated by incarceration, but Melville is not.[8]

White-Jacket is one in a series of antebellum maritime anatomies, including William McNally's *Evils and Abuses* (1839), Richard Henry Dana, Jr.'s *Two Years Before the Mast* (1840), Samuel Leech's *Thirty Years from Home* (1843), and J. Ross Browne's *Etchings of a Whaling Cruise* (1846), all of which Melville used as sources for his book. Each of these narrators evaluates the social order on ship and in state. Each asserts the specific character of his shipboard conditions: naval vessels, merchant ships, and whalers are represented as different spaces. Each narrator declares his maritime working-class position, insisting upon his inside perspective. Dana offers a "voice from the forecastle," Leech a "voice from the main deck," Melville a voice from the "maintop." In order to understand the genre of the seaman's narrative, we must reimagine the force conveyed in 1840 by Dana's title preposition: "*before* the mast"—that is, living in the forecastle and serving as a sailor. In the opening chapter of *Two Years Before the Mast,* Dana asserts that he provides the first detailed account from the perspective of a "common sailor." The seaman's narrative, ignited if not inaugurated by Dana's book, responded to mid-nineteenth-century readers' complexly motivated desires to stand in the place of the "common sailor." The seaman's narrative is a genre of position, a genre in which positions are specified, literalized, and navigated: the space between forecastle and captain's cabin, main deck and quarter deck, writer and reader, ship and state.[9]

The anatomical impulse—the effort to diagnose the national body in the decades before the Civil War—is shared by reformers, radicals, and reactionaries. It reaches a political climax in the probings and prescribings of the famous Senate speeches in 1850 delivered by Henry Clay, John C. Calhoun, and Daniel Webster over the issue of Clay's compromise for dealing with the question of slavery in the territories acquired in the war with Mexico. Acknowledging the present crisis, each speaker gives a version of the origin, condition, and development of the United States in the first sixty years of its existence—a different history and histology of the Union. As Calhoun writes, making explicit the therapeutic metaphors: "How can the Union be preserved? To give a satisfactory answer to this mighty question, it is indispensable to have an accurate and thorough knowledge of the nature and character of the cause by which the Union is endangered. Without such knowledge it is impossible to pronounce, with any certainty, by what measure it can be saved; just as it would be impossible for a physician to pronounce, in the case of some dangerous disease, with any certainty, by what remedy the patient could be saved, without similar knowledge of the nature and character of the cause which produced it."[10] Clay, Calhoun, and Webster offered separate diagnoses and performed their examinations from above rather than, like sailors or slaves, from below. Yet there is a shared sense of the need to make public an accurate and thorough knowledge of the national illness.

George Fitzhugh, the pro-slavery, anti-capitalist reactionary, published a caustic anti-anatomy four years before the collapse of the Union. He writes from a position inside the system of slavery. In the outrageous, infuriating, illuminating *Cannibals All!* (1857), Fitzhugh turns the terms of cultural difference against the civilized Northern elite. He argues that the system of capitalist "wage slavery" is far more savage and parasitic than the chattel slavery of the South. In the North, masters devour those under their charge without fulfilling their paternal obligations. Fitzhugh traces American analytical obsessions to the recognition of crisis in Europe and America after 1830, and in particular to the growing consciousness of the exploitation of labor and the unequal distribution of capital. Fitzhugh accepts the diagnoses of Northern social disease offered by Northern reformers and harnesses the force of their scathing critiques of "wage slavery" to justify the more "humane" order of chattel slavery. He embraces the analogy between wage and chattel slavery and turns that analogy against abolitionists. According to Fitzhugh, Northern social critics have exposed the putrid system not of slavery but of capitalist relations. The Northerners now should cease their efforts to reconstruct American society and instead call for the return to an earlier, healthier order:

> We are satisfied with our institutions, and are not willing to submit them to the *experimentum in vile corpus!* If the North thinks her own worthless, or only valuable as subjects for anatomical dissection, or chemical and phrenological experiments, she may advance the cause of humanity by treating her people as philosophers do mice and hares and dead frogs. We think her case not so desperate as to authorize such reckless experimentation. Though her experiment has failed, she is not yet dead. There is a way still open for recovery.

In the name of humanity, nature, and God, argues Fitzhugh, the age of anatomy must end. The national body must be spared further abuse and be allowed to function naturally. Fitzhugh is reacting to the acute political and literary probing of American institutions in the decades before the Civil War.[11]

In this outpouring of "reckless experimentation," a critical tool was analogy, and particularly the analogy with racial slavery. To understand "free" American society was to examine its relation to "unfree" American society. Across the range of antebellum political discourse, the condition of chattel slavery served as a defining, haunting concept. The analogy with slavery was the pivot for apologists such as Fitzhugh; Northern labor radicals such as Theophilus Fisk, George Henry Evans, and Mike Walsh; women's rights advocates such as Sarah Grimké, Margaret Fuller, and Elizabeth Cady Stanton; and nationalists such as John C. Cobden and Henry Carey. The analogy between sailors and slaves was made repeatedly in seaman's narratives by McNally, Dana, Leech, Browne, and Melville. African American writers who had been slaves, such as Frederick Douglass and William Wells Brown, refused to remain the silent term in such analogies. They argued for the incommensurability of the comparison between American chattel slave and

American, English, or Irish laborer or between enslaved and free American women. Slavery, argued Douglass, was about the prohibition of movement, the punishment of assembly, the silencing of voice, the lack of control over one's own body. It was a term and a status whose meanings were not easily transposable or interchangeable. "Slavery" was to be submitted to the exchanges of analogy with caution.[12]

It is not only the rhetorics of feminism and abolition, then, that "intersect" at the point of racial slavery, to use Karen Sánchez-Eppler's expression, it is also the rhetorics of anti-capitalism, labor radicalism, nationalism, and military reform.[13] At the heart of antebellum political anatomies is the analogy with racial slavery. The analogy is used to articulate the "parts" of antebellum society: geographical (North, South, and West), racial (white, black, and red), class (workers, masters, capitalists), and gender (men, women). Resonating like Jefferson's "firebell in the night," the specter of racial slavery echoed through antebellum debates on marriage, family, citizenship, work, social structure, military practice, and national character. The analogy was crucial but also volatile. Its terms, once animated, released unaccountable desires and fears and suggested unsettling links between white and black Americans. At the center of antebellum political discourse, at the core of the analogy, lurked the fundamental question: What does it mean to be "like a slave"?

SLAVES: THE SCENE OF FLOGGING
IN DOUGLASS, PENNINGTON, AND NORTHUP

What does it mean to be "like a slave"? This is the question at the heart of two related genres of antebellum anatomy, the seaman's narrative and the slave's narrative. Like Douglass's 1845 *Narrative* before it and his 1855 *My Bondage and My Freedom* after it, Melville's *White-Jacket* details mechanisms of intimate oppression, such as the use of alcohol as a regulatory tool and the function of holidays as a safety valve to release frustrated energies. Douglass and Melville describe the ways in which ordinary human activity is criminalized under chattel and naval systems. In Douglass's description of the whimsical floggings administered by the Reverend Rigby Hopkins and in Melville's portrayal of the arbitrary applications of the cat-o'-nine-tails on board the *Neversink,* both writers express outrage at a social order in which to be human is to be punished. Both Douglass and Melville test the integrity of the founding texts of American liberty—the Constitution and the Declaration of Independence—by applying them to the living and working conditions of the oppressed.[14]

Both sailor and slave narrators metaphorize position in their projects of urgent address: the emblematic stations in Dana and Melville, the resonant states and borders in Douglass, Solomon Northup, Mary Prince, and Harriet Jacobs. Both genres raise complex questions about mediation and access. Writers such as Dana and Melville voluntarily assume their "forecastle" points of view, temporarily inhabiting the world whose stories they tell. Figures such as Douglass, Northup, Prince, Jacobs, and Louisa Picquet struggle over verbal possession with the amanuenses who tell or the allies who attempt to shape their stories. These genres foreground the interpretive dilemmas of sojourners and fugitives. Whatever their differences—and there are many—both slave and sailor narratives seek to present readers on the "outside" with a view of the "interior life" within a system of domination. Both genres ask in urgent apostrophes or suggest through a skein of analogies that their readers consider the gaps and proximities between slave and free, South and North, sea and land, plantation, ship, and state.[15]

Both genres urge their readers to take action, yet both acknowledge that exhortation alone will not be effective. At the end of a chapter in *White-Jacket* titled "Some of the Evil Effects of Flogging," Melville appeals for joint action: "But what torments must that seaman undergo who, while his back bleeds at the gangway, bleeds agonized drops of shame from his soul! Are we not justified in immeasurably denouncing this thing? Join hands with me, then; and, in the name of that Being in whose image the flogged sailor is made, let us demand of Legislators, by what right they dare profane what God himself accounts sacred" (142). Yet the next chapter opens with a curious qualification: "It is next to idle, at the present day, merely to denounce an iniquity. Be ours, then, a different task" (143). The task different from "merely denouncing" is shared by antebellum sailor and slave narrators. Douglass insists that, in order to interpret the songs slaves sing on their way to the plantation house or the "contented" speech slaves offer to their masters, his readers must try to understand how these utterances are shaped by their contexts. Jacobs asks her readers to come to terms with the different discursive and moral situations of enslaved African American and "free" European American women. In *White-Jacket,* Melville contends that proper judgments can be reached and effective action taken only after an attempt is made to achieve an "interior" understanding of systems of domination. In addition to "merely denouncing," Douglass, Melville, and Jacobs provide immanent critiques.

Douglass evokes the rhetorical urgencies and perceptual dilemmas during his apostrophe to the white-robed vessels in Chesapeake Bay: "Alas! betwixt me and you, the turbid waters roll." Literally, Douglass addresses the boats, white and mobile; figuratively, he writes across the gulf that separates him from his readers, the gulf in opportunity and experience. It is such turbid waters that slave and sailor narrators seek to navigate. As Dana writes in *Two Years Before the Mast,* describing the imaginative crossing required for readers of sailor narratives: "We must come down from our heights, and leave our straight paths, for the by-ways and low places of life, if we would learn truths by strong contrasts; and in hovels, in forecastles, and among our own outcasts in foreign lands, see what has been wrought upon our fellow creatures by accident, hard-ship, or vice." "Betwixt me and you" is the fraught terrain of these narratives, which mine the tiny, crucial preposition "between." What lies betwixt me and you in slave narratives and sailor narratives? A body bound, stripped, and beaten.[16]

Such scenes of flogging are prominent in many slave narratives, which use them to focus attention on the physical cruelty of chattel slavery and the texture of broken, bleeding skin. The spectacle of black flesh being whipped had been conspicuous in abolitionist discourse since the late eighteenth century and was on display, with renewed intensity, in the anti-slavery agitation after 1830. In volumes such as George Bourne's *Picture of Slavery in the United States of America* (1834), the indictments are punctuated with lurid images of whipping. In Theodore Weld's best-selling compendium *American Slavery As It Is* (1839), the long section on "Floggings" leads the chapter entitled "Punishments." The "mark of the whip" is the refrain that runs through this section. There is an eerie aspect to Weld's collection, in which corporeal horror is textualized. The reader can consult the index for page citations concerning varieties of flogging ("for unfinished tasks," "of children," "of pregnant women until they miscarry") and encounter in alphabetical proximity "Ear-cropping," "Eyes struck out," and "Fingers cut off."[17]

In slave narratives, particularly those written by men, scenes of flogging often serve as emblems of slavery's inscriptions. In Douglass's *Narrative* (1845), the tableau of Aunt Hester being whipped forms "the blood-stained gate, the entrance to the hell of slavery" for the narrator and his readers. In *My Bondage and My Freedom* (1855), Douglass describes the record of the whip: "The overseer had written his character on the living parchment of most of their backs, and left them callous; my back (thanks to my early removal from the plantation to Baltimore,) was yet tender. . . . I was a 'graduate from the peculiar institution,' Mr. Collins [the general agent of the Massachusetts anti-slavery society] used to say, when introducing me, *'with my diploma written on my back!'*" The overseer writes his "character" on Douglass's back in the sense that he cuts lines of degradation in the skin and also in the sense that these marks are enduring evidence of his own sadistic personality. Yet the bodies of these African Americans, callous or tender, are already marked. They are "living parchment" before the whip ever touches them. Their character is already written on the surface of their bodies. As Hortense Spillers eloquently phrases it, African American bodies already contain an "American grammar book" of graduated meaning conveyed in the color of the skin, the proportions of the body, the contour of facial features, and the shape of the head. Douglass's fellow slaves are articulate texts redundantly and willfully re-marked by the lash.[18]

The vicious tautology of the whip is made vivid in the engravings in Bourne's *Picture of Slavery* (see figures 8 and 9). In *Flogging American Women* and *Torturing American Citizens,* the skins of the female and male African American slaves are already lined. The strokes of the whip are indistinguishable from the grooves of the burin that indicate their color. According to the text accompanying *Torturing American Citizens,* the farmer who is flogging the man has fastened a cat to his back to heighten the lacerating effects. Teeth, claws, whip, and burin all cut into this picture of slavery. The graphic torture extends beyond the boundaries of the slaves' bodies in these overwrought prints. The engravings in Bourne present a world composed and cramped by innumerable gashes. It is a world whose signature is the upraised, writhing whip.[19]

Scenes of flogging are supercharged by the effort to force different meanings on black and white flesh. In *Twelve Years a Slave* (1853), a ghost-written narrative, the kidnapped New Yorker Solomon Northup describes how he was imprisoned within sight of the United States Capitol and beaten with a paddle and a cat-o'-nine-tails by his captor Burch for insisting he was a free man. The louder Northup asserts his freedom, the more viciously he is scourged, as though the remarking of the whip

Flogging American Women. Page 100.

Figure 8. *Flogging American Women*, from *Picture of Slavery in the United States of America*, by George Bourne (1834).

Torturing American Citizens. Page 129.

Figure 9. *Torturing American Citizens*, from *Picture of Slavery in the United States of America*, by George Bourne (1834).

would subdue his claims. Northup is not merely whipped—he is flayed "until it seemed that the lacerated flesh was stripped from my bones at every stroke." The specter of free, defiant black skin is so infuriating and so unsettling to Burch that he must excoriate it. He must inscribe a new slave skin. Each stroke refutes Northup's claims, establishing the lines between freeman and slave.

The contest over status and color becomes acute later in *Twelve Years a Slave* when the master Edwin Epps lays into Northup, enraged at his request that he be sold away from the cotton plantation to a tanner and currier named O'Niel. Epps taunts as he flogs:

> "Feel above cotton-scraping, I 'spose. So you're going into the tanning business? Good business—devilish fine business. Enterprising nigger! B'lieve I'll go into that business myself. Down on your knees, and strip that rag off your back! I'll try my hand at tanning." . . . "How do you like *tanning?*" he exclaimed, as the rawhide descended on my flesh. "How do you like *tanning?*" he repeated at every blow. In this manner he gave me twenty or thirty lashes, incessantly giving utterance to the word "tanning," in one form of expression or another. . . . This time, he remarked, he had only given me a short lesson in *"tanning"*—the next time he would "curry me down."

Epps is provoked by Northup's racial and artisanal presumptions. He lacerates Northup with the word "tanning." With each word and welt, Epps asserts his power to enforce meaning. In response to Northup's request to learn a trade, he viciously puns on the terms of that trade. Relishing the redundancy, Epps tans a black man. He seeks to make Northup pliable by tearing his skin. With sadistic glee, he underscores the linguistic conjunction of skin and punishment, drawing on the dual meaning of "tan" as a noun denoting the exterior and as a verb describing an act of violence. Next time, he threatens, he will finish the job and "curry" him down. The flogger has the power to render the skin of his victim. Yet the inordinate skill the flogger displays also registers his insecurity, revealing the immense force necessary to install and maintain the difference in position between flogger and victim. Epps relies on his whip to articulate and lay open that difference. In scenes of flogging, African American skin is treated differently from European American skin. It is an affront that must be subdued.[20]

Douglass emphasizes the differential treatment of skin in *My Bondage and My Freedom*. An indignant Hugh Auld brings Frederick Douglass, his damaged personal property, before the magistrate Watson in order to secure the arrest of the shipyard workers who savagely beat him. Auld is frustrated by the court's refusal to accept Douglass's body of evidence:

> "Sir," said Watson, "I am sorry, but I cannot move in this matter except upon the oath of white witnesses."
>
> "But here's the boy; look at his head and face," said the excited Master Hugh; "*they* show *what* has been done."

In this scene, the difference in flesh that has been stamped by the fist and the lash is reinforced by the law. Douglass's body offers insufficient testimony. His face is not prima facie. His skin is not legally tender. Despite Auld's entreaties, in the eyes of the law Douglass's features do not show what has been done. In his serialized novel *Blake; or, The Huts of America* (1859, 1861–1862), Martin Delany bitterly unites flogging with the American flag, steeping the patriotic colors in blood and emphasizing the separation and subordination emblazoned in the national image: "high in the breeze from the flagstaff [of the slave prison in Washington, D.C.] floated defiantly the National Colors, stars as the pride of the white man, and stripes as the emblem of power over the blacks." [21]

In slave and sailor narratives, in abolitionist tracts and fiction, the pervasive scenes of flogging are explicitly staged as scenes. That is, on the soil of Pennington's Maryland and Northup's Louisiana, on the planks of Dana's *Pilgrim* and the boards of Melville's *Neversink*, flogging is a three-dimensional act performed by characters in front of an audience, unfolding in a deliberately ordered space. In *The Fugitive Blacksmith* (1849), James Pennington arranges actors and audiences in a succession of planes and gazes. Pennington watches as his father is beaten; then Pennington himself is beaten for catching his master's eye, while his mother observes the scene; then Pennington watches as a daughter sees her elderly father being flogged; and, finally, when his own mother is threatened, he decides that he must escape. In Pennington's scenes, flogging gains its force not only from the accumulating blows of the whip but also from the intensifying gazes of its witnesses. In the opening pages of his narrative, he depicts the intolerable social state of enslaved families, linked by the lash, as family member follows family member in the roles of victim and witness. With each new flogging, the violence, mortification, and rage escalate, until Pennington determines that he must break the cycle. [22]

In *Twelve Years a Slave,* the narrator displays a keen sense of flogging as theater. While imprisoned on Edwin Epps's cotton plantation in

Louisiana, the kidnapped Northup is forced to be a slave driver. He is expected to regulate the field hands with his whip. The narrator tells us that Northup did not dare show any lenity, "not having the Christian fortitude of a certain well-known Uncle Tom sufficiently to brave his [Epps's] wrath, by refusing to perform the office." Rather than absorbing his fellows' blows like the suffering hero of Stowe's popular novel, Northup "performs"—that is, fulfills and feigns—his office. He choreographs blows for his overseer's eyes:

> "Practice makes perfect," truly; and during my eight years' experience as a driver, I learned to handle the whip with marvelous dexterity and precision, throwing the lash within a hair's breadth of the back, the ear, the nose, without, however, touching either of them. If Epps was observed at a distance, or we had reason to apprehend he was sneaking somewhere in the vicinity, I would commence plying the lash vigorously, when, according to arrangement, they would squirm and screech as if in agony, although not one of them had in fact been grazed.

Having rehearsed the role of victim, Northup delivers a flawless performance as perpetrator. He satisfies his audience's craving for degrading spectacle while preserving the integrity of his actors' bodies. Northup recasts the roles. The beaten determine the effect and affect of their own blows, the beater colludes with his victims, and attention is turned to the spectators, whose appetites are foregrounded and manipulated. In revealing his plot, in sharing Northup's secret, the narrator also draws attention to the ambivalent desires of his readers, the audience that lies beyond the fourth wall of the scenes of flogging and conspires to produce their meaning.[23]

The drama of beater, beaten, and audience, of vulnerability, exposure, and inscription, of sadism and voyeurism, is played out again and again on the grounds of slave narratives and the decks of sailor narratives. These scenes raise a series of questions that resonate across antebellum culture. If, as Douglass figures it, the whip writes on the backs of African American bodies, then what are the messages it inscribes? If, as the seamen narrators repeatedly imply, the whip marks the analogy between white sailors and black slaves, then what is the character of this analogy? Seaman's narratives, and a range of imaginative writings in the 1830s, 1840s, and 1850s, offered their readers the opportunity to inhabit the position of the oppressed, using as a pivot the scene of flogging. The writer of "Mental Metempsychosis" urges, "Could we but persuade those with whom we plead, in behalf of the slave, to imagine themselves for a few moments in his very circumstances, to enter into his feelings, comprehend all his wretchedness, transform themselves mentally into his very self, they would not surely long withhold their compassion. . . . let the fetter be with its wearing weight upon their wrists, as they are driven off like cattle to the market, and the successive strokes of the keen thong fall upon their shoulders till the flesh rises in long welts beneath it, and the spouting blood follows every blow." [24] How are such imaginative acts possible? What are their effects?

In what senses is a white sailor like or unlike a black slave? For a series of sailor narrators who restage the scene of flogging in the 1840s (Leech, McNally, Browne, Dana, and Melville) the answer has to do with—and what lies betwixt me and you is—skin.

SAILORS: THE ANALOGY WITH SLAVERY IN LEECH, MCNALLY, BROWNE, AND DANA

When the *New York Daily Tribune* exulted two days after the Congressional prohibition of naval flogging, it described the gain of sailors at the expense of slaves thus:

> Henceforth, the backs of American freemen will no more be gashed and gored by the horrible "cat" and "colt" while they are exposing their lives and courting hardships in defense of the Starry Flag which would fain be held the symbol and stay of free and Equal Manhood. The stripes of that flag may henceforth be imaged on the writhing backs of black Slaves, but no longer on those of White Freeman.[25]

The *Tribune* passage comes at the climax of the national debate over sailors and slaves, at the end of the 1848–1850 Congressional session during which legislators argued over both the abolition of flogging in the United States Navy and the extension of slavery into the new United States territories gained in the war with Mexico. As in the slave narratives, here we are presented with a patriotic sadism in which national stripes are written on the backs of men. Yet the dynamics of representation differ. The indictment of chattel slavery is blunted by the channeling of outrage from the bodies of black slaves to the backs of white sailors and by the distinction made between plural slaves and a singular sailor. Here the white sailor—the Freeman—is juxtaposed with and freed from attachment to the mass of black Slaves. In the seaman's narratives of the 1840s, the analogy between sailors and slaves is forcefully drawn in a series of flogging scenes, and part of that force is exerted to redirect the reader's concern from South to North and from black to white in order to establish a hierarchy of suffering.

In *Thirty Years from Home* (1843), Leech gives perhaps the most graphic portrayal of flogging. Shifting to the present tense, he describes events he witnessed on board the British frigate *Macedonian*, on the passage from London to Spithead:

> The boatswain's mate is ready, with coat off and whip in hand. The captain gives the word. Carefully spreading the cords with the fingers of his left hand, the executioner throws the cat over his right shoulder; it is brought down upon the now uncovered herculean shoulders of the MAN. His flesh creeps— it reddens as if blushing at the indignity; the sufferer groans; lash follows lash, until the first mate, wearied with the cruel employment, gives place to a second. Now two dozen of these dreadful lashes have been inflicted: the lacerated back looks inhuman; it resembles roasted meat burnt nearly black before a scorching fire; yet still the lashes fall; the captain continues merciless. . . . Four dozen strokes have cut up his flesh and robbed him of all self-respect; there he hangs, a pitied, self-despised, groaning, bleeding wretch; and now the captain cries, forbear! His shirt is thrown over his shoulders; the seizings are loosed; he is led away, staining his path with red drops of blood.

Leech's description repels and fascinates, as does his later gruesome report on the practice of multiple floggings "through the fleet." Leech exhibits the sadism, humiliation, bodily rupture, rendering inhuman of human flesh, and draining of vital fluids at the center of the scene of flogging. He insists that a flogging does not end with the sheathing of the "cat" and the swathing in clothes. Later in his narrative, he describes the seaman Daily, scourged for an inconsequential pilot error, who continues to wear his ripped shirt in order to display his gashes as a rebuke to the captain. Daily seeks to convert his badge of shame into an accusation. These scenes of flogging are powerful, yet the sources of their power lie not merely in their vigorous descriptions.[26]

The spectacle of white flesh being whipped, set before American readers by seaman's narratives in the 1840s, invokes and is augmented by the spectacle of black flesh being whipped. The double character of African American bodies, their invidious difference engraved first by "nature" and then by human hands, makes the slave term of the analogy different from the sailor term. Flogging represents such an outrage in sailor narratives in part because the narrators imagine that European and American male bodies are not already stigmatized. The whip disfigures the white surface. In this sense, sailors are treated "like slaves"; that is, their bodies are cut with lines that eloquently reveal their vulnerability and viscerally expose their degraded character. In the

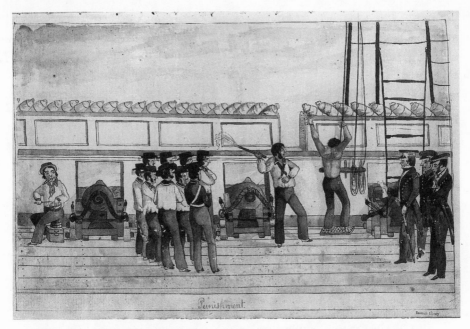

Figure 10. *Punishment*, watercolor by William H. Meyers, from his journal (1841–1844). Courtesy of the Bancroft Library, University of California, Berkeley.

comparative register that defines the analogy between sailor and slave, sailor narrators often argue for the deeper offense of scarring an unscathed body.

The depth of this difference is conveyed in William H. Meyers's watercolor *Punishment* (see figure 10). Meyers portrays a flogging on board the United States sloop-of-war *Cyane*, on which he served as a gunner from 1841 until 1844. *Punishment* may depict the penalty inflicted on one of three sailors whose flogging Meyers briefly, dispassionately describes in his journal during November 1841. (Meyers bound the watercolor into his journal near these entries.) Compared with the illustrations in Bourne's *Picture of Slavery*, Meyers's image makes clear that the lash violates the integrity of the body. The vicious pink curves traverse the cross formed by the sailor's spine and scapula. They manifest his incorporation in the grid of naval authority outlined by Meyers. He is fastened not only by the rope around his wrists but also by the gazes of the flogger, the officers, and his fellow sailors, except for the sailor on the extreme left who pauses from his whittling to watch the watchers. In contrast to the hyperbolic engravings in Bourne of black bodies tautologically scarred, Meyers's subdued watercolor shows how order is cut into pale, tender flesh.[27]

"A man should be secured the rights of a citizen, as well on the *planks* as on the *soil* of his country," argues Leech.[28] The status of the term "man" is key here, since it guarantees "citizenship" and "rights." This insistence that rights extend from shore to ship highlights a difference in the positions occupied by the sailor and the slave. A sailor has, at least theoretically, legal rights on shore, which are taken from him when he enters into service on a naval ship. A slave has no rights to lose and no choice about whether or not to serve. (Despite Congressional law prohibiting chattel slaves in the navy, enslaved African Americans did toil on U.S. naval vessels while their masters received their pay, as Melville notes in a chapter titled "The Manning of Navies.") In the analogy between sailor and slave, the term "slave" is definitive. While it makes sense for Leech, McNally, and Melville to complain that a sailor is treated like a slave, it would make no sense for them to complain that a slave was treated "like a sailor." This would be a nautical solecism.

"From the time he [the whaleman] leaves port he is beyond the sphere of human rights: he is a slave till he returns," writes Browne, delineating the spatial and racial distribution of rights. "Slave" signifies a position outside "the sphere of human rights," which the sailor may occupy for a time. In this model, there is no port to which the slave can return. H. Bruce Franklin describes nineteenth-century sailors as "temporary chattels," to distinguish their position from that of slaves and "free" laborers. Leech asserts: "Flogging may be needful to awe a slave writhing under a sense of unmerited wrong, but never should a lash fall on a freeman's back, especially if he holds the safety and honor of his country in his keeping." In the intricate way in which the analogy often works, Leech conveys a sense of the arbitrariness and cruelty of punishment to which a "slave" is subjected but he also uses the slave as a stable point of contrast to clarify the greater wrongs inflicted on the "freeman." "May be" and "never": the lash is seen as conditional for the slave, while an imperative is thundered to protect the freeman. In Leech's formula, it is unimaginable that a slave could hold the safety and honor of his country in his keeping.[29]

In *Evils and Abuses in the Naval and Merchant Service Exposed* (1839), William McNally makes explicit the hierarchy and asymmetry integral to the comparison between sailor and slave. In chapter 14, which opens with a call for the abolition of corporal punishment, McNally criticizes the attention lavished by reformers on chattel slaves and revaluates the "sailor" term:

> Never let American citizens in the Northern states rail at slavery, or the punishment inflicted on slaves, or say that it is wrong, so long as their own sons, their own flesh and blood, their own seamen, their own free citizens, and the men to whom they look for protection in case of war, are daily subject to the same treatment as the slaves, whose degraded situation in the southern states calls forth, so justly, the warmest sensibilities of the heart and nature of philanthropists. . . . Oh, Americans, to what are you coming! the blood of your ancestors is turned to water in your veins. Those who exclaim loudest against slavery, had better turn their attention to objects of suffering and benevolence at home, before they look for them abroad, hundreds of whom will be found to stand as much in need of their assistance, and emancipation from the yoke of tyranny and oppression, as the swarthy sons and daughters of Africa. At present, masters of merchant vessels are vested with greater authority than the magistrates or judges, and with the same power as the negro driver, or slaveholder, who has so often been stigmatized with the epithets of tyrants and brutes, by a society whose object is declared to be equal rights and privileges to all, and yet these men pass by the seaman, whom they daily see in the streets, and who is liable to, and often receives worse treatment than the slave, in whose behalf so many petitions have been presented, and such efforts been made as have nearly turned one half of the union against the other; if such men want objects of compassion, and their object is the welfare of mankind, let them turn to the common seaman. As long as this suffering class are permitted to remain as they now are, the efforts of anti-slavery societies can pass for nothing more than a wish on their part to join in the cry raised by individuals in Great Britain, who knew as little of slavery as their brethren on this side of the Atlantic. "Those who live in glass houses should be careful how they throw stones." Those who rail at negro slavery should take care that none of their own servants are receiving the treatment of slaves.

McNally castigates abolitionist hypocrisy (comparing Northern domestic servants and Southern chattel slaves) and the skewed philanthropic vision (the failure to see the exploitation taking place in Northern streets). Fueling the elaborate rhetoric of a passage such as McNally's is the effort to revise key terms of abolitionist discourse—"emancipation," "suffering," "tyranny," "oppression," "benevolence"—and to shift concern from black to white. His effort extends beyond the boundaries of the debate over naval reform, as is evident in the defining refrain "their own" and in the appositional series that extends from "sons" to "flesh and blood" to "seamen" and "free citizens." This passage participates in a broader attempt to redraw and reinvigorate the lines of male

American identity. McNally seeks to define who is and is not a member of the family of free citizens by exhorting readers on the ties of blood and race: "Oh Americans, to what are you coming! the blood of your ancestors is turned to water in your veins." [30]

McNally eloquently turns attention from slave to sailor. A suggestion at the beginning of the passage that sailors are "subject to the same treatment as the slaves" becomes, by the end of the passage, the assertion that sailors receive "worse treatment." Abolitionist regard for the plight of Southern slaves, first labeled a response "so justly" called forth, is finally characterized as "railing." "Americans" should look "home," before they look "abroad." McNally dilates the analogy between sailors and slaves, takes it apart, and recalibrates its levers. His analysis pivots on phrases of ranking and redirection: "rather than," "more than," "before," "worse than," "let them turn their attention to." He uses the analogy between sailors and slaves to elucidate a racial priority and to restrict the economy of compassion and the scope of political action. White sailors, not black slaves, should be the objects of sympathy.

I do not mean here to suggest that we should make a choice of oppressions, or to suggest that McNally and his fellow sailor narrators have made the wrong choice. I mean to reject such a contest between the claims of sailors and slaves. The choice was defined by naval reformers in the 1840s, who sought to establish a hierarchy of suffering. The scene of a white sailor being flogged at the mast, on display in many seaman's narratives of the 1840s, competes for attention and emotion with the flogging scenes in slave narratives and abolitionist polemics. In sailor narratives, energy is drained from the term "slave" and channeled to the term "sailor." [31]

The rhetorical and racial dynamics of this transfer of power are evident in the elisions, reversals, and forgettings that mark McNally's movement from "abroad" to "home." Abuse in the naval and merchant services is presented as the outrage that offers itself to awakened American senses. Chattel slavery is a foreign issue; naval oppression is a native one. Yet chattel slavery in the 1840s was manifestly a "home" issue, despite the efforts of McNally and many other Americans, Southern and Northern, to alienate its objects (Africans who do not belong in the United States or who deserve their position as chattel) and origins (blame the British for instituting and perpetuating the practice in its North American colonies).

McNally fails to remember that chattel slavery in America exists as a result of the "abroad" having been brought "home." He diagnoses an antebellum hypermetropia: the distant object of the black slave is seen more distinctly than the near object of the white sailor. Yet McNally's call for a refocusing of attention is premised on a distortion of space (the placement of slaves in the background or on the margins) and on a false choice (either sailor or slave but not both, since the eye can sharply perceive objects in only one plane). Attention is not just turned in *Evils and Abuses;* it is warped. This perversity is at the heart of McNally's tropes and his claims. McNally calls for American renewal and re-Union through a solidarity that crosses class lines and reinforces racial barriers. Seamen such as McNally and Leech articulate a version of what George M. Frederickson has called "white democracy," a white male bond of freedom that defines itself in racial terms.[32]

The passage in McNally obscures the shared abuse of sailor and slave, elides the economic appropriation of Africans, and redirects concern to the problems of "free" "white" "citizens." When McNally writes that "Seamen know that they are born free, and freemen will never submit to the lash of slavery," he conveys the knowledge at the core of the analogy between sailor and slave. Freemen know that they are free because of the lash of slavery. The existence of that lash, its infliction on others, and the threat of its bite all define and animate the condition of "freedom." The freeman will never submit to the lash of slavery, but that lash must persist for him to be made free.[33]

If McNally provides the finest calibrations of distance and hierarchy between the positions of sailor and slave in the seaman's narratives of the late 1830s and 1840s, then J. Ross Browne most emphatically impresses the rhetoric of abolition in the service of naval reform. Such coercions are unstable, suggesting the difficulty of maintaining the lines between sailor and slave. In *Etchings of a Whaling Cruise* (1846), Browne details his experience on a whaling ship, rather than on a naval vessel. Toward the end of the narrative, he describes the conditions to which a sailor was subjected while confined in the "run," a hole immediately under the cabin floor:

> In this dark and noisome hole an unoffending and friendless young man dragged out a weary confinement of SEVEN MONTHS. I ask the reader to pause and reflect upon his sufferings. Can any thing more dreadful be conceived? Within limits scarcely larger than a coffin—thousands of miles from his native land—breathing the thick and fetid air of a dungeon; surrounded by dense and perpetual darkness, without the power of escape should the vessel suddenly founder; without a friend to whom he could appeal; goaded by the insults of a tyrant; mocked by offers, which, as a man not totally dead to all sense of the dignity of human nature, he felt bound to reject with disdain;

days, and weeks, and months dragging their slow length along without a
change—what language can depict his sufferings! what heart is there that
does not sympathize with him!

Let no man say the age of inquisitional cruelty has passed away! Is it possible to conceive any thing more fiendish than this? Can the imagination picture a more malicious, a more brutal act of despotism?

Well, yes. The imagination can at least picture a comparably malicious
and brutal act: the confinement of Africans in the interior of slave trading vessels during the long "middle passage" across the Atlantic. Although Browne never names the referent, his prose is saturated in the
language of conventional depictions of the Atlantic passage. Echoing
anti-slavery texts, Browne asks his readers to acknowledge that language is inadequate to represent the horror of experience, and he insists
that his readers must respond with their hearts. It would be possible to
read Browne's portrayal of confinement in the "run" as an effort to supplement renderings of the "middle passage" were it not for his apostrophe to the "philanthropists" two paragraphs later, at which point it becomes clear that Browne wishes to supplant abolitionist discourse.
"Look to this, philanthropists!" he rails sarcastically, calling for a shifting of regard to "the slavish and degraded condition of a certain
class of your white countrymen. . . . They are but white men, it is true—
men of no influence or standing in society; men who have been so degraded by the lash that respectable people spurn them; but so much the
greater reason for the exercise of your magnanimity." The degrading
lash, Browne suggests, has obscured the whiteness of these sailors. Re-
placing slaves with sailors, Browne seeks to restore the luster of those
skins.[34]

Yet the terms and topics of slavery are not so easily disciplined. Despite Browne's effort, the repeated and excessive questions—"Can anything more dreadful be conceived?" "Is it possible to conceive anything
more fiendish than this?" "Can the imagination picture a more malicious, a more brutal act of despotism?"—have the effect of conjuring
the presence that he wishes to banish. The specter of black chattel slavery haunts these passages in Browne, serving as an expressive absence,
the kind of Africanist presence in American texts that Toni Morrison
has characterized as "invisible things" that "are not necessarily 'not-
there.'"[35] Despite Browne's attempt to eliminate the "black slave" term
of the analogy, that term continues to register its effects in his prose, like
a severed limb that persists in troubling its owner.

On the decks of the *Pilgrim* in Dana's *Two Years Before the Mast*

(1840), the analogy between sailor and slave becomes an explicit weapon used by the captain to subdue his sailors. The men who labor on the *Pilgrim* have spent difficult weeks trading along the California coast. Order is fraying, and the captain's need to enforce his authority erupts onto the bodies of two unfortunate sailors. Captain Thompson has developed an antipathy for a large, slow-witted sailor named Sam from the Middle States (a slave state, we are later told). Finding an excuse to charge Sam with impudence, the captain demands that Sam declare he will never again verbally challenge him:

> "Answer my question, or I'll make a spread eagle of you! I'll flog you, by G–d."
> "I'm no negro slave," said Sam.
> "Then I'll make you one," said the captain.

In this exchange, the equation between being flogged and being treated like a chattel slave is immediately apparent to the participants and immediately becomes the explicit object of their struggle. The captain vows that he will inflict the analogy, flogging Sam into a Negro slave. In a savage parody of the seaman's rights as an American citizen, the captain tells him that he will stretch out his limbs for punishment in a travesty of the national emblem.[36]

In a scene notorious for its eloquent sadism, Captain Thompson then dances about the deck, flailing John, a sailor who had questioned the grounds for Sam's flogging. Intoxicated with his demonstration and declaring that he, and not Jesus Christ, is the authority to whom sailors should appeal, Captain Thompson proclaims his mastery:

> "You see your condition! You see where I've got you all, and you know what to expect!"—"You've been mistaken in me—you didn't know what I was! Now you know what I am!"—"I'll make you toe the mark, every soul of you, or I'll flog you all, fore and aft, from the boy, up!"—"You've got a driver over you! Yes, a *slave-driver—a negro-driver!* I'll see who'll tell me he isn't a negro slave!"[37]

"You see your condition!"—this command propels the captain's scene of flogging. He displays to his audience his power to convert the meanings of their skin. Captain Thompson is a "slave driver" who turns white sailors into negro slaves through the strokes of his rope. If the sailors don't toe the mark, Captain Thompson will mark them. He will usurp the divine authority to designate types of mankind. Captain Thompson wields the analogy between captains and masters and between sailors and slaves as a lash itself.

Yet what, more precisely, does it mean to be made into a "negro slave" on board the *Pilgrim?* Dana gives an answer to this question in his report of the two very different fates of the Swede John and the Southerner Sam in the aftermath of the floggings:

> John was a foreigner and high-tempered, and though mortified, as any one would be at having had the worst of an encounter, yet his chief feeling seemed to be anger; and he talked much of satisfaction and revenge, if he ever got back to Boston. But with the other, it was very different. He was an American, and had had some education; and this thing coming upon him, seemed completely to break him down. He had a feeling of the degradation that had been inflicted upon him, which the other man was incapable of. Before that, he had a good deal of fun, and amused us often with queer negro stories,— (he was from a slave state); but afterwards he seldom smiled; seemed to lose all life and elasticity; and appeared to have but one wish, and that was for the voyage to be at an end. I have often known him to draw a long sigh when he was alone, and he took but little part of interest in John's plans of satisfaction and retaliation.[38]

John, the Swede, can dream of retribution. He is incapable of feeling the same sense of degradation that Sam felt because he did not have the same sense of superiority. He did not possess an American education. He did not occupy a position in a society with chattel racial slavery as its defining feature. For John, being treated "like a slave" is an abstraction. Despite the damage to his flesh, the captain's rope does not cut into the cutis vera. For Sam, the Southerner, being treated "like a slave" means something more literal, intimate, and devastating.

 After the flogging, Sam loses life and elasticity. His identity becomes brittle. He no longer amuses his shipmates with "queer negro stories," possibly because his experience has given him a new understanding of the position of enslaved Africans in American society, but certainly because the humor is lost. The jokes no longer work now that the distance between teller and object has collapsed. The stories don't seem as "queer." Although Sam is not a "negro slave," he is also no longer a "freeman." He now inhabits the space that intervenes between the terms sailor and slave. He occupies the anomalous position of the "white slave," neither free nor white nor black nor slave. He has become unmoored from his racial and social position. Sam is, if you will, not a tragic mulatto but a "tragic mariner" figure. With the blows of the rope, he has felt the class difference between him and the captain, between two white men, open up until it seems as permanent and vast as the racial difference between him and the "negro slave." Sam's skin does not protect him. His skin does not prevent his exposure at the gangway. It does not deflect or cushion the blows. It does not heal or erase his injury. The failure of Sam's white skin precipitates an inner collapse, a loss of faith that fantasies of revenge will not restore. Sam feels the force of the analogy between sailor and slave, and that force breaks him.[39]

The analogy breaks the career sailor Sam, but it repairs the temporary sailor Dana. That is, at the beginning of *Two Years Before the Mast* Dana's narrator tells his readers that he went to sea in order to repair a "weakness of the eyes . . . which no medical aid seemed likely to cure." In "Twenty-Four Years After," the appendix first published in 1869, the narrator assures his readers that his eyes did indeed recover after his return. His ailment is not only somatic (a severe attack of measles had weakened the actual Dana's eyes), it is also psychic. The narrator goes to sea to heal his sight and secure his identity. This emphatically descriptive, thinly plotted book is filled with distinctive sights: the different appearances and characters of Americans, Californians, Spanish, Indians, Sandwich Islanders, and Russians; the hierarchy of labors on board ship; the different positions occupied by narrator and sailors. Prominent in this sight-seeing cure is the scene of flogging he witnesses on the decks of the *Pilgrim*. The narrator goes to sea and finds himself. He finds that he is not a sailor (after the flogging, he writes "[I] vowed that if God should ever give me the means, I would do something to redress the grievances and relieve the sufferings of that poor class of beings, of whom I then was one") and not a slave. His experiences clarify his perspective through distance and difference. The narrator goes to sea a young, unfocused gentleman student and he returns a man, a white man, an American.[40]

In *White-Jacket*, Melville also presents a narrative of identity formation. Yet in Melville's version, the collapsing of distance between sailor and slave threatens the narrator himself, not just a minor character, and provokes a fantastic attempt at self-preservation. Unlike the unfortunate Sam, White-Jacket does get solace from visions of revenge, and he is the beneficiary of a miraculous reprieve from the cat-o'-nine-tails. White-Jacket's white skin does protect him, then fails him profoundly, then sacrifices itself for him.

FLOGGED FREE: WHITE-JACKET'S EMANCIPATION

In *White-Jacket*, Melville slices open the analogy between sailors and slaves and exposes its structures. Melville's denunciations of flogging are impassioned, yet, as Anderson and more recently Dimock have suggested, they are somewhat belated. That is, *White-Jacket* was published less that a year before the Congressional vote to prohibit flogging in the American navy, following two years of legislative debate on the issue and more than a decade of public agitation on the part of seamen and naval reformers. Even if we don't wish to reduce Melville's polemics to a savvy gesture of market manipulation, as Anderson does ("Melville simply got on the bandwagon of reform; he had an eye for the public taste"), we must acknowledge that his anti-flogging arguments are standard and safe.[41] "Merely to denounce," as Melville himself recognizes, is not the task of *White-Jacket*. Melville delves into the corporeal anxieties in the analogy between sailor and slave. At risk is the narrator's own skin.

According to White-Jacket, "Some of the Evil Effects of Flogging" include its indiscriminate, frequent, and severe application; the lack of proportion between punishment and offense; the absence of any trial or court of appeal; its restriction to sailors and the exemption of officers from the penalty; and the absolute authority it confers on the captain, who becomes legislator, judge, and executive (139–49). The most evil effect of flogging in the American navy is, as Melville puts it in a resonant pun, "an everlasting suspension of the Habeas Corpus" (144). Not only is the writ guaranteeing the right of an accused man to be brought before a court suspended, or rendered void, on naval ships, but the body of the accused is literally suspended: hung from the gratings, stripped, its flesh bared to the eyes of the entire crew and to the whip of the boatswain's mate. The writ of habeas corpus isn't simply ignored on United States men-of-war; it is rewritten, sadistically, on the exposed backs of the class of men called sailors.

The subjection to authority, the vulnerability, and the scarring all sharpen the analogy between sailor and slave in *White-Jacket*. The narrator describes the legacy that endures on the body of a flogged sailor, "a penalty the traces whereof he carries to the grave; for to a man-of-war's-man's experienced eye the marks of a naval scourging with the *cat* are through life discernible." Although White-Jacket affirms the "untouchable" zone of a sailor's "true dignity," this insistence is qualified by his identification with the seeping body: "But what torments must that seaman undergo who, while his back bleeds at the gangway, bleeds agonized drops of shame from his soul!" (142). The whip cuts the body, and drops of the soul leak out.[42] The slice of the whip gives the assembled viewers access to what the narrator earlier refers to as the "inmost soul" (47) and later as the interior "man's manhood" (280). The whip produces an intimate blood knowledge. The sailor's scars signify his degradation, a visceral exposure rendered permanently legible in the ruptures of his skin.

In this sense, flogging in *White-Jacket* presents a danger similar to that posed by tattooing in *Typee:* the prospect of indelible, invidious marking. In *Typee,* the narrator fixates not on the melodrama of cannibalism but on the horror of tattooing. Similarly, in *White-Jacket,* the narrator focuses not on the severing of the body—which is satirically rendered in a series of chapters describing the bungled operations of the naval ship's surgeon, the eager Dr. Cadwallader Cuticle—but on the outrage of flogging. As was the case with cannibalism in *Typee,* in order to understand Melville's concerns about corporeal inscription we need to examine his defining alternative in *White-Jacket:* dismemberment.

Taken from the satiric tradition of Molière, Swift, and Smollett, Dr. Cuticle is a myopic, verbose, overzealous specialist, an artificial shell of a professional man, a patchwork of prostheses, with a wig, one glass eye, and a set of false teeth. Dr. Cuticle is an epitome of technical reason and a human wreck. He is marvelously indifferent to the sufferings of his patients. Cutting off their limbs is always the preferred treatment. He is noted for the speed of his amputations: one minute and ten seconds to sever a leg, as clocked by his admiring assistants. "Amputation is the only resource," is his refrain (253, 256).

In "The Operation," Melville describes Dr. Cuticle at work. Seeking to remove a bullet from the thigh of an unnamed foretopman, who was shot while attempting to swim ashore, Dr. Cuticle opts, of course, for amputation. The good doctor addresses his surgical audience on the tortuous medical practices of the past and separates the joints on a model skeleton to pinpoint the site of his intervention, all in front of the patient, who repeatedly faints. White-Jacket details Dr. Cuticle's cut, the flow of blood down the patient's thigh, the "thrilling, rasping sound" of the saw, and the leg sliding into the arms of a surgical assistant. Later, after Dr. Cuticle delivers a disquisition on the route the ball must have taken in the foretopman's thigh and on the tangled paths of firearm projectiles through history, the steward enters, announcing that the patient has died.[43]

Melville presents a delicious caricature of medical myopia. Yet in *White-Jacket* amputation is funny, while flogging is not. Although Dr. Cuticle is a figure of corporeal punishment, his penalties are much

less severe than those inflicted by the boatswain's mate and his "cat."
While the final preparations are being made for the amputation, the doctor addresses the assembled surgeons:

> "Gentlemen," said he, taking up one of the glittering knives and artistically
> drawing the steel across it; "Gentlemen, though these scenes are very unpleasant, and in some moods, I may say, repulsive to me—yet how much
> better for our patient to have the contusions and lacerations of his present
> wound—with all its dangerous symptoms—converted into a clean incision,
> free from these objections, and occasioning so much less subsequent anxiety
> to himself and the Surgeon. Yes," he added, tenderly feeling the edge of his
> knife, "amputation is the only resource." (256)

Dr. Cuticle's operation is funny, as well as horrible, because it is so
quick, clean, and finite: cut and dried.[44] If Dr. Cuticle had politics, he
would be a Garrisonian, recommending the swift severing of the Union
so that the integrity of the North might be preserved. A "Morbid
Anatomist" fascinated with diseased parts (249), Dr. Cuticle does not
recognize systemic conditions. With a slash, the patient is separated
from his distressed flesh.

If Dr. Cuticle is an artist ("'Gentlemen,' said he, taking up one of the
glittering knives and artistically drawing the steel across it"), he is inferior to the tattooer Karky in *Typee*. He is less subtle and his work is less
enduring. Karky's incisions create, rather than tidily convert, wounds.
Karky's lines persist on his canvas and define his subject. Neither Cuticle's pains nor his patients last. Cuticle's venerable literary ancestors
reinforce the impression that he is an old-fashioned doctor. His instrument, his emblem, is the knife that separates limb from body, rather than
the invisible pencil that traces permanent lines of character. He is literally and figuratively an artist of the cuticle. His knife passes through
the dermis to the muscle and the marrow, but the marks are fleeting.
If Dr. Cuticle is a cannibal who cuts off and consumes flesh, whose
hungers, while intense, are brief, then Karky, in Melville's typology, is a
flogger who inscribes indelible lines and whose desires are limitless.
Alarmingly, Karky's patients and the boatswain's victims live. They survive their operations with vivid scars for all to see. The horror in *White-Jacket* is not the sundering of amputation but the eloquent intaglio line
cut of flogging.

On the boards of the *Neversink*, the fate of the analogy between
sailor and slave is played out with surprising twists. In calling for the
abolition of flogging in the navy, White-Jacket maneuvers among the arguments for the abolition of slavery. It is a question of immediate, not

gradual, abolition, he tells his reader. It is a question not of economics
or sentiment but of morality:

> It is not a dollar-and-cent question of expediency; it is a matter of *right and
> wrong*. . . . No sentimental and theoretic love for the common sailor; no ro-
> mantic belief in that peculiar noble-heartedness and exaggerated generosity
> of disposition fictitiously imputed to him in novels; and no prevailing desire
> to gain the reputation of being his friend, have actuated me in any thing I
> have said, in any part of this work, touching the gross oppression under
> which I know the sailor suffers. Indifferent as to who may be the parties con-
> cerned, I but desire to see wrong things righted, and equal justice adminis-
> tered to all. (146, 304)

Melville deftly positions his narrator in the contours of abolitionist discourse and punctures the self-indulgence of certain sentimental poses.
He criticizes the imputations of fiction, the ways in which character is
ascribed and projected. Yet while the narrator defines the white sailor
with the vocabulary and logic of abolition, he mutes the "slave" term.
The silencing is not as total or violent as in Browne. The terms slave and
sailor are briefly linked through the multivalent word "race" ("Nor . . .
is the general ignorance or depravity of any race of men to be alleged as
an apology for tyranny over them") and the suggestion, which Melville
had developed at length in *Typee*, that laws denominate and then punish their own victims (304). The specter of chattel slavery flickers in and
out of view in the "abolition" passages of *White-Jacket*.[45]

An actual chattel slave does appear on the decks of the *Neversink*.
Melville introduces "Guinea," a black slave from Virginia shipped as
a seaman, whose wages are collected by his owner. Guinea belongs to
the vessel's purser, a "southern gentleman" with a "good heart" (379).
Guinea becomes the focus of a comparative and evaluating gaze:

> Never did I feel my condition as a man-of-war's-man so keenly as when see-
> ing this Guinea freely circulating about the decks in citizen's clothes, and,
> through the influence of his master, almost entirely exempted from the disci-
> plinary degradation of the Caucasian crew. Faring sumptuously in the ward-
> room; sleek and round, his ebon face fairly polished with content; ever gay
> and hilarious; ever ready to laugh and joke, that African slave was actually
> envied by many of the seamen. There were times when I almost envied him
> myself. (379)

As sailor looks at slave, Melville literalizes and examines the terms of
the analogy. Guinea's circulation sharpens the sailors' sense of their
condition. "Guinea" is the name the sailors have bestowed upon him,
White-Jacket informs the reader (378–79). Guinea is the currency

whose exchange gives them value. He bears the stamp of geography (the west coast of Africa), economy (the slave trade), and race (Negro) that lends meaning to their lives. The bonds of sailorhood depend on the overstatement of Guinea's "freedom" (his sumptuous dining, his ample body, his polished surface), the downplaying of his restraints, and the incongruity of his citizen's attire. Comparing themselves with Guinea, the sailors compare "black" and "white" subjection. In their envy, they conclude: your "slavery" is not slavery, but mine is.[46]

The key, shifting word in the passage is the adverb "actually" in the phrase "that African slave was actually envied by many of the seamen." What are the implications of this modifier? In what manner did the sailors "envy" Guinea? Did they envy Guinea even though he was a slave? If so, their envy is a sign of their debasement, in which their judgment is so distorted as to produce the envy of a chattel slave. Or did they even envy a slave? If so, they envied Guinea because he was indeed treated better than they were. Were the grounds for envy imagined or real? Does the narrator deliver this line in a tone of sorrow or bitterness? We cannot determine. This unstable adverb registers the complicated lines of desire and resentment that extend from sailor to slave.

Guinea has become a critical touchstone for discussions of Melville's racial politics and literary practice in *White-Jacket*. H. Edward Stessel views Guinea as a figure used strategically by Melville to convey the degraded status of the sailors. For Carolyn L. Karcher, Guinea and the "happy sailor" Landless are both examples of slaves who learn to love their subjugation in a martial society, part of Melville's larger interest in how environment shapes character. Patricia Allen Zirker argues that Guinea is a figure taken from pro-slavery literature, who dramatizes the advantages enjoyed by the chattel over the wage slave.[47] Guinea's presumption in donning "citizen's clothes" does seem to evoke minstrel performances. Yet Stessel and Karcher also have a point: the comparison with Guinea involves the reversal of hierarchies and the unsettling of color distinctions. Whether one interprets Guinea positively or negatively, however, he is a device used by characters, narrator, and author. His value is instrumental. We cannot invoke the figure of irony to redeem Melville from his disturbing representations. Our disturbance is part of the interest of the representations, rather than the signal that we should seek to exonerate the author. The point is not to praise or blame as much as to acknowledge. Melville exhibits the attractions and costs of the analogy between sailor and slave. In his hands, the figure tends to enhance the position of the white laborer and diminish the position of the black slave. Yet ultimately in *White-Jacket* the analogy endangers its wearer.[48]

Among the exemptions granted to Guinea, White-Jacket tells us, was that he was excused from being present at the administering of the scourge. This is a privilege granted to Guinea alone among the crew except for the hospital steward and his patients. On the level of character, Guinea, a chattel slave, does not need to learn the personal and public instruction taught by the whip. On the level of figure, Guinea's presence at the scene of flogging would threaten the analogy between sailor and slave with incoherence. In seaman's narratives, the distance between sailor and slave is essential for the production of meaning. The analogy works when the term "slave" is out of sight, if not out of mind. For a sailor's peers, "men of his own type and badge," to watch his degradation at the mast is humiliating (135). For the slave Guinea to stand and watch a sailor being flogged would be to render the sailor not "like" a slave but beneath a slave. Before such an audience, the defining, hierarchical space between the two terms would collapse. The force of the blows would be concentrated in and then reflected by such eyes and would redouble on the white victim. The positions in the analogy are not symmetrical or reversible. All slaves, it would seem, are not created equal.

Melville represents and then reverses the visual dynamics of flogging in the chapter "White-Jacket arraigned at the Mast." White-Jacket and all the other sailors are called to witness the lashing of Rose-Water, a mulatto sailor who is being punished for unsanctioned combat with the black May-Day. (The captain only permits fighting at his command for the pleasure of the crew.) Melville stresses White-Jacket's condescension in order to prepare him for his fall:

> When with five hundred others I made one of the compelled spectators at the scourging of poor Rose-Water, I little thought what Fate had ordained for myself the next day. Poor mulatto! thought I, one of an oppressed race, they degrade you like a hound. Thank God! I am a white. Yet I had seen whites also scourged; for, black or white, all my shipmates were liable to that. Still, there is something in us, somehow, that, in the most degraded condition, we snatch at a chance to deceive ourselves into a fancied superiority to others, whom we suppose lower in the scale than ourselves.
>
> Poor Rose-Water! thought I; poor mulatto! Heaven send you a release from your humiliation! (277)

White-Jacket uses the occasion to reassure himself of his superior racial position. Yet, he reminds himself, the scourge does not recognize his difference. The superiority he has snatched does indeed prove to be "fancied" when, the next day, he himself is brought to the mast on a charge of failing to be at his proper station during the tacking of the ship. The spectator becomes the object of scrutiny.[49] White-Jacket is put in the position of Rose-Water—yet he is and he isn't.

In these scenes, Melville opens and closes and opens again the distance between "sailor" and "slave." The analogy—if not exactly between sailor and slave, since Rose-Water is not a slave but a "free" mulatto, then between white and black oppression—retains a verticality. Heaven *does* send White-Jacket a release from his humiliation, in the form of the deus ex machina of Corporal Colbrook and the maintop man Jack Chase. At the moment when the captain commands that White-Jacket be tied to the gratings in preparation for flogging, Colbrook advances from the crowd of assembled sailors and declares that White-Jacket is honest and reliable and would certainly have been at his station if he had been properly informed of his duties. After Chase seconds Colbrook's remarks, Captain Claret for the one and only time in the book aborts a flogging and retracts his authority. With uncharacteristic understatement, placing the captain's words in indirect discourse, White-Jacket tells the reader that the commander of the *Neversink* said to him, simply, *"you may go"* and then "sauntered aft into his cabin" (281).

The narrator's escape from flogging is a literary invention. During his actual voyage on the *United States,* the sailor Melville never faced a flogging, nor was the captain argued out of inflicting punishment on any sailor. White-Jacket emphasizes the strangeness of this moment. He observes that Colbrook's speech was "almost unprecedented" and that "Seldom or never before had a marine dared to speak to the Captain of a frigate in behalf of a seaman at the mast" (281). Only this once in the narrative do words have the power to alter the shipboard logic of merciless regulation and punishment. It is a moving but fantastic moment, its rhetorical investments reminiscent of Frederick Douglass's literary slave from *The Columbian Orator,* who talks his master into voluntarily emancipating him. White-Jacket's reprieve is preceded by his vision of revenge, in which he imagines hurling himself against Captain Claret and throwing them both into the ocean, in an ultimate act of murder and suicide.[50]

While White-Jacket escapes, the decks of the *Neversink* offer unremitting scenes of violence that are not bounded by chapters or contained in the ritual acts at the gangway. Three chapters detail the impositions of the despotic naval Articles of War, the nightmare Constitution that regulates the sailors' lives. The Articles are "an index to the true condition of the present civilization of the world," White-Jacket tells us (293). Standing at attention, bareheaded, listening to the monthly reading of the Articles of War "till the last sentence is pronounced" (292), White-Jacket reflects on the punitive persistence of martial sentences. Even after death, "the Martial Law might hunt you straight through the other world, and out again at its other end, following you through all eternity, like an endless thread on the inevitable track of its own point, passing unnumbered needles through" (296). All sentences pronounced on board the *Neversink* are barbed. The martial law knits all of its victims. Like Emily Dickinson's "Weight with Needles on the pounds" that coolly punctures flesh "That not a pore be overlooked," Melville here offers a remarkable image of pierced identity, "the sense of boundary inseparable from its violation," as Mary Loeffelholz nicely describes Dickinson's poem.[51] Like the tattooing implements wielded by Karky in *Typee,* these martial needles threaten to scar the sailors. Unlike Tommo in *Typee,* the sailors in *White-Jacket* have no place to flee. Tommo escapes to the decks of the whaler *Julia,* but whalers and frigates are the domains of disfiguring authority in *White-Jacket.* In the man-of-war world, the needles are wielded not by your enemies, not by the savage Typee, but by your countrymen.

Several chapters after the "escape," White-Jacket portrays the "great Massacre of the Beards," during which Federal supervision of sailors' bodies climaxes in the taking of blades to their faces. The recalcitrant old Ushant is jailed, lashed, and jailed again. In "Flogging through the Fleet," the narrator describes the spectacle of serially flogging an offending sailor from ship to ship. He writes: "To say, that after being flogged through the fleet, the prisoner's back is sometimes puffed up like a pillow; or to say that in other cases it looks as if burned black before a roasting fire; or to say that you may track him through the squadron by the blood on the bulwarks of every ship, would only be saying what many seamen have seen" (371). These chapters heighten the sense of claustrophobia, vulnerability, and mortification. White-Jacket writes that, like the poor artist who was impelled by Jove to paint Medusa, he "sickened at the sight of what his forced pencil had drawn" (386).

Despite White-Jacket's declaration in one of the flogging chapters that there is a "feeling of innate dignity, remaining untouched, though outwardly the body may be scarred for the whole term of the natural life" (142), and despite his intuition during his revenge fantasy—"I felt my man's manhood so bottomless within me, that no word, no blow, no scourge of Captain Claret could cut me deep enough" (280)—there are representations in *White-Jacket* that compete with these reports of an interior space beyond reach or theft. Responding to the first floggings described in the book, in which four sailors are punished for fighting, White-Jacket remarks that "not to feel scarified to the quick at these scenes would argue a man but a beast" (138). The sailors on board the *Neversink* do seem "scarified to the quick," not only by witnessing flogging and by becoming victims of flogging themselves, but also by serving on a naval vessel. The outrage at corporeal marking in *White-Jacket* starts as a demand that sailors not be treated like slaves, that white flesh not be exposed and disgraced like black flesh. It evolves into an apprehension that both sailors and slaves are arraigned at the mast with their bodies already scarred. The resistance to being "convert[ed] into slaves" (144) turns into a dislocating insight that you already may be a slave. To put this point another way, using Melville's own cutaneous metaphor, over the course of the book the narrator recognizes and is revolted by the fact that "his own hapless jacket forever proclaimed the name of its wearer" (120). The narrator's flesh is neither silent nor unseen. He wears an eloquent, vulnerable white jacket.

White-Jacket's "forced pencil" draws the analogy between sailor and slave, and over the course of the narrative that analogy eludes its author. As we have seen, analogy was often used by naval reformers and labor activists to appropriate the figure of the black slave and the experience of chattel slavery in order to advance the politics of white oppression and to establish a hierarchy of suffering. Comparing sailor or worker with slave, many reformers articulated a racial choice for sentimental response and political action. In *White-Jacket,* the trope is not so easily mastered. Rather than aggrandizing the figure of the sailor while protecting him from the taint of racial slavery, the intimate analogies in *White-Jacket* threaten to expose the sailors as slaves. The distance sustained in the hierarchical comparisons of McNally threatens to collapse. The "slave" term, elided in Browne, returns with a vengeance. The flow of meaning is no longer conducted through contrived channels. Instead, the floodgates open and the figure of the sailor is inundated. Melville renders this condition not only through the accumulating burden of exposition (Articles of War, Massacre of the Beards, Flogging through the

Fleet), but also through plot and figure: White-Jacket's loss of his balance on the yardarm, his fall into the ocean, and the almost fatal saturation of his white jacket.

The first chapter opens with the narrator describing how he manufactured his white jacket in order to protect himself from the harsh weather ahead in the *Neversink*'s trip around Cape Horn. Unable to obtain a pea-jacket from the purser's steward, he devises his own garment. He folds a white duck frock double at the bosom, slits it open, and pads it with old scraps of clothing. Both the narrator and his fellow sailors regard the jacket as a sign of his difference. One in a series of Melville's overwritten symbols, White-Jacket's white jacket has been read as an emblem of personal alienation, illusory independence, and class superiority. Melville describes the jacket in terms of his own literary fashioning: "bedarned and bequilted," "well-patched, padded, and porous" (4–5). He suggests ruefully that it is produced and also received like a Melville text. In "An Auction in a Man-of-war," after the ship has rounded the Cape and the weather has turned warm, the narrator surreptitiously gives his jacket to the purser to dispose of at auction. When the item is "submitted to the inspection of the discriminating public," the sailors recognize it as the work of the narrator, question its generic status as a jacket, and abuse its appearance (201). No one will buy it.[52]

Yet the jacket also has a more corporeal dimension. It is padded, porous—and white. The jacket is skin. It has a structure that contains secrets and invites inscriptions: "There were, also, several unseen recesses behind the arras; insomuch, that my jacket, like an old castle, was full of winding stairs, and mysterious closets, crypts, and cabinets; and like a confidential writing-desk, abounded in snug little out-of-the-way lairs and hiding-places, for the storage of valuables" (36). Like the elaborate architectures of the self in *Pierre*—the sarcophagus of the soul that lies in a central room deep in a pyramid and the stair of a man's heart that spirals endlessly down a dark shaft—the jacket is chambered and cryptic.[53] This skin is represented as a surface filled with recesses of meaning. So inviting a prospect is this surface and so eager are the other sailors to investigate those recesses and to pilfer their contents that the narrator takes drastic action:

> I noticed a parcel of fellows skulking about after me, wherever I went. To a man, they were pickpockets, and bent upon pillaging me. In vain I kept clapping my pockets like nervous old gentlemen in a crowd; that same night I

found myself minus several valuable articles. So, in the end, I masoned up my lockers and pantries; and save the two used for mittens, the white jacket ever after was pocketless. (37)

The narrator seeks to seal the apertures that make him vulnerable to greedy eyes and intrusive hands. He seeks to shield himself from pick-pockets of the skin.

Even with sealed pockets he is not safe. The very texture of the jacket exposes him to danger. Stuffed and quilted and not waterproofed, the jacket acts like a "sponge" and becomes a "universal absorber" (4). Its pockets may be sealed, but its pores are open: "Of a damp day, my heartless shipmates even used to stand up against me, so powerful was the capillary attraction between this luckless jacket of mine and all drops of moisture" (4). In wet weather it drips, releasing liquid that is reminiscent of the "agonized drops of shame" (142) that bleed from the soul of the flogged sailor. Soaked and heavy, the jacket is a continuous burden to bear.

Yet it is not just the structure and texture of the jacket but also its color that becomes filled with meaning and exposes the narrator to danger. As in the chromatic reversals of *Moby-Dick* ("The Whiteness of the Whale"), Melville here represents white skin as subject to the kind of anxious regard usually associated with black skin.[54] Unable to obtain a standard navy-blue jacket, the narrator repeatedly tries to requisition some black paint in order to waterproof his garment and to change its "complexion" to a "dark hue" closer to that of his comrades' jackets (78, 120). Again and again, his request is denied by the first lieutenant. The resonant joke here is that White-Jacket wishes to darken his skin so that he can conform to the appearance of the majority. The darker color will protect him and enable him to assimilate. Yet the narrator is unable to change his color and remains subject to the abuse of his peers. His mess mates "nourished a prejudice" against his white jacket (61). Neither blue nor black, White-Jacket is vulnerable. His whiteness makes him uncomfortably visible: "And thus, in those long, dark nights, when it was my quarter-watch on deck, and not in the top, and others went skulking and 'sogering' about the decks, secure from detection—their identity undiscoverable—my own hapless jacket forever proclaimed the name of its wearer" (120). Like Tommo in *Typee,* White-Jacket desires the freedom to move through his society undetected and unknown, but White-Jacket's own white skin, not the prospect of an alien tattooed skin, betrays him. Unlike Tommo, he is already a marked man.

In the chapter "The Jacket aloft," White-Jacket becomes a target of interpretation and the victim of an almost lethal misreading. Seeing him high on the main-royal-yard, where he has gone to stargaze wrapped in his white jacket, the narrator's shipmates mistake him for the ghost of the recently deceased ship's cooper and they collapse the sails, nearly causing him to fall:

> after hailing me, and bidding me descend, to test my corporeality, and getting no answer, they had lowered the halyards in affright.
>
> In a rage I tore off the jacket, and threw it on the deck.
>
> "Jacket," cried I, "you must change your complexion! you must hie to the dyers and be dyed, that I may live. I have but one poor life, White Jacket, and that life I can not spare. I can not consent to die for *you*, but be dyed you must for me. You can dye many times without injury; but I can not die without irreparable loss, and running the eternal risk." (78)

The narrator's white jacket invites the testing of his corporeality, an operation that almost proves fatal. The punning on "dye" and "die" extends the serious joke about the danger in which his white skin places him. A dye—a change of complexion—will, he hopes, save him from death. To dye is to live. Yet the wordplay is not the most notable feature of this passage. In this scene, the character has a jacket but the jacket also has a character. The narrator tears off his skin in a rage and speaks to it. The articulate skin, which "proclaims the name of its wearer" (120), here is personified only to be shouted down. The narrator has a close, quarrelsome, punning relationship with his skin. It's either you or me, he warns his skin. "Jacket! jacket!" the narrator laments and threatens later in the book, "thou hast much to answer for, jacket!" (334). His skin defines and endangers his character. The name of his skin is, after all, the name of his character—the only name he has—and the name of his story.[55]

White-Jacket tells the story of the struggle of a man with and in his skin. The book presages the meditation on skin in *Moby-Dick,* especially in the chapter titled "The Blanket." White-Jacket's cutaneous dispute in "The Jacket aloft" ends in a draw. His request for black paint is again refused by the first lieutenant, and he dons the white jacket once more. According to the log books of the *United States,* there was an ample supply of blue naval jackets, one of which Melville himself certainly wore during his service. In *Life on Board a Man-of-War* (1829), Melville's source for the final chapter about the jacket, the sartorial encumbrance is easily removed.[56] The white jacket on display in Melville's book is not the result of biographical exigencies or literary pilferings.

Melville's emphasis on the jacket—its confinement, capillary attraction, and color—evokes the treatments of skin color and texture in narratives of slavery and antebellum African American fiction.

Like black skin, the narrator's skin renders him visible and vulnerable. Like black skin, the narrator's skin becomes ominous: the sign of his difference and his degradation. White-Jacket's skin, like the white paper and the white skin produced in the factories of Melville's sketch "The Tartarus of Maids" (1855), is not blank. It bears the imprint of the man-of-war factory in which it was manufactured. In a pattern begun with the eloquent tattooed skin in *Typee,* intensifying with the personified skin in *White-Jacket,* and climaxing with the hieroglyphic skin in *Moby-Dick,* Melville examines how the surfaces of bodies become saturated with meaning. He shows the dangers for the observer when the distance between observer and object dovetails into proximity and implication threatens to overwhelm. In the short fiction collected in *The Piazza Tales* (1856), and especially "Bartleby," "Benito Cereno," and "The Piazza," Melville continues delving into subject-object relations and the dynamics of interpretation, although the danger of reversal is minimized. In these complex psychological profiles, the narrator protagonists retreat to a secure, if haunted, distance from their object enigmas: the forlorn Bartleby, the rebellious Babo, the restless Marianna. This distance is established not only through physical separation but also through Melville's strict and meticulous prose in these tales.[57] In the fraught symbols and overwritten scenes of *White-Jacket,* the white skin that was supposed to protect the narrator becomes a trap. The insulating distance between sailor and slave collapses, as the white sailor's skin becomes infected by association with blackness.

In a remarkable chapter of *The Garies and Their Friends* (1857), one of the earliest African American novels, Frank J. Webb describes a similar scene of epidermal betrayal in which the garment of the skin makes, and unmakes, the man. Webb sets up his sinister, racist Philadelphia lawyer George Stevens for a fall. Stevens is the bane of the interracial Garie family, the white Clary, the "light-brown" Emily, and their two children. Enraged by the Garies' amalgamation and eager to profit from their distress, Stevens descends into the working-class part of town in order to direct Irish American violence against African American residents in general and against the Garies in particular. Wearing a dilapidated coat he has purchased at a second-hand clothing store from the African American Kinch, Stevens endures the exasperations of skin. The coat turns out to have belonged to a member of one of the city's fiercely competitive fire companies. As Stevens returns from his mission, his jacket blazons its character to the "practiced eyes" of a rival company. "Oh, it is not *my* coat—I only put it on for a joke!" Stevens assures a group of men who have begun to assault him. He becomes the victim of his own joke, of his sartorial condescensions and violent machinations. He is identified, ridiculed, beaten, and tarred because of his garment. His hands and face coated with tar and his lips swelled from the beating, Stevens undergoes another conversion. When he sits down to rest on the steps of a mansion, he is taunted as a "darkey" by a group of drunken young aristocrats, some of whom he recognizes. The young men force him to jump in and out of a hogshead filled with water and streak his face with lime in order to make "a white man of him," "a glorious fellow citizen." In his own home, seeking to regain the safety of his skin, desperate to remove the layer of tar, Stevens crawls off to bed, "with the skin half scraped off from his swollen face." [58]

Webb punishes Stevens for his prejudice and his pride, forcing him to undergo a series of costume changes from gentleman to laborer to poor black to abraded white. The final transformation, an effort to regain his original appearance, almost costs him his precious skin. Webb violently moves his character through the stations of class and race. The lawyer's masquerade results in a minstrel-show joke turned against its teller. Stevens is temporarily put in the position of the men whom he will pit against one another in the ritualized racial violence that forms the centerpiece of the book, Webb's fictional account of the wave of Philadelphia riots between 1834 and 1849. Stevens becomes the inciting object of "practised eyes." He is briefly made the scapegoat of his coat. Like Melville, Webb in this scene explores the vulnerabilities of white skin, stripped of its protective veneer.

Unlike Webb, Melville places his character in radical corporeal jeopardy. Arraigned and arrayed before the mast of the shipboard world, marked and remarked by the lash of discipline on the *Neversink*, his jacket exposing him to view and emphatically proclaiming the name and character of its wearer, feeling like a slave, White-Jacket must escape. He can neither take off his coat like Webb's Stevens, nor remain bound in his scarred garment like Dana's Sam, nor flee to the temporary safety of an American ship like Melville's own Tommo. White-Jacket's deliverance must be even more dramatic and fantastic. His skin may at first betray him, but then it saves him. In the end, White-Jacket's skin *does* die for him.

At the close of the *Neversink*'s journey, near the Virginia coast, while the narrator is up in the rigging working the sails, his jacket fails him for the last time. The ship tilts in the swell of a wave and the narrator, mistaking the jacket which has blown over his head for the sail, tries to support himself by grasping the white fabric. He leans on his skin, and it falters. He plunges a hundred feet into the ocean and, like Pip, the castaway in *Moby-Dick,* undergoes a watery epiphany, suspended between life and death. Yet while Pip's epiphany drives him mad—"The sea had jeeringly kept his finite body up, but drowned the infinite of his soul"— White-Jacket's experience produces the opposite effect.[59] It results in the submersion of his skin and the buoying of his soul:

> I essayed to swim toward the ship; but instantly I was conscious of a feeling like being pinioned in a feather-bed, and, moving my hands, felt my jacket puffed out above my tight girdle with water. I strove to tear it off; but it was looped together here and there, and the strings were not then to be sundered by hand. I whipped out my knife, that was tucked at my belt, and ripped my jacket straight up and down, as if I were ripping open myself. With a violent struggle I then burst out of it, and was free. Heavily soaked, it slowly sank before my eyes.
>
> Sink! sink! oh shroud! thought I; sink forever! accursed jacket that thou art!
>
> "See that white shark!" cried a horrified voice from the taffrail; "he'll have that man down his hatchway! Quick! the *grains!* the *grains!*"
>
> The next instant that barbed bunch of harpoons pierced through and through the unfortunate jacket, and swiftly sped down with it out of sight. (394)

"The gash being made," Melville writes in the first chapter, describing the incision that changed white shirt into white jacket, "a metamorphosis took place, transcending any related by Ovid" (3). The gash made at the end of the book enables an even grander transformation. It heals the wound inflicted by the exposure of the affinities between sailors and slaves. It reorients the sailor who has lost his bearings. White-Jacket violently frees himself from the "shroud" of his skin. In a final act of misreading, his fellow sailors interpret the sloughed jacket as a white shark and pierce it with a barrage of harpoons. The life of the jacket ends in ritual slaughter, a celebration of the regenerative powers of white skin.[60]

The wrangle of man with skin in *White-Jacket* concludes in this chapter, entitled "The last of the Jacket." Here, the fall into the ocean that earlier had been averted is now endured, and the flogging that had loomed is elevated into an act of liberating self-evisceration. The fantasy of homicide and suicide that the narrator had directed at Captain Claret is now turned toward himself, as, breathtakingly, he murders his own skin and then is transfigured. When he could not unburden himself of his white jacket at the purser's auction, the narrator compared his garment to the white shirt of Hercules, which, steeped in the centaur Nessus's poisoned blood, had burned his skin and which, when Hercules attempted to tear it off, had taken large pieces of flesh with it: "So, unable to conjure it into the possession of another, and withheld from burying it out of sight forever, my jacket stuck to me like the fatal shirt on Nessus" (203). Yet this allusion seems more appropriate to the protagonist of Melville's *Pierre*, who is consumed by a searing consciousness of living in his own skin and in the skin of beliefs about genealogy, gender, and desire. White-Jacket, on the other hand, has the ability to cast off his vestments. When the joke about the narrator's articulate skin goes too far, he cuts it. These are the astounding properties of white skin as represented at the end of *White-Jacket*: its owner can silence it, dye it, remove it. White skin can be wiped clean.[61]

If in the polemics of naval reformers and the narratives of seamen the lash inscribes the analogy between sailor and slave on the backs of white sailors, then *White-Jacket* ultimately offers a fantasy by which that inscription may be erased: the vulnerable, revealing surface can be shed. White-Jacket rips himself open and steps outside of his skin. He can detach himself from his blighted parts. Unlike Ahab in *Moby-Dick*, who asks the blacksmith Perth if he can smooth the seams and dents in his forehead and is told that such damage cannot be repaired, White-Jacket does not need an artisan to effect his bodily reconstruction.[62] He has his own tools.

White-Jacket's gash exposes the ligaments between the flogging and the jacket chapters, between the anatomies of ship and narrator. In the course of Melville's analysis of martial society, the narrator realizes that his own body has become degraded. The jacket, marred by the punishment that had been inflicted and absorbed during the voyage, becomes the target of his knife. Since it is no longer pickpockets that endanger him but his skin itself, White-Jacket turns from sealing his pockets to slashing his garment. On the boards of the *Neversink*, off the coast of Virginia, the Old Dominion of chattel slavery, White-Jacket arrogates the power of the flogger to inscribe and define skin. In a spectacular scene, White-Jacket, the white slave, flogs himself free.

In *White-Jacket*, Melville shows the reader how a white man was almost made a slave and, incredibly, made a man again. Melville follows the logic of racial conversion threatened in antebellum political discourse

and especially prominent in seaman's narratives: "I'm no Negro slave. . . .
Then I'll make you one!" (Dana, *Two Years Before the Mast*); "There
are thousands of enterprising young men in this country who would be
glad to find employment in the whale fishery, if they could do so without becoming slaves" (Browne, *Etchings of a Whaling Cruise*); "[the
naval code] should not convert into slaves some of the citizens of a nation of freemen" (*White-Jacket*, 144).[63] Reflecting on the representations of writers like Leech, McNally, and Browne, Melville explores the
ways in which anxieties about likeness generate efforts at discrimina-
tion. He examines the hinges in the articulation of the analogy between
white men and black slaves. He shows the reversals and renewals enabled by that analogy. He reveals at the pivot, at the preposition "like"
around which the meanings turn, a crucial point of difference that the
analogy clarifies and reinforces. In the comparative anatomy laid bare in
White-Jacket, to be "like" a slave is to be encased in skin that you cannot remove. To be unlike a slave is to possess a white jacket that is
portable and divestible. We do not know the features of the narrator's
new jacket, since no further detail is given about his appearance. Fit-
tingly, after his exuviation he remains nondescript. *White-Jacket* ends
with a vehement fantasy of erased marks and renewed flesh.[64]

In *Typee* and in *White-Jacket*, Melville represents prominent scenes
in the drama of antebellum racial discourse, in which the male body
becomes charged with meaning. Melville's prose registers, amplifies,
explores, and recoils from this charge. In both books, the loading of
graded meaning onto the head, face, and skin is represented as dangerous, as an overloading that threatens to discompose the observer. Yet the
unsettling of distance and rank in the two books is different. In *Typee*,
Tommo's position is reversed when he is menaced by Karky's gaze and
by the touch of his needles. He flees to the decks of an American whaling vessel and regains his status. In *White-Jacket*, the hierarchies are collapsed rather than reversed. The collapse of the difference between sailor
and slave precludes the possibility of literal flight and restoration. The
threat to identity lies in the sailor's own skin. Such dangers require extreme solutions.

White-Jacket teaches that the analogy between black and white slaves
is treacherous. It establishes but does not control a set of relations. In
the hands of sailor narrators and naval reformers, the analogy was used
to sustain distinctions. For writers such as Leech, McNally, and Browne,
it helped to furnish a "white" choice for moral and political attention.

In *White-Jacket*, the analogy is turned back on its manipulator, as it reveals a shared vulnerability and an intimate, persistent subjection to authority. The stain of the analogy provokes the graphic assertion of difference.[65]

Yet the solution offered at the end of *White-Jacket* is too easy. If *Typee* ends with a physical flight from racial encounter and corporeal inscription, then *White-Jacket* climaxes with a figurative flight. In *Typee*, Tommo's effort to go native is cut short by the specter of punctured skin, and he violently takes his leave from Nukuheva. In *White-Jacket*, the prolonged encounter between the terms sailor and slave played out by the narrator is ruptured by the prospect of lacerated flesh, and White-Jacket bloodlessly flees from his skin. White-Jacket removes the mark of the lash through a series of incisions made "straight up and down" his abdomen (394). His operation is better than Dr. Cuticle's in that it does not produce "quivering flesh" and "thick streams" of blood (261). White-Jacket's "fatal knife" (261) is an obstetrical instrument, enabling a self-inflicted and self-generating Caesarean section performed in the cleansing amniotic suspension of the sea.[66]

White-Jacket's removal of his skin is a procedure, like the surgeon of the fleet's, directed at the cuticle and not at the quick. It offers a fantasy cure for the social and somatic diagnoses of *White-Jacket*. Severing and deanimating flesh, it resembles the anthropophagy of the Typees and the amputations of Dr. Cuticle, rather than the durable marking of living features in Karky's tattooing and the boatswain's flogging. Across Melville's texts, we find this pattern of superficial "cutting off" juxtaposed with profound "cutting in." White-Jacket's fantasy is dispelled in an extraordinarily grisly chapter of *Moby-Dick*, "Cutting In." This chapter details the strain on the crew and on the ship itself of the effort to extract the whale's skin: the hook and tackle are inserted, the blubber is ripped from the body, the "blood-dripping mass" is peeled to the height of the maintop and then sheared into "blanket-pieces" and lowered below deck. These sections are sliced into smaller and more manipulable "horse-pieces" and then "bible leaves"—veritable texts of whale flesh. In the corporeal logic outlined in *Moby-Dick*, flesh is penetrated physically and then philosophically. "Cutting In" is followed by the chapter titled "The Blanket," whose initial, inciting question is "what and where is the skin?"[67]

In the final chapter of *White-Jacket*, Melville suggests that the narrator's corporeal escape is illusory. At the beginning of a valedictory

sermon otherwise composed of commonplaces, White-Jacket offers an
eerie melding of cryptography, incarnation, and incarceration:

> And though far out of sight of land, for ages and ages we continue to sail with
> sealed orders, and our last destination remains a secret to ourselves and our
> officers; yet our final haven was predestinated ere we slipped from the stocks
> at Creation.
>
>   Thus sailing with sealed orders, we ourselves are the repositories of the se-
> cret packet, whose mysterious contents we long to learn. There are no mys-
> teries out of ourselves. (398)

The sailors in *White-Jacket* prefigure the Polynesian harpooneer Queequeg in *Moby-Dick,* whose tattooed skin offers the viewer a mystical
treatise on truth that Queequeg himself cannot read; they prefigure, too,
the young American heir Pierre Glendinning in *Pierre,* whose coat, between the cloth and the heavy quilted lining, contains the worn but still
legible philosophical pamphlet "Chronometricals and Horologicals,"
the insights of which Pierre had been carrying within himself all the time
he was searching for them. The sailors in *White-Jacket,* themselves the
repositories of the mysterious contents they long to learn, form part
of Melville's astonishing gallery of legible, tantalizing bodies, texts in
flesh that contain—despite their owners' ignorance or efforts at divestment—a world of secrets for the viewer.[68] There are no mysteries out of
ourselves because, in Melville's anatomy of antebellum racial discourse,
the deepest mysteries lie within ourselves, waiting, longing to be read on
the surface of our bodies.

SAILING ON

In contrast to the ragged and ominous analogies that have shaped the
narrative, *White-Jacket* concludes with an intensely conventional allegory of life as a voyage:

> As a Man-of-war that sails through the sea, so this earth that sails through
> the air. We mortals are all on board a fast-sailing, never-sinking world-
> frigate, of which God was the shipwright; and she is but one craft in a Milky-
> Way fleet, of which God is the Lord High Admiral. The port we sail from is
> forever astern. . . .
>
>   Oh, shipmates and world-mates, all round! we the people suffer many
> abuses. Our gun-deck is full of complaints. In vain from Lieutenants do we
> appeal to the Captain; in vain—while on board our world-frigate—to the
> indefinite Navy Commissioners, so far out of sight aloft. Yet the worst of our
> evils we blindly inflict upon ourselves; our officers can not remove them, even

if they would. From the last ills no being can save another; therein each man must be his own saviour. For the rest, whatever befall us, let us never train our murderous guns inboard; let us not mutiny with bloody pikes in our hands. Our Lord High Admiral will yet interpose; and though long ages should elapse, and leave our wrongs unredressed, yet, shipmates and world-mates! let us never forget, that,

 Whoever afflict us, whatever surround,
 Life is a voyage that's homeward-bound! (398–400)

Melville's senses of an ending are complicated here. The final passages of *White-Jacket* are one part evasion of what has come before, one part reminder, and one part inside joke. Here, analogy has clean, reassuring, and inspiring lines. God is the Lord High Admiral whose command of this earthly vessel will supersede the cruel stewardship of terrestrial captains. God will preside over a supreme court of appeal that will hear the pleas of abused sailors and offer ultimate satisfaction. The brutal dynamics of flogging are forgotten in the hackneyed affirmation of the abstract evils that sailors inflict upon themselves, whose mark can be removed only by the purifying hand of God. Such soothing words seem too little and too late and too forced. They are bestowed after several hundred pages portraying the prison that is an American man-of-war. These paragraphs culminate the buoyant critique of the book, as the distance between narrator and narrated reaches its most obtuse angle. The figurative space in the last chapter is not dense or adhesive or severe enough to require White-Jacket to use his knife to tear himself free.

 This tardy invocation of a regenerative future echoes the famous, or infamous, paean to American millennial destiny at the end of chapter 36:

The Past is dead, and has no resurrection; but the Future is endowed with such a life, that it lives to us even in anticipation. . . . Escaped from the house of bondage, Israel of old did not follow after the ways of the Egyptians. To her was given an express dispensation; to her were given new things under the sun. And we Americans are the peculiar, chosen people—the Israel of our time; we bear the ark of the liberties of the world. . . . God has given to us, for a future inheritance, the broad domains of the political pagans, that shall yet come and lie down under the shade of our ark. . . . God has predestinated, mankind expects, great things from our race. . . . We are pioneers of the world. (150–51)

This chauvinism follows three searing chapters describing the history of United States flogging and condemning its gratuitous cruelty. Although the celebration of life as a voyage and the paean to Manifest Destiny may be brief and may be asserted in the shadow of an immense critique of martial society, remarkably, these moments still stir the feelings.

White-Jacket's panegyric on America's destiny has become the focus of critical debate about whether Melville is being literal or ironic. Does he mean it or is he kidding? This seems a false choice, avoiding Melville's own fascination with the power of such consolatory gestures. Melville means it, deeply, but he also wonders how it means. To separate Melville from his words would be like dividing a sleeve from its lining. White-Jacket may be able to tailor such an outcome, but Melville never rests comfortably in such fantasies. *White-Jacket* is a testimony to the difficulty of standing outside of one's own corporeal and ideological skin. Although the concluding allegory is out of place, the book offers the possibility that this final flourish may be sufficient. The prospect of a redemptive future may be so affecting and so attractive that it has the power to eclipse what has come before. As John Gerlach has noted, some contemporary reviewers responded this way. In evaluating *White-Jacket,* the *Southern Literary Messenger* emphasized Melville's "fine thoughts nobly expressed" and quoted profusely from the final chapter. Gerlach observes the disjunction between the last and the preceding chapters and he analyzes the paean to Manifest Destiny as "a calculated exaggeration which exposes its own foolishness." For Gerlach, Melville's rhetoric at these moments is "ironic," conveying a surface acceptance beneath which lies the author's disavowal. I dissent from such appraisals of irony in Melville's fiction. I argue against an irony that escapes its context and secures a protective distance. In *White-Jacket,* the ultimate exaltation of life as a voyage and the tribute to America's destiny suggest not only that an argument may occur in "contexts which drain its purported significance," as Gerlach argues, but also that some arguments and some figures are so compelling that they may drain significance from their contexts. These passages may be calculated and they may be exaggerated, but they are not foolish.[69]

At the end of *White-Jacket,* Melville is susceptible to the range of possibilities. He seems caught up in the sweep of his rhetorical wave. He seems unable to resist the formal force of the banal and moving sermon. The effects are not predictable. As with the return to cannibalism at the end of *Typee,* the swerving to stock Christianity at the end of *White-Jacket* is a potent evasion. The shift into allegory and sermon may obscure the lesson of the anatomy. Or the shift may sharpen that lesson through contrast with a too-easy and too-arbitrary comfort. What are the effects of a passage or chapter or book ending? What different desires attach to an ending? Melville meditates on such issues in book 7 of *Pierre*, where he criticizes the "proper endings" of novels: they falsely cap gloom with gladness, they unravel intricacies and mysteries, they faithfully provide "wedding bells . . . in the last scene of life's fifth act." These endings sound like the conclusion of *White-Jacket*. Yet despite the narrator's dismissive tone in *Pierre*, Melville never dismisses either the allure of such consolations or their power to shape interpretation.[70]

The end of *White-Jacket* offers a dream analogy—Life is like a Voyage—in which the second term secures the first. The meaning flows smoothly. The body of *White-Jacket* offers a nightmare analogy— the sailor is like a slave—in which the second term disorders the first. Across the pages of *White-Jacket*, Melville catalogues the self-inflicted damage wrought by the analogy between black and white "slaves" and he represents a fantastic attempt to repair that damage. This drama of breakdown and recovery unfolds on the narrative stage as well as the figurative one. In *White-Jacket*, as in "Benito Cereno," *Battle Pieces*, and *Billy Budd*, abuse generates the specter of mutiny, which in turn elicits a narrative exercise of order.[71] If the text of the final sermon in *White-Jacket* is the analogy between ship and state and its doctrine is commonplace (Have faith, shipmates and world-mates, God is our Lord High Admiral), the application is anxious: Beware of analogies—they can invigorate and augment, but they also can implicate and contaminate.

The inside joke at the end of *White-Jacket* is at the expense of Thomas Cole, whose enormously popular four-canvas allegory in oil, *The Voyage of Life*, was completed in 1839–1840. Cole depicts the journey of a male pilgrim in a small boat on the river of Life. Over the course of the canvases, the pilgrim sails from a dark cavern into the rosy light and narrow banks of *Childhood*, then through the clear streams and airy horizons of *Youth*, and is confronted by the turbulent waters, menacing crags, and storm clouds of *Manhood*. His voyage climaxes in *Old Age* and the passage of his shattered boat from the mouth of the river into the ocean of eternity, as the clouds break and a heavenly radiance pours forth. The final chapter of *White-Jacket*, like the final frame of *The Voyage of Life*, displays the assurance of blinding light in a scene notably stripped of the detail that characterized previous settings. Melville alludes to Cole's trajectory from "our first embarkation, as infants in

arms" to the "blessed, placid heaven . . . in store for us all" (398–99).
The joke here is that Melville has composed his own "Voyage of Life,"
but in *White-Jacket* the terms of comparison—life as voyage, state as
ship, and sailor as slave—are literalized, politicized, taken apart, and
turned inside out, the structures of confinement painstakingly examined, before the picture is hastily put back together. *White-Jacket* is
"The Voyage of Life" limned not by Cole but by Piranesi.[72]

CHAPTER 3

Getting inside Heads
in *Moby-Dick*

In *Moby-Dick* (1851), Melville climaxes the intense racial inquiry begun in *Typee* and continued in *White-Jacket*. In *Typee*, the narrator recoiled from the prospect that his own face would be marked. In *White-Jacket*, he sought to escape from his damaged garment. In *Moby-Dick*, Ishmael neither averts his gaze nor flees the scene. Instead, he confronts the alien and alluring bodies of others and joins the ethnological quest. After the reversal of positions in *Typee* and the collapse of hierarchies in *White-Jacket*, Melville in *Moby-Dick* attempts to figure out ethnological fascinations by drawing out the figures of nineteenth-century racial discourse.

In the vast body of the whale, Melville illuminates ethnology's mysterious cyphers: the synecdoches, literalizations, analogies, and catalogues of Samuel George Morton, the preeminent United States scholar of human differences; the cartography and synesthesia of the Fowler brothers, who helped to disseminate ethnological ideas in their popular series of phrenology manuals; and the typology and typography of such popularizers of scientific racism as Josiah Nott and George Gliddon. In contrast, Melville suggests an epistemology of the body based not on visual penetration but on contact between individuals, the caress and the squeeze that take place in the dark.

Again and again in *Moby-Dick*, and across antebellum United States culture, a scene is enacted: a scene of bodily and especially cranial contemplation, in which the observer stands before another and seeks access. This is the primary ethnological scene. Its fantasies of exposure help to shape the obsessions of antebellum writers: the catalogues of body parts in Whitman, the embodied abstractions and eerie corporeal cosmologies in Dickinson, the spectacular bodily confessions in Hawthorne, the fixations on heads, hearts, and teeth in Poe. The scene is critiqued from the object position by writers such as William Apess, Frederick Douglass, and William Wells Brown, who condemn ethnology's errors and describe the experience of being sized up. It is critiqued from the subject position by European American writers such as Lydia Maria Child and Herman Melville, who evaluate the dissecting scrutiny of such observers as Morton but also acknowledge the desire to inhabit another's skin and to get inside another's head.

In *Moby-Dick,* Melville gives access to the excess of the extraordinary nineteenth-century quest for bodily knowledge. He offers an anatomy of anatomies, a viscerally immanent critique of nineteenth-century efforts to get inside the body, and to gauge and rank its character.

MIDDLE-AGED MAN WITH A SKULL: SAMUEL GEORGE MORTON AND THE QUEST FOR CRANIAL CONTENTS

In "Memoir of the Life and Scientific Labors of Samuel George Morton," published at the beginning of *Types of Mankind* (1854), the summa of antebellum ethnology dedicated to the recently deceased Morton, Dr. Henry S. Patterson sketches a remarkable scene of the renowned craniometrist in his study:

> Morton's study now was more than ever "a place of skulls." His correspondence, having been widely extended, was at last bearing its fruit. Contributions came dropping in from various quarters, not always accompanied with reliable information, and requiring careful deliberation before being assigned a place in his cabinet. Nothing short of positive certainty, however, would induce him to place a name upon a cranium. The ordeal of examination each had to undergo was rigid in the extreme. Accurate and repeated measurements of every part were carefully made. Where a case admitted of doubt, I have known him to keep the skull in his office for weeks, and, taking it down at every leisure moment, sit before it, and contemplate it fixedly in every position, noting every prominence and depression, estimating the extent and depth of every muscular or ligamentous attachment, until he could, as it were, build up the soft parts upon their bony substratum, and see the individual as in life. His quick artistic perception of minute resemblances or discrepancies of form and color, gave him great facilities in these pursuits. A single glance of his rapid eye was often enough to determine what, with others, would have been the subject of tedious examination.

Like Hamlet, whose meditation on the jester Yorick's skull Patterson surely had in mind when penning this scene, Morton's thoughts are stimulated by the cranium he holds in his hands. Yet unlike Hamlet, who recoils at the sight of Yorick's fleshless smile and who famously acknowledges the common mortality, Morton's gaze animates not only his thoughts but also their object. Under his rapid, calibrating eye flesh is restored to bone. Morton's stare reconstructs the lips on the maxilla and mandible, and the skull speaks to him, delivering a sermon on its character and capacities. Of course, this voice is provided by Morton. The scene as sketched by Patterson conveys the astonishing acts of ventriloquy and resuscitation performed by antebellum ethnologists on their corporeal objects.[1]

In his seminal works *Crania Americana* (1839) and *Crania Ægyptiaca* (1844), Morton reanimated crania in order to fix, separate, and rank human types. He gave skulls names in order to assign them a place in his cabinet. Through scrupulous measurements of the "internal capacity" of the cranium and its "facial angle," and with precise illustrations, Morton demonstrated the inferior characteristics and thus degraded character of American Indians and Negroes, and he argued for immutable racial differences. The human skull is not an emblem of mortality for Morton—it is the thing itself, the repository of human character whose "internal capacity" can be reckoned by stopping the orifices with cotton, turning the skull upside down, and pouring white pepper seed or lead shot into the foramen magnum until the cranial cavity is full, and then transferring the substance to a graduated cylinder in which the total cubic inches are tallied. Morton's labors drew on faculty psychology, which viewed the mind as divided into separate powers, and on phrenology, which located those powers in distinct mental organs. This scene of cranial contemplation is not about humility but about power, not about the limits of human consciousness but about its reach.[2]

Patterson's scene, like Shakespeare's, draws upon the rich iconography of Renaissance vanitas and memento mori traditions. In these meditations on death and consciousness, detail is lavished on the contours and textures of the human skull. Skulls were placed on display on shelves and tables in the still lifes of Pieter de Ring, Adriaen van Nieulandt, and Abraham van der Schoor. Skulls were represented as the attributes of saints—Dürer's St. Jerome and Zurbarán's St. Francis—or as the accouterments of young men, in portraits by Hans Holbein and in "Young Man with a Skull" pictures by Lucas van Leyden and Frans

Figure 11. *Portrait of a Young Man with Skull,* engraving by Lucas van Leyden (c. 1519), Volbehr 120, 18.3 x 14.4 cm (sheet), Clarence Buckingham Collection, 1940.1314. Photograph © 1997, the Art Institute of Chicago, All Rights Reserved.

Hals (see figures 11 and 12). Lucas's *Young Man,* gazing to the right of the frame, points with an extended left forefinger to an angled skull, half concealed in the folds of his cloak and supported by his right hand. Three of the six luxurious feathers attached to his hat extend downward,

Figure 12.   *Young Man Holding a Skull,* Frans Hals (c. 1626–1628). Courtesy of the National Galley Picture Library, London.

betokening the mortal. Hals's *Young Man,* also looking right at a prospect beyond the frame, holds a quarter-turned skull in the palm of his right hand. The fingers of his left hand are vertically spread, motioning toward the viewer. The distance between thumb and little finger echoes the distance between parietal and occipital bones. A long pink feather extends rightward from his red cap and droops over the skull, completing the circuit of gesture and the visual parallel between head and skull.[3]

Ethnological scenes draw upon the force of these memento mori but

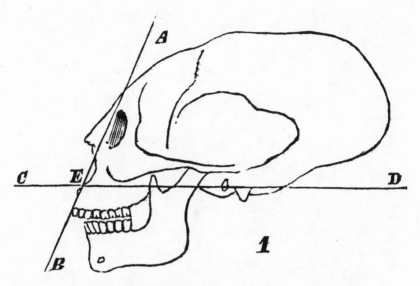

Figure 13. *Facial Angle,* from *Crania Americana,* by Samuel George Morton
(1839). Courtesy of the Bancroft Library, University of California, Berkeley.

also alter their meaning. In both kinds of scenes, composition and gesture focus on the skull. Both scenes meditate on the relations between
life and death and between self and other and examine the content and
scope of consciousness. Yet unlike Lucas's or Hals's young men, who
look beyond the frame, Morton bores into the skull. He overlooks the
intricate irony of young men with skulls—the inevitable transitions
from figure's head to death's head to the contemplating head of the
viewer, the implication of observer in the cycle of seeing and dying. In
Morton's crania, flesh does not decay into bone. Instead, bone confesses
to flesh.

Morton's gestures improve upon Lucas's index finger and Hals's
span. His reach is extended by calipers, protractors, and graduated
cylinders. If the fingers on the left hand of Hals's *Young Man* can be said
to measure the skull held in his right hand, it is a figurative measurement
of the tenuous distance between flesh and bone, between himself and the
object he holds and his audience, rather than the literal reckoning of
Morton.

Toward the end of the text of *Crania Americana,* Morton describes
the workings of the facial goniometer, an instrument designed to gauge
the "facial angle," an imaginary quantity formed by the intersection of
lines drawn from forehead to jaw and from ear to the base of the nos-

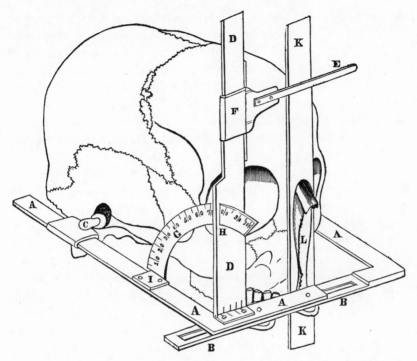

Figure 14. *Facial Goniometer*, from *Crania Americana*, by Samuel George Morton (1839). Courtesy of the Bancroft Library, University of California, Berkeley.

trils. The measure ostensibly indicated comparative beauty and intelligence (see figure 13). As pictured in an engraving, the skull is encased in the goniometer, pinned to the frame by conical pivots in the auditory meatus, and bound by brass slats and a curved ruler (see figure 14). A couple of pages later, Morton details how pencil marks are made on the skull, holes drilled, and wire inserted. He measures the distance between skull and viewer, but the conclusions he reaches are different from those of Lucas or Hals. Rather than suggesting a shared fragility and mortality, Morton proclaims natural separation and hierarchy. For Morton and his contemporaries in the "American school" of ethnology, race trumps death as the defining feature of human existence.[4]

These ethnological scenes—memento differre, if you will—are staged not to indicate what lies beyond flesh and bone but to demonstrate the lessons of difference taught by the body. In the nineteenth century, there were guidelines for contemplating skulls. When Patterson writes that Morton would examine a skull "fixedly in every position," he knows that such scrutiny was no amateur affair. As summarized in John Draper's *Human Physiology* (1856), there were four professional ways of looking at a skull to evaluate differences in structure: the lateral view specified by Petrus Camper, the vertical analysis of Johann Blumenbach, the basilar perspective of Richard Owen, and the front view practiced by James Prichard.[5] Morton pioneered a fifth "internal" view, in which lead shot and graduated cylinders were used to make visible the volume of the skull. These nineteenth-century Hamlets seek to measure Yorick's facial angle and to reach inside his cranial cavity.

While earlier ethnologists focused on complexion, many in the middle of the nineteenth century adduced the skull as better, more stable evidence of human difference. In *Crania Ægyptiaca*, Morton describes complexion as much less conclusive than skull structure for reconstructing the racial identity of the ancient Egyptians. In *Types of Mankind*, Nott describes cranial differences between the races as primary and representative. Draper in *Human Physiology* discusses complexion and cranium but emphasizes the latter, concluding his chapter on ethnology by analyzing how different skull forms manifest the intellectual qualities of different nations. As the revealing case for the brain, the support and protection for the eyes, nose, and mouth, and the architecture of apertures linking the inside of the body with the outside world, the thirty-two bones of the skull represented for Morton and his contemporaries the puzzle whose precise articulation would give access to the depths of human character and human difference. As the historian Reginald Horsman writes, "The physical structure of the head explained all."[6]

Morton's office at the Philadelphia Academy of Natural Sciences, with the largest collection of crania in the world, was an American Golgotha. His meticulously researched, exhaustively detailed, lavishly illustrated works, *Crania Americana* (1839) and *Crania Ægyptiaca* (1844), showed how racial and national character were written in bone. *Crania Americana* and *Crania Ægyptiaca* are elaborate, scrupulous authentications of prejudice. In *Crania Americana,* Morton "proved" through the measurement of crania from more than forty Indian groups that American Indians were a separate race, not descended from Asian migrants or from the peoples who had built massive, ancient earthworks. In *Crania Ægyptiaca,* intervening in the great question of the day concerning the racial identity of the ancient Egyptians and "whether civilization ascended or descended the Nile," Morton "proved" through comparisons of nearly six hundred human crania and physiognomic portrayals on

Egyptian monuments that the ruling inhabitants were Caucasians and not Negroes and that Negro slavery was a venerable practice. Neither the ancestors of Native Americans nor those of African Americans were capable of advanced social organization or cultural production, and so their present subjection on the North American continent had historical warrant. Morton's skulls, to use Patterson's eerie, apt conceit, bore fruit.[7]

Despite Morton's assurance in the dedication to *Crania Americana* that he would present "the facts unbiased by theory, and let the reader draw his own conclusions," his facts are saturated with racial theory and his conclusions are already drawn. This determinative relation between theory and facts is evident in the racial epitomes at the beginning of Morton's long "Introductory Essay on the Varieties of the Human Species":

> The Caucasian Race is characterised by a naturally fair skin, susceptible of every tint; hair fine, long and curling, and of various colors. The skull is large and oval, and its anterior portion full and elevated. The face is small in proportion to the head, of an oval form, with well-proportioned features. The nasal bones are arched, the chin full, and the teeth vertical. This race is distinguished for the facility with which it attains the highest intellectual endowments.

This seamless move from description to evaluation, from physical characteristics to intellectual character, structures Morton's argument in the two volumes. Morton's rapid eye and artistic perception produce a measured corporeal aesthetics. The American race is marked by a brown complexion, long black hair, deficient beard, low brow, high cheek bones, large and aquiline nose, tumid and compressed lips, and small, wide skull, and it is averse to cultivation, slow in learning, restless, and revengeful. The Ethiopian race is characterized by a black complexion, black, wooly hair, broad and flat nose, thick lips, long and narrow head, low forehead, projecting jaws, and small chin, and it is joyous, flexible, and indolent. Morton's facts are fused with adjectives. Stereotypes are substantiated. Twisted details present themselves as objective evidence advancing toward irrefutable conclusions.[8]

The suturing of characteristics and character is repeated at the levels of paragraph, section, and chapter, and in *Crania Americana* as a whole. In the "Introductory Essay on the Variety of Human Species," Morton ranks the five races, as defined by Blumenbach, in descending order of cranial capacity. In the 150 pages on American Indian crania, Morton outlines the history, culture, and appearance of different Indian groups.

In a final chapter on "Anatomical Measurement," he explains his techniques and offers tables summarizing his results. In the "Appendix," the phrenologist George Combe asserts that cognitive racial differences can be read in the surface of the head. Combe thus joins the two preeminent antebellum sciences of the head, phrenology and craniometry, in the service of racial scholarship.

In *Crania Americana* and *Crania Ægyptiaca*, Morton wields his calipers and straps and graduated cylinders and a vast amount of learning in order to verify a wicked cycle in which the individual embodies the race and anatomy recapitulates history and aesthetics. At the end of *Crania Ægyptiaca*, Morton makes explicit the conclusion impelling both volumes: "The physical or organic characters which distinguish the several races of men are as old as the oldest records of our species." No external cause—not climate, not the state of society, not the manner of living—and not even the misguided, if well-meaning, interpreters of Scripture who insist upon the unity of the human species can alter the fact that character is organic and that the human body, the oldest and most revealing record, teaches the lesson of inherent, hierarchical difference.[9] In the whale anatomy chapters of *Moby-Dick*, Melville will tease a different application from his corporeal text, driving a wedge between description and evaluation and rendering the natural strange.

Morton's texts and the other texts of the "American school" abound with corporeal detail. *Crania Americana* and *Crania Ægyptiaca* catalogue the internal capacity of the cranium, the facial angle, the structure of the cranial bone, the face, chin, forehead, eyes, eyebrows, teeth, nose, lips, mouth, hair, and ears. These incantations of difference attempt to secure separation through a cordon of precedent and evidence.

The anatomical catalogue is a feature of nineteenth-century racial discourse, and one catalogue in particular is repeated. (Racial science teems with repetition of facts, claims, errors, and anecdotes.) Although the German anatomist Samuel Soemmerring concluded that Europeans and Negroes belonged to the same species, his inventory of differences appealed to ethnologists, who quoted extensively from his *Über die Korperliche* (1785) to support their polygenetic arguments. Soemmerring's catalogue specifies forty-seven points of anatomical difference between Europeans and Negroes, including face, tongue, ribs, chest muscles, shoulders, navel, and pelvis. Soemmerring focuses on the architecture and contents of the skull: the height and circumference of the zygomatic arch, the depth of the orbits and the nasal cavity, the dimensions of the mouth, the angle of the jaw, the length and grain of the bones that form the cranial cavity, the weight and texture of the brain, the thickness of the cranial nerves.[10]

Walt Whitman captures this kind of minute corporeal fascination in his own catalogues of the body in the fifth poem of the 1855 edition of *Leaves of Grass,* and especially in the revised and expanded version published as "Poem of the Body" in 1856. Toward the end of both versions, Whitman's speaker assists an auctioneer in placing male and female bodies on display, stripping the flesh from red, black, and white limbs and probing to the blood and heart. In 1855, the speaker announces that the initial object of his interest is "a slave at auction!" In 1856, Whitman seems to have had second thoughts about such confining regard, and he alters the noun from "slave" to "man." In the 1856 version, Whitman has his speaker restore organs, flesh, and features to the bodies he had stripped. Across sixty-seven lines, the speaker names the parts of male and female bodies from head to toe, from finger-balls to man-balls to toe-balls, from breast to lung-sponges, stomach-sac, and bowels.[11]

In the figure of poet as auctioneer and in his anatomical catalogue, Whitman displays the charges—tactile, visual, intellectual, emotional, and economic—that galvanize the observer's attractions to the human body. Yet Whitman not only taps his ethnological sources, he also redirects them. Ethnological catalogues treat bodies as repositories of graded meaning and emblems of inherent difference. Whitman does not calibrate his body parts or assemble them into types of mankind. He refuses to rank or decipher. Whitman's catalogue is not an ethnologist's effictio, not an inventory of inequality, confounding characteristics and character. Nor is it a traditional lover's effictio, a metaphoric unfolding of his beloved's charms. This auctioneer does not flaunt the body as metaphor, symbol, or commodity. Instead, he presents it as "naked meat":

> Head, neck, hair, ears, drop and tympan of the ears,
> Eyes, eye-fringes, iris of the eye, eye-brows and the waking or sleeping of
>   the lids,
> Mouth, tongue, lips, teeth, roof of the mouth, jaws, and the jaw-hinges,
> Nose, nostrils of the nose, and the partition,
> Cheeks, temples, forehead, chin, throat, back of the neck, neck-slue . . .

He does not seize the jaw and inspect the teeth or test the body's muscles or appraise the cranium with lead shot. He deflects attention from the skull, alluding to its contents only briefly, while listing a series of internal organs: "The lung-sponges, the stomach-sac, the bowels sweet and clean, / The brain in its folds inside the skull-frame." [12]

If the body is a text for Whitman, it is literally a catalogue, a list of items. His speaker identifies the parts of the body without classifying them. In "Poem of the Body," the catalogue is composed almost entirely of nouns, prepositions, and conjunctions, bereft of adjectives. Unlike the catalogues of trees and rivers in the "Preface" to the 1855 *Leaves of Grass,* in which the thesaurus-like enumeration weighs down Whitman's project of animating America, or even the catalogues of American characters and occupations in "Song of Myself," in which the endless tally threatens to erase the differences among the items, in "Poem of the Body" Whitman uses the exhaustive gesture to strip significance strategically from the human body and restore an innocent wonder to its contemplation. Whitman's speaker evacuates meanings here in response to a culture that has saturated its bodies with vicious denotation. [13]

If it seems peculiar to juxtapose Walt Whitman and Samuel George Morton, the singer of the body electric and the quantifier of crania, it may be because I have not yet begun to give you a full account of *Crania Americana.* It is one of the most beautiful books published in the United States in the first half of the nineteenth century. Printed on large folio pages with wide margins, the book climaxes with seventy-six near-life-size lithographic plates of human skulls, Native American skulls, prepared by the Philadelphia artist John Collins. These prints rival the vibrant, meticulous anatomical wood engravings in Andreas Vesalius's *De Humani Corporis Fabrica* (1543), the unsparing stipple engravings of skin diseases in Jean-Louis Alibert's *Clinique de l'Hôpital Saint-Louis* (1833), and the searing etchings of exposed flesh and bone by Otto Dix in *Der Krieg* (1924). Morton writes in his preface that neither care nor expense was spared in achieving accuracy in the plates, and his assurance is borne out in the magnificent illustrations. In an advertising circular inserted at the end of the volume, Collins explains that he spent two years working almost exclusively on executing the prints. [14]

Exploiting the graphic potential of lithographs to detail texture and shading, Collins brings Morton's cranial cabinet to life. Collins represents the human skull as an extraordinary terrain. He delicately models the ridges and slopes of the parietal, the articulations of suture, the inviting temporal recesses and veiled orbits and interstices (see figures 15 and 16). He is fascinated with surface texture and suggested depths, with

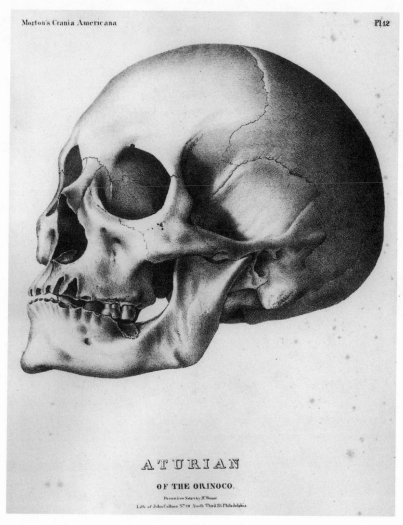

Figure 15. *Aturian of the Orinoco,* lithograph by John Collins, from *Crania Americana,* by Samuel George Morton (1839). Courtesy of the Bancroft Library, University of California, Berkeley.

standard contours and their deviations. In his representations, bone is treated like skin, given qualities of graininess and smoothness that encourage the viewer's eyes to caress the surface and invite the hand to reach under and inside the skull. *Crania Americana* begins with the geography of the globe, with a world map colored to designate the

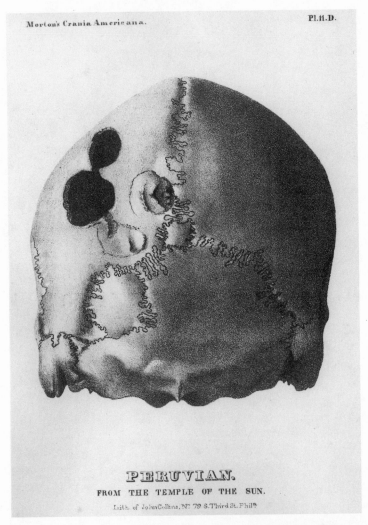

Figure 16. *Peruvian from the Temple of the Sun,* lithograph by John Collins, from *Crania Americana,* by Samuel George Morton (1839). Courtesy of the Bancroft Library, University of California, Berkeley.

distribution of the races, and ends with the geography of the head. As the volume expands in detail, it contracts in scope, finally locating the world in a skull.[15]

Collins's lithographs illustrate and substantiate Morton's cranial analyses. Collins inscribes on stone the natural messages Morton reveals in bone. Yet the discoveries in Collins's skulls are not circumscribed by

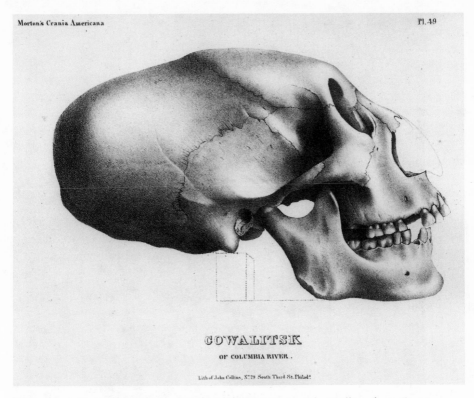

Figure 17. *Cowalitsk of Columbia River,* lithograph by John Collins, from *Crania Americana,* by Samuel George Morton (1839). Courtesy of the Bancroft Library, University of California, Berkeley.

Morton's calipers. Unlike the skulls in Morton's text, which are pinned, marked, drilled, wired, filled, emptied, and measured in an effort to force them to yield their contents and fix their character, the skulls in Collins's lithographs exceed, and even contradict, such definitions. Seen in the context of the European memento mori or danse macabre, stripped of the color and modeling of flesh, the skulls Collins holds out to the viewer speak of the equality of death rather than of the racial hierarchies of the nineteenth-century United States. Seen in the context of the practices among some Native American groups of compressing and reshaping the heads of infants, Collins's lithographs suggest that skulls can be as much a work of art as a work of nature. Plate 49 represents a horizontally altered Cowalitsk cranium (see figure 17). Plates 20 and 21 depict a vertically elongated Natchez skull seen from two perspectives (see figures 18 and 19). Such extraordinary images call into question

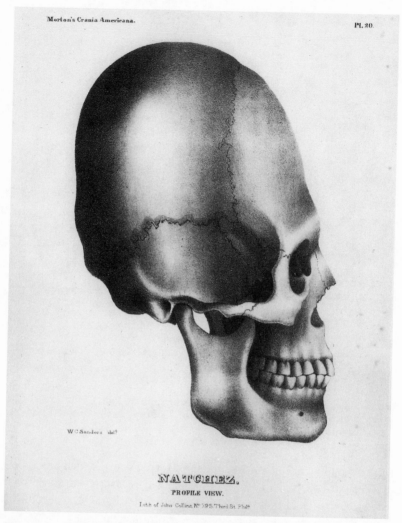

Figure 18. *Natchez: Profile View,* lithograph by John Collins, from *Crania Americana,* by Samuel George Morton (1839). Courtesy of the Bancroft Library, University of California, Berkeley.

Morton's principle of enduring natural and national sculpture. With some urgency, Morton tries to explain away the Natchez manipulations as merely emphasizing national characteristics. Yet the spectacle of refashioned crania haunts his system of stable facial angles and sacred cranial space. The parade of beautiful, bleached skulls and the prospect of

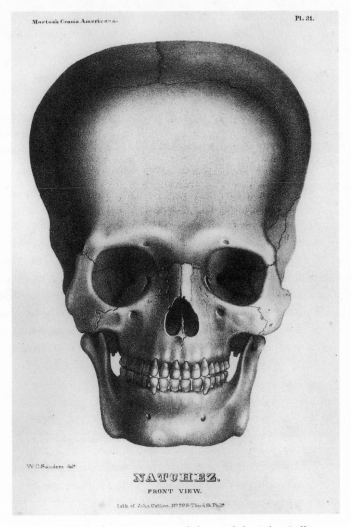

Figure 19. *Natchez: Front View*, lithograph by John Collins, from *Crania Americana*, by Samuel George Morton (1839). Courtesy of the Bancroft Library, University of California, Berkeley.

the grinning anamorphic skull confronting the viewer in plate 21, with its astounding phrenological measurements (indicating an unusual degree of cautiousness and secretiveness, as Morton explains), suggest that Morton's faith in the holy grail of craniometry may be misplaced.[16]

Yet such suggestions are neither acknowledged nor developed by Morton in the text of *Crania Americana*. Instead, Morton reinforces the lesson of disparity:

> However much the benevolent mind may regret the inaptitude of the Indian for civilisation, the affirmative of this question seems to be established beyond a doubt. His moral and physical nature are alike adapted to his position among the races of men, and it is as reasonable to expect the one to be changed as the other. The structure of his mind appears to be different from that of the white man, nor can the two harmonise in their social relations except on the most limited scale.

However regretful and however qualified by tentative verbs and by a later remark that education might enable the Indian to approach the Caucasian, Morton's conclusion is clear: the Caucasian pondering the skull of the Indian recognizes the structural gap between them. The space between subjects is charged and fractured by pervasive notions of racial difference. Yet this insistence on a gulf gives rise to a range of desires in European American observers: a craving for access in order to reveal the contents of that difference; a curiosity about what lies behind the barriers of bone and skin; a regret at the costs of separation; and a search for other ways of knowing bodies besides the calibrating gaze.[17]

DRY BONES: THE LAWS OF ANATOMY IN ANTEBELLUM ETHNOLOGY

Types of Mankind (1854), the massive recapitulation of antebellum ethnology edited by Josiah Nott and George Gliddon, is dedicated "To the Memory of Morton," who had died three years earlier. An engraved portrait of Morton forms the frontispiece for the volume. In the preface, Gliddon describes the book as a "literary monument" to Morton and explains that he and Nott seek to "make known the matured views of the father of our cis-Atlantic school of Anthropology." Along with Morton, Nott and Gliddon formed the core thinkers and teachers of the "American school" of ethnology in the two decades before the Civil War. The "American school" developed a theory of racial difference based on anatomical and historical fact and ultimately concluded that human races had been separately created by God.[18]

It is not surprising that Morton should have been celebrated in America and in Europe. His two volumes sliced through debates about historical and contemporary racial relations. Morton presented his findings not in the register of speculation or anecdote or personal animosity, but in the cool, irrefutable register of corporeal facts. In an 1851 eulogy published in the *Charleston Medical Journal,* Morton was remembered fondly: "we of the South should consider him as our benefactor, for aiding most materially in giving to the negro his true position as an inferior race." The key terms here are "materially" and "true." In evaluating the material of the human body, Morton had demonstrated the truth about racial hierarchy. He had certainly earned what a reviewer of *Crania Americana* in the *London Medico-Chirurgical Review* called the "meed of a Caucasian reputation." [19]

Morton claimed he was a man of facts and was hesitant to draw social and theological conclusions from his work. Nott and Gliddon had no such reluctance. Proclaiming where Morton suggests, reckless where he was cautious, boasting where he was regretful, vigorously enlisting him in the polygenetic cause and the contest between true austerity of science and the false benevolence of theology, Nott in his introduction and essay on the "Comparative Anatomy of Races" argues that the facts of anatomy sanction the social violence in American society. The difference in tone and emphasis between Nott and Morton can be attributed partly to the difference between 1839 and 1854, between the initial statements of the "American school" and their recapitulation, between debate in the first decade of the abolitionist movement and the rupture over slavery in the 1850s. *Types of Mankind* is a vicious book, with none of the complex fascination evinced in Morton's volumes and none of the conflicted interplay between text and illustrations.

Types of Mankind is one major part anatomy book, compiled by Nott, and two smaller parts biblical ethnography and philology, provided by Gliddon. It is an enormously learned and vastly myopic effort to prove that moral and intellectual character are fused to physical characteristics and that there are permanent human types. As Nott explains, Caucasian dominance in the past and conquering destiny in the future are corporeally determined: "No philanthropy, no legislation, no missionary labors, can change this law: it is written in man's nature by the hand of his Creator." Nott specifies the nature of this law later when, discussing the paucity of written records left by human hands, he asserts the priority and superiority of human structure as evidence of divine intention: "*Anatomy* . . . possesses its own laws independently of history." *Crania Americana, Crania Ægyptiaca,* and *Types of Mankind* seek to promulgate the laws of anatomy.[20]

When the Louisiana physician Samuel A. Cartwright argues that the Creator has a predilection for puns—"In the anatomical conformation of his [the Negro's] knees, we see 'genu flexit' written in his physical structure, being more flexed or bent, than any other kind of man"—it seems that the good doctor must be joking. Yet Cartwright's punning articulations of human anatomy are symptomatic of the zealous reading by the "American school" of racial character in physical characteristics. Preparing to analyze an ancient Egyptian skull from Morton's cabinet, Nott assures his readers that "Science can make 'these dry bones speak.'" The ethnologist is a nineteenth-century Ezekiel who outperforms the biblical prophet. The ethnologist's bones not only speak, they tell racial jokes.[21]

In the faceted term "types" used for the title of their book, Nott and Gliddon provide their most elaborate ethnological pun. In Nott's definition, "types" refers to "those primitive or original forms which are independent of Climatic or other Physical influences. All men are more or less influenced by external causes, but these can never act with sufficient force to transform one type into another." Here, the discourses of biology, theology, and printing converge. "Types" are the Creator's original, indestructible forms, composed of physical characters in which moral and intellectual character has been visibly, permanently cast. "How indelible is the image of a *type* once impressed on the mind's eye!" Nott exclaims, asserting the legibility of the Jew's face. "Types" is the term of choice for Nott and Gliddon, rather than the earlier nineteenth-century designation "Varieties," used by such writers on ethnology as the environmentalist Samuel Stanhope Smith. In the shift from "Varieties" to "Types," we see the shift from diversity within the human species to diversity between different species of humans; from the unity of humankind to separate creations; from superficial distinctions to radical difference; and from skin to bones. In Nott and Gliddon's vision, God is not only a printer, He is a stereotyper. In their magnum opus, they set out to publish a gloss on the Creator's corporeal typography.[22]

"Your head is the type of your mentality," reads the first epigraph on the title page of the Fowler brothers' *Illustrated Self-Instructor in Phrenology and Physiology* (1852). The Fowler brothers made popular and practical the craniology of Franz Joseph Gall and Johann Kaspar Spurzheim. The Fowlers trained their readers to recognize types of mentality by examining the relief characteristics of the skull. As historians recently have reminded us, phrenology and ethnology were closely linked. Phrenological research in the 1820s and 1830s directed attention to the head and set the stage for the craniometrical examinations of the 1840s and 1850s. Both phrenologists and craniometrists held that the size and shape of the skull corresponded to the capacities of the brain. Although phrenologists encouraged readers to exercise their faculties and improve their characters, such improvement was bounded by the mental distinctions that set apart the races. Beginning in the 1840s, phrenology was discredited as a science after discoveries that brain structure did not correspond to the "organs" described by phrenologists. Nevertheless, it continued to attract a wide audience throughout the nineteenth century. The Fowler brothers' phrenology manuals instructed their readers how to read character in the privacy of their own homes. The only tools required were an educated eye and discriminating fingers. In these manuals, we can grasp the visions of nineteenth-century ethnology.[23]

In the "Rules for Finding the Organs" section of *The Self-Instructor,* the Fowlers provide guidelines for ruling the head. This section follows a map of the mental faculties, essays describing how physiology and phrenology indicate character, and analyses of the specific faculties. In the "Rules," the Fowlers explain how to discern spirituality in someone else's head:

> On each side of Veneration, SPIRITUALITY is located. It may be found by the following rules: Standing behind the subject, who should be seated, so place your fingers that the first fingers of each hand shall be about an inch apart—that the ends of your second fingers shall be about three quarters of an inch forward of a line drawn across the middle of the head from side to side, and the balls of your fingers will be on Spirituality. Or reversing your position, so as to stand in FRONT of the subject, so place your hands that the first fingers of each hand shall be as before, about an inch apart, and the ends of your longest fingers shall just touch the fore part of Hope, and the balls of your second and third fingers will rest on Spirituality.

Here the ethereal has been made material. This fantasy embodies character and offers specific directions for fulfilling the quest for knowledge. Eyes are focused, digits extended, lines drawn, and—eureka!—you can put your finger on Spirituality. According to the Fowlers, there are regions that remain to be charted, unknown organs that incite further pursuit: "Between Hope, Cautiousness, and Approbativeness, there probably exists an organ, the natural functions of which has [sic] not yet been fully established. There are doubtless other organs yet undiscovered, especially in the middle line of the head, between Benevolence and Philoprogenitiveness, and also between Imitation and Causality." Crania incognita still beckon the corporeal traveler. Again, the specific locations and the merging of the material and spiritual may seem like a joke

to modern sensibilities—Spirituality is located on each side of Veneration; I'll meet you between Hope and Cautiousness; Individuality, the
brothers explain, is found directly above the root of the nose and
between the eyebrows—but these reductions and couplings reveal
the deep nineteenth-century investments of hope and desire in the human body.[24]

The "Rules for Finding Organs" are almost poetic in their vivid images, rhythmic anaphora and isocolon, and lyrical yearning. They
poignantly express the desire for tangible truth. They are poetic also in
their drawing out of elaborate conceits: that Spirituality can be located,
that Hope has foreparts, that cranial organs are analogous to bodily
organs, that the skull reflects its contents. Although the poems of
Emily Dickinson are often seen as idiosyncratic in their literary context,
they share the eccentricities of nineteenth-century phrenology. In both
Dickinson and the Fowlers, we find weird corporeal geographies and
geometries, bodily violence practiced as a matter of routine, and speakers who calmly offer perverse instructions to their readers. Dickinson,
like Melville, does not merely reproduce these gestures, she also reworks
them. Yet the writers and ethnologists share a corporeal terrain.[25]

Governing the "Rules for Finding Organs" is the core ethnological
conceit: the insistence that characteristics of the body specifically, literally, and permanently reveal hierarchical differences in human character. Outside and inside are violently yoked. This defining, confining
bond is naturalized in pervasive images of the body as landscape, map,
text, and treasure chest. In the Fowlers and in Morton, vision is extended into the fingertips. As the Fowlers put it, readers who follow
their advice will be able to "test [their] sight by touch."[26] In *Crania
Americana* and *Crania Ægyptiaca,* the reach of the eyes is augmented
through prosthetic calipers and straps. Part of Melville's project in the
whale-anatomy chapters of *Moby-Dick* is to unhinge these catachreses
in which characteristics are confounded with character, head with person, and sight with touch. Melville restores a sense of the physical and
cognitive violence that these articulations enable and conceal.

Ethnologists wield calipers, straps, charts, and tables—and they also
wield the knife. This instrument is conspicuous in the writings of the
virulent popularizers of scientific racism such as the Louisiana doctor
Samuel A. Cartwright and the New York physician and editor John H.
Van Evrie. Cartwright laments the lack of response to Jefferson's call, in
the famous "Query XIV" of *Notes on the State of Virginia* (1787), for
a scientific comparison of the black, red, and white races as an aid to set-

tling America's urgent social questions. Cartwright insists that anatomy will provide the answers: "But no effort has since been made to draw the distinctions between the black and the white races by the knife of the anatomist, but much false logic has been introduced into our books and schools, to argue down the distinctions which nature has made. It is to anatomy and physiology we should look, when vindicating the liberty of human nature, to see that its dignity and best interest be preserved." Cartwright repeatedly invokes the vindicating knife. He describes the "revelations" of the knife as a "rewriting" of Scriptural sanction for racial slavery. He catalogues the "proof" of immutable racial difference the knife offers and the "errors" about equality it corrects. In opening the "sealed book" of African American anatomy, Cartwright's knife draws its distinctions not only between the races but also into soft tissue.[27]

In a dictated narrative, the African American slave John Brown describes how his master's doctor attempted to open his sealed book. The doctor placed Brown in a heated pit five or six times to test a remedy for sunstroke, bled him every other day, and repeatedly blistered him in an effort to "ascertain how deep [his] black skin went." This gauging of depth and attempt to bring the lower layers to the surface characterizes much nineteenth-century ethnological practice. Virey, translated by Guenebault, reports that black skin color indicates darker blood, muscles, brain, and bile. Cartwright concurs, asserting that in Negroes "the flesh and the blood, the membranes and every organ and part of the body, except the bones" are "a darker hue than in the white race." This extraordinary, spurious, desperate fantasy is graphically rendered at the beginning of Van Evrie's pamphlet "Negroes and Negro Slavery" (1853):

> Stripping off the skin of the negro, he [Van Evrie] proposes to demonstrate to the senses, as well as the reason, that he [the Negro] is not a black white man, or a man merely with a black skin, but a different and inferior species of man;—that this difference is radical, and total, and relatively, as great in the primordial arrangement of elementary particles, or the single globule of blood, as in the color of the skin, or the grosser facts, palpable to the senses;—that it is original, invariable, and indestructible, as long as the present order of creation itself lasts.

The anatomist probes to fundamental particles. He reveals a world of racial difference that seethes beneath the skin.[28]

Similarly minute and inordinate fantasies of corporeal exposure are present in the literary texts of the period even when "race" does not appear to be an issue. At the conclusion of *The Scarlet Letter* (1850), the narrator has a stunning vision of something inside the body eating its way out. Meditating on the possible explanations for the "A" revealed on Dimmesdale's breast during the final scene upon the scaffold—was it the result of a self-inflicted wound? Of Chillingworth's medical necromancy?—the narrator emphasizes a theory of involuntary confession, a literal unbosoming of oneself: "Others, again,—and those best able to appreciate the minister's peculiar sensibility, and the wonderful operation of his spirit upon the body,—whispered their belief, that the awful symbol was the effect of the ever active tooth of remorse, gnawing from the inmost heart outwardly, and at last manifesting Heaven's dreadful judgment by the visible presence of the letter."

The consuming mysteries of the body are driven to seek the light. The narrator wonders if Dimmesdale's marks are the result of compunction. Yet as is the case with other such signifiers in Hawthorne's fiction, such as the crimson stain on Georgiana's cheek that represents "mortality" in "The Birthmark" (1843) or the reptilian dweller inside Roderick Elliston that stands for "diseased self-contemplation" and "jealousy" in "Egotism" (1843), Hawthorne's explicit formulae never adequately explain the hold that bodily symbols have on his narrators and his characters. Whether read as a badge of adultery or one of ability, an emblem of shame, guilt, or redemption, whether imposed by the Salem authorities, embroidered by Hester, or appearing on the flesh of Dimmesdale, the "office" of the scarlet letters is to reveal the body's secrets. The scarlet letters tantalize the viewer with the prospect of legibility. The narrator describes Dimmesdale's letter as "his own red stigma," "the type of what has seared his inmost heart." Here Hawthorne employs the tangled terms of theology, printing, law, and ethnology: the stigma is at once a stain on the reputation, a mark of disease, and the brand of a criminal or a slave; the type is a character carved in flesh.[29]

Hawthorne offers startling metaphors to convey restless subcutaneous forces. Inside the body, traversing the space between depth and surface, there are other bodies or parts of bodies. In *The Scarlet Letter*, the "tooth of remorse" cuts from the heart out to the skin to incise its character on Dimmesdale's breast. In "The Birthmark," Dr. Aylmer dreams of chasing the hand-shaped print on Georgiana's cheek with his knife until it grasps her heart. In "Egotism; or the Bosom Serpent," something is alive inside the haunted Roderick Elliston, and it is hungry. In these nineteenth-century tales, which draw on Puritan efforts to make sanctity visible, Hawthorne details contemporary preoccupations with seeing and knowing the human body. The search for signs of grace has been inflected by the quest for signs of race.[30]

Poe provides a gallery of narrators whose vision is deranged by their bodily fixations. In "The Tell-Tale Heart" (1843), the old man's "Evil Eye" leads the narrator to murder and then confession when he imagines that the victim's heart is telling the story of his guilt, beating through the floor planks beneath which the body is buried. In "Ligeia" (1838), the narrator idealizes his beloved's features: her skin of the purest ivory, her glossy black hair, her gently prominent forehead, her sweet mouth, her large expressive eyes. At the end of the story, he attempts to resurrect Ligeia by decomposing the body of his abhorred second wife through what Richard Wilbur nicely describes as a "remorseless and dematerializing gaze." In "The Man of the Crowd" (1840), the narrator is thwarted in his "craving desire" to classify London types by interpreting their faces. He becomes compelled by the figure of a decrepit old man, whom he follows and studies for a full day, but whose physiognomic secrets remain sealed. The old man's face is a book that "does not permit itself to be read." [31]

In "Berenice" (1835), the narrator's "frenzied desire" focuses on his cousin's teeth, which he ultimately wrenches from her mouth. The narrator's peculiar disease, which he labels a "monomania," draws him to frivolous objects, which assume, "through the medium of [his] distempered vision, a refracted and unreal importance." The narrator is engrossed: "The teeth!—the teeth!—they were here, and there, and every where, and visibly and palpably before me; long, narrow, and excessively white, with the pale lips writhing about them, as in the very moment of their first terrible development." He contemplates the teeth: "I held them in every light. I turned them in every attitude. I surveyed their characteristics. I dwelt upon their peculiarities. I pondered upon their conformation. I mused upon the alteration in their nature. I shuddered as I assigned to them in imagination a sensitive and sentient power, and even when unassisted by the lips, a capability of moral expression." The narrator's symptoms (morbid, overwrought attention), objects (the teeth! the teeth!), procedures (the gaze that violently appropriates), and investments (the detached teeth that speak volumes) all resemble the condition of the ethnologist and the anatomist. In "Berenice," Poe diagnoses and seems to delight in the "distempered vision" that was being directed at human bodies in the expanding professional effort to construe differences in race and gender.[32]

I am not arguing here, as I do about Melville in *Moby-Dick* or about

Frederick Douglass and William Apess, that Hawthorne and Poe strategically respond to ethnology; rather, I am arguing that their concerns are
shaped by the prominent discourses of bodily inquiry.[33] Hawthorne's
corporeal exposures, Poe's abstracted body parts, both writers' fervent
observers who offer lethal cures to their patients, the parsed bodies in
Whitman, Dickinson's corporeal enigmas—to an extent that remains to
be examined, the ethnological revolution helped to transform content,
form, and technique in nineteenth-century United States literature. The
bodies that absorb literary attention are already texts that have been
defined, inscribed, interpreted, and publicized. The writers' accounts of
these bodies are twice-told tales, at the least.

SKIN DEEP: THE ETHNOLOGICAL CRITIQUES
OF DOUGLASS, BROWN, AND APESS

The judgments of ethnology did not go unchallenged. In "American Ethnology" (1849), a review of research on Indian character and origins,
the archaeologist Ephraim G. Squier criticizes as premature and partial
the arguments for natural Indian inferiority. He emphasizes past cultural achievements by the ancient Mexicans, the Iroquois confederation,
and the Peruvians. He adduces the example of the contemporary Southwest, where fruitful exchanges were occurring between Indians and
whites. The Charleston minister and naturalist John Bachman attacked
Nott's argument for separate creations. Bachman was offended by the
polygenetic threat to the accuracy of the Bible, not by the idea of permanent racial hierarchy. In response to the often-reprinted catalogues of
anatomical difference, Bachman enumerated twenty-one correspondences in human structure. In 1855, *Putnam's Monthly* published the
ironically titled "About Niggers," an essay in which a genial narrator
repeats racial stereotypes about innate black inferiority, unmasking
their inherent contradictions. Yet these challenges were often blunted by
an inability to repudiate the ultimate conclusions of the "American
school" about racial character. Squier is a progressive polygenist. Bachman defends the unity of humankind and the institution of slavery. The
Putnam's writer frames his critique in stereotypes. Irony does not quite
erase their print.[34]

  Less equivocal is James Russell Lowell's essay "The Prejudice of
Color" (1845). Lowell characterizes as "pitiably ludicrous" the attachment to such physical differences as color, "an accidental difference in

the secreting vessels of the skin." He assails the ethnologist's appeal to natural "facts":

> Meanwhile, as a prophecy is sometimes known to bring about its own fulfill-
> ment, the national prejudice against the colored race is fast producing a plen-
> tiful crop of statistical facts on which to base an argument in its own favor.
> The colored people of the so-called free states are still held in slavery by
> something stronger than a constitution, more terrible than the cannon and
> the bayonet,—the force of a depraved and unchristian public opinion. We
> shut them rigidly out from every path of emulation or ambition, and then
> deny to them the possession of ordinary faculties.

Lowell argues that the methods of racial science reveal not divine plan but self-fulfilling prophecies in which prejudice disfigures evidence. The "American school" discovers secrets it already knows. Lowell decries the silent violence that degrades and then punishes its victims.[35]

The sharpest rejoinders to ethnology were delivered by its objects. In an address at Ohio's Western Reserve College in July 1854, Frederick Douglass presented his own ethnological treatise, relying on the work of the monogenist and Egyptologist James Prichard. In "The Claims of the Negro Ethnologically Considered," Douglass asserts that "the Negro is a MAN" and that all human beings share a common ancestry. He targets the figures of the "American school"—Morton, whose "contempt for Negroes" is evident throughout his work, and Nott and Gliddon, whose "compendious and barefaced" *Types of Mankind* would require several lectures to expose.[36]

In a series of deliberately titled sections, Douglass elucidates ethno-logical biases and errors. In "The Bearings of the Question," he suggests that polygenists are not disinterested observers but are overwhelmingly supporters of racial slavery, seeking to justify oppression by discrediting its victims. In "Ethnological Unfairness Towards the Negro," Douglass describes how Morton's prejudice, his "genuine American feeling," dis-torted the ways he selected and interpreted evidence. He questions Morton's separation of Negro from Egyptian and his denial of any black contribution, other than in the form of slave labor, to ancient civiliza-tion. He charges that ethnological illustrations regularize Caucasian fea-tures, while distorting Negroid characteristics. In the hands of the "American school," according to Douglass, science is caricature.[37]

In the section entitled "Superficial Objections," Douglass shows how cultural ignorance leads ethnologists to misguided judgments. Using Charles Hamilton Smith's *Natural History of the Human Species* (1848,

1851) as an example, he demystifies claims about the suitability of the spherical Ethiopian head for carrying burdens (if Smith ever stood at Douglass's door, he would have seen hundreds of German and Irish people whose heads successfully bore their own burdens); about the feeble and hoarse voice of the male Negro (if Smith ever stood in the shoes of a slave, he would understand the minor tone as a self-protective strategy); and about the absence of any African alphabet (to demonstrate Smith's illiteracy, Douglass during his lecture held up a published grammar of the coastal West African Mpongwe language).

Employing his favorite trope of chiasmus toward the end of the address, Douglass argues for the role that environment plays in shaping human characteristics and in molding the apparently neutral conclusions of ethnology: "A man is worked upon by what *he* works on. He may carve out his circumstances, but his circumstances will carve him out as well." Douglass concludes that even if he were unable to prove that Egyptians were dark-skinned or that the human races descended from a common origin, essential similarity and shared destiny oblige equal treatment.[38]

In *Clotel* (1853), William Wells Brown skewers the medical trade in African American bodies. Around a thin plot, Brown stitches a comprehensive display of racial convention. He collects, arranges, and evaluates pieces of antebellum culture—fictional plots, characters, and scenes, lines of poetry, snatches of written and rumored history, quotes from Jefferson, advertisements, legal documents, newspaper clippings, passages from sermons—to convey the racist texture of American society.

In chapter 11, "The Parson Poet," Brown reprints two passages that had already been excerpted in the "Public Opinion" section of Theodore Dwight Weld's abolitionist compilation *American Slavery As It Is* (1839). The first passage is a prospectus from the South Carolina Medical College in Charleston that boasts the unparalleled opportunities "for the acquisition of anatomical knowledge": "Subjects being obtained from among the coloured population in sufficient numbers *for every purpose,* and proper dissections carried on *without offending any individuals in the community!*" The second excerpt is from an advertisement by a Dr. T. Stillman offering to pay the "*highest cash price*" to "Any person having *sick Negroes,* considered *incurable* by their respective physicians, (their owners of course,) and wishing to dispose of them." Both Brown and Weld expose the naturalized violence of a "public opinion" that can read and not recoil from the syntax of these advertisements. Weld frames the passages with statements about vulnerable bodies, the "experimenting knives" of southern physicians, and the surgical gaze of doctors and the southern public. Brown seems less assured of the contrast between South and North and more skeptical of the pedagogical power of declamation.[39]

Brown situates the medical notices in a conversation between the Connecticut native the Reverend Peck, now settled and slaveholding in Mississippi, and his daughter Georgiana and his old New England school-friend Mr. Carlton, both of whom have anti-slavery leanings. In this context, bound by ties of family, friendship, and race, Carlton can quiver at the advertisements and at Peck's defense and Georgiana can deliver an arch sentence about the "iniquity of the institution," but neither character can or will take forceful action.

There is no easy release in this chapter for characters or readers. The Reverend Peck cuts short the conversation by giving Carlton a poem he has written for his sister's album. Georgiana insists that Carlton read aloud this "domestic piece." Entitled "My Little Nig," a sample of plantation sentiment, the poem illustrates the caricatured charms of Peck's favorite slave boy. Through this seeming diversion from politics to poetry, Brown joins types of violence—medical and literary, professional and popular, clinical and sentimental. Both advertisement and poem dissect their African American objects. Juxtaposed, the medical advertisement seems less aberrant and the sentimental poem more vicious. Since the chapter ends with the end of the poem, there is no sign in characters' dialogue or authorial comment of Georgiana's or Carlton's responses beyond their anticipation. (Carlton "laughed as his eyes glanced over it" and Georgiana says that her father " 'gets off some very droll things at times.' ") Whether they were satisfied or whether they acknowledged the symbiosis between surgery and poetry Brown leaves unanswered in the silence at the bottom of the page.[40]

Both slave narrative and Native American autobiography, *The Life of Okah Tubbee* (1852) responds baroquely to the characterizations of antebellum ethnology. The *Life* is written in a collaboration between Tubbee, who dictated the story, his Native American wife Laah Ceil, who wrote it down and revised and expanded it twice, and the Reverend Lewis Allen, who edited an earlier version. Tubbee attempts to use the ambiguity of physical distinctions to alter his identity and transfer his allegiance from African American to Native American in order to ascend the racial hierarchy.

Born Warner, the son of a black slave woman in Natchez, Mississippi, Tubbee in his life and in his textual and oral performances sought to reconstruct his racial character with the support of his European American audiences. Tubbee's *Life* pivots on the lacunae in the ethnological argument. Seizing upon the diversity of human colors and features and reversing the interpretive trajectory from characteristics to character, Tubbee argues that he has been wrongly typed. His proud, free, and pure character identifies his characteristics as those of an Indian, rather than an African American slave. In fact, he claims, he is the son of a Choctaw chief. The usual plot lines are tangled in Tubbee's story. His black mother enforces her authority as his master by flogging him. The Indian in him emerges in narrative retrospect. He performs his Indian "character" on stage, telling the story of his life and playing the flute, along with Laah Ceil, who lectures on behalf of Indian rights. These performances win him an appreciative European American audience, for a time. He is not the object of United States scientific inquiry but a medical authority himself, a purveyor of "Real Indian Medicines." The life and the *Life* indicate the price of a challenge that reinforces racial categories. Tubbee denies his maternal heritage and he searches for certification from an often suspicious or hostile white audience. He ceaselessly presents his credentials.[41]

Before the cranial breakthroughs of Morton and the popular triumphs of the "American school," when skin still seemed the lens of difference, William Apess, a Pequot Indian who became a Methodist minister, published "An Indian's Looking Glass for the White Man" (1833). Interested, as Melville would be, in anatomizing terms and reversing positions to expose the exposures of nineteenth-century ethnology, Apess argues that the European American viewer does not penetrate into the mysteries of Native American character when he inspects colored skin, but instead sees himself. For Apess, ethnology's emblem is not the calipers or the scalpel or the microscope; rather, it is the mirror, the looking glass that magnifies not the object but the subject of the gaze.[42]

Apess structures his essay with an antithesis between "skin" and "principles." Principles lie "under" the skin for Apess, but the preposition does not indicate a fixed site. Instead, he refers to a moral sense without latitude or longitude. Apess inverts the color scale. Jesus Christ was a Jew and thus dark-skinned and he sought to save the whites, the most degraded people then on earth. Thus Apess cautions his readers, "you are not indebted to a principle beneath a white skin for your religious services but to a colored one." Rather than being impaled by his reader's stare, Apess "penetrate[s] more fully into the conduct of those who profess to have pure principles." In Apess's looking glass, the viewer is meant to draw back from the hypocrisy between white ideals and acts, rather than from the stain of color on character.[43]

Apess does not merely denounce Christian hypocrisy. As a sign of his ethnological times, he figures that hypocrisy as recorded on the skin:

> Assemble all nations together in your imagination, and then let the whites be seated among them, and then let us look for the whites, and I doubt not it would be hard finding them; for to the rest of the nations, they are still but a handful. Now suppose these skins were put together, and each skin had its national crimes written upon it—which skin do you think would have the greatest? . . . I should look at all the skins, and I know that when I cast my eye upon that white skin, and if I saw those crimes written upon it, I should enter my protest against it immediately and cleave to that which is more honorable. And I can tell you that I am satisfied with the manner of my creation, fully—whether others are or not.

In this singular image of an ethnological congress, a cutaneous judgment day, national skins are collected and compared. As Melville will do in the "Whiteness of the Whale" chapter in *Moby-Dick*, Apess here makes white skin the object of discriminating curiosity usually reserved for dark skin. Apess inspects, abstracts, and degrades. Pointedly, this assembly takes place in imagination, not in nature. The writing is not indelible. The crimes are historical, not inherently racial.[44]

In "An Indian's Looking Glass for the White Man," Apess urges his European American readers to see and know Native Americans and themselves in unconventional ways. He joins his key terms, "skin" and "mirror," in a final pun. "By what you read, you may learn how deep your principles are," Apess writes, referring to the looking-glass properties of ethnology, of Scripture, and of his own reflective text. "I should say they were skin-deep," he concludes. Apess has taken great pains to demonstrate that this is not deep at all. Yet his impassioned exposures of superficiality were followed by three decades during which American ethnology extended its sway over the skins, heads, hearts, and minds of the United States. The "tree of distinction" that Apess demands "be leveled to the earth" at the very end of his essay instead ramifies across American science, politics, and culture.[45] Almost two decades later, Melville sets it as his task in *Moby-Dick* to anatomize the racial quest and to understand how very deep skin-deep is. In pursuit of this knowledge, Melville journeys into the belly, and the head, of the whale.

A SIGHT OF SIGHTS TO SEE:
CETOLOGY AND ETHNOLOGY IN *MOBY-DICK*

While it may seem strange in this argument to move from human to
whale anatomy, it is a move that Melville makes repeatedly in *Moby-
Dick*. It is neither arbitrary nor idiosyncratic. As he suggests in his web
of allusions and figures, the two efforts were bound together in the late
eighteenth and nineteenth centuries. Both Thomas Beale and Frederick
Debell Bennett, the meticulous observers of whale anatomy whom
Melville used as sources, were surgeons on English whaling ships in the
South Seas. The renowned British anatomists John Hunter and Richard
Owen were also pioneering whale anatomists, on whom Beale, Bennett,
and Melville all relied. Hunter inspired the British comparative anatomist Charles White, who conceived of charting "the regular gradation
in man" after seeing a series of skulls Hunter had arranged in ascending
order from dog to monkey to African to American to Asiatic to European. Hunter was also the main source for Beale's chapter on the "Anatomy and Physiology of the Sperm Whale."[46]

In *Moby-Dick*, Melville employs the whale's massive corpus as the revealing stage on which to play out the tragedy and comedy of nineteenth-century bodily investigation. As Melville emphasizes, the whale,
the largest species of mammal known to exist, offers immense possibilities for unlocking the secrets of the skin and head. The whale's skin, up
to fifteen inches thick, can be peeled from its body and sliced into leaves;
its epidermis is detachable, its rete mucosum preservable, and precious
fluid can be distilled from its blubber, the cutis vera. The sperm whale's
head is one-third the size of its entire body; it can be split open and its
contents carried away in pails.

Both cetologists and ethnologists debated the proper classifications
to make among specimens and whether they were dealing with one or
many species. In *Moby-Dick*, these categorical difficulties unsettle confidence in defining human types. The cetological axiom that the skeleton
of the whale does not accurately reflect the shape of the whale's body
(Melville makes the point three times) raises questions about the ethnologist's abilities to make dry bones speak. Melville represents the process of cutting into the skin and head of the whale as extraordinarily violent and liquid, violating the integrity of the object and threatening to
inundate the observer. He associates knowledge with appropriation,
representing the ways in which anatomy enables commodity and the
parts of the body become vendible.[47]

At the center of *Moby-Dick*, the cetology chapters do not merely serve as "keel" or "ballast." They do not simply form the documentary base that moors Melville's speculation, as much of the criticism has it. They are a vital part of the book. In these chapters, Melville anatomizes the features of ethnological discourse: the excess, literalization, catalogues, analogies, personification, synesthesia, and catachreses that structure the object of knowledge. The cetology chapters do not reject the "scientific method," as several critics suggest. If Melville sought to dismiss ethnology, he could have done so in one or two chapters—in "Cistern and Buckets" or "The Nut" or "A Bower in the Arsacides." Twenty chapters would seem excessive, even for a writer of Melville's notorious verbosity. Rather than dismiss, however, Melville inhabits and defamiliarizes nineteenth-century corporeal inquiry. He savors ethnology's pleasures, tests its limits, and makes palpable its dangers. In a self-deprecating letter to Richard Henry Dana Jr., dated May 1, 1850, and thus penned during the early stages of writing *Moby-Dick*, Melville himself belittled his cetology. He complained about the difficulties of extracting poetry from blubber: "It will be a strange sort of a book, tho', I fear; blubber is blubber you know; tho' you may get oil out of it, the poetry runs as hard as sap from a frozen maple tree." Such disparagements are often echoed in critical rankings of the different registers of the book. Yet in *Moby-Dick* Melville is passionate about blubber. *Moby-Dick* is about the similarity not the difference between blubber and poetry. It is about the epic poetics of the body. It is not about the gap between expendable surface and philosophical depth but about how bodies became saturated with meaning and how "race" was seen as the key to it all.[48]

Although critics often separate the cetology from the tragedy or romance, Melville in *Moby-Dick* refuses such distinctions. His anatomy chapters bear an intimate and substantial, rather than tangential, digressive, or parodic, relation to the narrative. *Moby-Dick* tells the story of a quest for knowledge anchored in bodies and animated by the search for racial secrets—at once an ocean quest, a vision quest, and a body quest. In *Moby-Dick*, Western quest narratives climax in the labyrinthine skeleton, in the inscribed skin, and especially in the capacious, inviting head of the whale. Conveying both the reach and the risks of the ethnological enterprise, Melville alludes, especially in the cetology chapters, to the stories of Jonah, who spent three days and three nights inside the body of a great fish, and of Job, who sought to know the power of his God, was chastised for his inability to draw out Leviathan

with a hook or discover his garment or open the doors of his face, and
was left to contemplate his own frangible skin.⁴⁹

Between "Cetology" (chapter 32) and "Does the Whale Diminish?"
(chapter 105), Melville takes the reader on a fantastic voyage around the
surface and inside the body of the whale. During this journey, the action
is continually suspended and probed. At the beginning of this sequence,
Melville punctuates his narrative with cetology chapters—"Cetology,"
"The Quarter-Deck," "Moby Dick," and "The Whiteness of the
Whale"—that establish the terms and analyze the psychodynamics of
the corporeal quest. Then—in "Stubb Kills a Whale" through "The
Shark Massacre"—he describes the crew's pursuit and killing of a sperm
whale, the second mate Stubb's devouring of a whale steak, and the car-
nivorous appetites shared by human beings and sharks. These ravenous
scenes incite a long sequence of anatomy chapters, as though fixing the
whale to the side of the ship and feasting upon its flesh do not satisfy the
narrative hungers. Ishmael attempts to decipher the text of the whale,
from skin ("The Blanket") to head ("The Sperm Whale's Head"
through "The Nut") to tail ("The Tail"), and finally inside the skeleton
("A Bower in the Arsacides" through "The Fossil Whale").

The deeper we penetrate into the mysteries of the whale's body, the
more we learn about the obsessions of the observer. If the cetology chapters do not fulfill the desire for anatomical epiphanies, they do reveal the
structures of compulsion, as Ishmael returns again and again to the
whale, despite his repeated failures and his incessant irony about the endeavor. In "A Squeeze of the Hand," Melville suggests an alternative
epistemology based not on sight but on touch. The sequence culminates
in the spectacular scene of "Queequeg in his Coffin," in which Ahab,
Ishmael, and Melville all stare at the Polynesian harpooneer's body,
bristling with significance.⁵⁰

♦   ♦   ♦

After the "Pequod" has been "launched upon the deep," in order to
prepare readers for the "special leviathanic revelations and allusions of
all sorts which are to follow" (134), Ishmael broaches the difficulties of
definition. In "Cetology," he describes the effort to catalogue whales as
"the classification of the constituents of a chaos" (134). Taking much of
its detail and argument from Beale, this chapter is filled with jokes about
the encrustations of precedent, the arbitrariness of names, and the elu-
siveness of the whale's features.⁵¹ Making an argument he will repeat at
the end of "The Funeral," Ishmael challenges the "law of precedents"

(309). He doubts claims made by experts who have not seen whales themselves or who have merely repeated the verdicts of their predecessors. Authority gains its authority from the reproduction of error. Fact becomes fact with repetition. Names preserve the mistakes of their bestowers: the sperm whale is prized not for its semen but for the oil in its head, which was confused with semen; the narwhale does not have a horn but a tusk; the killer whale is unfairly stigmatized for a violent nature shared by sea and land creatures. The features on which observers conventionally found their distinctions—baleen, hump, fin, and teeth—are not confined to separate species of whales, but are "peculiarities" "indiscriminately dispersed" among all sorts of cetaceans (140). The whale, Ishmael insists, has not yet been accurately or fully represented in words.

Although this chapter swells with the rhetoric of incompletion, climaxing in the famous account of *Moby-Dick* as "but the draught of a draught" (145), the point is that such exegeses have been misguided or distorted, not that they are unnecessary or impossible. Far from it. In the first of many graphic images, Ishmael describes his yearning for the interiors of whales. He desires "To grope down into the bottom of the sea after them; to have one's hands among the unspeakable foundations, ribs, and very pelvis of the world" (136). To know the whale is to follow him to his depths. To grasp the anatomy of the whale is to lay one's hands on the framework of the cosmos.

In "Cetology," Ishmael postpones the journey to the interior in favor of examining the external features of the body. He classifies whales on the basis of blunt differences in size, borrowing bibliographical terms: folio, octavo, duodecimo. The governing conceit in this chapter, and in all the corporeal chapters that follow, is that the body is a book of secrets, waiting to be read by the observer. *Moby-Dick* inflates this ethnological conceit, offering the most voluminous of volumes.[52]

Ishmael divides whales into three primary divisions, or "books," subdivided into "chapters." While describing the characteristics of "Folio," "Octavo," and "Duodecimo" whales, Ishmael suggests the economic motives that partly fuel such classifications. The sperm whale is the most valuable in commerce, providing the emollient spermaceti; the grampus is prized for its illuminating oil; the huzza porpoise (Melville's own coinage) is known for the lubricating fluid extracted from its jaws. The reduction of difference to size does not liberate whales. It focuses attention in profitable ways. In analyzing the semantic and somatic effects of the "middle passage," Hortense Spillers suggests that the enslaved

Africans carried across the Atlantic were subjected to a "total objectification" that stripped them of associations with gender, will, desire, and feeling. Reduced to quantities, these bodies then became ripe for vicious distinction. In Melville's "Cetology" chapter, the quantification of cetacean bodies similarly opens them for discriminating investments. The joke about whales and books, about eloquent flesh, is a joke with a long genealogy in European and American culture and with enduring consequences for the narrative.[53]

If "Cetology" articulates the corporeal quest in a jaunty register, "The Quarter-Deck" gives it furious voice. Ahab, explaining his mania to Starbuck, famously calls attention to the "little lower layer" and describes all visible objects, and the broad white visage of Moby Dick in particular, as "pasteboard masks" through which "some unknown but still reasoning thing puts forth the mouldings of its features." Ahab sees in Moby Dick "outrageous strength" and "inscrutable malice," and he vows to return the insult and "strike through the mask" (164). These obsessions are epistemological (the surface infuriatingly concealing the depths) and theological (involving natural and possibly divine malevolence), but as always in *Moby-Dick,* philosophy and theology are melded with flesh. Inside Ahab's pasteboard masks lurk presences that press against the surface. In this phrenological nightmare, Ahab sees facial features as projections of malice. He takes them as insults. From Ahab's point of view, then, Starbuck is certainly wrong when he describes Moby Dick as a "dumb brute" (163). Though the whale cannot talk, his features speak for him. The inscrutable things are what Ahab hates, the things that resist searching examination. Ahab responds to the affront by thrusting his own rage through his body. Such self-defenses can result in carnage, as Ishmael imagines: "He piled upon the whale's white hump the sum of all the general rage and hate felt by his whole race from Adam down; and then, as if his chest had been a mortar, he burst his hot heart's shell upon it" (184). This is a visceral retort to the insult of inscrutable difference. In his drive to expose the whale and his corrosive vision of forces that distort the features of others, Ahab eviscerates himself.

"Cetology" and "The Quarter Deck" are companion chapters, weaving together corporeal desires. Although Ishmael's playfulness seems unlike Ahab's frenzy, the distance is not so great between the fantasy of reaching down into the body and grasping its foundations and the fantasy of striking through the mask. Ishmael's ardor and Ahab's hatred, knowing and killing, will come for a time in the narrative to seem more alike than different in terms of their effects on other bodies. The paired characters and passions are further developed in "Moby Dick" and "The Whiteness of the Whale."

In these chapters, Ishmael analyzes first Ahab's preoccupations with the whale and then his own. In "Moby Dick" Ishmael unfolds Ahab's violent object relations, his "sudden, passionate, corporal animosity":

> ever since that almost fatal encounter, Ahab had cherished a wild vindictiveness against the whale, all the more fell for that in his frantic morbidness he at last came to identify with him, not only all his bodily woes, but all his intellectual and spiritual exasperations. The White Whale swam before him as the monomaniac incarnation of all those malicious agencies which some deep men feel eating in them, till they are left living on with half a heart and half a lung. That intangible malignity which has been from the beginning; to whose dominion even the modern Christians ascribe one-half of the worlds; which the ancient Ophites of the east reverenced in their statue devil;—Ahab did not fall down and worship it like them; but deliriously transferring its idea to the abhorred white whale, he pitted himself, all mutilated, against it. All that most maddens and torments; all that stirs up the lees of things; all truth with malice in it; all that cracks the sinews and cakes the brain; all the subtle demonisms of life and thought; all evil, to crazy Ahab, were visibly personified, and made practically assailable in Moby Dick. (184)

Confessing his sympathy with his captain, Ishmael explains the pathological processes of "incarnation." Torments are transferred from subject to object. Then the object is attacked as the embodiment of malicious agencies. The self is "pitted," a response whose verb implies both onslaught and mutilation. Project, personify, and assail—these acts describe not only obsessions with whales but also obsessions with humans. Ishmael identifies the psychodynamics of racism. "Visibly personified" nicely conveys the ways in which features are activated by the eye. "Practically assailable" suggests that scapegoating enables trauma to be targeted, but it also precludes victory. The practical assault can practically, but never quite, succeed. Melville's allusions to ancient fetishism and his catalogues ("all that most maddens and torments," "all that stirs up the lees of things," "all truth with malice in it," "all the subtle demonisms of life and thought") indicate the genealogy, density, and reach of such projections.

In "The Whiteness of the Whale," Melville continues to analyze "visible personifications," specifically the imputations of color. Ishmael focuses on the chromatic characteristics of Moby Dick, singularly and disturbingly white among a species known for its blackness.[54] In this chapter, Melville amplifies his techniques of allusion and inventory, as

Ishmael traces the appalling significance of "whiteness" for him and in history. The chapter shifts concern from black to white skin. Ishmael signals this reversal in the extended concessional clause that forms the entire second paragraph. "Though" white is often associated with the sweet and the honorable and the sublime, Ishmael argues, "yet" there "lurks an elusive something in the innermost idea of this hue" that affrights (188–89). Between the "though" and the "yet" and for twenty paragraphs following the "yet," Ishmael sounds the disconcerting "incantation of this whiteness" (195). In this chapter, Melville performs a thought experiment. He imagines the effects of turning withering scrutiny upon the body of the observer. We all know what black signifies and what red signifies in United States culture. We all know the investments of meaning, the stock responses, and the warrants for subjection. Now let's think about what it would mean to think about what white "means." In Ishmael's analysis, it means elusive ghastliness, nameless terror, the pallor of the dead, the expressive hue of the shroud. The devotees of whiteness, he suggests, may be worshipping not God but the Devil.[55]

Yet this is not an anti-white chapter. Melville does not blacken whiteness to discredit Caucasians. Through his alienating effects, he seeks to open to view the peculiar and powerful notion of a rule of pigment. "Though" the chapter begins by repeating the truism that "this preeminence in it [whiteness] applies to the human race itself, giving the white man ideal mastership over every dusky tribe" (189), "yet" it goes on to unsettle the idea of a natural hierarchy of color and to question the ideological grounds of mastership. If color is to be attached to character, then it must be acknowledged that the "whiteness" of Caucasian skin is subject to impurities like all other colors. That "white" skin is colored, rather than beyond color, is the message conveyed by the repeated pun on "appalling": "It was the whiteness of the whale that above all things appalled me" (188, see also 195). Contemplating whiteness drains the color from Ishmael's face. Ishmael's blanching is the complement to the shadow cast on Benito Cereno by "the negro" at the end of Melville's novella "Benito Cereno" (1855). In Melville's assay of whiteness, racial anxiety alters the Caucasian complexion.[56]

The chapter ends by questioning the very idea of color as a stable characteristic. According to Ishmael, "whiteness is not so much a color as the visible absence of color, and at the same time the concrete of all colors" (195). Ishmael's whiteness exposes the betrayal of all colors, which promise substance but deliver emptiness. "A dumb blankness, full of meaning" (195), he labels whiteness, suggesting the persistence of racial knowledge, despite—or maybe because of—the vacancy of its categories, a vacancy that enables these categories to be vast. This "dumb blankness, full of meaning," discursive structures that are both empty and compelling, is an epistemological paradox that preoccupied Melville and that becomes the focus and the undoing of *Pierre*. According to Ishmael, not only are the investments in whiteness misplaced, so is the belief in the significance of color in general: "all other earthly hues . . . are but subtle deceits, not actually inherent in substances, but only laid on from without" (195). Ishmael explains that natural philosophers have argued that color is a property of light, not a property of bodies themselves. Drawing upon Locke, Ishmael outlines how color, a secondary quality, has become interpreted as primary. Surface has been taken as substance. In Ishmael's model, unlike Locke's, secondary qualities do not clarify substance, they confound it. Ishamel bitterly complains about the loss of color as a foundation for meaning: "all deified Nature absolutely paints like the harlot, whose allurements cover nothing but the charnel-house within" (195).[57]

The image of the harlot, the painted woman, reminds us that the study of sexual anatomy took place alongside and in relation to the study of racial anatomy. The bodies in the cetology chapters are not conspicuously gendered, with the notable exceptions of the phallic trophy borne in "The Cassock" and the gestating, lactating, and copulating whales in "The Grand Armada." Melville concentrates on differences marked as racial. Such features consume the observer's attention, as they consumed the attention of ethnologists such as Morton and Nott. The body of "Nature" from which Ishmael recoils at the end of "The Whiteness of the Whale" deceives his eye. It allures and then disappoints. Yet in *Moby-Dick* corporeal disenchantment is always followed by renewed interest. To analyze the articulation of difference is not to exorcise the desires that fuel it. Neither the psychoanalysis of the "Moby Dick" chapter nor the reversals and exposures of "The Whiteness of the Whale" satisfy Ishmael. If he cannot grasp the vast body of the whale, he will attempt to probe its parts. Though the secrets of the body may not be revealed by the color of the skin, they may be revealed by its structure ("The Blanket"), or by the design of the head ("The Great Heidelburgh Tun"), or by a pail full of its contents ("Cistern and Buckets").[58]

In a series of chapters about pictures of whales ("Monstrous Pictures of Whales," "Less Erroneous Pictures of Whales," and "Of Whales in

Paint, in Teeth, &c."), Ishmael demonstrates that the whale's body resists representation. The whale swims out of the sight of most observers,
and even when seen, nearly all of its body lies under water. Most illustrations have been based on the carcasses of dead whales or whale skeletons, which misrepresent the whale's living shape. The three chapters
move from less accurate to more accurate pictures, from the hilarious
"amputated sows," "hippogriffs," "squashes," and "Richard III whales,
with dromedary humps" produced by artists and scientists to the more
reliable outlines made by French sailor artists and British seamen cetologists such as Thomas Beale, and from there to the crude but truest images on whalebone and painted boards made by sailors. For the most
precise views, Ishmael explains, one must go to sea. These chapters
point toward Melville's own picture of the sperm whale: Stubb's whale
fixed by Tashtego's harpoon and moored to the side of the *Pequod*.[59]

The scenes in which Stubb kills and eats the whale and the sharks devour it are extraordinarily grisly (from "Stubb Kills a Whale" through
"The Shark Massacre"). They establish the setting, object, instruments,
and appetite for the cetology chapters that follow. In "Stubb Kills a
Whale," the pipe-smoking second mate leads the charge against a sperm
whale, whose body, pierced by dart after dart and then by Stubb's pry-
ing lance, releases a torrent of liquid:

> The red tide now poured from all sides of the monster like brooks down a
> hill. His tormented body rolled not in brine but in blood, which bubbled and
> seethed for furlongs behind in their wake. The slanting sun playing upon this
> crimson pond in the sea, sent back its reflection into every face, so that they
> all glowed to each other like red men. . . .
> And now abating in his flurry, the whale once more rolled out into view;
> surging from side to side; spasmodically dilating and contracting his spout-
> hole, with sharp, cracking, agonized respirations. At last, gush after gush of
> clotted red gore, as if it had been the purple lees of red wine, shot into the
> frighted air; and falling back again, ran dripping down his motionless flanks
> into the sea. His heart had burst! (285–86)

Ishmael emphasizes the surge outward of the whale's clotted contents.
As he explains later in the book, there are no valves in the whale's cir-
culatory system. When a blood vessel is pierced by a harpoon, the absence of "flood-gates" combines with the pressure of the surrounding
water to produce "incessant streams" (357).[60] Yet hydraulics alone does
not account for the excessive absorption and flow in this scene. Stubb is
hungry and he is searching. He probes the whale's flank: "Stubb slowly
churned his long sharp lance into the fish, and kept it there, carefully

churning and churning, as if cautiously seeking to feel after some gold watch that the whale might have swallowed" (286). This is one of many images representing the whale's body, and particularly the head, as a container of value: chest, wine cask, cistern, citadel, temple. In the sailors' darts and Stubb's lance, Melville depicts the violent penetrations by the body's treasure hunters. When the whale, saturated with meaning, is pierced, liquid pours forth, gush after gush. The crimson operation literally reflects on the sailors, as their faces are stained by the color of blood and they become "red men," white savages, a portrayal that will be developed in the set-piece cannibal feast on whale flesh in "Stubb's Supper."

In a poem resonating with the killing of Stubb's whale, Emily Dickinson illustrates the risks incurred by the seeker after bodily secrets. If in *Moby-Dick* Melville expands his field of vision to encompass the largest mammal, in "Split the Lark" Dickinson focuses on one of the smallest avian bodies. The yield of both bodies is similar. Given the difference in size, the quantity of liquid produced by Dickinson's lark is astounding:

Split the Lark and
you'll find the Music—
Bulb after Bulb, in
Silver rolled.
Scantily dealt to the
Summer Morning
Saved for your Ear when
Lutes be old.

Loose the Flood—
you shall find it patent—
Gush after Gush,
reserved for you—
Scarlet Experiment!
Sceptic Thomas!
Now, do you doubt
that your Bird was
true?

My point is not that Dickinson was specifically revising Melville (although in addition to the similarity in scene there is the verbal echo of "Gush after Gush"), but that both writers reworked the prominent antebellum scene of bodily contemplation. Dickinson's poem is about knowledge and faith, a knowledge that pierces and a faith that abjures the instruments of sight and touch. It is a particularly cruel poem, choosing to inflict its "Scarlet Experiment" on a merry little bird. (In one of her "Master" letters, which also links bird, Thomas, knowledge, faith, and rupture, Dickinson shoots the bird.) Dickinson associates this dissecting knowledge with the male "Sceptic Thomas." A descendant of Doubting Thomas of John 20:24–25, this nineteenth-century Thomas also insists upon ocular and manual proof to certify his belief. Dickinson's "Sceptic Thomas" seeks to make truth "patent" by splaying it. His knowledge is septic as well as skeptic, rotted and contaminating as well as suspicious, as Dickinson suggests in her choice of spelling (offering the possibility of pronouncing a soft "sc") and her aligning of "Sceptic" and "Scarlet." Her "Thomas," as she explains in the third "Master" letter, has a misplaced faith, a "faith in anatomy."[61]

Although the moral of the poem would seem to be the comforting "have faith, don't pry," the speaker both castigates Thomas's "Scarlet Experiment" and commands it. "Split the Lark," she insists, "Loose the Flood." The speaker shares in the poem's assault. Violence is inflicted on the lark, lashes back at Thomas, and rebounds on the imperative speaker. This accumulating force is figured in the poem as a surge of liquid, out of all proportion to the volume of the victim's body. "Now, do you doubt that your bird was true?" we imagine the speaker asking Thomas, as he—and she—drown. The red tide, gush after gush, is not quite the regulated access to the body's contents that Thomas had in mind. "Scarlet Experiment" is an apt term not only for Dickinson's "Sceptic Thomas" splitting his lark and for Melville's sailors puncturing their whales but also for the "faith in anatomy" that impelled the ethnological quest.

The scarlet experiment of the *Pequod*'s sailors is followed by a cannibal feast whose scenes of bloodletting make the gore in "Stubb Kills a Whale" seem understated. In "Stubb's Supper," the sailors fill Leviathan's skin with barbed irons, tow the carcass to the *Pequod,* and moor it to the side of the ship, head to stern. Stubb orders the harpooneer Daggoo to cut a steak from the body. Ishmael paints a lurid, beautiful diptych in which the sailors' carving and glutting on deck is mirrored in the sharks' gouging of the carcass below the waterline. In "The Whale as a Dish," Ishmael explains the custom of splitting the skull of a small sperm whale with an ax, removing the two whitish lobes, mixing them with flour, and serving them as an epicurean treat. In "The Shark Massacre," he describes how, in an effort to reduce the loss of whale flesh to the thousands of feeding sharks, Queequeg and a sailor from the forecastle pierce skull after skull with their long whaling spades. In these chapters, Melville wields the conventions of cannibal narratives not to vilify uncivilized Polynesians but to illuminate the savagery of American body—and especially head—hunters. Resembling neither the melodramatic glimpses into flesh pots in *Typee* nor the satiric dismemberings of *White-Jacket,* the cannibalism in these middle chapters of *Moby-Dick* reveals vehement, unsettling appetites. One is reminded of the "horrible repast" described by Captain Krusenstern, the rage to tear apart the body and sip blood from the skull. This time, though, the cravings are indulged by sailors on an American whaleship, pointedly described by Melville as a "cannibal of a craft, tricking herself forth in the chased bones of her enemies" (70).[62]

This cluster of chapters ends with an image of hunger that persists even after death. The sharks, their skins gashed by the whaling spades, find new objects for their appetites:

> They viciously snapped, not only at each other's disembowelments, but like flexible bows, bent round, and bit their own; till those entrails seemed swallowed over and over again by the same mouth, to be oppositely voided by the gaping wound. Nor was this all. It was unsafe to meddle with the corpses and ghosts of these creatures. A sort of generic or Pantheistic vitality seemed to lurk in their very joints and bones, after what might be called the individual life had departed. Killed and hoisted on deck for the sake of his skin, one of these sharks almost took poor Queequeg's hand off, when he tried to shut down the dead lid of his murderous jaw. (302)

The hunger in these cannibal chapters has many sources: economic (flesh as profit), philosophical (flesh as barrier or window), theological (flesh and spirit), psychological (flesh and personal identity). As I have been arguing, ethnology, the science of the age, channeled these attractions and focused them on the human body defined in racial terms. "Race," declared the Scottish anatomist Robert Knox in 1850, "is everything: literature, science, art, in a word, civilization, depend on it." [63] The corporeal quest in *Moby-Dick* is an ethnological quest, not in the narrow sense of distinguishing human characteristics, but in the comprehensive nineteenth-century sense in which the racial body was seen to contain the secrets of the world and the effort to decipher its parts was seen as crucial for the articulation of the national order. That the urgent violence of this quest consumes not only its object but also the subject is figured in Melville's spectacle of the sharks disgorging and devouring their own entrails.

In the narrative logic and ethnologic of *Moby-Dick,* bodily hungers are not satisfied by eating flesh. To eat flesh is to incorporate it. The goal of the cetology chapters, the desire of nineteenth-century ethnology, is to define the distance between bodies. In the pattern begun in *Typee,* where cannibalism is subsumed by tattooing, and continued in *White-Jacket,* where amputation is eclipsed by flogging, the body in *Moby-Dick* is represented first as meat and then, more satisfyingly and disturbingly, as text. "Stubb's Supper" is followed by "Cutting In," which describes the removal of the whale's skin, and by "The Blanket," which opens this surface to view. Eating is followed by reading.

"Cutting In" presents an ethnologist's fantasies come true. The *Pequod* provides a vast operating table and elaborate systems of hooks and tackles to hold and manipulate the huge body. There are arsenals of probing instruments—spades, swords, knives, lances—and there is an entire crew to wield them. After a hook and line have been inserted just above the nearest of the whale's two side-fins, the sailors strain to turn the windlass and the ship careens until at last the skin of the whale snaps and the hook draws up the first strip of blubber. The sailors continue to turn the windlass as the mates Starbuck and Stubb cut a "scarf" line that allows the blubber to be peeled from the body like the rind from an orange. Thus the sailors of the *Pequod* draw out Leviathan with a hook. When the strip of blubber reaches the height of the maintop, another hook and line are attached to its base and the blubber is cut in two with a "scientific dash" of the boarding-sword. This action forms the severed "blanket-piece," which is lowered beneath the main hatchway, leaving the next strip ready for flaying. The process is grimy and dangerous, not the clean removal of skin imagined at the end of *White-Jacket.* Melville describes the swaying of the "prodigious blood-dripping mass" attached to the maintop rope, as it threatens to knock unwary sailors overboard (303–04). The whale's skin is animated, not only in its initial resistance to being removed and its aggressive movements while bound, but also when it is in the form of a long blanket-piece, resting uneasily in the hold, "as if it were a great live mass of plaited serpents" (304). Hooked, drawn, peeled, sliced, coiled, and stored, alive with significance, the skin is ready for inspection.[64]

"What and where is the skin of the whale?" Ishmael asks at the beginning of "The Blanket" (305). In this chapter, at the exact midpoint of *Moby-Dick,* Ishmael inaugurates his meticulous corporeal journey. In "The Blanket," Ishmael attempts to discover the face of Leviathan's garment. What is the skin? Melville asks, seeking, like William Apess, to understand how the somatic has become semantic. Yet for Melville, the skin is more than a "looking glass" whose surface reflects the distorted desires of the viewer. Such an account ultimately may be true, as Melville implies in his reference to the Narcissus story as "the key to it all" at the beginning of the book (5), but in its abstract form it does not begin to explain the enduring compulsions of the skin. The skin may be a looking glass, but, in Ishmael's series of metaphorical attempts to expose cutaneous investments, it may also be window, lens, commodity, container, hieroglyphic. Melville drains color from his analysis of skin in "The Blanket," omitting the emphasis found in past cetological and ethnological commentary. He does so because earlier, in "The Whiteness of the Whale," he sought to undermine pigment as a fundamental category and because in the cetology chapters he is tracing the beliefs of ethnologists who by mid-century had discounted color and elevated structure as the guarantee of human difference.[65]

Ishmael suggests that fascination with the skin springs in part from an inability to locate it. Is the enveloping layer, the extremely thin transparent layer that is easily detachable after death, the skin of the whale? No, concludes Ishmael, this is the "skin of the skin" (306). He compares this outer covering to isinglass, a gelatin obtained from the bladders of certain fish and used as an adhesive and as a clarifying agent. He claims to have used dried bits of whale skin for bookmarks. He imagines that these slices of skin augment the type when they are laid upon the printed page. Magnifying glass as well as looking glass, the skin opens the whalebook to view. As he does again and again, Melville takes an observation in his cetological sources—here, Bennett's interest in the transparent, removable whale epidermis—and amplifies it, making visible the ethnological implications.[66]

From the skin of the skin, Ishmael moves to the lower layer, the blubber, which, concurring with Beale, he labels the true skin of the whale. He estimates its "yield" (306). Between ten and fifteen inches thick and weighing over ten tons, the blubber of a very large sperm whale can produce one hundred barrels of oil. "Yield" is a resonant term in this chapter and in the book as a whole, with frequent reference being made to the "yield" of the body: the blubber, the lip, the tongue, the head (142, 144, 334, 355, 340, 342). In "The Blanket," the skin yields literal profit, as the figurative distillations of skin do in the antebellum economic and social order. Melville painstakingly represents this order in the two "Knights and Squires" chapters, which detail the hierarchy of Caucasian officers and their Polynesian, Native American, and African subordinates on board the *Pequod*.[67]

As represented in "The Blanket," the skin renders a profit not only in barrels of oil but in knowledge. According to Ishmael, there are riddles in the skin:

> Almost invariably it is all over obliquely crossed and re-crossed with numberless straight marks in thick array, something like those in the finest Italian line engravings. But these marks do not seem to be impressed upon the isinglass substance above mentioned, but seem to be seen through it, as if they were engraved upon the body itself. Nor is this all. In some instances, to the quick, observant eye, those linear marks, as in a veritable engraving, but afford the ground for far other delineations. These are hieroglyphical; that is, if you call those mysterious cyphers on the walls of pyramids hieroglyphics, then that is the proper word to use in the present connexion. By my retentive memory of the hieroglyphics upon one Sperm Whale in particular, I was much struck with a plate representing the old Indian characters chiselled on the famous hieroglyphic palisades on the banks of the Upper Mississippi. Like those mystic rocks, too, the mystic-marked whale remains undecipherable. (306)

Hatched and cross-hatched, the skin of the whale is scored with significance. Its marks, viewed through the window of isinglass, are not scratched on the surface but engraved on the dermis. Unlike the tattooing in *Typee*, these line cuts allure rather than repel the viewer. The keen observer recognizes that they constitute sacred writing. Melville has drawn out the "linear impressions" Beale describes on the sides of the sperm whale's body into a revealing metaphor of engravings and hieroglyphics. Allusions link exegesis of the whale to the geographical and corporeal sites of Egypt and Native America, the foci in antebellum ethnological debates. Although Ishmael cannot interpret the dermal marks, they incite his curiosity. The suggestiveness of the skin drives his quest deeper.[68]

The desires of Ishmael and Ahab for bodily knowledge overlap in the next chapters. In "The Sphynx," at noon, when the deck of the *Pequod* is deserted, Ahab emerges from his cabin, paces the quarterdeck, then gazes over the right side of the ship, where the huge severed head of the sperm whale has been suspended half out of the sea. Inserting the sharp end of Stubb's spade into the lower part of the whale's head and placing the other end under his arm, Ahab leans over and addresses his object: "Speak, thou vast and venerable head . . . which, though ungarnished with a beard, yet here and there lookest hoary with mosses; speak, mighty head, and tell us the secret thing that is in thee" (311).

Instead of Hamlet in the graveyard holding Yorick's skull and acknowledging their common mortality, Melville presents Ahab interrogating the whale's head with a spade and searching for secret things. Melville emphasizes the space between viewer and head, a gap that spurs the search for access and answers. Like Samuel George Morton, Ahab does not view the severed head as a reminder of the evanescence of earthly desires. Instead, the panorama of the whale's head intensifies Ahab's desire to get inside, to fulfill the vision of striking through the mask he eloquently outlines in "The Quarter-Deck." The joke of Melville's scene, of course, is that the sperm whale's head is too large for Ahab to seize. He is dwarfed by its mass. The entire ship strains and leans in the effort to hold it. In order for this head to be examined, it must be secured by hooks, tackles, and cables. In "The Sphynx," Melville foregrounds not only the vehement desires of observers like Morton to decipher the characters of heads but also the elusive, precarious grasp of the observer. In *Crania Americana* and *Crania Ægyptiaca*, Morton does make his heads speak and reveal their secrets of inherent difference. In *Moby-Dick*, despite Ahab's imperative, the sperm whale's head remains mute. This silence generates Ishmael's avalanche of words about whales.[69]

After Stubb and Flask kill a right whale, the sailors sever its head and attach it to the left side of the *Pequod,* thus balancing the pull of the sperm whale's head on the starboard side. These two heads remain suspended at the sides of the ship for the next several chapters, during which they are literally and figuratively probed. Melville has some fun linking heads to philosophers, comparing the weight shifting on either side of the *Pequod* to the unstable alternation between the empiricism of Locke and the idealism of Kant and identifying the right whale as a Stoic and the sperm whale as a Platonian (327, 335). Yet the craniological chapters focus not on the philosophy abstracted from heads but on the philosophy embodied in them.

In "The Sperm Whale's Head—Contrasted View" and "The Right Whale's Head—Contrasted View," Ishmael conducts comparative cetology, evaluating the heads, and particularly the eyes, ears, and mouths, of two prominent kinds of whales. These chapters initiate a series of spectacular entries into whale bodies:

> Let us now with whatever levers and steam-engines we have at hand, cant over the sperm whale's head, so that it may lie bottom up; then, ascending by a ladder to the summit, have a peep down the mouth; and were it not that the body is now completely separated from it, with a lantern we might descend into the great Kentucky Mammoth Cave of his stomach. . . . Over this [right whale's] lip, as over a slippery threshold, we now slide into the mouth. Upon

my word, were I at Mackinaw, I should take this to be the inside of an Indian wigwam. Good Lord! is this the road that Jonah went? The roof is about twelve feet high, and runs to a pretty sharp angle, as if there were a regular ridge-pole there; while these ribbed, arched, hairy sides, present us with those wondrous, half vertical, scimetar-shaped slats of whalebone, say three hundred on a side, which depending from the upper part of the head or crown bone, form those Venetian blinds which have elsewhere been cursorily mentioned. . . .

But now forget all about blinds and whiskers for a moment, and, standing in the Right Whale's mouth, look around you afresh. Seeing all these colonnades of bone so methodically ranged about, would you not think you were inside the great Haarlem organ, and gazing upon its thousand pipes? For a carpet to the organ we have a rug of the softest Turkey—the tongue, which is glued, as it were, to the floor of the mouth. It is very fat and tender, and apt to tear in pieces in hoisting it on deck. This particular tongue now before us; at a passing glance I should say it was a six-barreler; that is, it will yield you about that amount of oil. (331, 334, 335)

At first, it seems as though this descent and return will be much more civilized than the route taken by Jonah. Levers and steam-engines manipulate the body for easy access. Ladders and lanterns make the trip safer. Yet although these conveniences open the whale to view in new and improved ways, the view itself is uncomfortable. The exotic spaces seem inviting enough, individually—Mammoth Cave, Indian wigwam, the great Haarlem organ, twelve-foot ceilings, Venetian blinds, and plush carpet—but the conglomeration of detail overdecorates the oral cavity. The mouth may suggest the Haarlem organ, but, as Ishmael's pun reminds us, the mouth is an actual organ. We are being taken on a tour of organs.[70]

The unpalatable effects of Melville's metaphors are epitomized in that very strange tongue, which first is compared to a "rug of the softest Turkey." Melville plays on the geographical and avian meanings in the phrase "of Turkey," suggesting the edible appeal of the substance that covers the floor of the mouth. Then that substance is strangely reified, glued to the floor. Then it is disembodied, hoisted from the mouth. Finally, the tongue is quantified as yielding six barrels of oil. Unlike the ethnological puns of Josiah Nott or Samuel Cartwright, which fasten meanings to the parts of the body, Melville's puns often dislocate their anatomies. With Ishmael, the reader strolls on an organ that is edible and that might, in turn, eat the observer. The carpet of the tongue neither provides traction nor cushions the path. One might slip on this tongue. In the trajectory from tourist site to commodity and the attendant inflation and deflation of metaphors and mixing of analogies, Ish-

mael's oral journey unsettles the ground beneath the body quest. Corporeal spaces that seem tempting are revealed to be treacherous. Desires
for knowledge are entangled with desires for profit, as Melville makes
clear in his linkage between knowing and "owning" the whale in the
next chapter (338). The body gives up its yield only after tearing and
rendering. And the cost of this yield is made vivid. In the metaphor that
looms over this passage, bodily knowledge is predicated on the disarticulation of the object. Ishmael and the reader take stock of the whale's
mouth by standing on its tongue.

Comparing sperm whale and right whale heads, Ishmael announces
that the two are "almost entirely different" (335) and he ranks the
sperm whale's head above the right whale's in terms of "mathematical
symmetry," "character," and "dignity" (329). While this may seem to
be an anatomical verdict about types as firm as that of Charles White,
J. H. Guenebault, or Samuel George Morton, Ishmael's judgment is
qualified by the bluster of his delivery (he takes Beale's side against
Scoresby in the long-standing debate about which whale should be
crowned monarch) and by the cognitive obstacles he describes in the
very next chapter. The guiding metaphor of "The Battering-Ram" is
that the front of the sperm whale's head is a powerful weapon, a "dead,
blind wall, without a single organ or tender prominence of any sort
whatsoever," twenty feet of "enormous, boneless mass" resisting the
penetrations of the sharpest harpoon or lance (336–37). Employing the
tactics of rear assault, the following chapters enter the whale's head
from behind, appraising its interior structure ("The Great Heidelburgh
Tun") and unloading its contents ("Cistern and Buckets"). These chapters achieve Ahab's desire to "strike through the mask" (164), but they
do so by cutting in from behind rather than by piercing the front.[71]

"The Battering-Ram" ends with advice for the reader and a glimpse
of the revelations to come: "For unless you own the whale, you are but
a provincial and sentimentalist in Truth. But clear Truth is a thing for
salamander giants only to encounter; how small the chances for provincials then? What befel the weakling youth lifting the dread goddess's veil
at Sais?" (338). By "own" the whale Ishmael certainly means his reader
must admit its power, but ownership in these chapters is also linked with
possession. To own the whale is to know the whale, and in order for us
to know the whale, Ishmael will take us inside its head. "What befel the
weakling youth" in the poem "The Veiled Statue at Sais" in J. C. F. von
Schiller's *Poems and Ballads* (1844), a volume Melville acquired in
1849, is that when he secretly entered an Egyptian temple and lifted the

veil of Truth, he was struck senseless and died soon after. In the incarnations of the subsequent chapters, Melville locates the temple in the whale's body, and he associates the veil with the envelope of blubber. In *Moby-Dick,* lifting the veil and glimpsing the cranial sanctum sanctorum is a perilous enterprise in which seeing is linked with drowning.[72]

In "The Great Heidelburgh Tun," Ishmael compares the appearance and function of the whale's head to the celebrated wine cask, elaborately carved in front, which held thousands of gallons of choice liquid. Like the face of the Heidelburgh Tun, the Sperm whale's "vast plaited forehead" is formed of "innumerable strange devices" (340), which Ishmael will attempt to interpret in the chapters "The Prairie" and "The Nut." Behind the "strange devices" lies the repository of cranial treasure: the upper part of the whale's head known as the "case," more than twenty-six feet deep, sheltering five hundred gallons of precious spermaceti (340).[73]

In the next chapter, "Cistern and Buckets," Ishmael describes the dangerous process of removing the contents of the head. The Native American Tashtego climbs aloft and then lowers himself with a rope onto the severed end of the inverted whale head. He searches with his cutting spade for the proper point of entry into the Tun, "like a treasure-hunter in some old house, sounding the walls to find where the gold is masoned in" (341). A bucket is hoisted up to the Indian, who forces it down into the head with a long pole until it fills with spermaceti. Tashtego then signals his fellow seamen to raise the bucket out of the head, carefully lower it to the deck, and decant it in a large tub. While he is "baling the case," after the eighteenth or nineteenth load, when the head has been nearly drained of spermaceti, Tashtego is the victim of an accident. He drops "head-foremost" into the head and "with a horrible oily gurgling, went clean out of sight" (342). The African Daggoo tries to save him by ramming the bucket into the head for him to grasp, but himself narrowly avoids falling into the ocean when one of the two hooks used to suspend the massive whale's head tears loose and the head plunges into the water.

It is no accident here that the two potential victims of the effort to extract the contents of the whale's head, a Native American and an African, were also the two targets of the antebellum effort to probe the interior spaces of the human head, the explicit objects of racial study in Morton's *Crania Americana* and *Crania Ægyptiaca.* The crucial chapter "Cistern and Buckets" is Melville's effort to get inside the head of craniometry and the first of three chapters concentrating on techniques of cranial inquiry. Through a series of literalizations in "Cistern and Buckets," Melville makes palpable the desires, procedures, and costs of this celebrated attempt to make the body yield its racial secrets. The thirst for capital knowledge is given a liquid referent in the limpid, aromatic, and valuable spermaceti. In Melville's description of "baling the case," Morton's filling and draining of cranial capacity are rendered material and profitable. Instead of artificially pouring pepper seed or lead shot into a skull and then calibrating its volume in graduated cylinders, the sailors on board the *Pequod* work with a huge, fleshy head whose natural contents need to be measured by the hundreds of gallons. "Cistern and Buckets" presents the craniometrist's dream come true: a head filled with treasure that can be scooped out in buckets.[74]

Yet this dream includes a cruel twist. In "Cistern and Buckets," the observer gets what he desires, but it is not what he expected and it threatens to overwhelm him. So you want to get inside the head, runs the wicked logic of the chapter. You want to know and rank its capacities. You want to own its contents. You hold a skull in your hands or gaze at the heads of others and desire access. All right—but, remember, you asked for it. And what is it like inside the head, according to Melville? There is no orderly and revealing internal architecture. The whale's head is filled with junk and sperm. It's disgusting. It's oily. It's gurgling. And you're drowning in it. The inside of the head might offer a sweet death, as Ishmael implies—"a very precious perishing; smothered in the very whitest and daintiest of fragrant spermaceti; coffined, hearsed, and tombed in the secret inner chamber and sanctum sanctorum of the whale" (344)—but it is a death nonetheless. Craniometry, as figured in "Cistern and Buckets," is an "almost fatal operation" (340).

The operation is almost fatal not only for the observer, who is in danger of losing his footing and his identity in his corporeal quest, but also for the objects of this quest. The near deaths of Tashtego and Daggoo signify the cognitive and physical violence directed by antebellum ethnologists toward Native Americans and Africans. From this perspective, the whale's head is figured as the perceiving subject. In a remarkable passage, Melville describes Tashtego's predicament in the submerged head of the whale, a nineteenth-century Native American Jonah literally trapped inside another's head: "Looking over the side, they saw the before lifeless head throbbing and heaving just below the surface of the sea, as if that moment seized with some momentous idea; whereas it was only the poor Indian unconsciously revealing by those struggles the perilous depth to which he had sunk" (342). Here Melville offers a strik-

ing, writhing image of racial ideology: an inert head animated by the
idea of an "Indian" and an actual Indian struggling in a cognitive cage.
"Cistern and Buckets" is filled with such elaborate puns on the notions
of "head," "contents," and "consciousness." The observer's cranial
penetration does not extend the reach of his vision but undermines his
own position. Tashtego falls "head fore-most" into the head, which falls
into the ocean, thus marking the dangerous depths of racial consciousness. In this chapter, Melville contemplates the heads of others and the
heads of observers.

The ultimate puns occur when Ishmael describes the rescue of Tashtego by his fellow harpooneer Queequeg:

> diving after the slowly descending head, Queequeg with his keen sword had
> made side lunges near its bottom, so as to scuttle a large hole there; then
> dropping his sword, had thrust his long arm far inwards and upwards, and
> so hauled out our poor Tash by the head. He averred, that upon first thrust-
> ing in for him, a leg was presented; but well knowing that that was not as it
> ought to be, and might occasion great trouble;—he had thrust back the leg,
> and by a dexterous heave and toss, had wrought a somerset upon the Indian;
> so that with the next trial, he came forth in the good old way—head fore-
> most. As for the great head itself, that was doing as well as could be expected.
> (343–44)

Rather than craniometry, physiognomy, or phrenology, Queequeg performs a Caesarean operation on the head of the whale, slashing it open
and delivering Tashtego. Melville stages this drama of rescue with a cast
of characters usually relegated to bit parts—the three racial subordinates, the harpooneers Tashtego, Daggoo, and Queequeg. The deliver-
ies performed in "Cistern and Buckets" are complicated. Queequeg effects both a literal release from the whale's head and a figurative release
from conceptual cages. Ishmael describes the sensuous experience of the
spermaceti, which, when encountered outside the head in the chapter "A
Squeeze of the Hand," will offer a tactile and olfactory reprieve from the
visual obsessions of the book. Invoking Hephaestus's ax, which begat
Athena from the head of Zeus, Melville suggests that all human beings
share a common ancestor (or at least a common head).[75] Melville's
mixed metaphors at the end of the chapter represent Queequeg's operation as some bizarre blend of obstetrics and brain surgery, thus suggesting the violence that generates and sustains ethnological conceptions.
While White-Jacket antiseptically emancipates himself from his own
skin, Queequeg labors to deliver Tashtego from a premature burial in

the viscous head of another. Queequeg performs his operation in deeper and more turbid waters.

With the failure of craniometry, Ishmael, with the reader at his side, turns to the two other nineteenth-century sciences of the head, physiognomy ("The Prairie") and phrenology ("The Nut"). He seeks to open the doors of Leviathan's face. Yet the longer Ishmael stares at the whale's body, the stranger it looks and the more arbitrary the interpretive impositions come to seem. Practicing whale physiognomy and whale phrenology, the observer does not "own" the body but loses title to it.

In "The Prairie," Ishmael describes the allure of the whale's face and head, invoking the founders: "Such an enterprise [reading the whale] would seem almost as hopeful as for Lavater to have scrutinized the wrinkles on the Rock of Gibraltar, or for Gall to have mounted a ladder and manipulated the Dome of the Pantheon" (345). Such a huge surface promises to magnify the corporeal achievements. Melville's phrenologist in the Pantheon probably was inspired by a similar passage in Cheever's *The Whale and His Captors* (1850):

> Is it not a little surprising, that in the researches of comparative phrenology the cranium of the great sperm whale should be overlooked?
>
> For the matter of room, a phrenologist might keep shop in it, and light it up, if he chose, with its own brains, and there point out to visitors by the lamp-light the places in the walls and ceiling where the different organs lay. It would be like a painter at Rome who should open his studio in the Parthenon; the celestial gods would be eying him from the ceiling; deified men and the infernals would be looking on him from all around.

Cheever here sketches the ultimate phrenological fantasy: a self-illuminating body displaying its mental faculties on its interior walls, so spacious that the observer could set up house and offer tours. Cheever depicts not a young man with a skull but a young man *in* a skull. Both Cheever's cranial artist and Melville's Franz Joseph Gall fingering the dome of the Pantheon suggest how cetology offered vast and tantalizing opportunities for the fulfillment of ethnological desires.[76]

Yet Ishmael's hopes for cetacean physiognomy and phrenology are thwarted. The whale's head resists manipulation. "Physiognomically regarded," Ishmael concludes, "the Sperm Whale is an anomalous creature. . . . phrenologically the head of this Leviathan, in the creature's living intact state, is an entire delusion" (345, 349). The problem in conducting whale physiognomy, Ishmael discovers, is that the whale has no nose. The whale's face exhibits no prominent structure around which to organize the features and anchor interpretation: "as in landscape gardening, a spire, cupola, monument, or tower of some sort, is deemed almost indispensable to the completion of the scene; so no face can be physiognomically in keeping without the elevated open-work belfry of the nose" (345–46). Nothing can be as clear as the nose on one's face. Where there is no nose, there is no clarity. While Tommo panicked at the prospect of facial incoherence in *Typee,* Ishmael responds humorously in "The Prairie." In *Typee,* Melville flinched at the idea of losing the face as we know it. In *Moby-Dick,* he evaluates knowledge about the face and finds it wanting. In fact, Ishmael explains, the sperm whale has no face: no nose, eyes, ears, or mouth, to speak of. He is all forehead. That forehead is "sublime," "mystical," and "pleated with riddles," enticing but enigmatic.[77]

If the lack of physiognomical analogy between facial features and moral and spiritual character is figured in the whale's slippery visage, the problem with phrenology is different. Here the claim is not that the lineaments symbolize internal capacities but that these capacities mold the very structure of the brain and shape of the skull. Ishmael's attempt at whale phrenology exposes this misplaced faith in structure. In "The Nut," the whale's head is compared to a nut that cannot be cracked, not because of an impenetrable shell but because of the incommensurability between outer form and inner contents. As Ishmael explains, in an adult sperm whale, between the forehead and the skull there lie at least twenty feet of space and several tons of head matter. The brain itself, "hidden away behind its vast outworks, like the innermost citadel within the amplified fortifications of Quebec," is tiny (348). Thus the brain cannot shape the head unless it pushes through twenty feet of material. Even if the researcher could breach the formidable defenses of the whale, he would find the "choice casket" (348) a disappointing prize. The meager brain itself cannot either analogically or actually be taken to represent the dignity and power of the whale.[78]

Melville does not reject the idea of the body as meaningful, nor does he once and for all repudiate physiognomy and phrenology. Although many critics see "The Prairie" and "The Nut" as discrediting systematic bodily knowledge, in *Moby-Dick* the failure of one perspective to disclose secrets stimulates other efforts. Dermatology gives way to craniometry and physiognomy and phrenology, and finally to skeletal anatomy. In *Pierre* (1852), Melville associates Pierre's pursuit of truth with a Lavater-like faith in physiognomy and portraiture. Melville charts his protagonist's disastrous readings of facial character, and he meditates on the compulsions of error, the ways in which human beings are moved to do what they know they should not do, again and again. In *Moby-Dick*, Melville describes the persistent search for answers in the features and recesses of the body, despite patent absurdity and calamity. "But there is no Champollion to decipher the Egypt of every man's and every being's face," Ishmael declares, or, possibly, laments (347). In this view, every being's face is an "Egypt," containing the mysteries of human identity, antiquity, and destiny. No observer has yet discovered the key. "I but put that brow before you. Read it if you can," Ishmael writes at the end of "The Prairie," having confessed his own inability to do so (347). These final lines do not dismiss; they invite. You probably cannot read the whale's brow any more accurately than I can, Ishmael suggests, but maybe, just maybe, someone, someday . . .[79]

Ishmael wonders why practitioners cease their inquiries at the borders of the brain: "Now, I consider that the phrenologists have omitted an important thing in not pushing their investigations from the cerebellum through the spinal canal. For I believe that much of a man's character will be found betokened in his backbone. I would rather feel your spine than your skull, whoever you are" (349). Phrenology is both skull gauge and spinal tap. Melville makes the synesthesia uncomfortable, as the gaze reaches through the brain and down into the vertebrae. When Ishmael locates firmness of character in the "backbone," he suggests that phrenology is a science grounded in clichés, validating the stereotype. The last line favors an alternative approach to feeling the spine: not through the brain but around the back, in an embrace.[80]

"The Fountain" and "The Tail" are about dangers and limits. In "The Fountain," Melville transforms the cetological debate over the substance of the whale's spout—is it water swallowed and ejected or is it the vapor of the whale's breath?—into Ishmael's musings on the difficulties of perception ("you might almost stand in it, and yet be undecided as to what it is precisely") and his warning that some inquiries can burn and blind: "You cannot go with your pitcher to this fountain and fill it, and bring it away. For even when coming into slight contact with the outer, vapory shreds of the jet, which will often happen, your skin will feverishly smart, from the acridness of the thing so touching it. And I know one, who coming into still closer contact with the spout, whether with some scientific object in view, or otherwise, I cannot say, the skin peeled off from his cheek and arm" (373). This cistern is not easily emptied. When the caustic contents of this body are expelled, the observer may find his own anatomy exposed. Ishmael imagines that the spout represents the vapors of contemplation, thought externalized and condensed—a revealing conceit, since in the cetological chapters Melville himself seeks to give substance to nineteenth-century ideas about race and bodies.[81]

In "The Tail," Ishmael celebrates the extent, symmetry, texture, strength, and beauty of the whale's tail. He confesses his own descriptive shortcomings: "The more I consider this mighty tail, the more do I deplore my inability to express it. . . . Dissect him how I may, then, I but go skin deep; I know him not, and never will. But if I know not even the tail of this whale, how understand his head? much more, how comprehend his face, when face he has none? Thou shalt see my back parts, my tail, he seems to say, but my face shall not be seen. But I cannot completely make out his back parts; and hint what he will about his face, I say again he has no face" (378–79). Unlike Moses, who in *Exodus* is permitted to see God's back parts but not His face, Ishmael, like Sir Thomas Browne in *Religio Medici,* claims that he is not even granted this posterior apprehension. Yet in the cetology chapters Ishmael alternates between accepting, Job-like, divine embargoes against the pursuit of knowledge and continuing to search for corporeal answers. "I but go skin deep," he writes, but chapters such as "The Blanket" and "Queequeg in his Coffin" suggest that this is very deep indeed. Ishmael's journey does not end with the exasperated dissection of "The Tail." The next anatomical step he takes is to "penetrat[e] very far beneath the skin of the adult whale" and, like Jonah, to literally stand inside its skeleton (448–49).[82]

In "A Bower in the Arsacides," Ishmael finally gets inside the whale, past the barriers of skin and spermaceti and junk to the open, inscribed spaces of the interior. What is left when the body is stripped down to the skeleton? A temple, and a tourist site. Ishmael explains that once, while staying with his friend Tranquo, king of Tranque, in the Arsacides atoll in the southwest Pacific, he was invited to visit the skeleton of a stranded whale that had been transported to a glen and transformed into a place of worship:

> The ribs were hung with trophies; the vertebrae were carved with Arsacidean annals, in strange hieroglyphics; in the skull, the priests kept up an unextinguished aromatic flame, so that the mystic head again sent forth its vapory spout; while, suspended from a bough, the terrific lower jaw vibrated over all the devotees, like the hair-hung sword that so affrighted Damocles. (449)

The body is a shrine. The skull has become an altar. Ishmael parts the vines, breaks through the ribs, and walks through the passageways of the body, threading his way with the aid of a ball of Arsacidean twine, like Theseus through the labyrinth. Using a yardstick cut from island foliage, he calibrates the height of the ribs, thus taking the measure of the Arsacidean deity, to the consternation of his hosts. The islanders enter into a dispute among themselves over the exact dimensions and end up cracking each other's heads with their rulers.[83]

Melville develops his serious joke about yardsticks and tourist sights in the description of the sperm whale skeleton owned by Sir Clifford Constable. Unlike Tranquo's whale, which is a figment of Melville's imagination, Constable's skeleton was actually on display in Yorkshire, England. Ishmael imagines that it will be developed for maximum comfort and gain:

> Sir Clifford's whale has been articulated throughout; so that, like a great chest of drawers, you can open and shut him, in all his bony cavities—spread out his ribs like a gigantic fan—and swing all day upon his lower jaw. Locks are to be put upon some of his trap-doors and shutters; and a footman will show round future visitors with a bunch of keys at his side. Sir Clifford thinks of charging twopence for a peep at the whispering gallery in the spinal column; threepence to hear the echo in the hollow of his cerebellum; and sixpence for the unrivalled view from his forehead. (451)

This anatomy is open to the public. The ribs and jaw are hinged for easy access. A guide will be provided for the choicest locations, which will be placed under lock and key and be available for viewing under a graduated system of admission fees. The observer will pay at the door to get inside the head. This eloquent anatomy is filled with the whispers and the echoes of its explorers. It is an improvement over the sites promoted by Morton, Nott, and the Fowlers. There are no secret chambers that cannot be seen. The features are thoroughly explicated. The grounds and figures are regularly maintained. Unlike Jonah, the sojourner in this body can have all the privilege of corporeal witness with none of the risk. Unlike Job, this seeker *can* open the doors of Leviathan's face, and even swing on his jaw (for a price).[84]

When Melville writes that Constable's whale has been "articulated throughout," he is making an intricate pun. The skeleton is articulated in the sense that it has been hinged and stepped for the convenience of its visitors and the profit of its overseers. More deeply, it has been articulated in the sense that its structure has been made expressive. This is the ethnological sense, in which graded meanings have been fastened to parts of the body. In Melville's vision of Constable's skeleton, anatomy has been made accessible but also drained of interest. Ascribed, inscribed, prescribed—the attraction has been muted. The site no longer holds any allure or danger. In "Measurement of the Whale's Skeleton," Ishmael takes the reader on an arid tour of an attenuated body. The quest has ended in a pile of dry bones.

If "A Bower in the Arsacides" is about the articulations of anatomy, then "The Fossil Whale" is about Melville's own articulations and particularly about the intimacy between discourse and object in his extended fiction. In this chapter, Ishmael reinvests the whale with flesh and significance. "From his mighty bulk the whale affords a most congenial theme whereon to enlarge, amplify, and generally expatiate," he begins, with appropriate verbosity, as he reflects on the provocative form and figure of the voluminous corpus (455). The peculiar preposition "whereon" here indicates that in his amplifications, Melville writes on and about, inscribes and extracts meaning from, the body of the whale. This dovetailing of discursive and corporeal excess is evident when Ishmael describes the breadth of his regard: "not overlooking the minutest seminal germs of his blood, and spinning him out to the uttermost coils of his bowels" (455). The body, perceived as embodying the secrets of difference, origin, and destiny—and Ishmael at the end of the chapter links whale fossils, as ethnologists linked human fossils, to the mysteries of ancient Egypt and Africa—generates a discourse and tactics of inquiry. In *Moby-Dick*, observer and body become engrossed in a spiral of hyperbole articulated grandiloquently by Ishmael:

> One often hears of writers that rise and swell with their subject, though it may seem but an ordinary one. How, then, with me, writing of this Leviathan? Unconsciously my chirography expands into placard capitals. Give me a condor's quill! Give me Vesuvius' crater for an inkstand! Friends, hold my arms! For in the mere act of penning my thoughts of this Leviathan, they weary me, and make me faint with their outreaching comprehensiveness of sweep, as if to include the whole circle of the sciences, and all the generations of whales, and men, and mastodons, past, present, and to come, with all the revolving panoramas of empire on earth, and throughout the whole universe, not excluding its suburbs. Such, and so magnifying, is the virtue of a large and liberal theme! We expand to its bulk. (456)

In contemplating the whale, Melville contemplates ethnological procedures and discourse and also his own literary operations, in particular the revealing excess that expands to inhabit and illuminate its subject. Melville's extravagance bears an intimate relation to the overwrought practices it magnifies. Thus there is a triple excess in *Moby-Dick*—corporeal, ethnological, literary. In *Moby-Dick*, Melville offers an anatomy of a nineteenth-century anatomy that saw the world—history, geography, philosophy, anthropology, zoology, archaeology, empire—a whale of meaning—in a skull.

TO LOOK AND TO KNOW

Earlier I wrote that the sensuous experience in "Cistern and Buckets" suggested an alternative to the obsessive visual seizures of the body. Melville expands this suggestion in the "Squeeze of the Hand" chapter, in which Ishmael joins the other sailors on the *Pequod* in squeezing the crystallized lumps of sperm back into fluid to prepare for boiling in the try-pots. Immediately following the isolation of the cabin boy Pip in "The Castaway" and preceding the slicing portrayal of manhood in "The Cassock," "A Squeeze of the Hand" has been analyzed by critics as depicting a different kind of male relation: communal, reciprocal, playful, sensual. A remarkable feature of this chapter is the lack of emphasis on sight. It is one of the few scenes in Melville's intensely visual work that could take place in the dark:

> After having my hands in it for only a few minutes, my fingers felt like eels, and began, as it were, to serpentine and spiralize. . . . as I bathed my hands among those soft, gentle globules of infiltrated tissues, woven almost within the hour; as they richly broke to my fingers, and discharged all their opulence, like fully ripe grapes their wine; as I snuffed up that uncontaminated aroma,—literally and truly, like the smell of spring violets; I declare to you, that for the time I lived as in a musky meadow; I forgot all about our horrible oath. (415–16)

In this scene, fingers are extended and boundaries stretched. The monumental difference represented by the whale is caressed and inhaled rather than dissected, calibrated, or deciphered. The substance that threatened to overwhelm the cranial inquisitor in "Cistern and Buckets" provides the medium of exchange for sailors outside of the head. In this unctuous, fragrant salve, Ishmael imagines that the edges of the self are soothed for a moment and he calls upon the sailors to squeeze themselves into each other.[85]

In the early chapters of *Moby-Dick*, Melville represents male exchange through touch as an alternative way of knowing other bodies. The initial encounter between Ishmael and Queequeg is a choreographed comedy of racial expectations, a mixture of bedroom and ethnological farce that highlights and overturns clichés about the racial significance of the skin and head. The landlord of the Spouter-Inn in

Nantucket has manipulated Ishmael's anxieties about his unseen bedmate, telling him that the harpooneer is "dark complexioned," eats only
rare steaks, is out late peddling his head (which is broken), and will beat
Ishmael "brown" if he hears him slandering his head (14–18). When the
Polynesian Queequeg finally enters Ishmael's shadowy room, Melville
portrays the transforming contact of racial presumptions with actual
bodies.

Holding a candle in one hand and the embalmed New Zealand head
he has been marketing in another, Queequeg arrives, puts down his burdens, and sets to work undoing the knotted cords of his large seaman's
bag. After some time, during which Ishmael becomes eager to see his
face, Queequeg at last turns around and presents a shocking spectacle:
"good heavens! what a sight! Such a face! It was of a dark, purplish,
yellow color, here and there stuck over with large, blackish-looking
squares" (21). Not any distinct color in an ethnological spectrum,
Queequeg is represented as a categorical nightmare. As Ishmael, pretending to be asleep in the bed, scrutinizes Queequeg's face and head in
the candlelight, he tries to interpret the strange markings in terms of familiar categories: He must have been in a dreadful fight. He must be a
white man tattooed by cannibals. He must be a sailor bizarrely burned
by the South Pacific sun. Evoking a gaze like Morton's, Ishmael compares Queequeg's "bald purplish head" to "a mildewed skull" (21). As
Queequeg undresses and Ishmael sees more and more of his patchwork
body, he abandons his strained effort to normalize Queequeg's features,
and he acknowledges that he must be confronting an "abominable savage," a Polynesian cannibal who might take a fancy to his own head
(22). The perceptual horror climaxes as Queequeg extinguishes the
candle, gets into bed, and begins feeling his unexpected bedmate.[86]

Yet the absence of light and the presence of touch alter Ishmael's evaluations. In the dark, being fondled, manipulated rather than manipulating, Ishmael ultimately relents. In the dark, the ethnological charge is
drained from bodies, replaced by a less defined erotic intensity. Foreheads pressed together, waists clasped, with Queequeg making the
moves, the two become "bosom friends," "a cosy, loving pair" (51, 52).
Ishmael is not judging on the basis of what he sees because, as the perspectival comedy in the bedroom demonstrated, what he sees is inextricably bound up with what he has been taught to know about Queequeg's color, cranium, and character. In the dark, Queequeg's skin is not
a symbol, not a sight, but a texture and an aroma, as skin was for the islanders when they first encountered Tommo and Toby in *Typee*: "They

felt our skin, much in the same way that a silk mercer would handle a remarkably fine piece of satin; and some of them went so far in their investigation as to apply the olfactory organ" (74). In the bedroom at the Spouter-Inn, touch is not the extension of sight, as it is in Morton's craniometric calibrations or the Fowlers' gauging fingers. Touch, detached from light and sight, is represented as another way of making out the differences between bodies. Ishmael suggests this alternative epistemology when he describes the reason he always keeps his eyes shut in bed: "Because no man can ever feel his own identity aright except his eyes be closed; as if darkness were indeed the proper element of our essences, though light be more congenial to our clayey part" (54).[87]

In *Moby-Dick,* touch transforms not only character relations but also racial diction and syntax. After feeling Queequeg, there is no more talk of "mildewed skulls," "abominable savages," and "checkered" skin (21, 22). Instead, Melville pens the famous lines in which ethnological convictions are reversed: "Better sleep with a sober cannibal than a drunken Christian" (24), "certain it was his [Queequeg's] head was phrenologically an excellent one. . . . Queequeg was George Washington cannibalistically developed" (50), and "as though a white man were anything more dignified than a whitewashed negro" (60). These aphorisms refuse to identify character with characteristics. They displace qualities from fixed nouns into portable adjectives. Here "cannibal" does not naturally mean undisciplined and underdeveloped; "Christian" does not automatically mean moderate and civilized. Judgments of character are made on the basis of behavior and bearing and not according to permanent types. Superior features are not racially ascribed but, instead, dispersed indiscriminately among Polynesian and American royalty. The divine palette does not recognize a fixed ground and figure; it may paint black on white or white on black or mix purple and yellow. White skin may be not a chaste mantle but a whitewash. In Melville's transformational grammar, neither adjectives nor nouns embody permanent qualities.[88]

Yet the clean reversals and displacements in Melville's lines are complicated in the narrative, which begins rather than ends with images of interracial, homosexual marriage and the jumbling of racial syntax. From the start of the book, Melville acknowledges the difficult, persistent desire to understand another racial position. Ishmael's initial effort to stand inside Queequeg's skin ends in estrangement. Inspecting the contents of the room at the Spouter-Inn before Queequeg's arrival, Ishmael finds something resembling a "large door mat" or "South

American poncho" (20). One in a series of Melville's metaphorical jackets, including Redburn's shooting jacket and White-Jacket's duck frock, Queequeg's garment is figured as skin. Melville explicitly links skin and poncho in the "Blanket" chapter: "For the whale is indeed wrapt up in his blubber as in a real blanket or counterpane; or, still better, an Indian poncho slipt over his head, and skirting his extremity" (307). In the room at the Spouter-Inn, Ishmael decides to see how it feels to wear the harpooneer's garb:

> I put it on, to try it, and it weighed me down like a hamper, being uncommonly shaggy and thick, and I thought a little damp, as though this mysterious harpooneer had been wearing it of a rainy day. I went up in it to a bit of glass stuck against the wall, and I never saw such a sight in my life. I tore myself out of it in such a hurry that I gave myself a kink in the neck. (20)

Here Melville's protagonist does not flee from the riddled skins of others as he does in *Typee,* nor does he attempt to escape from his own inscribed skin as he does in *White-Jacket*. Instead, Ishmael tries on a strange skin but does not find it a comfortable fit. Sleeping with Queequeg eases but does not eliminate his anxiety. Awakening with Queequeg's arm around him, Ishmael compares his sensations to those he had while a child when he dreamed of unsettling contact with a supernatural hand. In the scene before the mirror at the Spouter-Inn, Melville complicates a genealogy of European American literary declarations, not of independence but of racial empathy, ranging from Robert Beverly's "I am an *Indian*" to Whitman's "I am the hounded slave" to Ishmael's own "I myself am a savage" (270). In *Moby-Dick,* Melville examines the gap between speaker and spoken, saying and being. He rejects the ethnological discriminations of character and describes the allure of other bodies, but he does not depict an untroubled interracial fraternity. In *Moby-Dick,* there is no easy identification with others. It is a difficult thing to see oneself in another's skin, especially if that skin has been marked as radically different and inferior.[89]

The imaginative challenge is confronted not only in the plot of *Moby-Dick* but also on the level of character representation. That is, it is not only Ishmael as protagonist, it is also Melville as author who attempts to construct Queequeg's character. Over the course of the book, Queequeg is not a character in the same sense as Ishmael, Ahab, or Starbuck. Melville does not represent Queequeg's consciousness with the detail and depth he employs for the Caucasian sailors. Queequeg is always seen from the outside: unpacking the contents of his bag, performing his rituals, carving his coffin. He is sketched sympathetically but without an effort at internal development. Whether a result of inability or strategy (Queequeg often seems to serve as a cultural alternative to the sinful, self-conscious West) or a judicious refusal to get "inside" the character, to claim he knows a subjectivity like Queequeg's, Melville's discrete portrayal of the Polynesian forms a part of the racial conundrum explored in *Moby-Dick*.[90] In this sense, Melville's analysis of the ethnological effort to discern human character in bodily characteristics and his fictional effort to represent character on the surface of the page illuminate one another. That they are not the same revelatory procedure in Melville's mind is clear in his extended critique of racial science in the cetology chapters; that they are not exclusive approaches is evident in his continuing desire for intersubjective access, particularly across racial lines, and in his refusal to relinquish the vision of the eloquent, distant racial body. If fiction is intimately concerned with conveying character, with offering the reader the possibility of standing in the skin and getting inside the heads of others, then in the nineteenth century, when the racial lines were vividly drawn and announced to be indelible, "race" was the test case for the reach of the fictional endeavor.

The ethnological, fictional, and interpersonal stakes are high in the magnificently overwritten scene in "Queequeg in his Coffin," in which Queequeg copies the tattooing symbols from his body onto the coffin he has transformed into a sea chest. Taking place after the chapters on the whale's skeleton, this scene culminates the previous bodily inquiries. The viewer returns to the outside and gazes once again at flesh, not bones. Ishmael has painstakingly demonstrated the limits, dangers, biases, and violence of the quest, and yet Queequeg's articulate body still fascinates. Early in the narrative, Ishmael describes Queequeg with apparent redundancy as "a very sight of sights to see" (51). This repetition of parts of speech formed from the verb "to see" stresses the enormous visual investments that Melville analyzes in the cetology chapters. The nominalizations signal that the racial body has become the focus for the penetrating eye, a site of revealing physical sights.

While "disembowell[ing]" the damp hold, Queequeg catches a chill and then a fever that consume his body (477). His fellow sailors undertake a deathwatch, and the carpenter is ordered to construct a coffin according to the harpooneer's wishes. Queequeg is chalked and measured with the carpenter's rule, the coffin is built, and Queequeg tries it out for size. When he unexpectedly recovers his health, he decides to use his coffin as a chest in which to store his clothes, and he spends hours carving the surface of the wood. Ishmael imagines that Queequeg is copying the designs incised on his body:

> And this tattooing, had been the work of a departed prophet and seer of his island, who, by those hieroglyphic marks, had written out on his body a complete theory of the heavens and the earth, and a mystical treatise on the art of attaining truth; so that Queequeg in his own proper person was a riddle to unfold; a wondrous work in one volume; but whose mysteries not even himself could read, though his own live heart beat against them; and these mysteries were therefore destined in the end to moulder away with the living parchment whereon they were inscribed, and so be unsolved to the last. And this thought it must have been which suggested to Ahab that wild exclamation of his, when one morning turning away from surveying poor Queequeg—"Oh, devilish tantalization of the gods!" (480–81)

The chapter begins with a deathwatch and ends with a lifewatch. Like the lined skin of the whale—"all over obliquely crossed and re-crossed with numberless straight marks in thick array" (306) and "mystically carved" (339)—Queequeg's skin is riddled with mystery. Queequeg is an anthology of textual metaphors used by Melville to describe the whale and by nineteenth-century ethnologists to describe their vastly significant human bodies: scripture, encyclopedia, cosmography, rune—the key to it all. Queequeg's body tantalizes because it promises answers yet balks access. Queequeg cannot read himself, yet he demands to be interpreted. He requires observers to explicate him, yet they cannot spell out his secrets. Seen, his answers are never touched. Desire is incited and frustrated and thus intensified, giving the passage its erotic, melancholy charge. Skin deep appears very deep, after all.[91]

Ahab, Ishmael, and Melville share the fascination in overlapping, but not identical, ways. Their link is signaled by the dash that substitutes for words that would tie a specific speaker to the chapter's final line: " 'Oh, devilish tantalization of the gods!' " Certainly this is Ahab's outburst, as Ishmael implies, but it also hovers at the end of the chapter, syntactically detached from any particular voice. For the Ahab of "The Quarter-Deck" and "Moby Dick," Queequeg is an enigma whose solution offers the possibility that the captain will be able to restore his lost corporeal and psychic integrity. Ahab's observations in "Queequeg in his Coffin" are bracketed by his exchanges with the carpenter and the blacksmith, during which he imagines dissolving himself into a single vertebra or mending the dents and seams in his skull bone or ordering the manufacture of an entirely new physique. By fixing the meaning of Moby Dick or of Queequeg, Ahab hopes to secure his own identity.

For the Ishmael of "Cetology," Queequeg is an enticing text whose multiple meanings are to be caressed. Ishmael does not have a splintered body in need of repair. He has an insubstantial body that requires confirmation in the communion with Queequeg. In contrast to the pages devoted to the details of Ahab's aspect and ailments, the regard for Queequeg's figure and figures, and chapter after chapter lavished on the whale, no words in *Moby-Dick* describe the features of Ishmael. Ishmael is the only character whose appearance is concealed from the reader. And so when in "A Bower in the Arsacides," the one hundred and second chapter of the book, Ishmael reveals that he has the measurements of a whale skeleton tattooed on his right arm, the fact that he has a tattoo, and even the fact that he has a right arm, come as something of a surprise. Ishmael says that he had only the feet and not the inches inscribed since "I was crowded for space, and wished the other parts of my body to remain a blank page for a poem I was then composing" (451). Limited to his arm, Ishmael's tattooing is a different order from Queequeg's or from the Marquesan tattooing in *Typee*. Most of Ishmael's surface is left as a "blank page" awaiting his own invention, while Queequeg is envisioned as already having been completely embellished by a prophet. The marks on Ishmael are easily read facts about length, height, and width, not mystical emblems of truth. Ishmael is a commonplace book rather than a wondrous work in one volume. The cetacean dimensions on his arm give heft to his body. For Ishmael, gazing at Queequeg seems to involve an imaginative effort to transcribe some of the Polynesian's characters in order to fill his own blank spaces.[92]

For Melville in *Moby-Dick,* the characteristics of Queequeg's body still fascinate, even after his meticulous critique of the ethnological crusade. Melville does not, as he might, translate Queequeg or his tattoos. There is no attempt to fix his color in the great spectrum of being, or to decipher the grammar of his visage or the landscape of his brow, or to measure the capacity of his cranium. If Melville wishes to know Queequeg through the medium of his eloquent body, it is a wish shaped but not contained by the pervasive racialism of the nineteenth century. It is the longing for exchange between subjects increasingly defined as incommensurable.

Lydia Maria Child offers a similar longing critique in one of her "Letters from New York," published in March 1843. Child's thoughts are prompted by a visit to Barnum's American Museum, where she sees on display fifteen western Indians from the Sac, Fox, and Iowa tribes. Like

many of her "Letters," this one unfolds in a series of perspectival shifts
that test the writer's and reader's responses. She suggests, conventionally, that the robust and noble figures are a "keen satire" on the debility
of civilized society; she attacks Americans' fondness for proving the inferiority of their victims, using as an example the cranial and facial evidence offered by the "American school"; she regrets that human beings
are exhibited in a "two-shilling show"; she recoils from the "animal-
ism" of war dances performed at the Museum; she feels her own tribal
sympathies reawaken as she imagines the perils of the Puritan settlers;
she enlarges her sentiments, embracing Native Americans as potential
Christians, "children of the same Father"; and she reports, in a jarring
postscript, the illness of several of the chiefs and the deaths of two Indian women who had been on display, including the niece of the Sac
chief Black Hawk. Child frames the scene in the museum as a synecdoche for the United States' treatment of its native inhabitants, in which
a fatal gaze objectifies, exposes, and contaminates. Her contemplative
turns are in part the result of Child's own ambivalences and in part the
result of rhetorical strategy. As with Melville, it is often difficult to distinguish ambivalence from strategy. Both writers remain uneasy with
their perceptions.[93]

Although Child criticizes the findings of the "American school"
about permanent racial inferiority, she cannot escape the terms of
their proof. That is, she argues that physical differences are produced
by accumulated environmental effects and that all races are capable
of improvement under the proper social circumstances. Yet like many
nineteenth-century Americans, Child accepts the idea that physical differences connote moral and intellectual differences. She reprints a vertical list of races and their corresponding facial angles, even though she
offers a different account of causes. Although Melville detaches feature
from meaning in the cetology chapters, he remystifies the racialized
body in the enthralling vision of Queequeg as a wondrous work in one
volume. In their fraught restagings, both Child and Melville, writers of
extraordinary trenchancy, demonstrate the difficulty of seeing around
the compelling structures of ethnology.

Standing before the Sac, Fox, and Iowa Indians in Barnum's museum,
Child craves inside knowledge:

> I would suffer almost anything, if my soul could be transmigrated into the
> She Wolf, or the Productive Pumpkin, and their souls pass consciously into
> my frame, for a few days, that I might experience the fashion of their
> thoughts and feelings. Was there ever such a foolish wish! The soul *is* Me,

and *is* Thee. I might as well put on their blankets, as their bodies, for purposes of spiritual insight. In that other world, shall we be enabled to know
exactly how heaven, and earth and hell, appear to other persons, nations, and
tribes? I would it might be so; for I have an intense desire for such revelations.
I do not care to travel to Rome, or St. Petersburg, because I can only look *at*
people; and I want to look *into* them, and *through* them; to know how things
appear to *their* spiritual eyes, and sound to *their* spiritual ears. This is a universal want; hence the intense interest taken in autobiography, by all classes
of readers.

Child wishes for a transmigration of souls, but she acknowledges that
such a passage is impossible. Nor is it possible to fathom others by wearing their blankets or putting on their bodies, as she recognizes and Ishmael discovers in his awkward attempt before the mirror at the Spouter-
Inn. Like Melville in "Queequeg in his Coffin," Child in her "Letter"
contemplates a figure of another race, conceived as essentially different,
and wishes to see deeply. The desire for such revelations is remarkably
"intense." Melville imagines "a complete theory of the heavens and the
earth" before his eyes, just beyond his reach. Across the "Letter," Child
raises her bid for racial insight, from "I would have given a good deal to
know their thoughts" to "I would suffer almost anything" to "I would
give the world to know."[94]

The "universal want" that Child describes may not be shared equally
by all, since racial lines are not drawn symmetrically. It would be hard
to imagine William Apess or Frederick Douglass experiencing the same
"intense desire" to know the racial interior while contemplating the
bodies of Child or Melville. Nevertheless, it is a want expressed by both
Child and Melville and encouraged by demands like William Apess's
that white observers appreciate Native American points of view and
by imaginative overtures like those extended by Frederick Douglass to
his European American readers. Douglass writes in *My Bondage and
My Freedom* (1855) that "to *understand,* some one has said a man must
stand under." In his autobiographies, speeches, essays, and fiction,
Douglass offers exacting invitations to sojourn in his place.[95]

Both Child and Melville find themselves bound to what Kwame Anthony Appiah has described as the ideological "axis" of race, in which
"race" is identified as the essential human characteristic and defined in
a system of oppositions. For many European American observers in the
nineteenth-century United States, this axis had come to seem natural.
Despite their critiques, Child and Melville continued to see and feel
the effects of ethnological axioms. Nor is it difficult to understand their
perceptual dilemma, since "race" was not and is not merely axis or

axiom—it is a set of beliefs and responses given substance in human bodies and enacted in political, economic, and social practice. The literary careers of Child and Melville were marked by an acute engagement with issues of ethnology and intersubjectivity. Their "intense desires" and "devilish tantalizations" were a product of and an answer to the claims of craniometry, physiognomy, and phrenology.[96]

When Child and Melville restage the scene of contemplation, they do so with a difference. Viewing bodies charged with racial significance, they reject the hierarchical claims of ethnology and seek ways of knowing, without owning. They suggest alternatives to visual access: the metempsychic, the tactile, the imaginative. Their figures are vital and resisting, not inert and pliable. In their scenes, comprehension is often frustrated, as it is in Shakespeare's prototypical scene of Hamlet pondering Yorick's skull in the graveyard. Child and Melville restore the potent traditional emphases of the scene that had been eclipsed in ethnological views. In Barnum's museum and on the decks of the *Pequod*, the observers' positions are insecure. Their conduct is appraised. Subjective thought is revealed, rather than objective contents.

Melville is less willing than Child to detach soul from body and to relinquish the allure of enigmatic flesh. He is more skeptical than Child about the power of sympathy to bridge difference. In the fiction of the 1840s and 1850s, he often focuses on racial encounters, in which the European American observer's perceptions are strained and tested: Tommo's disfiguring fears among the Typee, White-Jacket's prophylactic analogy with slavery, Ahab and Ishmael's rapt survey of Queequeg. In these texts, the mind that Melville probes most deeply is his own. In opening himself to such scrutiny, Melville is not engaging in solipsism, or if he is it is a solipsism of national proportions. Delving into his own permeable consciousness, Melville exposes structures of thought and feeling that he shares with his compatriots.

This currency of perceptions is dramatized in the chapter of *Moby-Dick* entitled "The Doubloon." "The Doubloon" begins with two acts of looking. Ahab's "riveted glance" fastens "like a javelin" on the piece of gold stamped with strange figures and characters, "the white whale's talisman," that he had nailed to the mainmast as a prize for the first man who sighted Moby Dick; and Ishmael observes about the doubloon that "some certain significance lurks in all things" (430–31). As they do throughout the book, these two gestures—the penetrating gaze and the investment of concealed meaning—cooperate to propel the quest for knowledge. Ishmael describes the physical features of the coin: the let-

ters "REPUBLICA DEL ECUADOR: QUITO" around its border, the
partitioned zodiac, marked by a blazing sun, that arches over three sum-
mits, upon which rest a flame, a tower, and a crowing cock. Melville famously marches his characters to the mast one by one, in order of their
shipboard station. (Ishmael, the narrator, watches and reports, sees
without being seen.) Facing the doubloon, each character reveals himself. Ahab reads a message of ego, power, and anguish, while Starbuck
discerns the comforts and failures of the Trinity. Stubb, who conceals
himself behind the try-works and interprets the subsequent interpreters,
sees the doubloon as an allegory depicting the jolly wheel of life. The
practical third mate Flask calculates that he could buy nine hundred and
sixty cigars with the coin. Aligning the doubloon with a horse-shoe
nailed on the other side of the mast and reading the two signs together,
the Manxman predicts when the *Pequod* will encounter Moby Dick.
Queequeg remains silent, comparing the marks on the coin to the designs on his body. Whatever significance the symbols may bear for him,
it is certainly not conveyed by Stubb's patronizing dismissal: "No: he
don't know what to make of the doubloon; he takes it for an old button
off some king's trowsers" (434). When the Parsee Fedallah confronts
the doubloon, Stubb imagines him bowing to the sign of the sun in an
act of fire worship. Finally, the cabin boy Pip steps up and repeats three
times the lines that are often read by critics as Melville's credo of solipsism and relativism: "'I look, you look, he looks; we look, ye look, they
look'" (434).[97]

"The Doubloon" both recapitulates and predicts. In this chapter,
Melville summarizes the characters' interpretive biases. The elaborate
mise-en-scène—with Ishmael looking at both Ahab and Starbuck looking at the doubloon and then Ishmael watching Stubb watching Flask,
the Manxman, Queequeg, Fedallah, and Pip as they all inspect the
coin—calls attention to the mediated expanse between reader and object. Stubb's lens conspicuously distorts the reception of the Polynesian
Queequeg, whose gestures are interpreted as comic befuddlement, and
of the African American Pip, whose strange words are discounted as in-
sane muttering. Disturbed by Pip's insinuating litany and possibly by remorse over having abandoned the cabin boy after he fell from a whaleboat into the ocean, Stubb departs during the middle of Pip's speech.

The pattern of gazes in "The Doubloon" points forward to the elaborate choreography of balked access in the last section of the book,
when Ahab finds no image in the "vacant pupils" of Pip's eyes (522); is
locked in fixed gazes with Fedallah (537–38); seeks the "magic glass" of

human comfort in Starbuck's eye, but averts his sight and then finds that
Starbuck has fled and that he is looking into the reflection of Fedallah's
eyes (544–45); and, finally, fatally, sees Moby Dick (547). Apart from
the gazes that seek to connect, interpret, or penetrate is the singular
moment of ocular detachment in *Moby-Dick* when, in the "Grand Armada" chapter, the young nursing whales look past the sailors who have
been temporarily stranded in their whaleboat within the herd: "looking
up towards us, but not at us, as if we were but a bit of Gulf-weed in their
new-born sight" (388). As Ishmael explains earlier, the whale's eyes
are unsuited for scrutiny. With one small eye on each side of its head,
the whale simultaneously embraces two opposing prospects (330). The
whale cannot see directly.

Yet Melville's interest in *Moby-Dick* lies not in this moment of maternal nurture and innocent sight, but in nineteenth-century American
looks fraught with significance that fasten like javelins on their marks.
" 'I look, you look, he looks; we look, ye look, they look' "—Pip's words
do not emphasize distinct perspectives but, instead, define perception as
a shared, structurally linked activity. Pip, we are told, has been watching each of the viewers of the doubloon, Stubb included. At the end of
the chapter, he comes forward to deliver his interpretation of interpretation by conjugating the verb "to look." The African American Pip has
not only been studying the popular "Murray's Grammar" (434), as
Stubb remarks before his anxious departure; he has also been studying,
and, one assumes, has himself been the object of study in, the visual
grammar and corporeal logic of the nineteenth century. (After his conjugation, Pip tells a joke about bodily disarticulation: He asks, What
happens when you unscrew your navel? The unspoken answer: Your ass
falls off.)

In Pip's morphology, the verb "to look" may take different forms, but
the acts of looking are yoked together. When Ishmael eyes Queequeg,
when Ahab contemplates and addresses the sperm whale's head, when
Ishamel catalogues the whale's body, and when Ahab, Ishmael, and
Melville gaze at Queequeg, individuals see and know in their own ways,
but their ways are not entirely their own. Pip's choice of the verb "to
look," rather than "to see," suggests that he is describing a state that
precedes seeing, a setting of the eyes. The term "look" also reflects upon
the viewer's appearance, joining aspect and prospect. Pip's choice may
imply a yearning for the kind of unaccountable vision described in "The
Grand Armada" that looks toward but not at.

In *Moby-Dick*, Melville conjugates the verbs "to look" and "to know" in nineteenth-century America, trained on human bodies and inflected by ethnological zeal. He parses the "sight of sights to see," showing how racial meaning was concentrated in and extracted from bodies. He anatomizes the subjects and objects in this epic pursuit. He examines the difficult desire for intersubjectivity, heightened by the nineteenth-century mania to secure bodily boundaries. The legacy of this mania is a sense of eloquent racial difference. In the huge and revealing looking glass that is *Moby-Dick,* Melville offers an intimate, excessive reflection on the corporeal obsessions that continue to skew our vision.

CHAPTER 4

Penetrating Eyes in *Pierre*

At the start of *Pierre; or, The Ambiguities* (1852), the reader is placed in the role of urban visitor embarking on a rejuvenating picturesque stroll:

> There are some strange summer mornings in the country, when he who is but a sojourner from the city shall early walk forth into the fields, and be wonder-smitten with the trance-like aspect of the green and golden world. Not a flower stirs; the trees forget to wave; the grass itself seems to have ceased to grow; and all Nature, as if suddenly become conscious of her own profound mystery, and feeling no refuge from it but silence, sinks into this wonderful and indescribable repose.[1]

Yet the prospect offered in the first books of *Pierre* is not what the viewer has been taught to expect. Instead of the pleasures of manipulated perspective and distanced contemplation, the viewer in *Pierre* is drawn into the picture. Despite the assurance of the opening lines that the personification of natural features will be held in check, over the course of the first books the grass and flowers of Saddle Meadows throb with ominous intensity. The trees resemble less the signature blasted trunks of Thomas Cole and more the sinuous, entwining limbs of, say, the late-nineteenth-century artist Edvard Munch. The sojourner from the city finds himself at the mercy of a recalcitrant, vengeful landscape. Strolling forth into the fields of *Pierre,* the reader is greeted with a summer morning in the country that is very strange indeed.

Melville's exorbitant landscape is a response to antebellum efforts to define the American difference through representations of nature. The writers and artists of the New York City cultural establishment—"so-journers from the city"—shaped and popularized the new perceptions. They concentrated on northeastern landscapes, and particularly on the Hudson River and its environs. Such efforts included Irving's *Sketch Book* (1819–1820), Bryant's poetry, the paintings of Thomas Cole and Asher B. Durand, aesthetic treatises such as Cole's "Essay on American Scenery" (1835), and landscape gift books such as Nathaniel Parker Willis's popular *American Scenery* (1840) and the anonymously edited *Home Book of the Picturesque* (1852). In the sentimental education outlined by these literary and visual artists, Americans were trained to see the difference between American and European prospects. For many viewers in the 1850s, the American land was not the site of historical struggle between competing interests but an Eden paradoxically urging its own manipulation and destruction. By contrast, the landscape of *Pierre* presents a hyperbolic version of the American picturesque, in which the tropes of visual possession are pressed to revealing—and rup-turing—limits.

In the opening books of *Pierre*, Melville focuses on the eye, examin-ing its structures while the pupil is dilated under the stimulation of the American landscape. Continuing his cognitive inquiries, he shifts em-phasis in *Pierre* from the faculty psychology in *Moby-Dick,* which imagined that the powers of the mind were embedded in the brain, to an associationist psychology, which saw the contents of consciousness as linked by principles of relation, such as similarity, contiguity, and frequency. Associationist ideas influenced nineteenth-century painters, writers, and nationalists who exalted the American scene. Turning to landscape, Melville expands his scrutiny of the links between the indi-vidual, the natural, and the national.

In *Pierre*, Melville delves behind the eyes and deep into the cavity of the chest. He further tests the epistemology of character and character-istics, first in the body of the landscape and then in the hidden landscape of the body.[2] In the end, the narrator and author pull back from their in-timate exposures. *Pierre* begins by gazing outward, at Saddle Meadows, and ends by staring inward, at the seared landscape of Pierre, character and writer. Ultimately, Melville turns the figure of the eloquent body in-side out. In the most encumbered prose of Melville's career, his narrator reads the lines written not on Pierre's face, skin, or head but on his own heart. In the next two chapters, I will chart these movements outward and inward and suggest how such unfolding concludes the first phase of Melville's career.

AMERICAN VIEWS:
NATURAL FEATURES AND NATIONAL CHARACTER

From the very first pages of *Pierre,* there is something strange in the "green and golden world" of Saddle Meadows, the manorial estate that is the title character's patrimony. The problem is not exactly a serpent in the garden, since on the level of plot things seem quite fine, maybe even too fine. As the *Boston Post* described the situation: "Pierre Glendinning and his proud but loving mother are living together, surrounded by everything the world, intellect, health and affection can bestow. The son is betrothed to a beautiful girl of equal position and fortune, and everything looks brightly as a summer morning." Yet the gap is vast between this abstract epitome and what actually happens in the viscous medium of Melville's prose. Several of the contemporary reviews, which were almost uniformly negative, used the plot summary as a vehicle for parody, letting the self-evidently absurd excesses and reversals of the story speak for themselves.[3] And on one level this parody works. The story *is* bizarre, and one does look forward to perusing the entries in the literary contest to "Describe the Plot of *Pierre* in Ten Sentences or Less." Yet the parodies fail to indicate just how strange *Pierre* is. They normalize the book, even in their gestures of warning. In their stylizations of *Pierre* as a movement from rural golden age to urban wasteland, sentiment to idealism, dilation to collapse, they avoid confronting the ways in which the opening books are implicated in the antebellum nightmare that follows.[4]

Saddle Meadows is not the site of innocence but the intersection of intense political, patriarchal, and sexual anxieties. The explicit rhetoric of rural paradise in the opening sections is repeatedly challenged by displacements, overstatements, anticlimaxes, and the mingling of categories. In the first of a series of prodigiously developed metaphors, the narrator describes the inspiration Pierre receives from nature:

> [Nature] blew her wind-clarion from the blue hills, and Pierre neighed out lyrical thoughts, as at the trumpet-blast, a war-horse paws himself into a lyric of foam. She whispered through her deep groves at eve, and gentle whispers of humanness, and sweet whispers of love, ran through Pierre's thought-veins, musical as water over pebbles. She lifted her spangled crest of a thickly-

starred night, and forth at that glimpse of their divine Captain and Lord, ten thousand mailed thoughts of heroicness started up in Pierre's soul, and glared round for some insulted good cause to defend. (14)

Clearly, this is one part joke—we can almost hear the straining of nature's lungs—but it is also play with a purpose: the rhetoric molds the character's thoughts and provides the contours for his actions. Pierre doesn't simply have a mind stirred by nature's call. In Melville's revealing neologism, he has "thought-veins," channels through which ideas flow.[5] Like the conventional figures of English and American Romanticism, Melville's natural metaphors exalt in the aesthetic realm a relation to nature that had become debased in the economic sphere by the early nineteenth century. Yet Melville's excess here verges on distortion, and his metaphors threaten to collapse. His aeolian harp is too leaden (with such nominalizations as "humanness" and "heroicness"), too literal (Pierre seems practically metamorphosed, half-man and half-horse, as he "neighs" out his "lyrical" thoughts, and his "soul" seems overpopulated, not to mention overdressed, with all those "mailed thoughts of heroicness" milling about), and too mixed (with war horses, foaming lyrics, deep groves, musical water rushing over pebbles, spangled crests, and massed armies all occupying the same ground). Melville's excess does not subvert Romantic cliché but breathes new life into it, conveying its fervent antebellum American invocation.[6]

In examining representations of the land in the antebellum period, we need to remember that the very terms of the discussion—"landscape," "scenery," and "picturesque"—are aesthetic constructions, particular orientations of perspective and detail that became current during the rise of landscape painting in Europe in the seventeenth and eighteenth centuries and in America during the early nineteenth century. They are painters' terms, separating observer from view and abstracting land from human labor or occupancy. E. H. Gombrich argues that landscape painting is more a conceptual than a visual art, privileging aesthetic attitude over subject matter and requiring "some pre-existing mould into which the artist could pour his ideas." The rise of landscape painting marks what Dieter Groh and Rolf-Peter Sieferle call "an epochal transformation" in the cultural meaning of nature: nature is made alien while the capitalistic manipulation of the world is naturalized. As the natural world was objectified and contracted, nature appreciation was discovered and manifested in landscape painting, prints, and gift books, travel literature, lyric poetry, prose sketches, and fiction. In America, it is in the first decades of the nineteenth century that we find such an "epochal transformation"—what the influential New York City editor and writer Nathaniel Parker Willis referred to as "a direct revolution" in American perspective. In the northeastern United States, and especially among New York academicians in the 1840s and 1850s, there was an urgent call for American viewers to turn their attention to the distinctive, defining qualities of American scenery.[7]

Both British and American understandings of the picturesque drew upon associationist psychology, following Hobbes and Locke. Uvedale Price and Richard Payne Knight argued that aesthetic ideas resulted from the transformation of sensory data through mental associations. Writers disputed the origin and quality of these associations. Agreeing on the predominant role of abstract visual qualities in shaping aesthetic response, Price argued that associations with line and color had their source in human feelings, while Knight maintained that the associations with light and color were defined and sharpened by the viewer's experience of the art of painting. In contrast to Price and Knight, the landscape gardener Humphrey Repton stressed the role of personal or historical circumstances in determining aesthetic response. These theorists were interested in visual training. In a resonant passage, Knight described the complex act of perception: "The spectator, having his mind enriched with the embellishments of the painter and poet, applies them, by the spontaneous association of ideas, to the natural objects presented to the eye, which thus acquire ideal and imaginary beauties; that is, beauties that are not felt by the organic sense of vision, but by the intellect and the imagination through that sense." Knight sought to analyze the ways in which the eye becomes a vehicle for the mind.[8]

The discussion of American scenery became comparative and nationalistic. European and especially British writers asserted that American scenery lacked the historical or cultural associations of high civilization and that the picturesque scenery of the eastern United States was insufficient to stimulate thoughts of the sublime. Americans debated the character of their landscape and nation. Some, such as Walter Channing, Jared Sparks, and George Bancroft, agreed that American scenery was wanting and hoped for future development. Others, such as William Tudor, Samuel Gilman, W. H. Gardiner, and William Cullen Bryant, felt that American national associations could stimulate aesthetic response and support literary and artistic production. Often such associations had a manufactured quality, such as the "fanciful associations" put forth by the contributors to *The Home Book of the Picturesque* (1852). In a powerful synthesis of the two positions, some observers validated the "absence" of historical associations and celebrated the American land as a divinely inscribed tabula rasa. In the redemptive Edenic landscape was written not the burden of the past but divine assurance of the nation's glorious future. Spared the scars of the aristocratic Old World, Americans would write their own history. In these nationalistic visions, aesthetics, religion, and politics were conflated, and the sublime promise of the United States was seen as fulfilled in the cultivated scenery of picturesque America.[9]

Like the picturesque theorists, Melville is fascinated with form and response, with the shaping of views. Accepting the analysis of consciousness as composed of ideas linked by associations, Melville revises the terms and principles of connection. In his Saddle Meadows, historical associations are not absent but hauntingly present. His narrator in *Pierre* repeatedly alludes to the centuries-long struggle for possession of the American land. Melville examines how this kind of history is obscured and how the landscape is transformed. Melville offers the associative principle of historical contiguity: the tenacious, contentious bond between present and past. In *Pierre,* he demonstrates the important role played by "association" and its rhetorical analogue "allusion" in the antebellum debate over the nature of America. Does America have a past? Do its citizens bear the weight of history? Who "owns" the land? Is there a divine sanction for American internal colonization? Is there an American "difference," and what difference does that difference make? In this debate, the control over "association" or "allusion" is the control over American absences and presences, the ability to mask and to invigorate. Melville tells us that the scenery at Saddle Meadows was "the perfect mould" (5) for Pierre's mind, and he shows how such "moulding" operated: how the antebellum ideology of the imperative American landscape both compelled and incarcerated.

Melville was not the only writer to rework the American picturesque, of course. In several of his novels, and particularly in *The Pioneers* (1823), James Fenimore Cooper depicts the ravages of human appetite and the class and ethnic struggles over rights to the land and its products. Often, though, these scenes are caught up in Cooper's narrative about the inevitable and miraculous transformation of New York State. In *Hope Leslie* (1827), Catharine Maria Sedgwick seeks to alter the perspectives of her readers on contemporary racial questions by overlaying seventeenth- and nineteenth-century landscapes and presenting the decisive colonial victory against the Pequot Indians as unsanctified slaughter. In such prose sketches as "Domain of Arnheim" (1847) and "Landor's Cottage" (1849), Edgar Allan Poe profiles radical devotees of the picturesque, obsessive manipulators of nature who contrive overwrought landscapes. In *Walden* (1854), Henry David Thoreau stares at the natural world with such an intensity and grants it such a density that he risks losing himself in it. In "The Panorama" (1856), John Greenleaf Whittier unrolls not a glorious American procession but the corrupting spread of slavery from sea to sea. Narrators of slavery offer alternative views of American scenery. Solomon Northup describes his grinding schedule of labor on a cotton plantation in Louisiana in *Twelve Years A Slave* (1853). Emily Burke, a northern schoolteacher, details the relentless cycle of chores performed by African American women on southern plantations in *Reminiscences of Georgia* (1850).

Contributing to the ferment of debate about natural features and national character, Melville examines the deep structures of the picturesque gaze. He does not consecrate American scenery, endow it with legends, naturalize its violent past, or lecture his audience on their myopia. Instead, he makes vivid the framings, veilings, animations, and dissolutions of American views. In the Saddle Meadows sections of *Pierre,* Melville examines the trope of feeling through the eyes. The central gesture of *Pierre* is to reveal cliché as catachresis.[10]

THE LOVING EYE:
THOMAS COLE AND THE VISUAL EMBRACE

With a confidence not often present in his conflicted canvases, Thomas Cole writes about the assurances inscribed in the landscape in his "Essay on American Scenery" (1835). Cole repeatedly emphasizes the importance of "cultivating a taste for scenery," of seeing the American land in a way that elides the stories of struggle. "We are still in Eden," he encourages his readers, if only we learn how to look. Cole focuses on Hudson River features, training his gaze on the very ground over which tenants were struggling with their feudal landlords for right of occupancy during the bitter Anti-Renter conflicts of the 1830s and 1840s. He describes the sublimities of American scenery at the very time that the machinery of the federal government, under orders from President Jackson and in defiance of the Supreme Court's decision in *Worcester v. Georgia* (1832), was forcing the "Five Civilized Tribes" from their homes in the southeast to the newly appointed reserved lands in Oklahoma. Cole entreats his readers to appreciate the "wildness," "variety," and "vicissitudes" of American scenery, yet the details of controversy and displacement are precisely those that cultivated viewers are taught to crop from the frame. The American eye should be attuned not to the story of a landscape but to its "sublimity": "He who stands on Mount Albano and looks down on ancient Rome, has his mind peopled with the gigantic associations of the storied past; but he who stands on the mounds of the West, the most venerable remains of American antiquity, *may* experience the emotion of the sublime, but it is the sublimity of a shoreless ocean un-islanded by the recorded deeds of man." This "Western sublime" involves a peculiarly American myopia. The viewer, taking his vantage point on what is either a mountaintop or one of the massive Native American earthworks that fascinated antebellum observers, is taught that the land is boundless and unmarked, taught *not* to people his mind with the associations of the actual American past.[11]

Native American earthen mounds played a role in nineteenth-century debates about American associations. Some mounds, containing skeletons or ashes along with ceremonial objects, were used for burial purposes. Others served unknown functions. Were the builders of these prominent structures the ancestors of contemporary Indians who had degenerated from the character of their predecessors, or were they a separate, more civilized people whom the Indians supplanted? Did these impressive features of the western and southern landscapes entitle contemporary Native Americans to some measure of respect? (As we have seen, these are questions Samuel George Morton sought to answer in the researches of *Crania Americana*.) Defenders of the national honor offered Native American mounds as evidence of American antiquity, in response to European assaults on America's infancy and primitiveness.[12]

In his 1832 prospect poem, "The Prairies," William Cullen Bryant has his speaker stand before the vast and empty fields of the midwest, his heart swelling and his eyes dilating, and wonder how to interpret the visible traces of human hands:

> Are they here—
> The dead of other days?—and did the dust
> Of these fair solitudes once stir with life
> And burn with passion? Let the mighty mounds
> That overlook the rivers, or that rise
> In the dim forest crowded with old oaks,
> Answer. A race, that long has passed away,
> Built them . . .

For Bryant, as for many others, the mounds evoked a distant, vanished race, who had been overthrown by the "red man," who, in natural turn, was being displaced by European settlers. Toward the end of Bryant's poem, the domestic hum of a passing bee incites an aural association with a swarming future: "The sound of that advancing multitude/ Which soon shall fill these deserts." Native American mounds offer to such observers a principle of dissociation. They sever links between the American past and present. They announce the discontinuity of Native American civilizations. Like Cole standing on the mounds of the West, Bryant is unable or unwilling to see the palpable evidence of "the recorded deeds of man" before his eyes and beneath his feet.[13]

Cole does not endow his American vistas with the kinds of literary or historical references, the poetical scenes and inscribed ruins, that often mark his canvases of Europe, such as *Landscape Composition: Italian Scenery* (1831–1832), *A View Near Tivoli* (1832), *The Departure* and *The Return* (1838), *Dream of Arcadia* (1838), and *L'Allegro* and *Il Penseroso* (1845). In his "Essay," Cole offers "taste" as the counterforce to the rampant accumulation of Jacksonian America: "The pleasures of the imagination, among which the love of scenery holds a conspicuous place, will alone temper the harshness of such a state; and, like the atmosphere that softens the most rugged forms of the landscape, cast a veil of tender beauty over the asperities of life" (101). Here, concealment is represented as one of the "pleasures of the imagination," as a natural feature of American landscape aesthetics. "Veiling" is an operation of the atmosphere itself. In order to develop what Cole calls a "loving eye" (100), the American viewer must learn to keep secrets.[14]

Such veiling enhances the beauty of Cole's luminous, panoramic canvases. The gesture is allegorized in Cole's monumental historical cycle *The Course of Empire* (1836), which tells the story of the rise and fall of a civilization corrupted by wealth and vice, as nature reasserts its authority over the disfigurements of human history. (The references to Jackson's America are clear in these European scenes.) The series moves from the shadowy dawn of *The Savage State,* to the morning of *The Pastoral or Arcadian State,* through the intense light of day in the third canvas, *The Consummation of Empire,* filled with human structures and figures, to the smoky conflagration of the fourth scene, *Destruction,* and finally to the gelid *Desolation* of night. Cole's paired views of *The Past* and *The Present* (1838) repeat this moving lesson about the cloaking hand of nature and of the artist. From the radiant morning light of the past, which illuminates the view of a medieval European festival taking place before a turreted castle, we move to the shadowy twilight of the present, which obscures the details of the scene and shrouds the ruins of the castle in murky silhouette.[15]

In the "Essay on American Scenery," Cole provides a feature-by-feature gazetteer for American landscape appreciation: mountains, lakes, waterfalls, rivers, and forests (102–108).[16] These natural sights may not evoke the range of European historical allusions, but they are unmatched in their religious and moral associations. Cole asserts that the American difference is an asset. He climaxes his catalogue with a paean to America's "skies," which out-Europe Europe's, encompassing the entire geographical and visible spectrum:

> as we have the temperature of every clime, so have we the skies—we have the blue unsearchable depths of the northern sky—we have the upheaped thunder-clouds of the Torrid Zone, fraught with gorgeousness and sublimity—we have the silver haze of England, and the golden atmosphere of Italy. And if he who has travelled and observed the skies of other climes will spend a few months on the banks of the Hudson, he must be constrained to acknowledge that for variety and magnificence American skies are unsurpassed. (108)

Cole writes of American scenery that "It is a subject that to every American ought to be of surpassing interest . . . it is his own land; its beauty, its magnificence, its sublimity—are all his; and how undeserving of such a birthright, if he can turn toward it an unobserving eye, an unaffected heart!" (98). The "loving eye" functioning in the imperative mood is the end of this sentimental education—the eye *must* observe in a certain way, the heart *must* be affected. The "loving eye" must acknowledge and must embrace its inheritance: the unscathed, apotheosized Eden yearning for its Adam. Pierre labors under such a territorial imperative in Saddle Meadows. In Cole's essay, the circuit is forged between perception, emotion, and action. Thus the "cultivation of a taste for scenery" does not quite "temper" the "harshness" of the American state, in the sense of moderating or alleviating that Cole implies. Instead, aesthetics here transmutes the "harshness," sets the terms and relations for a system, inspired but castigated by Cole, in which cultivation and destruction are linked and naturally inevitable.[17]

At the end of the essay, Cole elevates his reader so that he or she may gain a wide prospect. This is one in a series of prominent antebellum images of visual ascendancy. Cole gives directions for the eye:

> Seated on a pleasant knoll, look down into the bosom of that secluded valley, begirt with wooded hills—through those enamelled meadows and wide

waving fields of grain, a silver stream winds lingeringly along—here, seeking the green shade of trees—there, glancing on the sunshine: on its banks are rural dwellings shaded by elms and garlanded by flowers—from yonder dark mass of foliage the village spire beams like a star. You see no ruined tower to tell of outrage—no gorgeous temple to speak of ostentation; but freedom's offspring—peace, security, and happiness, dwell there, the spirits of the scene. On the margin of that gentle river the village girls may ramble unmolested—and the glad school-boy, with hook and line, pass his bright holiday—those neat dwellings, unpretending to magnificence, are the abodes of plenty, virtue, and refinement. And in looking over the yet uncultivated scene, the mind's eye may see far into futurity. Where the wolf roams, the plough shall glisten; on the gray crag shall rise temple and tower—mighty deeds shall be done in the now pathless wilderness; and poets yet unborn shall sanctify the soil. (108–109)

Here we have the guidelines for the construction of American "scenery." Landscape is cleared of European "associations"; its features are imbued with the consecrated aura of a rural golden age; and the eye and interest of the viewer are directed to future cultivation. Although the poet has yet to sanctify this soil, the artist has already done so with pen and brush. The meadows Cole presents are indeed "enamelled," the product of surfaces layered and lustered, beautiful and opaque.[18]

In his paintings and his private writings, Cole was less sanguine about the rise of temples and towers and the groove of the glistening plow. In "Essay on American Scenery," the claims seem strained and the faith too fervent, as though Cole were attempting to talk himself into a confidence that he could not see. Such ambivalence about American prospects is on display in his famous 1836 oil painting of the Connecticut River, *View from Mount Holyoke, Northampton, Mass., after a Thunderstorm (The Oxbow),* composed at the same time as the "Essay" (see figure 20). Cole arranges and frames his view to convey the lessons of the American landscape: the eye sweeps along the diagonal of the composition from the blasted tree and gray storm clouds in the left foreground, down the sun-tinged green of the hillside, and back into the glowing golden river valley, in which wisps of smoke climb from the few homesteads. The viewer is directed from the sublime to the picturesque, from gray green to golden yellow, from wilderness to cultivation. At the center of visual interest in the frame is a circle of green and golden land almost severed from the bank by the loop of the river: a stage set for transformation by human hands. A tiny figure in the foreground, marked as Thomas Cole by his physiognomy and by his signature on the

Figure 20. *View from Mount Holyoke, Northampton, Massachusetts, after a Thunderstorm (The Oxbow)*, by Thomas Cole (1836). Courtesy of the Metropolitan Museum of Art, gift of Mrs. Russell Sage.

nearby portfolio, faces the viewer, his brush raised in his fingers. Presiding over the scene, rising above the ring of water, a hillside in the golden valley has swaths cut into its foliage, forming Hebrew characters, which have been interpreted to signify either "Noah" or the "Almighty." In *The Oxbow*, it appears that Cole has inscribed divine assent to cultivation on the land itself.[19]

Yet, as Angela Miller observes, the circle of land in the center of the painting forms not only a stage or yoke but also a question mark. The storm, like the river, might reverse course. The clouds still cast shadows over the land. The divine writ may not be good news. The eye may follow the smooth path along the diagonal of the hillside, but it also may be interrupted by the recessional plunge between precipice and valley. The brilliance of *The Oxbow* lies in the two paths offered by its split composition and particularly in the indeterminate gap that divides the foreground and the middle landscape. In *Pierre*, Melville achieves the rhetorical equivalent of Cole's visual ambiguities. Many of Cole's successors fill the gap and smooth the transition from wilderness to cultivation. They choose the hillside route rather than the precipice. Many painters and printmakers used *The Oxbow* as a formula for progress through American space. They felt Cole's longing and anticipation but not his misgivings.[20]

THE HUNGRY EYE: NATHANIEL PARKER
WILLIS AND THE TASTE FOR SCENERY

In Nathaniel Parker Willis's *American Scenery,* a popular landscape gift book published in 1840, the loving eye is represented as a particularly calculating and hungry eye. Willis was editor of the "Knickerbocker" *New York Mirror,* popularizer of the digest periodical in the *Home Journal,* travel writer, novelist, playwright, poet, and shaper of middle-class taste. *American Scenery* consists of text by Willis accompanying 121 engravings made from the drawings of English artist W. H. Bartlett, whom Willis accompanied on his American sketching trips. Willis and Bartlett's book provides views of, among other locations, the Hudson River, the Catskills, the Erie Canal, the White Mountains, Albany, and Boston. The boundaries of "America" in *American Scenery* are restricted to the northeast. In over 100 brief sections, the text ranges from accounts of the middle-class tourist's comical discomfiture at the indignities of American travel ("Albany"), to historical anecdotes that embellish Revolutionary scenery ("View of the Ruins of Ticonderoga"), to Indian tales and archaeology ("Descent Into the Valley of Wyoming [Pennsylvania])," "Lockport—Erie Canal," "Hudson Highlands, from Bull Hill"), to advice on the quality of service and food at popular resorts ("Two Lakes and the Mountain House on the Catskills"). In the section on Albany, Willis refers to "old Enceladus." For Willis, however, the figure is not the tortured, amputated Titan of book 25 in *Pierre,* but a "worky," a potent laborer whose arms are likened to the Erie and Champlain canals stretching out from the Hudson.[21]

In his preface, Willis makes the familiar assertions about America as divine and original creation and about the uniqueness of American natural features, but then announces that his goal is to domesticate the American sublime, to bring it to the fireside so that his readers can have all of the pleasure of traveling with none of the inconvenience that comes with leaving home. As Willis puts the matter, in advertising lingo: "So great a gratification is seldom enjoyed at so little cost and pains" (v). In his introductory essay "American Scenery," Willis repeats the clichés in a closely packed series of metaphors: "It strikes the European traveller, at the first burst of the scenery of America on his eye, that the New World of Columbus is also a new world from the hand of the Creator.... [H]e may well imagine it an Eden newly sprung from the ocean. The Minerva-like birth of the republic of the United States, its sudden rise to independence, wealth, and power, and its continued and marvellous increase in population and prosperity, strike him with the same surprise, and leave the same impression of a new scale of existence, and a fresher and faster law of growth and accomplishment" (3).

The argument takes an unusual turn, as do the terms, when Willis describes his version of the different European and American "associations." Linking artist and tourist, Willis argues that there has been an American "revolution" in perspective, in "the soul and centre of attraction in every picture" (3). In a set piece of national distinction, the kind of chorographia through antithesis often delivered in antebellum America, Willis echoes and amplifies Cole's commanding view of the rural valley. He makes contemporary and material Cole's glimpse of American progress:

> Instead of looking through a valley, which has presented the same aspect for hundreds of years—in which live lords and tenants, whose hearths have been surrounded by the same names through ages of tranquil descent, and whose fields have never changed landmark or mode of culture since the memory of man, [the American] sees a valley laden down like a harvest waggon with a virgin vegetation, untrodden and luxuriant; and his first thought is of the villages that will soon sparkle on the hill-sides, the axes that will ring from the woodlands, and the mills, bridges, canals, and railroads, that will span and border the stream that now runs through sedge and wild-flowers. The towns he passes through on his route are not recognizable by prints done by artists long ago dead, with houses of low-browed architecture, and immemorial trees; but a town which has perhaps doubled its inhabitants and dwellings since he last saw it, and will again double them before he returns. Instead of inquiring into its antiquity, he sits over the fire with his paper and pencil, and calculates what the population will be in ten years, how far they will spread, what the value of the neighbouring land will become, and whether the stock of some canal or railroad that seems more visionary than Symmes's expedition to the centre of the earth, will, in consequence, be a good investment. He looks upon all external objects as exponents of the future. In Europe they are only exponents of the past. (4)

Here, as in Cole's "Essay on American Scenery," there is a willful forgetting of the social history of the land. The viewer refuses to see what lies before his eyes: the "lords" and "tenants" actually struggling over the land of the Hudson River Valley. Yet Willis's tone is different. He is palpably impatient with the same old views and the faded renderings of musty architecture and obsolete trees. There is appetite in the eye that sees "a valley laden down like a harvest waggon."

Several of the genteel engravings in *American Scenery* register these desires. In one significant compositional pattern, seen in such images as *Albany, Hudson Highlands, from Bull Hill,* and *Villa on the Hudson, Near Weehawken,* the space is divided into three characteristic planes: foreground, in which small human figures manipulate the scenery (viewing or cultivating or conducting commerce upon it); middleground, consisting of watery band; and background, marked with signs of civilization, such as domestic or commercial structures (see figures 21 and 22). This mise-en-scène tells a story, a processional narrative about navigating the gap and consuming the middle landscape. The engraving of the *Hudson Highlands* bears no visual trace of the legend Willis invokes in his accompanying prose sketch. (It is a tale of the loyal bond between a white family and their Indian friend, who warns them of an impending massacre and is killed by his peers for his betrayal.) Several of Willis's prose pieces allude to Native American or Revolutionary War stories, yet Bartlett's images are insistently contemporary and resist such references. Willis's associations are merely ornamental. They do not inhere in the view. Word often slides from image in *American Scenery.*[22]

Although many of Bartlett's scenes are compositionally similar to Cole's theatrical landscapes, and particularly to *The Oxbow,* the eye is permitted to traverse the space with greater ease. Instead of being situated on the uneven precipice of *The Oxbow,* Bartlett's observers are lodged on the level shore or the sculpted promenade. In place of Cole's knotted river, Bartlett delineates courses of water that flow uninterrupted from foreground into background. This visual passage is emphasized in several prints by sailboats gliding into the distance. In the last scene of the book, *Faneuil Hall, from the Water,* such vessels are depicted as reaching their destination: the landfilled Boston harbor whose streets are crowded with people and over which preside the sublime domes and towers of Faneuil Hall, the pinnacle of liberty and commerce, the port of once-and-future American glory (see figure 23).[23]

In Willis's opening prose sketch of the rural valley, there is eagerness in the images of the linked transportation and industrial revolutions: "the valley laden down like a harvest waggon," the "villages that will soon sparkle on the hill-sides," "the axes that will ring from the woodlands," and "the mills, bridges, canals, and railroads that will span and

Figure 21.   *Hudson Highlands, from Bull Hill,* engraving by W. H. Bartlett, from *American Scenery,* vol. 1, by Nathaniel Parker Willis (1840).

Figure 22.   *Villa on the Hudson, near Weehawken,* engraving by W. H. Bartlett, from *American Scenery,* vol. 1, by Nathaniel Parker Willis (1840).

Figure 23. *Faneuil Hall, from the Water,* engraving by W. H. Bartlett, from *American Scenery,* vol. 2, by Nathaniel Parker Willis (1840).

border the stream." There is excitement at the prospect of geometric in-crease that extends beyond the frame: the population which doubles and redoubles, the soaring value of land and stocks. Sitting by the fireside with paper and pencil, Willis's observer itemizes the landscape. He cal-culates the future in terms of multipliers and dividends. The "revolu-tion" in perspective that Willis describes is a change in the way nature is viewed. Willis's natural features are exponents of the future. They put forth their own meanings; they interpret themselves; they advocate their own manipulation and transformation. They proclaim not a religious sublime but a commercial one. They deliver a sermon on the exertion and increase of power, on the enchantments of American capitalism. In a particularly bizarre preface to his volume of scenic engravings, Willis outlines a vision of the natural destroying itself.[24]

A similarly potent oxymoron is at work in the rural vision from William Cullen Bryant's "The Ages" (1821) that Willis uses to conclude his opening remarks. "The Ages" is a long, versified providential his-tory, which begins with an evocation of "Those pure and happy times— the golden days of old," then comforts the reader who fears a narrative of decline with good news about the lessons of history. Bryant teaches these lessons through vignettes in twenty-seven stanzas, describing "the genial cradle of our race" in the ancient Near East, the conventional eras of Western history (Egypt, Greece, Rome, the Middle Ages, the Reformation), and the advent of America. It is, of course, a story of progress and expansive destiny, yet it is not a story with a simple trajectory nor one that conveys the cozy natural supernaturalism often associated with Bryant. In selecting stanzas for placement at the end of his remarks, Willis seems to have been attracted to the language of a particular kind of progress:

> Look now abroad—another race has fill'd
> These populous borders—wide the wood recedes,
> And towns shoot up, and fertile realms are tilled;
> The land is full of harvests and green meads;
> Streams numberless, that many a fountain feeds,
> Shine, disembowered, and give to sun and breeze
> Their virgin waters; the full region leads
> New colonies forth, that toward the western seas
> Spread, like a rapid flame among the autumnal trees.[25]

We recognize the visual imperative to acknowledge the American advance. Striking here is the violence contained within the conventional form and meter. This march of progress is an enlightenment through conflagration. America's most beloved nature poet celebrates the recession of the Native American race and the destruction of the land. And, in a remarkable moment, the word "disembowered," Bryant's neologism for natural ravage—a word which bears an uncanny resemblance to "disemboweled"—is inserted in the poetic line without missing a beat. Without "disembowered," the stanza reads like dozens of antebellum imperial romantic effusions. With "disembowered," progress is naturally linked with evisceration. What seems a solecism, a jarringly inappropriate turn of phrase, apparently for Bryant and for the audience of his very popular poem was a part of the verbal texture.[26]

American Scenery and the American picturesque operate on the basis of such transformations, reorientations, and naturalizations. American Scenery is eulogy and elegy, nostalgia and assault, Baedeker and epitaph. American Scenery is about devouring American scenery. Through antithesis, hyperbole, incarnation, and division, and in a remarkably genial, understated, and delicately ironic style, Willis channels the energy of the sublime to the hearthside and uses it to promote a taste for the land. Nature is appreciated and destroyed; that is, appreciated in such a way that it can, in fact *must*, be destroyed. In the perverse final paragraph of this elegant gift book, cultivation becomes extirpation. Willis briefly laments the disappearance of the oyster boats and vendors that once clustered before Faneuil Hall, but then he realizes that such "poetry" encumbers "improvement." In the place where we would expect Willis to sentimentally mourn or imaginatively recover the past, he offers not an ode on melancholy or immortality or a nightingale but a call to purge the American soil: "So flee away before the advances of improvement all that reminded us of other days; and it is by this resolute plucking up of old associations, and resolute modernizing and improving, even upon the most sacred habits and usages of our forefathers, that this new nation keeps its unchecked headway, with neither rooted superstition nor cherished prejudice to restrain it" (362).[27] No associations with the past clog Willis's view or impede American progress. He recommends that such nuisances be eradicated. The book does not offer a panoramic view of the northeast, nor is it structured according to a strategy of geography or theme or chronology. Instead, *American Scenery* is divided and isolated into over one hundred discrete units, each consisting of an illustration and no more than a couple of pages of text. America is imagined for the domestic traveler in such a way that the land can be carved up into scenery and appropriated for private pleasure.

THE DISSOLVING EYE:
SUSAN COOPER AND THE PERSISTENCE OF VISION

Published in 1852, the same year as *Pierre, The Home Book of the Picturesque* stands at the peak of three decades of attention directed toward the landscape of the northeastern United States. This popular gift book reproduced engraved scenes by the foremost landscape painters, including Cole, Durand, Kensett, Church, and Huntington, and published reflections by the most prominent prose artists of the antebellum period, now at the end of their literary careers. James Fenimore Cooper compares the colors and compositions of English, French, and American scenery, concluding that while American scenery may be wanting in sublimity it is superior to that of Europe in its picturesque blending of cultivated and savage. Washington Irving mines the legendary interior of the Catskill mountains for "fanciful associations" with the Indian and Dutch pasts. William Cullen Bryant displays word pictures of scenes along the Housatonic River. The *Home Book* opens and closes with didactic essays by two popular lecturers, E. L. Magoon and G. W.

Bethune, who illustrate the ways in which natural scenery stamps national character. A contribution to the public taste, the *Home Book* summarizes the scenic gains in the sixteen years since Cole's insistence in his "Essay on American Scenery" that Americans learn to appreciate their distinctive landscape. The most revealing meditation in this compendium is not by the patriarchs Cooper, Irving, or Bryant, it is by a member of the next generation of American observers, Cooper's daughter Susan.[28]

In "A Dissolving View," Susan Cooper shows how difficult it is to sustain the picturesque lessons she has learned. "A Dissolving View" is not only about veiling but also about the persistence of vision. It is not only about extirpation but also about the tenaciousness of roots. Susan Cooper's literary legerdemain dissolves the human traces on the American land. Yet her manipulations also threaten to dissolve the frame that separates the American from the European scene.

Seated on a fallen pine near a projecting cliff that overlooks a valley, the observer in Cooper, like the observers in Cole and in Willis, commands a wide prospect. Susan Cooper's sketch reworks the elevated views and scenic desires that structure her father's novel *The Pioneers* (1823). Like James Fenimore Cooper's Elizabeth Temple, Susan's observer stands before a scene whose details have been arranged "like a beautiful map" for her aesthetic contemplation (81). Unlike Elizabeth Temple, who insists to Oliver Edwards that she and her father could not, even if they wished, reverse the course of development and return the land to its pristine state, Susan sets in motion such a conversion, although its results are not exactly what she imagined.[29]

Scanning the valley, the observer's mind wanders to Europe, and she laments the labored texture of its landscapes: "there is not in those old countries a single natural feature of the earth upon which man has not set his seal" (88). In contrast, she assures her readers and herself, the appearance of America is youthful and unlined: "How different from all this is the aspect of our own country! . . . there is no blending of the old and the new in this country; there is nothing old among us" (88–89). Yet Cooper has to exert herself to preserve her natural and national distinctions. Standing upon the cliff, she waves a sprig of witch hazel and then presides over a spectacle of transformation. In Cooper's hands, the magic of the picturesque is rendered visible and literal. Like the artist figures of Cole and Bryant on the promontory in Durand's famous painting *Kindred Spirits* (1849), both of whom wield staffs that seem to configure the Catskills scenery around them, Cooper casts her spells over the landscape, dissolving and reconstituting what lies before her eyes.[30]

First her sweeping hand and scanning eye raze the village: "The wooden bridge at the entrance of the village fell into the stream and disappeared; the court-house vanished; the seven taverns were gone; the dozen stores had felt the spell; the churches were not spared; the hundred dwelling-houses shared the same fate, and vanished like the smoke from their own chimneys" (91). America's lines are not clean enough, even in comparison with the belabored European surface. Yet these demolitions only begin to fulfill her "ambition" (91). Next, she passes the witch hazel over the valley again, and, in a turn of events that would have warmed the heart of Natty Bumppo, the forest is regenerated. Trees that had been lost to settlers and builders resume their original height. The scars that had been cut into the land seem to heal. And if the autumn reverie ended here, Cooper merely would have provided another diverting fantasy of Eden. Yet she does not seek an original state of nature as much as she attempts to ward off the specter of European associations.

Cooper tells the reader that she wished to view the American valley as if it had been the product of European history—"how, in such a case, would it have been fashioned by the hand of man?" (92). With another wave, her wish is granted and she beholds the European fate of the American scene:

Many of the hills had been wholly shorn of wood. The position of the different farms and that of the buildings was entirely changed. Looking down upon the little town we saw it had dwindled to a mere hamlet; low, picturesque, thatched cottages were irregularly grouped along a wide grassy street, and about a broad green which formed the centre of the village; in this open grassy green stood a large stone cross, beautifully designed and elaborately carved, doubtless a monument of some past historical event. . . . The church, the largest building in the hamlet, was evidently very old, and covered a good deal of ground—its walls were low, of hewn stone—one large and rich window occupied the eastern end, and a graceful spire rose in the opposite direction. Two or three small, quiet-looking shops represented the trade of the place. The bridge was of massive stone, narrow, and highly arched, while the ruins of a tower stood close at hand. The fields were parted by hedges, which lined the narrow roads on either side. . . . Then just without the village was a place of some size, evidently an old country house, dating perhaps some six or eight generations back, with its brick walls, quaint chimneys, angles, cornices, and additions; this place could boast its park, and deer were grazing on the lawn. Yonder in the distance, upon the western shore of the lake, stood a castle of gray stone, its half dozen towers rising a hundred feet from the hill-side. (92–93)

The "hand of man" (92) has written all over this landscape of partitioned spaces and vertical tiers, although the signs of its exhaustion are evident in the bare hills, dwindled villages, and crumbling structures. This village is one of at least nine the observer can see. Several of them have been built on the former sites of feudal castles. Emblems of writing mark the scene: cross, spire, towers. The land has been shaved and graded. Fields have been parted by hedges. The village is surmounted by a country house, boasting occupants generation after generation. A castle reigns over all. The historical strata and feudal traces—the ruins, the castles, the lords, and the tenants—are visible in Cooper. Then again, her prospect is conjured from European materials. Or is it?

Rather than confirming difference, the shifts between America and Europe blur the line she seeks to draw. A "dissolving view" that begins by purging the American scene ends by superimposing Europe on America, mingling the marks of history and class. Despite Cooper's claim that there is no blending of old and new in America, her own alternations imply a merging of prospects. In Cooper, we can see how the American landscape is "enamelled," to use Cole's evocative phrase. Cooper attempts to ornament and protect the American scene through a layering of surfaces. Yet the strain in her gestures calls attention to the resemblance. The view of an American Eden is obstructed by the prominence of Cooper's own hand in the foreground of her picture. Threatening to dissolve before Cooper's hand and eye are not the historical "associations" of America but the frame that divides America from Europe.[31]

The sketch ends when a roving bee, attracted by the sprig of witch hazel, stings the observer's finger and recalls her wandering attention: "the spell was over; the country had resumed its every-day aspect" (94). Well, not exactly. While the view resumes its clarity after the bee's sting, the ache persists. The dissolving eye erases, veils, and layers, yet traces persist on the retina. Such a persistence of vision and such a retrospective ache are major symptoms in the pathology of *Pierre*.

STRANGE EYE-FISH WITH WINGS: MELVILLE'S CLOGGED OPTICS

If Cole sets the stage and Willis forcefully animates it and Cooper provides the special visual effects, then Melville scripts the picturesque's

most overwrought performance. In *Pierre,* he scrutinizes its constructions: the stage properties, the characteristic stances, gestures, and dialogue, the transactions between viewer and object. In *Pierre,* a different
taste for scenery is cultivated. The landscape of Saddle Meadows is neither tractable nor nourishing. Pierre chokes on it. American prospects—
the links between vision, scenic possession, and progress—are dimmed.
The "associations" of Saddle Meadows are not "wanting." References
to sustained conflicts over the land circulate through the opening pages,
echoing and reinforcing one another and indicating the patterns of European and American encroachment. The style of *Pierre* does not seam-
lessly connect cultivation and destruction. The figurative excess clogs
and warps the system, illuminating the twists and turns in the American
"revolution" in perspective. One source of the excess in *Pierre* is the fric-
tion produced by the contradictions in the system described, the energy
expended in massive gestures of erasure and intervention, displacement
and expansion.

In the opening sections, we are presented with Pierre as young heir to
the estate of Saddle Meadows, "the only surnamed male Glendinning
extant," as we are told twice in the same paragraph (7–8). Pierre is the
sole bearer of the precious Glendinning legacy, shaped by its rural and
sentimental entailments: "It had been his choice fate to have been born
and nurtured in the country, surrounded by scenery whose uncommon
loveliness was the perfect mould of a delicate and poetic mind; while the
popular names of its finest features appealed to the proudest patriotic
and family associations of the historic line of Glendinning" (5). Here, at
first glance, Melville apparently celebrates the glories of the family line
and of rural education, particularly the education through landscape
championed by antebellum painters and writers. (The narrator repeats
his assertion—"it had been the choice fate of Pierre to have been born
and bred in the country"—a few pages later.) The conventional terms
are introduced—"scenery," "associations," and "a delicate and poetic
mind." Saddle Meadows seems picturesque, in the tradition of Irving's
sketches or Willis's views. Yet over the course of the first two books the
key terms for framing the American land are anatomized and revised so
that "choice fate" is seen as a historical curse; "the perfect mould" de-
forms; "a delicate and poetic mind" is represented as divided, dependent, and guilty; proliferating "popular names" and "family associations" inspire but also occlude; and "the historic line of Glendinning"
becomes a garrote.

The landscape of Saddle Meadows is repeatedly described as sentimentalized and owned by Pierre: "But not only through the mere
chances of things, had that fine country become ennobled by the deeds
of his sires, but in Pierre's eyes, all its hills and swales seemed as sanctified through their very long uninterrupted possession by his race . . .
Pierre deemed all that part of the earth a love-token; so that his very
horizon was to him as a memorial ring" (8). Here, through diction
and juxtaposition, terms are not simply inverted or reversed, they are
pressed to revealing limits. Connotations invoke repressed significances.
Etymologies restore forgotten histories. "Sires" and "swales," words ostensibly alien to the democratic American landscape, suggest anachro-
nism and privilege. Sanctification here is conferred not only through the
divine mandate often invoked in nineteenth-century American civil religion but also by right of "possession." And "possession" is asserted
in the name of "race," evoking not only the legacy of Pierre's great-
grandfather, the Dutch patroon ("race" in the older sense of a group of
persons descended from a common ancestor), but also Anglo-Saxon authority in the struggle over the American land ("race" as defining the na-
tures and places of different human types, a meaning with particular
force in the context of nineteenth-century justifications of racial slavery
and displacement).

The emphasis on "race" in the opening pages of Pierre—in addition to being told that the landscape is "possessed by his race," we
are told that Pierre views Saddle Meadows as "the background of his
race" and that he has descended from a "martial race" (6)—reminds
us that Saddle Meadows has been "sanctified" through blood, particularly the blood of Indian battles, and that the Glendinning possession
of the land has not exactly been "uninterrupted"—that is, undisputed.
We are told that the blood of Pierre's great-grandfather had seeped
into the grass of the sloping meadows, as he exerted his claim against
Native Americans during the colonial period. Pierre's grandfather
had spilled the blood of the Iroquois in his effort to retain control
over the region during the Revolutionary War, in a battle that echoes
the celebrated success of Melville's own maternal grandfather, Peter
Gansevoort, in defending Fort Stanwix, near present-day Rome, New
York, in 1777.[32]

In an extended digression on the "large estates" and "long pedigrees"
of England and America, Melville twists the rhetoric of American exceptionalism. The narrator insists that America surpasses the mother

country in the natural power of its political institutions and the strength of its ruling class, finding an "apt analogy":

> For indeed the democratic element operates as a subtile acid among us; forever producing new things by corroding the old; as in the south of France verdigris, the primitive material of one kind of green paint, is produced by grape-vinegar poured upon copper plates. Now in general nothing can be more significant of decay than the idea of corrosion; yet on the other hand, nothing can more vividly suggest luxuriance of life, than the idea of green as a color; for green is the peculiar signet of all-fertile Nature herself. Herein by apt analogy we behold the marked anomalousness of America; whose character abroad, we need not be surprised, is misconceived, when we consider how strangely she contradicts all prior notions of human things; and how wonderfully to her, Death itself becomes transmuted into Life. So that political institutions, which in other lands seem above all things intensely artificial, with America seem to possess the divine virtue of a natural law; for the most mighty of nature's laws is this, that out of Death she brings Life. (9)

Both "the democratic element" and "the subtile acid" appear to corrode original structures but actually reinvigorate them in a new form. Here, in an argument for America's equality in the family of nations, Melville unravels the progress and originality that distinguish the American narrative. Like Susan Cooper's "dissolving eye," Melville's democratic acid disintegrates in order to constitute difference. Yet Melville's acid is more effective, achieving its result through conversion rather than incomplete erasure. In Melville's analysis, America out-Englands England, managing to transmute its structures of property and class into more potent elements through the agency of its difference. These structures are thus rendered "natural," in contrast with the "artificial" and so more fragile distinctions of England. The "aptness" of the analogy between "the democratic element" and "a subtile acid" lies in its apparent incongruity yet functional success. Progress is linked with corrosion in a narrative of "natural law." Out of revolutionary "Death" comes new "Life" for old institutions. *Pierre* is steeped in the language of such antebellum alchemy. Yet there is also something not quite right about the analogy— as there is often something jarring about the rhetoric in *Pierre*. Here, "new" democracy is associated with the antique aura of a patina, and the process described, despite Melville's winking assurance at the climax of the paragraph, is not natural but explicitly artificial: the French, he explains, induce verdigris by pouring grape-vinegar on copper plates. And there is at least a slight mocking of early American Athenian pretensions when Melville compares democracy to vert-de-Grice, literally the green crust of Grecian artifacts.[33]

Melville ends his digression not with a paean to absence but with a figure of salience. The "Revolutionary flood," he writes, did not clear the land but receded to reveal the "mighty lordships" fortified and defended by the state militia, surviving the deluge like "Indian mounds" (11). Hudson river estates are associated with Ohio and Mississippi Valley earthworks, Dutch manors with Native American burial mounds.[34] Unlike the observers in Cole's "Essay on American Scenery," Bryant's "Prairies," Willis's *American Scenery,* or Cooper's "Dissolving View," the narrator-observer in *Pierre* sees a pattern of references to social struggle in the features of the landscape, which here signify the tenacity of privilege and the death of civilizations. Melville's American swagger induces queasiness. The reader is more dizzied than captivated by the tacking and yawing in an argument for American equivalence that becomes an argument for American exceptionalism by transforming the American difference from a badge of inferiority into a mark of efficiency.

We are reminded of the force needed to claim and retain possession of the American land through Melville's strangely oblique allusion to the Anti-Renter struggles in the Hudson River Valley. During this conflict, tenant farmers rioted against the feudal practices of their landlords, in particular protesting the restrictive clauses in land leases and the demand for payment of "rents," or yearly tributes in produce, labor, or money. Such practices had been in place in the Hudson Valley since the early seventeenth century. In the 1760s, and especially from 1839 until 1846, tensions between tenants and landlords simmered to violent climaxes. The Anti-Renter "wars" of 1839–1846 were critical events in New York history with broad political implications, including the adoption of a new state constitution in 1846 that abolished the feudal system. In December 1839, during a fierce outbreak of resistance, Governor Seward sent the state militia to suppress a large gathering of Anti-Rent farmers. In August 1845, Governor Wright sent three hundred troops to collect rents.

As Melville's narrator explains, "regular armies, with staffs of officers, crossing rivers with artillery, and marching through primeval woods, and threading vast rocky defiles, have been sent out to distrain upon three thousand farmer-tenants of one landlord, at a blow. A fact most suggestive two ways; both whereof shall be nameless here" (11). Melville's archaic irony ("primeval woods," "vast rocky defiles," "to distrain upon") does not simply subvert the feudal pretensions of the Hudson Valley landlords, although certainly one effect of the diction and the syntax is to distance the events as reactionary. Coming at the

climax of the digression on the creation of "mighty lordships in the heart
of a republic," the inflated diction and antiquated syntax indicate the
success of the retrogressive venture, as landlords and tenants contend
against an epic backdrop—an anachronistic venture in supposedly new
and democratic nineteenth-century America, to be sure, but an anachro-
nism that seems to work. When Melville represents Saddle Meadows as
a "manor," the portrayal is charged with a mid-nineteenth-century political meaning.[35]

The narrator comments on the class structure of Saddle Meadows in
book 20, when he describes the "povertiresque" lives of the Millthorpes,
the Glendinnings' tenants, who must abandon their farm because they
cannot pay the manorial rent. The irony is much easier to track here, as
Melville attacks the violent complacency of those writers and artists
who employ "poverty" as a piquant element in their compositions. (Possible targets might include male sentimentalists such as Irving, Willis,
and Donald Grant Mitchell.) Melville had made a similar point in the
"Launcelott's-Hey" section of *Redburn* (1849), in which the young narrator strolls down a narrow Liverpool street and discovers not one of
Irving's insulated urban retreats but instead a cellar and the still lifes of
a dying mother and children, a view unheralded in his picturesque old
guidebook. In "Poor Man's Pudding and Rich Man's Crumbs" (1854),
Melville depicts the ways in which poverty ruptures the verbal and visual frames of its representations. This diptych represents the inability
of euphemism to contain its object and climaxes with a spectacle of
charity that is rent by scorn. Not a dark revelation about the golden
Saddle Meadows of books 1 and 2, the mention of the penurious Millthorpes in book 20 serves more as a redundant reminder of the fraught
opening scenes.

Toward the end of the book, in the "Mount of Titans" section, the
narrator alludes to rents both of and in the landscape (342–46). Taking
the reader on a tour of the manor and invoking the picturesque impera-
tives ("you would see," "you saw"), the narrator journeys across fields
and foothills and up to the "impregnable redoubt" (344) of the mountain that reigns over the meadows. He imagines hearing the cries of tenants who implore their lady to abate their rents because a blanket of
amaranth is choking their pastures. He sees ruptures in the terrain:
"long and frequent rents among the mass of leaves revealed horrible
glimpses of dark-dripping rocks, and mysterious mouths of wolfish
caves" (343). Enormous boulders, broken from the face of the mountain, litter the hills, prompting the narrator and Pierre to think of the

defiant, thwarted Titans of classical mythology. The closer one looks at Saddle Meadows, the more one sees "a spectacle of wide and wanton spoil" (344). This desolate landscape resounds with echoes of rebellion, suppression, and disinheritance.[36]

Some of the ways in which the "fact" of the landlords summoning troops against their tenants might have seemed "most suggestive" to Melville are personal. His mother was a direct descendant of the first patroon, Killian Van Rensselaer. His cousins, the Van Rensselaers, were the largest and wealthiest landowners in the Hudson Valley, the only retainers of a patroonship (or, we might say, a "mighty lordship") after the "Revolutionary flood." They were the family most centrally involved in the Anti-Renter "wars."[37] Living in Albany or the Albany area from 1830 until 1840, Melville would have known firsthand of the conflict. In waging their guerrilla attacks on the legal authorities, the Anti-Renters assumed a calico "Indian" disguise, allying themselves explicitly with the savage "Indians" of Boston Harbor in 1773; they also allied themselves, by association if not intent, with displaced Native Americans and centuries of struggle over the American land involving the competing interests of colonial, federal, and state governments, Native Americans, large estate holders, entrepreneurs, and poor whites.

When Melville alludes in book 1 to the regular armies sent out to subdue masses of farmers, the remark suggests not only the Anti-Renter resistance of the 1830s and 1840s but also the most notorious class revolt in the early years of the United States: Shays' Rebellion, the 1786–1787 civil and military resistance of small farmers in western Massachusetts to the severe economic measures taken by the state during the postwar depression. In the wake of the unfinished American Revolution, both Hudson Valley and Berkshire County were battlegrounds over economic justice and land ownership. Across Massachusetts in the 1780s and particularly in the western counties, small farmers protested the increasing imprisonment for debt, the spread of peonage, and the levying of heavy taxes. The poor farmers of western Massachusetts, like the tenant farmers of New York, were associated by their enemies with Native Americans. In October 1786, Secretary of War Henry Knox requisitioned federal troops on the pretense that they would be used against Indians in the northwest, but stationed them in Massachusetts in order to quell a different kind of native revolt. As in the case of New York State resistance, in Massachusetts military defeat was followed by legislative victory. Shaysites in the state legislature reformed debt collection and court procedure and reduced the tax burden.[38]

The Berkshires retained personal significance for Melville. He wrote *Pierre* while living on his farm, Arrowhead, in Pittsfield, Massachusetts. (Melville named his property for the Indian relics found on the land.) *Pierre* is dedicated to Mount Greylock in the Berkshires, also known as Mount Saddleback or Saddle Mountain, and Melville used other local features as models for the topography of Saddle Meadows, such as Balance Rock (the "Memnon Stone" in *Pierre*). Like the Hudson River Valley, the Berkshires were a mecca for travelers in search of the picturesque combination of wilderness, pastoral landscape, and civilization. Here, too, the pleasures of viewing were bound up with acts of framing and veiling. Berkshire observers praised the ways in which the sloping topography of the Housatonic River Valley hid mills and factory villages. (In 1851, Melville visited a paper mill at Dalton, Massachusetts, which he made part of the explicit scenery in his 1855 sketch "The Tartarus of Maids.") Both the Berkshires and the Hudson River Valley housed a developing tourist industry and a community of writers and artists who marketed their views. Around Stockbridge and Lenox clustered such figures as Bryant, Sedgwick, Holmes, and Longfellow. The painters Cole, Church, Durand, and Kensett all visited the region and produced Berkshire canvases. Church even transplanted Cole's classic *Oxbow* in his streamlined 1848 *View Near Stockbridge*. Melville's Saddle Meadows is a composite landscape, bringing together the manors, landlords, and tenants of the Hudson River Valley, the visual and verbal lessons of the Hudson River School, and the contested terrain of the Berkshires.[39]

As did those involved in the rebellions in western Massachusetts and eastern New York, Melville associates the possession of land with the exploitation of poor whites and Native Americans. In describing the terms offered to tenant farmers by their Hudson Valley lords, he twice uses the notorious phrases of President Jackson's 1829 "Message" to the Creek Nation. The "Great Father" promised that the Creeks would be able to occupy the Oklahoma land to which they were being banished "as long as grass grows or water runs":

> consider those most ancient and magnificent Dutch Manors at the North, whose perches are miles—whose meadows overspread adjacent counties—and whose haughty rent-deeds are held by their thousand farmer tenants, so long as grass grows and water runs; which hints of a surprising eternity for a deed, and seems to make lawyer's ink unobliterable as the sea. . . . These far-descended Dutch meadows lie steeped in a Hindooish haze; an eastern patriarchalness sways its mild crook over pastures, whose tenant flocks shall there feed, long as their own grass grows, long as their own water shall run.
> (10–11)

Melville's Jackson allusion links the federal displacement of Native Americans in the southeast with the state-supported exploitation of the tenant farmers in the northeast. Both are subject to the sway of the "Great Father." Here, Manifest Destiny is ironically given a legal formula ("fee simples" "cotemporize[d] with eternity"), and the Native American contrast between white and Indian land rights is echoed (spiritual claim as vastly more enduring than legal title). Jackson's promise was masterful: sentimental, hypocritical, paternal, poetic, a pillaging of natural metaphor to sanctify expulsion, a metonymy backed by the full faith of the U.S. government. His phrases were fixed upon and turned back against their owner in several nineteenth-century responses: by the Creek chief Speckled Snake, who, in a speech to his people, sarcastically translated Jackson's message into "Get a little farther; you are too near me" (1829); by Thoreau, at the start of his *A Week on the Concord and Merrimack Rivers* (1849); by Melville, not only in the opening pages of *Pierre* but also in chapter 27 of *Typee* (1846), where he uses Jackson's rhetoric to criticize the French colonial seizure of the Marquesas; and, implicitly, by a long line of Native American orators, who underscored the discrepancy between American words and actions.[40]

The landscape of Saddle Meadows, then, is not merely embellished with images of Pierre's ancestors—"on those hills his own fine fathers had gazed; through those woods, over these lawns, by that stream, along these tangled paths, many a grand-dame of his had merrily strolled when a girl" (8)—nor cloaked in the qualities of "this new Canaan" (33). It is saturated with reminders of those who were dispossessed. Melville's Saddle Meadows is Washington Irving's landscape of "storied and poetical association" represented with a vengeance. Melville provides in his American landscape "the shadowy grandeurs of the past" and "the accumulated treasures of the age" that Irving's Geoffrey Crayon seeks in Europe, but in Saddle Meadows the shadows compete with the grandeurs and the accumulation encumbers the view. "Associations," excessive and violent, circulate through the opening pages of *Pierre:* the colonial struggles between European colonists and Native Americans; the Revolutionary War battle of Fort Stanwix, pitting the American rebels against the English and the Iroquois; the post-revolutionary skirmishes against courts and banks waged by debtor farmers; the Anti-Renter wars between landlords and tenants; and Jackson's forced removal of the Creeks. These associations thicken the atmosphere of Saddle Meadows. They seep into its soil. They point to the past, not to the future. Pierre does not possess the landscape; instead, the land itself is possessed by the specters of the displaced, made intractable by the weight of their stories. Allusion in *Pierre* is a conduit for the historical memory often erased from depictions of the American land. It is a pathway for the reentry of ghosts. Thus we might view *Pierre* as a key text in the literature of insistent memory, an example of an emphatically American gothic.[41]

In "Love, Delight, and Alarm," Pierre takes his betrothed, Lucy, on a phaeton ride over his domain. An extended pun governs this journey: as the ancestral vehicle rolls over the ground of Saddle Meadows, Melville examines the vehicles, tenors, and grounds of the metaphors that shape picturesque views. During this literal and figurative ride on a strange summer morning in the country, figures are stretched to the breaking point. The terms of the book's title—"Love," "Delight," and "Alarm"— are not merely items in a series. They augur the alarming results of the loving and delightful associations invoked during Pierre and Lucy's sightseeing trip, and they suggest the rhetorical technique of unsettling exorbitance that marks *Pierre*.

Pierre and Lucy embark at a particularly liquid time of day: "That morning was the choicest drop that Time had in his vase. Ineffable distillations of a soft delight were wafted from the fields and hills" (32). As the morning elapses, effusions of a more unsavory sort fill the air: "high in heaven you heard the neighing of the horses of the sun; and down dropt their nostrils' froth in many a fleecy vapor from the hills" (35). Toward the end of the outing, warm tears flow from Lucy's "over-charged lids" (36). This morning begins with choice drops and ineffable distillations and ends in nasal drips and seeping eyelids.

During the ride, the narrator delivers a piercing tribute to Nature and Love. Two successive paragraphs begin with the apostrophe "Oh, praised be the beauty of this earth, the beauty, and the bloom, and the mirthfulness thereof!" (32). In Saddle Meadows, to bend one's ear to the music of nature is to risk rupturing the eardrum: "Love has not hands, but cymbals; Love's mouth is chambered like a bugle, and the instinctive breathings of his life breathe jubilee notes of joy!" (33).[42] The narrator continues, breathlessly: "So on all sides Love allures; can contain himself what youth who views the wonders of the beauteous woman-world?" (34). This cacophonous paean to the "new Canaan" (33), in the course of which neither observer nor landscape can contain themselves, is delivered in the isocolon, antithesis, and syntax of a sermon, emphasizing how the American land is gendered, sentimentalized, and sanctified. It is as if the volume in Cole or Willis were turned up to the point of distortion.

Yet it is not only the faculty of hearing that is tested on that green and golden morning, it is also the sense of smell. In a tender exchange, Pierre and Lucy trade compliments:

> On both sides, from the hedges, came to Pierre the clover bloom of Saddle Meadows, and from Lucy's mouth and cheek came the fresh fragrance of her violet young being.
>
> "Smell I the flowers, or thee?" cried Pierre.
>
> "See I lakes, or eyes?" cried Lucy, her own gazing down into his soul, as two stars gaze down into a tarn. (33)

Lucy's natural perfume spills over Pierre. She implies that his eyes hold huge volumes of water, a visual immersion invoked again a couple of pages later, when Pierre risks drowning after he "dives deep down in the Adriatic" of her own eyes (35).

The analogies between facial and landscape features are not accidental or occasional in these sections of *Pierre*. Such analogies structure the representation of character. Lightning forks upward from Pierre's brow. Pierre sees stars and clouds in Lucy's eyes and the seasons in her face. Lucy's eyes contain unparalleled scenic wonders: "All the waves in Lucy's eyes seemed waves of infinite glee to him. And as if, like veritable seas, they did indeed catch the reflected irradiations of that pellucid azure morning; in Lucy's eyes, there seemed to shine all the blue glory of the general day, and all the sweet inscrutableness of the sky" (35). Like Cole's American skies, Lucy's eyes reflect the unique variety and magnificence of America. Lucy is a walking encyclopedia of landscape features—clouds, seasons, waves, seas, lakes, skies. In Melville's picturesque twist on the sentimental effictio, or "fashioning" of a female figure, Lucy is an overstocked embodiment of individual, natural, and national characteristics. The land does not merely lie before Pierre; it rises up and embraces him in the form of an inordinate, geomorphic angel. Pierre declares that a god has decreed his "unchallenged possession" of Lucy. She will be his "inalienable fief" (36).

When Pierre observes the atmospheric effects in Lucy's eyes, he cannot contain himself—or, to be more precise, he cannot contain his eyes—or, to be even more precise, his eyes cannot contain their pupils: "Then would Pierre burst forth in some screaming shout of joy; and the striped tigers of his chestnut eyes leaped in their lashed cages with a fierce delight. Lucy shrank from him in extreme love; for the extremest

top of love, is Fear and Wonder" (35). Here, the pleasures of perception
are rendered disturbing through the insinuating amalgam of adjective
and noun ("screaming shout of joy," "fierce delight," "extreme love").
The love in Pierre's eyes is given a savage shape and appetite. Melville
represents the blinding fulfillment of the picturesque goal of feeling
through the eyes, as Pierre's eager pupils threaten to rupture the aque-
ous humor, tear through the lashes, break out of their ocular confinement, and pounce upon their victim. The extremes are taken to their extremity, as Melville maps the contours of the sublime and ambivalent
peaks of Love.

Melville presents his most telling visual figure immediately after
Pierre and Lucy gaze into one another's eyes. In place of the "loving eye"
or the "hungry eye" or the "dissolving eye," all of which link sight and
desire in a metaphorics of possession, Melville offers the catachrestic
"lovers' eyes" of book 2. In these eyes, the hypnotic transaction between
viewer and object—what Melville calls at the beginning of *Pierre* "the
verdant trance" and "the trance-like aspect of the green and golden
world [of Saddle Meadows]" (3)—is dispelled and the picturesque
optics are strained. As in the other antebellum landscapes we have examined, topographia in *Pierre* is linked with optigraphia, praise of land
with power of vision, but in Melville's "eyes" the visualization of desire
leads to metaphorical overextension and collapse. "'See I lakes, or
eyes?'" asks Lucy, as she gazes down into Pierre, and the answer
Melville gives is neither:

> No Cornwall miner ever sunk so deep a shaft beneath the sea, as Love will
> sink beneath the floatings of the eyes. Love sees ten million fathoms down,
> till dazzled by the floor of pearls. The eye is Love's own magic glass, where
> all things that are not of earth, glide in supernatural light. There are not so
> many fishes in the sea, as there are sweet images in lovers' eyes. In those
> miraculous translucencies swim the strange eye-fish with wings, that some-
> times leap out, instinct with joy; moist fish-wings wet the lover's cheek.
> Love's eyes are holy things; therein the mysteries of life are lodged; looking
> in each other's eyes, lovers see the ultimate secret of the worlds; and with
> thrills eternally untranslatable, feel that Love is god of all. (33)

In terms of nationality, class, and trade, the Cornwall miners would
seem to have no place in Saddle Meadows. Yet Melville represents them
as an integral part of the scene. The Cornwall miners come to tear the
canvas.

As eyes look into eyes in Melville's defamiliarizing passage, the intervening medium is filled with ridiculous creatures. In this heightened and

revealing version of the "loving gaze," the eye is not at all a receptive organ but becomes an active, violating force, and its projections are ab-
surdly literalized. Neither particle nor wave, the "light" from the lover's
eye is composed of "strange eye-fish with wings." The mood is broken
here. The mystifications are materialized. Love's eyes are "holy things,"
Melville insists, after representing them as profane fish ponds. The eye
is "Love's own magic glass," he proclaims, and then he shatters the delicate vessel. Visual penetration is compared to the sinking of mine shafts,
and visual transaction threatens to become a literal "driving through":
when eyes bore into eyes, the shaft, one assumes, must be sunk through
the cornea.

As Melville implies in his linking of the Glendinning phaeton with the
ill-starred Phaeton, Pierre and Lucy's carriage offers an exhilarating,
dangerous ride. Melville heightens the senses of his characters. Noses fill
with liquid. Eardrums distend. Eyes blind. Figures are drawn out to the
point of rupture. From this perspective, we can appreciate the ways in
which meaning is shaped and distorted. During the wild phaeton ride,
Melville mines the grounds of picturesque perception. Metaphorical vehicles unsettle their tenors and the reader feels the force of the impact:
the crash of the striped tigers of Pierre's eyes against their lashed cages,
the thud and splash of the Cornwall miners performing their ocular ex-
cavations, the slap of strange eye-fish with wings against the lover's
cheek.

In the first section of "Nature" (1836), Emerson, too, joins an absurd
visual figure with praise of the landscape. After an exalted account of the
poetic possession of the land ("There is a property in the horizon which
no man has but he whose eye can integrate all the parts, that is, the
poet") and immediately following the assertion that the visual faculty is
the sine qua non of human existence—"In the woods . . . I feel that nothing can befall me in life,—no disgrace, no calamity, (leaving me my
eyes,) which nature cannot repair"—Emerson offers his famous catachresis: "I become a transparent eye-ball. I am nothing. I see all. The
currents of the Universal Being circulate through me; I am part or particle of God." Yet the bizarre physicality of Emerson's "eyeball" does
not interfere with the metaphorical dynamics of the passage. The "transparent eyeball" stands as a desire for all-encompassing vision, for the
removal of barriers to visual participation in the world, for the ultimate "integrity of impression made by manifold natural objects." It
is the strategically preposterous epiphany of Emerson's "occult relation between man and the vegetable." In Melville's figure of the "strange

eye-fish," such an "integrity of impression" is fractured; the "occult relation" is occluded; and the correspondence between viewer and landscape is converted to narcissistic projection. In *Pierre,* the disorders
of antebellum eyes are foregrounded in strained and viscous images.
Melville offers no Pisgah prospect, unlike Emerson, Cole, Willis, Bryant,
and Cooper. The most striking metaphor in *Pierre* describes eyes looking into eyes, in a twisted visual tautology.[43]

In a spectacular passage in "The Ponds" chapter of *Walden* (1854),
Thoreau describes an erotic meeting of gazes. In his "mind's eye,"
Thoreau recalls being seated in a boat on the pond and marveling at the
natural composition of the scene before him: the reflective foreground of
the water, the sculpted shores, the subtle gradations guiding the eye
from the low shrubs at the water's edge back and up to the highest trees.
For Thoreau, this is an intimate moment: "A lake is the landscape's most
beautiful and expressive feature. It is earth's eye; looking into which the
beholder measures the depth of his own nature. The fluviatile trees next
the shore are the slender eyelashes which fringe it, and the wooded hills
and cliffs around are its overhanging brows." In *Walden,* when the
"mind's eye" looks into "earth's eye," neither party blinks. There is
mutual recognition. When the "mind's eye" looks into "earth's eye," it
is love at first sight. When Lucy and Pierre look into each other's
"lakes, or eyes," the scene is not measured in recessional planes. In the
ocular waters of *Pierre,* not fringed but caged by lashes, there swarm
strange eye-fish with wings. In Melville's American scenery, the observer's reverie may be interrupted by a moist touch extending out from
the view.[44]

The phaeton ride ends abruptly, when Pierre and Lucy flee the hills
encircling Saddle Meadows to the level safety of the plains. Fearing that
"too wide a prospect" meets them on the slopes, Lucy insists they de-
scend (38). Lucy's anxieties are spurred by her thoughts about the mysterious face Pierre saw at the Pennie sisters' sewing circle. Remembering,
she loses the inspiration of the morning and sheds some tears. This is the
first of Melville's many references to the "riddle" of Isabel's face (37).
Associated with Europe, with the lordly sins of the fathers, and with illegitimate acts of possession and dispossession, Isabel's features weigh
on Pierre's mind. Under their pressure, the enamel of Saddle Meadows
cracks. The "discovery" of an abandoned sister casts Pierre's patrimony
in a new light. In the picturesque plot of *Pierre,* the onerous associations
of Isabel alter Pierre's views and propel the narrative toward renuncia-
tion, flight, incarceration, and death.

Melville's Saddle Meadows is a Hudson River and Berkshire landscape with a twist, or rather a tilt. From one angle, that is, read from the perspective of explicit statement, it seems simply to celebrate the apotheosized, imperative American land. However, read with attention to the strange stylistic motions, the topography of Saddle Meadows looks quite different from the golden fields of *The Oxbow* or the pliant vistas in *American Scenery*. *Pierre* is not the story of a fall from a golden age to an age of lead, from country to city, from Eden to Tartarus. Rather than a lament about the contemporary generation squandering its noble inheritance, *Pierre* tells the story of how the past suffuses and encumbers the present, how the present is scored over and over with the lines of the past. Pierre is both the heir of the first part of the book and the victim of the second part—the victim, we should say, of his inheritance. And *Pierre* is the anatomy of that inheritance, an exposure of the seams in the construction of Saddle Meadows.

CHAPTER 5

Inscribed Hearts in *Pierre*

Pierre is a victim not only of the landscape inheritance outlined in the opening pages but also of a larger inheritance, a broader education of the feelings represented across the book. If Melville begins by surveying the grounds of Saddle Meadows, he goes on to mine the grounds of Pierre's feelings, "the charred landscape within him." *Pierre* offers an overheated analysis of the production of emotion.[1]

Having focused from *Typee* through *Moby-Dick* on structures of feeling about race, nationalism, and gender, Melville's explicit turn to the feelings in *Pierre* seems logical. Logical, but surprising. The quest for ultimate secrets launched in *Typee* and continued in *White-Jacket* and *Moby-Dick*, which sought its treasure in the figures and bodies of others, ends with an intimate journey into the self. Melville's narrators had revealed themselves during the earlier books. Yet self-exposure, graphic and devastating, is at the core of *Pierre*.

Exploring "deep, deep, and still deep and deeper" into "the heart of a man" (288), Melville finds that the territory has already been mapped. When Isabel tries to convey her distress to Pierre in book 8, Melville provides the reader with a salient spectacle:

> Oh, my dear brother—Pierre! Pierre!—could'st thou take out my heart, and look at it in thy hand, then thou would'st find it all over written, this way and that, and crossed again, and yet again, with continual lines of longings, that found no end but in suddenly calling thee. (158)

This is how the corporeal quest ends in *Pierre:* with a vital organ whose surface is densely inscribed and whose depths are vacant. Melville holds out Pierre's heart to the reader, not "sister" Isabel's or fiancée Lucy's. Melville charts the lines of desire, representing Pierre's constricting development in unfolding discursive registers: the Sentimental, the Gothic, and the Romantic. *Pierre* reels from Melville's recognition that these lines both move and bind.

Pierre is not, as many of its critics would have it, a parody of the sentimental novel. Instead, it is a sentimental text taken to the *n*th degree, elevating to revealing and disturbing proportions the "heart of a man." For Melville's man of feeling, unlike Mackenzie's Harley or Sterne's Yorick or the American Donald Grant Mitchell's Ik. Marvel, the problem lies not in the gap between a vulgar world and exquisite sentiments but in the haunted chambers of his own heart. In a peculiar scene at the end of the book, after Pierre has been jailed for the killing of his cousin Glen, Melville describes a world in which feeling has become alienated and confining: "His immortal, immovable, bleached cheek was dry; but the stone cheeks of the walls were trickling" (360). His flesh petrified and his tear ducts parched, Pierre's prison weeps. In *Pierre*, Melville seeks to read the writing on the walls of nineteenth-century hearts.

In the scenes of reading and writing in *Pierre*, Melville reflects on the production of sentiment and the marketing of literary texts, he expresses doubts about the efficacy of his relationship with his audience, and he reaches the limits of the type of interior critique, the revelation through excess, that he had pursued in the first phase of his writing career. Thus *Pierre* stands as both acme and finale, the text in which Melville most ardently inhabits antebellum discourse and the text whose discoveries prompt his withdrawal from such an enterprise. An anatomy of inscriptions, *Pierre* moves from landscape to heart to Melville's own pages.

SENTIMENT AMERICAN STYLE: THE HEART ON THE PAGE

"Sentiment" in nineteenth-century American culture is a complicated and treacherous object of inquiry. Given the persistent cultural dichotomy between cognition and affect, sentimental analysis has proved conceptually difficult. The term "sentiment" itself is unstable, often detached from its specific contexts, such as eighteenth-century British

moral philosophy or nineteenth-century British and American evangeli-
cism, and often unmoored from its specific referents: maternal and
paternal sentiment, conjugal sentiment, religious sentiment, fraternal
and sororal sentiment, sentiment for the poor or oppressed. Critics often take the term to epitomize a gender (Fred Lewis Pattee, E. Douglas
Branch, Helen Papashvily) or a genre (Herbert Ross Brown) or a politics (Ann Douglas, Jane Tompkins, Philip Fisher). In *The Feminization
of American Culture* (1977), Ann Douglas argues that the "test" that
distinguishes romantic from sentimental self-exaltation is that "[roman-
tic] language, its rhetoric, no matter how strained or foreign to modern
ears, has not . . . 'gone bad'; language, like that of the sentimentalists,
which has utterly capitulated to the drift of its times invariably 'goes
bad.'" Yet this reliance upon a sentimental detector makes twentieth-
century taste the measure of nineteenth-century literary performance.
And the sentimentometer has not yet been invented whose wires would
not tangle and burn under the challenge of a single line from Melville's
Pierre.[2]

Douglas's notion of sentimental surrender has shaped the current debate. She argued that liberal ministers and women, in the roles of both
literary consumers and producers, helped to fashion an anti-intellectual
middle-class culture of the feelings that appeared to contest the emerg-
ing capitalist order but that, in fact, reinforced that order through its
self and class indulgence, its casting of the victims of oppression as martyrs and heroes, and its call for emotional response rather than political
analysis and action. In *Sensational Designs* (1985), Jane Tompkins
countered that female sentimental fiction did not surrender to capitalism but resisted it. According to Tompkins, such fiction offered not a di-
luted compensatory theology but an alternative domestic ideology for
antebellum American women, embracing the opportunities for female
authority in evangelical Protestantism and reversing and inverting male
concepts of power. Douglas's "capitulation" and Tompkins's "power"
have become the two poles in the debate about the function and value
of women's "sentimental" writing. Cast in these terms, the debate has
often sustained the venerable binaries of literary criticism: masculine
versus feminine, self-conscious versus self-indulgent, subversive versus
submissive. While American critics have at last directed serious attention to popular writing by women and to the substance of sentiment,
the choices offered in terms of gender and politics have seemed too
narrow. Critics such as Nina Baym, Mary Kelley, and Cathy Davidson
seek to avoid making such choices; instead, they examine the roles

played by women's writing in the lives of nineteenth-century writers and readers.[3]

Recent efforts to reconstruct the nineteenth-century literary and historical context give us a more complex sense of U.S. culture and loosen the grip of the gender, genre, and style caricatures. David S. Reynolds argues against identifying gender-specific forms of American literature, questioning the dominance of sentimental and socially conservative literature written by women for women. Reynolds discusses the popularity of more sensational genres and the diversity of women's roles in antebellum literature. He observes that several men were prolific and popular authors of sentimental and domestic fiction. Lora Romero characterizes the "feminization of American culture" as the effect of nineteenth-century propaganda and twentieth-century critical back formation, rather than as a historical fact.[4]

Contrary to the stereotypes in either their old or their new forms, antebellum American culture was not polarized between two camps—sentimental and anti-sentimental—and "sentiment" was not a genetically or generically female practice. Instead, both female and male writers participated in an urgent, subtle exchange with their readers, whose aim was to shape a language that would convey the motions and responses of the heart. Stirred by an expanding literary market, writers tested their powers and gauged their influence over their readers. Edgar Allan Poe calibrated his verbal structures in order to achieve emotional "effects" and fantasized that, during the hour of perusal of a short prose narrative, the "soul of the reader [was] at the writer's control." Harriet Beecher Stowe dreamed of a sentimental millennium and she capped the immensely moving contrivance that is *Uncle Tom's Cabin* with the summons to her northern female readers to "feel right." In "Calamus," withdrawn to the margins of a pond, Walt Whitman confided "the scented herbage of my breast" and the "blossoms of my blood." Frederick Douglass interrogated and orchestrated his readers' affect in the versions of his autobiography and in speeches such as "What to the Slave is the Fourth of July?" Donald Grant Mitchell and Fanny Fern, the best-selling sentimentalists of the 1850s whose work I will examine in the following sections, were masters of emotional manipulation. Melville created *Moby-Dick,* the epic novel of shipboard domesticity and titanic male confession ("Ahab never thinks; he only feels, feels, feels"), and *Pierre,* the period's most enthralled ode to sentiment.[5]

By arguing that both men and women shared a sentimental project and that sentiment did not have a categorical conservative or subversive force, I do not mean to deny the gender differences described within the writings of women and men or to deny that texts generated social effects. Instead, I mean to insist that these differences do not divide along the lines of women who practice "sentiment" and men who refuse it. Karen Sánchez-Eppler has described sentimental fiction as "an intensely bodily genre" concerned with both the corporeality of its characters and the physical responses produced in its readers. I will focus on another level of embodiment: the rhetorical procedures and ideological discoveries involved in representing the recesses of the heart on the surface of the printed page. While most late-twentieth-century critics speculate on the responses elicited by sentimental texts, I will analyze the conditions that allow those responses. Mitchell, Fern, and Melville each reflect on sentiment as they practice it; they dissect as they represent.[6]

American sentimentalism of the 1850s comes at a late stage, not only after decades of sentimental response in the United States but also after the heyday of British sentiment and its criticism in the eighteenth century. The best-sellers of the American 1850s tend to follow one of two different strategies. Works such as Susan Warner's *The Wide, Wide World* (1850) and Maria Cummins's *The Lamplighter* (1854) represent their female protagonists' educations in plain styles emphasizing plot and character. The conspicuous narrators of works such as Mitchell's *Reveries of a Bachelor* (1850), Stowe's *Uncle Tom's Cabin* (1852), and Fern's *Ruth Hall* (1855) savor the sentimental exposures of their characters and authors.

In the 1850s, Mitchell, Fern, and Melville each address in different ways the concerns of sentiment: the reciprocal investments of form and feeling, anxieties about sentiment out of proportion to its referent, the gendering of feelings, the distance and proximity between writer and reader, the pleasures and dangers of self-exposure, the adequacy of literary performance. Mitchell's *Reveries of a Bachelor,* Melville's *Pierre,* and Fern's *Ruth Hall* are all partly autobiographical, partly fictional, acutely conventional, and self-reflexive studies of the lines written on and of antebellum hearts. Each writer stages scenes of reading, in which the character's or narrator's receipt of a letter becomes the occasion for the author to meditate on sentimental dynamics and on his or her own literary practice. These tableaux signify the exchanges that the writers envision taking place between themselves and their readers.[7] In *Reveries of a Bachelor* and *Ruth Hall,* both best-sellers, Mitchell and Fern represent scenes of electric contact between writer and reader in which the writer's ability to reproduce the texture of the reader's heart results in a moving embrace. In *Pierre,* a colossal public failure, Melville represents a world tangled in sentimental lines and a scene of reading in which tears, ink, and blood mix and texts are wielded like knives. In *Pierre,* sentimental communion issues in murder and suicide.

MEN OF FEELING: DONALD GRANT MITCHELL'S TREATISES CONCERNING THE SENTIMENTAL AFFECTIONS

Recent American literary critics have tended to forget the prominent mid-nineteenth-century figure of the man of feeling. As in British senti-mentalism, in the United States there were two archetypal figures, the suffering woman and the sensitive man. Sharing the popular literary stage in the 1850s with Susan Warner's Ellen Montgomery and Maria Cummins's Gertie were Donald Grant Mitchell's Ik. Marvel, the delicate young narrator of *Reveries of a Bachelor,* and the daydreaming, uxori-ous husband who narrates George W. Curtis's *Prue and I* (1856). De-scendants of Sterne's Yorick and Irving's Geoffrey Crayon, steeped in nostalgia for lost youth, innocence, and power, the narrators in Mitchell and Curtis describe the predicament of the sensitive man who recoils from the assault of a sordid and materialistic world. The narrators of *Reveries of a Bachelor* and *Prue and I* dilate and examine their re-sponses, anxiously defend their vocations as literate men of feeling, and plead for the significance of reverie in an entrepreneurial society.[8]

Washington Irving, the father of American male sentimentalism, po-sitioned a retreat at the center of his influential *Sketch Book* (1819–1820): a literal retreat into the secluded spaces of "Westminster Abbey," "Bracebridge Hall," "London Antiques," and "Little Britain"; a figura-tive retreat into a comforting English antiquity; and an intellectual re-treat from the "male" arena of interest and ambition to the "female" sphere of the affections. Irving's retreats were vantage points from which he could attempt to gild the harsh world with his imagination. Mitchell and Curtis's narrators speak from such an angle of retreat. They con-struct insular, exquisite realms of affection and they invest in the pow-ers of the imagination not just to gild but to generate their worlds. Mitchell's *Reveries of a Bachelor* consists of four fantasies about mar-riage, women, love, and aging spun out by the young unmarried narra-tor at the fireside and at the graveside. In *Prue and I,* the narrator, a bookkeeper in a worn cravat, offers seven reveries in which he wonders about the measures of manhood in mid-nineteenth-century America: the possession of women, title to great estates, geographical mobility (the topic of two sketches), social performance, illustrious ancestry, and worldly success. Although his mind and his eyes wander, each time Curtis's narrator returns to his true wife, Prue, realizing that domestic space and spousal companionship are the ultimate achievements. Over the seven sketches, the moral is the same, predictable and yet moving: there is no place like home and there is no one like Prue. In his book, Curtis contracts the fictional world to the domestic and sentimental bond between the two title characters: Prue and I. Fantasy offers refuge from the mutable world and recompense for the sacrifices of married life. The withdrawals of Mitchell's bachelor and Curtis's husband are not only spatial, they are also tonal. Although both writers were relatively young when their texts were published (Mitchell was twenty-eight and Curtis thirty-two), they fashioned prematurely aged narrators, sensitive, melancholy male speakers who accepted their diminished physical and practical capacities and reflected on their imaginative satisfactions. In *Reveries of a Bachelor* and *Prue and I,* the sensibilities of youthful bachelorhood and middle-aged matrimony converge.[9]

Mitchell and Curtis project and caress their affect. Their sympathy is directed inward, as they observe their own responses. In analyses of sympathy and conscience that influenced the development of Anglo-American sentimentalism, Adam Smith in *The Theory of Moral Sentiments* described the self theatrically. According to Smith, human benevolence springs from the desire to identify oneself with others and to win and keep their sympathy. The acting self is viewed by a second self, an internal "impartial spectator" who guides and evaluates the self's conduct according to the standards and expectations of others. The "impartial spectator" is a "mirror" or "looking-glass" in which the acting self can view itself "at the distance and with the eyes of other people." The relations between actor and spectator model the behavior and feelings of the self. In the sketches of Curtis and especially of Mitchell, the theatrical dynamics are preserved but reversed. The self watches itself feel without the restraining internalized gaze of others. The self represents itself in the theater of its imagination, enacting its own sentiments for the reader. The self does not monitor itself, but sits back to relish its own performance. The self feels for itself and seeks the reader's communion.[10]

Mitchell and Curtis, the most popular male sentimental writers of the 1850s, wrote sketches rather than extended fictional narratives like those of Warner, Stowe, and Cummins. Given their strategic withdrawal into the constricted, feminized space of the hearth, they rendered themselves ineligible for the typical masculine plots of travel or adventure. Their arrested development thwarted the trajectories of the male and female bildungsroman and the popular narratives of reform. At the fireside, Mitchell and Curtis were left with the fragmentary, subjective form of the literary sketch, which they used to examine their own feelings. The problem, of course, is that their feelings are not their own, not only in Adam Smith's sense that the sentiments are always shaped by external pressures, but also in the sense that cultural arbiters in mid-nineteenth-century America had defined the feelings as the stereotyped property of women. Writing in *Putnam's Monthly,* Fitz-James O'Brien sharply characterized Mitchell's literary project and criticized him for his gender deviation. Acknowledging that Mitchell "writes essentially from the heart . . . continually gazing inward, picking up what he finds there, and displaying it . . . to the world," O'Brien laments his infinite regress. Mitchell "rolls an endless chain of reveries, like the long perspective of receding mirrors, that we see when we place two looking-glasses face to face." O'Brien associates this intricate self-absorption with "the almost feminine delicacy of Mr. Mitchell's nature" and sighs "for the sterner fields of thought that we forsook to join him in his dalliance." In Mitchell's prose, responses are not regulated. The face is not guided by its image. Instead, mirror faces mirror and reflections proliferate.[11]

The impulses to retreat and to dally in Mitchell and Curtis have many sources. Like the "American Renaissance" authors David Leverenz discusses in *Manhood and the American Renaissance,* Mitchell and Curtis diverge from dominant ideas of manhood, particularly from new middle-class ideas about entrepreneurial obligation and competition. They seek to forge intimate bonds with their readers in order to offer alternative styles of manhood and to stake claims to the territory of the feelings. In making the literary sketch a vehicle for emotional exposure, they sought to counter arguments such as those of Tocqueville in *Democracy in America* that "No men are less addicted to reverie than the citizens of a democracy, and few of them are ever known to give way to those idle and solitary meditations which commonly precede and produce the great emotions of the heart."[12]

Mitchell and Curtis were literary insiders who felt outside the mainstream of American male activity. Mitchell published the immensely successful *Reveries of a Bachelor,* the first sketch of which had appeared in the *Southern Literary Messenger* in September 1849, and which then was reprinted in *Harper's New Monthly Magazine* in October 1850. He began the "Editor's Easy Chair" feature in *Harper's* in 1851, the same year in which he brought out a popular sequel of sketches, *Dream Life: A Fable of the Seasons.* He serialized "The Fudge Papers," a satire of New York society, in the *Knickerbocker Magazine* between 1852 and 1854. Curtis was a founder and editor of *Putnam's Monthly,* where he accepted pieces from Melville and Thoreau. He succeeded Mitchell in 1854 as a writer of the "Editor's Easy Chair" column in *Harper's* and wrote for *Putnam's* a series of satiric New York sketches published in 1853 as *The Potiphar Papers,* as well as a series of sentimental and domestic sketches expanded and published as the popular *Prue and I* in 1856. Unlike Hawthorne, Melville, and Whitman, Mitchell and Curtis were not ambivalent about participating in the new literary market; they helped to create it. In seeking to shape the tastes of their readers and to defend the role of the imagination and their own roles as men of literary feeling, they had at their disposal the primary periodical outlets of New York culture.[13]

Hawthorne's *Blithedale Romance* (1852) provides a context for the male sentimentalists' responses that is lacking in the sketches of Mitchell and Curtis. *Blithedale* is another text in which a heavyhearted man retrospectively narrates his withdrawal from the gender turmoil of antebellum society. Hawthorne's Coverdale performs a double retreat, first from town to the rural Blithedale community and then from Blithedale up into his leafy "hermitage." Coverdale worries about powerlessness, vulnerability, and exposure. Setting the novel in a communitarian experiment, thus evoking the dozens of utopian endeavors in the decades before the Civil War and the transcendentalist and then Fourierist Brook Farm in particular, Hawthorne implies that his narrator's anxieties are exacerbated by the range of antebellum efforts to alter traditional structures of male dominance and to reform male and female character. Such efforts are represented in the novel by the feminist challenge of Zenobia, the obsessive institutional reforms of Hollingsworth, the mesmeric manipulations of Westervelt, and the unorthodox living arrangements and multiple, escalating erotic attractions at Blithedale. In these contexts of reform, Hawthorne suggests, it is no wonder that Coverdale wishes to climb up a tree. Confronted with entrepreneurial rivalry and an assault on male authority, the prominent male sentimental narrators of the 1850s—Mitchell's Ik. Marvel, Hawthorne's Coverdale, and Curtis's husband—share an embattled status, a desire to retreat, and an obsession with their own feelings. In *Prue and I,* Curtis's narrator makes the correspondence explicit, writing that Miles Coverdale would be the featured guest at his fantasy banquet of writers and literary characters.[14]

While sympathetic to his narrator's anxieties, Hawthorne, unlike Mitchell and Curtis, is also skeptical about the quality of Coverdale's sympathy and the validity of his projections. In particular, Hawthorne questions Coverdale's irony, his avowed distance from the action of the novel and abilities to evaluate the experience of others and his own experience. Although Coverdale declares himself to be the "calm observer" and "the Chorus in a classic play," Hawthorne presents these theatrical analogies as self-serving. Coverdale's spectatorship is repeatedly described in terms of stage properties. When he inspects Zenobia and Priscilla's boarding house, his views are literally framed and curtained. Zenobia tells Coverdale that he makes an "opera-glass of [his] imagination" when he looks at women. Coverdale, and Hawthorne himself, worry about the distorting lens of interpretation. (Coverdale's qualms neither prevent him from proceeding with his "fancy-work" nor cause him to withhold his ultimate, evasive confession of love for Priscilla.) As Coverdale watches himself, his feelings seem to be scripting his judgments, inverting the authority established in Adam Smith's scene. Coverdale's two selves do not preserve Smith's defining and regulating distance but, instead, collapse into self absorption and deception. By the time Coverdale announces, at the beginning of chapter 17, that he is "a devoted epicure of [his] own emotions," Hawthorne has already raised grave doubts about his narrator's taste.[15]

Melville evaluates the male sentimentalists' retreat in several sketches published in the mid-1850s in the same literary periodicals that brought out Mitchell and Curtis. In "Bartleby, the Scrivener," published in *Putnam's* in November and December 1853, Melville represents the bachelor lawyer narrator's sequence of responses to the passive copyist who disrupts his "eminently *safe*" life and whose "wonderful mildness" not only "disarms" but also "unmans" the narrator. Exhausting the available sentimental resources, moving from moral complacency to fraternal melancholy to fear and denial to nervous resentment to charity to rejection, the lawyer is thwarted in his attempts to reach the scrivener. Having failed in all his efforts to represent Bartleby in his imagination, he becomes haunted by the limits of his own sympathy. In "The Paradise of Bachelors and the Tartarus of Maids," published in April 1855 in *Harper's*, Melville tears the paper-thin walls insulating the delicate bachelors from the laboring maids. In "I and My Chimney," published in *Putnam's* in March 1856, the besieged male narrator, "a dozy old dreamer," fights to protect his beloved structure from being remodeled or dismantled at the zealous hands of his reform-minded wife and daughters. The few critics who discuss the relationship between these sketches and the male sentimentalists of the 1850s argue that Melville covertly parodied his models, concealing his hostility toward figures such as Mitchell and Curtis and toward his imagined reader, the "superficial skimmer of pages," beneath a veneer of geniality. Yet these sketches are steeped in male sentimentalism, drawing upon its points of view, its sensibilities, its scenes of domestic retreat, and its emotional props. Melville participates in the anatomy of male feelings and in Mitchell's punning attachment to male anatomy; he criticizes the gesture of retreat; he worries, like Hawthorne, about the deforming power of the imagination; and he shares male sentimentalist anxieties about female labor in the multiple senses of work, reform, and reproduction. These anxieties are registered in "The Tartarus of Maids" in the infernal characterizations of female work and also in the lurid violence of the protracted analogy between bloody, barren landscape and the female reproductive system.[16]

If it is clear that Mitchell and Curtis appropriate the domestic spaces, cloistered poses, and regard for the affections that were associated with middle-class women, the motives and effects of these appropriations remain to be explored. Certainly Mitchell and Curtis sought to profit from the popular interest in female sentimental scenes and formulas. In a scene of breathtaking gender assumption in *Reveries of a Bachelor,* Mitchell's narrator weaves the tale of a young man trapped in a loveless arranged marriage who hides his emotions, endures his calculating, flirtatious wife, and wastes away, unfulfilled, as a tear drops from his repentant spouse's eyes, too late. Yet to consider *Reveries of a Bachelor* merely an act of theft would be to accept the claim that the feelings were psychologically and literarily the property of women and to forget the enduring model of Irving's *Sketch Book* and the genre of male and female sentimental sketchbooks it helped to inaugurate. Mitchell participated in the widespread project of sentimental exposure. He, Fern, and Melville all address questions about who "owns" the feelings.[17]

Mitchell's *Reveries of a Bachelor* is not simply a retreat into the personal and subjective nor the act of an "overtly emasculated and covertly vengeful" male persona, as Douglas argues.[18] Mitchell's book is part of an imaginative effort, shared by male and female writers, to make the personal public and to scrutinize the subjective. As Fanny Fern will do in the pages of *Ruth Hall,* Mitchell shamelessly confesses and exhibits his ability to move readers by manipulating conventional plots, characters, scenes, and props, and he forges an intimate bond between writer and reader. In *Reveries of a Bachelor,* whose subtitle is *A Book of the Heart,* Mitchell takes the reader on a backstage tour of his sentimental production. This exposé enhances, rather than diminishes, his performance.

Across the four reveries that constitute the book, Mitchell examines aspects of feeling. In the first three, each of which is staged by a hearth, he conjures up a series of scenes based on the associations between fire and feeling. In the first reverie, "Over a Wood Fire," which takes place in a country farmhouse, the narrator's reflections on marriage are enkindled by contemplating the phases of flame: smoke (doubt), blaze (cheer), and ashes (desolation). In the second reverie, "By a City Grate," Marvel thinks about women as he watches the two different flames produced by sea-coal and anthracite (the flirt and coquette versus a woman with a true and earnest heart). The fantasies in the first part of this reverie are extinguished when the maid enters and pours her pan of anthracite on the fire. Although this violent gesture is given to the maid and directed at the images of the flirt and the coquette, the responsibility for it rebounds on Marvel, not only because of his role as the self-conscious choreographer of the scene but also because the artful sentiment for which the flirt is punished is the arch transgression of the narrator himself. The third reverie, "Over His Cigar," takes place before the fire at the house of the narrator's forty-year-old, unmarried Aunt Tabithy. Marvel succeeds in winning her permission to smoke his cigar on her front porch by demonstrating the usefulness and richness of a cigar for producing uplifting reveries about boyhood love, youthful love, and the love match.

The fourth and final reverie, "Morning, Noon, and Evening," which forms the second half of the book, departs from the elaborate fire analogies. Having sold the family farmhouse, Marvel returns to the country to visit his old haunts. Sitting down on a bench in the cemetery beside the graves of ancestors and friends, he writes a story describing the life of a man ("Paul"), which unfolds according to the stages of the day. This extended reverie is a *Pilgrim's Progress* for the 1850s sentimental Christian rather than the seventeenth-century Puritan. An allegory of life's voyage, it is intensely conventional and remarkably moving. Marvel's relentlessly projected and withheld future is finally realized in the present with a comforting marriage and faith in the consolations of an afterlife. The domestic and sympathetic spaces finally have been filled.

Yet at the end of the book, Mitchell twists open the narrative once more: it was all a dream. The narrator Marvel, who is not the protagonist of "Morning, Noon, and Evening," takes his gun, his shot-pouch, and his dog, and he departs into the sunset: "I dreamed pleasant dreams that night;——for I dreamed that my Reverie was real" (298). Such an ending, whose pleasures eclipse those of wife, home, and heaven, reestablishes the writer's power to produce feeling in the absence of experience. Such an ending clears the space for the infinite exercise of this authority. In fact, Mitchell's next book, *Dream Life: A Fable of the Seasons* (1851), begins where *Reveries* stopped, opening with the line: "–Pshaw!–said my Aunt Tabithy,–have you not done with dreaming?" Marvel's magic is that there is no end to reverie.[19]

Reveries of a Bachelor doesn't "end" in the sense that the characters succeed or fail or die or live happily ever after. Instead, Mitchell's plot, the story he takes up in *Dream Life,* the same story he tells over and over again, is about his own incessant sentimental manipulations. At the beginning of the "Sea-Coal" section of the second reverie, the narrator encourages his male readers to produce their own reveries:

> Or if your feelings are touched, struck, hurt, who is the wiser, or the worse, but you only? And have you not the whole skein of your heart-life in your own fingers to wind, or unwind, in what shape you please? Shake it or twine it, or tangle it, by the light of your fire, as you fancy best. He is a weak man who cannot twist and weave the threads of his feeling—however fine, however tangled, however strained, or however strong—into the great cable of Purpose, by which he lies moored to his life of Action. (67)

Unraveling the cliché of "heart-strings," Mitchell recommends the pleasures of dilating and caressing feelings. In *Dream Life,* he explicitly characterizes this sentimental exposure as an alternative to the "curdled affections" (24) of masculinity and to social pressures that insist on "the isolation, the unity, the integrity of manhood" (208) and that insist that manhood be "integral, fixed, perfect" (205). He asks for a wider latitude of response and for other measures of satisfaction than those offered by the standards of entrepreneurship and heterosexuality. "It is true there is but one heart in man to be stirred," he argues in the introduction to *Dream Life,* "but every stir creates a new combination of feeling, that like the turn of a kaleidoscope will show some fresh color, or form" (18). The "threads" of manly feeling may be strong, but they also may be fine, tangled, or strained. It is these latter qualities that Mitchell examines, insisting that they, too, are part of the masculine fiber. In the final turn of the "heart-strings" metaphor in the *Reveries* passage, Mitchell's narrator urges his male readers to weave their sentimental strands into the great cable of manly Purpose. Yet this gesture seems a lagniappe thrown by a narrator anxious about the reception of his unorthodox advice. The moorings that most interest Mitchell do not bind man to Purpose or Purpose to Action, but tie man to man and, in the operative trope of this passage, man to his own sexual organ.

Something crucial has been missing from my account of the reveries in Mitchell's books. Along with Whitman in the 1850s, in the poems that would come to be titled "Song of Myself" and "Crossing Brooklyn Ferry," Mitchell is a master of the rhetoric of "I" and "you," the intimate choreography between writer and implied reader. In the first three sketches of *Reveries of a Bachelor,* Mitchell's narrator shuttles confidentially between the first and second persons. In his emotional tableaux— mourning over a lost son and wife, savoring the self-possession that comes with the possession of wife and home, lamenting an empty marriage—the narrator does not represent his own exclusive feelings. Instead, he stages scenes, imagines the responses he shares with his readers, and then voices these responses in the reflected aspect of the second person.

Here, for example, is the narrator's comment on the plight of the young man trapped in a loveless marriage:

> And is this the intertwining of soul, of which you had dreamed in the days that are gone? Is this the blending of sympathies that was to steal from life its bitterness; and spread over care and suffering, the sweet, ministering hand of kindness, and of love? Aye, you may well wander back to your bachelor club, and make the hours long at the journals, or at play—killing the flagging lapse of your life! . . . Never suffer your Charlotte to catch sight of the tears which in bitter hours, may start from your eye; or to hear the sighs which in your times of solitary musings, may break forth sudden, and heavy. Go on counterfeiting your life, as you have began. It was a nice match; and you are a nice husband! (141)

Assuming the customary female position, the male narrator gains title to his feelings of disenchantment, discomfort, and resentment. He establishes a bond with both a male and a female "you" suffering under a sense of constraint. In passages like these, the "you" is multiply figured. It is the narrator's second self, projected and separated, performing before him and the object of his empathy. The "you" is also the narrator's audience, cast as both spectator and actor. The "I" enunciates the "you"; the "you" is scripted into the "I." Such splittings and enmeshings of subjects and objects enable Mitchell's sentimental exchanges.

Discussing Mitchell's acts of calculated sincerity, Wayne R. Kime describes his texts as compositions "in an almost musical sense," "modulating the reader's responses with deft ease." Mitchell's skillful, moving displays reached a wide audience. *Reveries of a Bachelor* was popular not only among female readers—the presumed audience, then and now, for sentimental literature—but also among young men.[20]

As Whitman will do in the long poem first published in the 1855 edition of *Leaves of Grass* and later titled "Song of Myself," Mitchell seeks in the early 1850s to bring his readers to themselves and to extend the range and reach of sentiments. Both writers insist that between the "I" and the "myself" lies the "you." Both assume that the reader will recognize himself or herself in their pronouncements. Mitchell's Marvel is more decorous than Whitman's speaker and more agitated about the prospect of physical intimacy. Both Mitchell and Whitman need the "you" to substantiate their personae, not just because, like all authors in the marketplace, they need customers, but also because they define their literary performances as a mingling of roles and an exchange of sentiments, a mutual exposure.

In *Dream Life,* Mitchell describes his primary rhetorical gesture with a touch of what we have come to regard as Whitmanian hyperbole:

> It has very likely occurred to you, my reader, that I am playing the wanton in these sketches;—and am breaking through all the canons of the writers, in making YOU my hero.
>
> It is even so; for my work is a story of those vague feelings, doubts, passions, which belong more or less to every man of us all; and therefore it is, that I lay upon your shoulders the burden of these dreams. If this or that one, never belonged to your experience,—have patience for a while. I feel sure that others are coming, which will lie like a truth upon your heart; and draw you unwittingly—perhaps tearfully even—into the belief that YOU are indeed my hero. (120)

Like Whitman, Mitchell sings not of arms and the man or of man's first disobedience but of the intimacy between "I" and "you." You are my hero, Mitchell whispers into his reader's ear. Although Mitchell's gesture is not unprecedented (the sentimental prose epic had been written in the Anglo-American tradition since Richardson), *Reveries of a Bachelor* and *Dream Life* do mark a period of explicit sentimental exposure and urgently sought exchange. Mitchell's narrator reassures his reader, here figured as male, that he will recognize feelings that belong to him. If at first he doesn't see one that he likes, he should be patient until Mitchell has displayed his entire stock. What I feel you shall feel, asserts Mitchell, for every feeling belonging to me as good belongs to you.

Mitchell shares with his implied male readers elaborate double entendres often dealing with masturbation. Invoking a long line of sentimental men attached to their pipes and cigars, Mitchell in *Reveries* enjoys the sexual overtones. A cigar is Ik. Marvel's main prop in the third reverie. He flourishes it at the beginning and end of each of the three narratives he spins for his Aunt Tabithy. It punctuates his accounts of frustrated heterosexual love. If Marvel satisfies his Aunt Tabithy's desire for moral narratives, then she will leave him alone to enjoy his cigar. The cigar suggests the allure of narrative and also physical manipulations. As G. J. Barker-Benfield points out, in mid-nineteenth-century American tracts on male sexuality, such as the popular advice manuals of the Reverend John Todd, "revery" was commonly, and negatively, associated with masturbation. In such a context, it is hard to imagine that Mitchell did not intend his readers to view his paeans to sentimental retreat and self-absorption as a winking invitation: "And have you not the whole skein of your heart-life in your own fingers to wind, in what shape you please? Shake it or twine it, or tangle it, by the light of your fire, as you fancy best." As Melville does in *Redburn* and *Moby-Dick,* Mitchell in *Reveries* employs the double entendre as a counterstroke to calls for disciplined, productive manly activity. When Marvel tells his Aunt Tabithy and his implied male readers the tale of the young man who is trapped in a loveless marriage and living a counterfeit life, and who longs to return to his bachelor club, Mitchell suggests feelings and practices that his culture discredits.[21]

Mitchell tightens his bond with his implied male readers at the expense of his implied female readers. In *Reveries of a Bachelor,* he clears a space for male affect by assuming conventional female scenes, plots, and positions, and by conjuring and then extinguishing women in a burst of flame or a cloud of smoke or under a pan of coal or by the more usual narrative means of a "natural" death. When describing his audience, Mitchell subordinates rather than excludes female readers. At the beginning of *Dream Life,* the narrator distinguishes between an imagined male reader, an "indulgent friend" whom he "button-hole[s]" in a "garrulous humor," and a female reader, before whom his gestures are extravagantly innocent and mannered (29–30). Marvel must perform for Aunt Tabithy to earn his peace, but his most heartfelt addresses are made "to every man of us all" (120). Aunt Tabithy may be a difficult audience, tidy and practical, but she is susceptible to his reverie spinning.

She sheds a tear after his final tableau, and permits him to smoke. Mitchell figures two other kinds of female reader in *Reveries,* one negative and one positive. In the "Smoke—Signifying Doubt" sketch, the narrator envisions being married to a bluestocking with a "sluttish" "ink stain on the fore finger" who takes literature so seriously that she neglects her family and soils his treasured copy of Tasso with baby gruel (27). In the "Anthracite" sketch, he sees a sculpted wife sitting by the fire whose charms are highlighted by the slim sentimental gift-book she holds in her hand: "The arm, a pretty taper arm, lies over the carved elbow of the oaken chair; the hand, white and delicate, sustains a little home volume that hangs from her fingers. The forefinger is between the leaves, and the others lie in relief upon the dark embossed cover" (87). This female reader, whose textual pleasures may be especially gratifying, as Mitchell's description implies, is as delicate and ornamented as the volume she reads. Yet as a model of affection and attention, this imagined reader is too static.

In *Reveries,* Mitchell represents the dynamic contact he seeks with his readers in the exchange of letters. At the beginning of the second chapter, he explains that the appearance of the first reverie, "Smoke, Flame, and Ashes," in the *Southern Literary Messenger* produced sympathetic letters from female and male readers who had "seen a heart in the Reverie" and had "felt that it was real, true" (55). He cherishes these notes and delivers an ode to epistles:

> Blessed be letters!—they are the monitors, they are also the comforters, and they are the only true heart-talkers! . . . there you are, with only the soulless pen, and the snow-white, virgin paper. Your soul is measuring itself by itself, and saying its own sayings . . . nothing is present, but you and your thought. . . . Utter it then freely—write it down—stamp it—burn it in the ink!——There it is, a true soul-print! . . . heart-talk blazing on the paper. (53–54)

The defining units of sentimental narrative in Richardson and much subsequent eighteenth-century fiction, letters carry a generic charge and emotional force that Mitchell, Fern, and Melville all harness and analyze. As will Fern in *Ruth Hall* and Melville in *Pierre,* Mitchell in *Reveries* takes the personal letter as a synecdoche for the transaction between writer and reader. In Mitchell's scene, the "soulless" pen is a conduit for the flow from the heart through the fingers and onto the unmarked surface of the page (a "virgin" paper, as Mitchell figures it, without "sluttish" stains of ink). Writing is a private performance, in which the soul gauges and articulates itself. The soul prints itself on the surface of the paper, whose characters preserve the clarity and bite of the writer's responses. Through these acts of correspondence, the page blazes and the ink burns with feeling that is communicated to the reader.[22]

Mitchell is grateful for readers who complete the sentimental circuit, who write back to him expressing how they were stirred by his pages: the mother who shed many tears over his description of losing his son, the "young, fresh, healthful girl-mind" who believed in the truthfulness of his "love-picture"; the father who laid down the book in tears (54–55). Mitchell does not describe responses from the audience he most earnestly addresses in *Reveries,* the young men who are, or whom he hopes to render, men of feeling. This omission may result from the lack of such letters (thus proving the necessity for his sensitizing literary project) or from their privacy. Mitchell does represent another kind of response, from a male reader who is indifferent to Mitchell's charms. This "cold critic" (57) does not see a heart in his reverie and does not feel that it is real and true. Such critics question Mitchell's eloquent melancholy over a lost son and wife, neither of whom ever existed. They object to his impersonations. They resist the congress of the "I" and the "you." They refuse to buy his sentimental product.

In response to such critics, Mitchell delivers an impassioned defense of his literary endeavors and of the market for feelings:

> What matters it pray, if literally, there was no wife, and no dead child, and no coffin in the house? Is not feeling, feeling; and heart, heart? Are not these fancies thronging on my brain, bringing tears to my eyes, bringing joy to my soul, as living, as anything human can be living? What if they have no material type—no objective form? All that is crude,—a mere reduction of ideality to sense,—a transformation of the spiritual to the earthly,—a levelling of soul to matter. (53)

In this treatise concerning the sentimental affections, Mitchell justifies his responses as the valid product of the motions of his mind. Like Jonathan Edwards defending the religious affections of the Great Awakening, Mitchell insists that intense thoughts materially affect the body, apart from the judgments and facts of the world. Unlike Edwards, Mitchell asserts the primacy of human consciousness and he is unconcerned about discriminating between true and false affections. Not God's grace but human "fancies" transform the human heart. For Edwards, the degree of response was not necessarily a sign of truth. For Mitchell, and for many contemporary male and female sentimentalists, ardor was proof enough. Mitchell's tautological question—"Is not feeling, feeling; and heart, heart?"—indicates the closed, self-confirming structure of his system. Against his critics, he adduces letters from readers who have been altered by his words. According to Mitchell, the responses of readers and writers validate one another. You can't argue with effects, he claims. You can't argue with success. In answer to the cold critic who will say "'it was artfully done,'" Mitchell answers, "A curse on him!—it was not art: it was nature" (57). Heart naturally responds to heart and feelings circulate. Words have the power to carry this charge. Sentiment moves in mysterious ways.[23]

According to Mitchell, carping critics misunderstand the sentimental transaction when they impugn his credibility by pointing to the absence of mundane causes for his responses. His fancies need not have a material type or an objective form because they have a conventional form. The death of a child, the loss of a wife, the coffin in the parlor—these scenes, played again and again in the home, on the stage, and in the pages of books, have a cultural resonance for him and for his readers, whether or not he or they have actually experienced them. Form gathers meaning and produces feeling.

In one of the opening sections of *Dream Life*, "With My Reader," Mitchell confronts the critics who have labeled *Reveries* "an arrant piece of imposture" (26) and he extends his defense of the veracity of sentiment. These critics are among the "thousands of mole-eyed people, who count all passion in print—a lie" (24). They are fearful of themselves being subject to sentimental scrutiny, of having their own "emotions unriddled" and their own "heart[s] laid bare" (24–25). The debate between Mitchell and his critics is an instance of the larger concern in the mid-nineteenth century about the unstable boundaries in popular culture between feeling and action, the imagined and the true, and the hypocritical and the sincere. In "With My Reader," Mitchell declares his allegiances. He asserts that "if I have made the feeling real, I am content that the facts should be false" (15). The question of whether his scenes are true is "an impertinent one" (26). He tells his critics that readers should have "Faith," instead of probing for facts (28). In this theology of sentiment, Mitchell insists that his readers must rely on the evidence of things felt. He is not retailing his autobiography or submitting an "affidavit" (26), he is offering sentimental communion.[24]

In *Dream Life*, Mitchell supplements his theology with a semiotics of sentiment:

A single affection may indeed be true, earnest, and absorbing; but such an one after all, is but a type—and if the object be worthy, a glorious type—of the great book of feeling: it is only the vapor from the cauldron of the heart,

and bears no deeper relation to its exhaustless sources, than the letter which
my pen makes, bears to the thought that inspires it. (17)

The printing terms here link sentiment with its technology. Pens, letters,
type, books: these are the means through which sentiment is circulated.
Single affections are but characters in the book of common feeling, types
of the heart, which is the ultimate anti-type. Of this "rare storehouse,"
no one can say that "he has exhausted the stock of its feeling" (17–18).
Mitchell depicts the heart as a magnificent volume, a steaming cauldron,
and a boundless storehouse, and he has previously depicted it as a ball
of yarn, with a metaphorical overload that also will characterize the cor-
dial figures of Fern and Melville. Mitchell meditates on the dissemination of feeling: "One train of deep emotion cannot fill up the heart: it ra-
diates like a star, God-ward and earth-ward. It spends and reflects all
ways. Its force is to be reckoned not so much by token, as by capacity"
(17). Again, he insists that feeling is not tied to a specific referent; it
spreads out, up, down, and across, forming sentimental networks; it is
measured by its reach.

In *Reveries of a Bachelor,* the shifts of mood from sketch to sketch,
the asymptotic narratives, the slides from signifier to signifier, and the
canny handling of convention generate feeling and help to invest the
flimsy structures of plot and character with affect. The narrator basks in
his web of feeling, winding and unwinding the "skein of his heart-life"
(67) in his fingers, manufacturing reveries, playing upon heartstrings,
enmeshing his readers. What Mitchell writes in *Reveries of a Bachelor*
about the texts of the British man of feeling Henry Mackenzie is also
true of his own sentimental productions: "your eye, in spite of you, runs
over with his sensitive griefs, while you are half-ashamed of his success
at picture-making" (66). Such recognitions about the potent and inex-
haustible stock of feeling will cause Fern to revel and Melville to balk.

A LITTLE HALF-WORN SHOE:
FANNY FERN'S EMOTIONAL INVESTMENTS

Recent critics of Sara Willis Parton's *Ruth Hall: A Domestic Tale of the
Present Time* (1855), written under the pen name Fanny Fern, and of her
anthologies of newspaper articles, *Fern Leaves from Fanny's Port-Folio*
(1853, second series 1854), have been intrigued by the rhetorical maneuverings in these texts and, in particular, by the shifts between "sentiment" and "satire." The 1853 *Fern Leaves* is divided into two untitled
parts, the first consisting of sketches on sentimental themes (abandoned

women, religious moods, caring for and training children, losing children to early deaths, the pleasures of home). This part constitutes three-quarters of the book and is followed by sketches that satirize social hypocrisy, gender inequalities and double standards, and the corrupt, pretentious, male-dominated New York City literary world. The 1854 *Fern Leaves* contains longer pieces in a wider variety of genres (scenes, soliloquies, narratives, reflections). In this second collection, sentimental and satiric sketches are mixed together, rather than separated, and the persona behind the sketches, "Fanny," is more sustained and strategic. *Ruth Hall*, like *Pierre*, is the partly autobiographical story of a protagonist's journey from country to city and baptism in the New York City literary market place, a story in which sentimental, satiric, and literary plots are intertwined; yet unlike Pierre, Ruth is successful in publishing her magnum opus and in playing the marketplace game.

The details in *Ruth Hall* closely parallel the details of Parton's own life. Ruth marries Harry Hall, a financially irresponsible young man who dies leaving her and her children without money (as did Parton's first husband, Charles Eldredge). She is subjected to the hostility of her father, her in-laws Mr. and Mrs. Zekiel Hall (Hezekiah and Mary Eldredge), who treat a dependent widow as an embarrassment and burden, and her vain and venal brother Hyacinth (modeled on Parton's famous brother, the editor and writer Nathaniel Parker Willis), who rejects her literary aspirations. Ruth struggles to support her family, and eventually allies herself with a sympathetic editor and publisher, John Walter of the *Household Messenger* (in Parton's life, Oliver Dyer of the *Musical World and Times*). She ultimately conquers an antagonistic male literary establishment, gaining profitable renown, under the pseudonym "Floy," as a controversial writer who boldly speaks her mind. Sharply written, exposing Parton's well-known family to ridicule, and aggressively marketed by the publisher Mason Brothers, *Ruth Hall* became a scandalous best-seller.[25]

Taking their cues from Fern's own statements about the necessity for female "stratagem" and "cunning" in a man's world, critics have articulated a split between satiric and sentimental registers in Fern's writing, disagreeing about its effects. Ann Douglas diagnoses an "artistic schizophrenia" in *Fern Leaves*, a confused shuttling between "the sentimental and the mischievously Satanic" and an awkward employment of sentiment to criticize the limits of a sentimental culture. Douglas sees this split utilized, if not healed, in *Ruth Hall*, in what she characterizes as a shift from sentiment to satire across the narrative. In separate essays,

Nancy Walker and Zita A. Dresner take Douglas's terms and make dia-
metrically opposed arguments about the strategies in *Fern Leaves*. For
Walker, Fern offers satire as an antidote to the sentimental powerlessness represented in the first three-quarters of *Fern Leaves*. For Dresner,
Fern uses both sentiment and satire in *Fern Leaves* in order to fashion a
new domestic woman, extending her reforming influence into the public sphere. Joyce W. Warren keenly analyzes the formal experiments in
Ruth Hall, the abrupt tonal changes and breaks across chapters, the
shifting points of view, and the vibrant understatement. Warren argues
that Fern "had thrown off the straitjacket of convention." She endorses
Douglas's view of the book as moving from sentiment to satire. Susan K.
Harris invokes Douglas's split, but she argues that Fern strategically de-
ployed her stances. Harris describes Fern as using a sentimental voice in
order to disguise her unorthodox portrayal of a female protagonist who
becomes physically, emotionally, and financially independent through
the force of her will and her words.[26]

Yet the hierarchy of "satire" over "sentiment" is a critical effect
rather than an accurate account of rhetorical practice in *Ruth Hall*. Only
in the first series of *Fern Leaves* does Fern separate her sentimental and
satiric pieces, and when she does so, she emphasizes the former. *Ruth
Hall* does not contain two distinct voices, one literal and the other
ironic, one benighted and the other clear-sighted, one inside and the
other outside prevailing ideas about femininity. Instead, Fern demonstrates the variety and suppleness of sentimental positions. She shows
the confinements of conjugal and parental attachments, invigorates maternal, sororal, and theological affections, and extends her readers' feelings in unaccustomed directions.

"Irony" here is not the achievement of a superior stance on "convention" but a sign of the critical distance within sentimentalism: the space
between the self who observes and the self who performs feelings, the
space in which feelings are displayed as common possessions and into
which the reader is drawn. These distances and doublenesses characterize sentimental texts and are foregrounded in Fern's flourishes. They are
signs of the theatrical dynamics of sentiment rather than the "artistic
schizophrenia" described by Douglas. When Ruth visits a phrenologist
at the urging of her friend John Walters, the professor tells her that her
predominance of the reflective over the perceptive intellect would make
her an excellent actress. Fern has her protagonist properly demur, citing
a puritan displeasure at the prospect of such base exposure. Yet despite
the character's and writer's disclaimers, *Ruth Hall* is a sentimental tour

de force. (The phrenological chapter is a way for Fern to place her fully developed head on display while insisting that she has "not the slightest faith in the science.")[27] For Fern, convention is more than a "strait-jacket." It is a constricting garment but also an often-sustaining garment and a network of possibilities in which to maneuver. She harbors no "White-Jacket" illusions that this ideological apparel can be cast off. Fern's texts challenge the inert categories of much recent criticism on "sentiment," "convention," and "subversion," with its metaphors of divestment and disguise. Fern wears her heart on her sleeve.[28]

Fern's range and control are vivid in an early chapter of the book. Ill after the birth of her first child, Ruth is subjected to the emotional tyranny of her mother-in-law, who complains about Ruth's having agreed to the hiring of a servant girl:

> "Pooh! pshaw! stuff! no such thing. You are well enough, or will be, before long. Now, there's a girl's board to begin with. Servant girls eat like boa-constrictors. Then, there's the soap and oil she'll waste;—oh, the thing isn't to be thought of; it is perfectly ruinous. If you hadn't made a fool of Harry, he never could have dreamed of it. You ought to have sense enough to check him, when he would go into such extravagances for you, but some people *haven't* any sense. Where would all the sugar, and starch, and soap, go to, I'd like to know, if we were to have a second girl in the house? How long would the wood-pile, or pitch-kindlings, or our new copper-boiler last? And who is to keep the back gate bolted, with such a chit flying in and out?"
>
> "Will you please hand me that camphor bottle?" said Ruth, laying her hand upon her throbbing forehead.
>
> "How's my little snow-drop to-day?" said Harry, entering Ruth's room as his mother swept out; "what ails your eyes, Ruth?" said her husband, removing the little hands which hid them.
>
> "A sudden pain," said Ruth, laughing gaily; "it has gone now; the camphor was too strong."
>
> Good Ruth! brave Ruth! Was Harry deceived? Something ails *his* eyes, now; but Ruth has too much tact to notice it.
>
> Oh Love! thou skillful teacher! learned beyond all the wisdom of the schools. (27)

In this carefully paced and spaced scene, Fern assays her characters' sentiments. The movement from paragraph to paragraph describes the dilemma of Ruth, in unpronounced pain, caught between her mother-in-law's pinched self-indulgence and her husband's myopia. Fern focuses on the ways in which Harry's endearment, complete with diminutive pet name—"How's my little snow-drop to-day?"—becomes cruel in the context of the strained affections and relations in the Hall household.

Speaking the lines of a devoted husband, Harry deepens Ruth's confinement. In this scene, Fern shows how his diminutive diminishes Ruth,
how conjugal sentiment can blind and bind. (Fern is always interested in
detailing how context shapes the ways in which sentiment is expressed
and received.) Several of Fern's periodical essays attend to clichés, using
a piece of conventional wisdom overheard or read to unfold the sexism
of syntax and diction.[29]

Fern does not explicitly reprove Harry; instead, she skewers him in
the movements from sentence to sentence and across the paragraph
breaks. Fern often combines transition, juxtaposition, and ellipsis to
evaluate sentiment and to validate her portrayal of Ruth's inner world.
Harry's obliviousness, Mrs. Hall's contracted heart, Hyacinth's postur-
ing—the shallowness of these characters is communicated through
spare, revealing dialogue and in choreographed contrast with the narrator's and protagonist's emotional depth. The intervals between words,
sentences, paragraphs, chapters—Fern points to these and fills them
with meaning. They become spaces of implied authorial comment and
understood exchange between writer and reader. Thus much of the writing and the reading of *Ruth Hall* takes place between the lines. In the
sickroom scene, Ruth inflicts her discomfort on herself. She feels the effects of her submission to her mother-in-law and husband and her re-
pression of anger in the throbbing headache that she develops. The scene
culminates in Fern's ambiguous apostrophe to the self-effacing lessons of
"Love!" whose tactful instructions Ruth will learn to transgress.[30]

In her essays and in *Ruth Hall,* Fern portrays the periodical editors
who shape New York literary culture as the members of a boys' club
who stroke each other's egos, pander to wealthy patrons and the religious press, profit from their opinions, and exclude women. In a sketch
entitled "Editors," Fern gives her readers a glimpse into such male
precincts:

> They go down to the office in the morning,—after a careful toilette and
> a comforting breakfast,—make up a fire in the stove hot enough to roast
> an Icelander, "hermetically seal" every door and window, put on a pair of
> old slippers, light a cigar, draw up a huge easy-chair, stick their feet up twice
> as high as their heads, and—proceed to business (?); that is to say, be-
> tween the whiffs of that cigar they tell excruciatingly funny stories, poke each
> other in the ribs, agree to join the mutual admiration society, retail all the
> "wire-pulling" behind the scenes, calculate which way the political cat is
> going to jump, and shape the paragraphs accordingly;—tell who threw that
> huge bouquet, at last night's concert, to Madam Fitz Humbug;—shake
> hands, and make room for all the "hale-fellows-well-met" that drop in to see

them;—keep their intellects sharpened up by collision with the bright and the gifted,—in short, live in one perpetual clover-field, and when they die, all the newspapers write nice little obituary notices, and give them a free pass to Paradise.

Drawing upon images of male retreat, complete with cigars and editors' easy chairs, Fern parodies the tones, scenes, and props of male senti-mentalism. In *Ruth Hall,* she caricatures the man of letters in the figure of Hyacinth, a barely disguised portrait of her brother, Nathaniel Parker Willis. Along with Mitchell and Curtis, Willis formed the reigning New York City male literary triumvirate in the 1850s. She even gestures to the grand old man of feeling, placing Hyacinth at the helm of the (Washington) *Irving Magazine.* According to Fern, whose critical terms echo those of Melville in the "Young America in Literature" sections of *Pierre,* the literary men of the 1850s amuse, move, and manipulate one another, all the while keeping their doors locked, sealing out sentiments and writers they have not authorized.[31]

Fern's satires of "Male America in Literature" are delicious, but they are not the whole story in *Ruth Hall.* She does not argue against a liter-ary market per se but against a market controlled by men. The anger that fuels her portraits of the male mutual admiration society proceeds from her sense that because she is a woman she has been denied access to the money and authority such a society confers upon its members. Fern describes how it feels to be outside the office door looking in. Over the course of *Ruth Hall,* Fern retells the story of her own success at play-ing a man's game. Like Fanny Fern, Ruth Hall boosts her salary by mak-ing editors compete for her increasingly valuable services. Like Fanny Fern, Ruth refuses to sell the copyright for a collection of her articles; in-stead, she opts for royalty payments, thus reaping a large profit when her book becomes a best-seller. Susan Geary has detailed the aggressive and innovative methods Fern's publishers used to market not only *Ruth Hall* but also the persona and autobiography of its author.[32]

Fern's allegiance to the market for feelings is evident when she de-scribes Ruth's persistent mourning for her first-born child Daisy, who has died of croup. Fern outlines the characters "written in the secret chamber of many a bereaved mother's heart" (48):

Eight years since the little Daisy withered! And yet, to the mother's eye, she blossomed fair as Paradise. The soft, golden hair still waved over the blue-veined temples; the sweet, earnest eyes still beamed with their loving light; the little fragile hand was still outstretched for maternal guidance, and in the wood and by the stream they still lingered. Still, the little hymn was chanted at dawn, the little prayer lisped at dew-fall; still, the gentle breathing mingled with the happy mother's star-lit dreams. (49)

Although eight years have passed, Ruth still feels the presence of her lost child. Now, Ruth's touching memories are all well and good, but the fact is that Daisy is a much more vivid character dead than alive. She appears in only a few scenes. The reader is given glimpses of mother and daughter rambling among the rural scenery and Daisy teaching Ruth a lesson about God's benevolence when she observes that God created and loves the ugly caterpillar. From the first, the narrator hints at the child's mortality. Daisy is born, takes a walk, finds a caterpillar, develops a cough, and dies. Fern presents a brief tableau of her death, with Daisy lying still on Ruth's lap, Harry kneeling at their side, and the housekeeper Dinah watching grimly with folded arms. Unlike, say, the famous prolonged death of Eva in Stowe's *Uncle Tom's Cabin* (1852) and many other deathbed set pieces, in which attention is lavished on the motions of the spirit, Daisy's death scene in *Ruth Hall* is understated and elliptical. Daisy is a device: the perfect child. The reader hardly knows Daisy well enough to weep over her demise.[33]

Yet this lack of intimacy is the point. The response here does not depend on specific character or event. Fern is playing on her readers' heartstrings. She demonstrates the power of gesture to call forth emotion. She recognizes the force of convention to signify even in the absence of a specific signified. And so, despite the fact that readers have never been acquainted with its wearer, Fern displays a certain article of the departed Daisy's clothing that she is confident will affect her readers deeply. It is an object described as almost unrepresentable in its clarity and resonance:

in her [Ruth's] lap lay a little half-worn shoe, with the impress of a tiny foot, upon which her tears were falling fast.

A little half-worn shoe! And yet no magician could conjure up such blissful visions; no artist could trace such vivid pictures; no harp of sweetest sounds could so fill the ear with music. (49)

Daisy's tiny foot has left a heavy print. Her half-worn shoe is creased with desire and longing. Fern is fascinated with the ways in which objects conjure feeling. She savors her power to display props, scenes, characters, and phrases that will elicit feeling. She knows that she can dangle that little shoe in front of her readers' eyes and captivate them.

Like the curls of Stowe's Eva, Fern's little shoe takes on a life of its own. In *Uncle Tom's Cabin,* the dying Eva asks her Aunt Ophelia to cut

off several of her ringlets, and she then bestows them as gifts to the assembled slaves. In a chapter entitled "The Tokens," Stowe tells the history of one of these curls, which has been given to Tom. He wears it
around his neck on a string and it sustains him during his beatings at
Legree's plantation. The curl is taken for a "witch thing" by Legree's
slave Sambo, who brings it to his master in a piece of paper. When
Legree opens the paper, the lock of hair "like a living thing, twine[s] itself round Legree's fingers." It carries a charge of reproach, reminding
Legree of the insinuating curl he received in the last letter from his
mother, whom he had abandoned but who, dying, forgave him. Eva's
filaments burn Legree's fingers. Seeking relief, he tears the strands from
his fingers and throws them on the coal in the fireplace. He assures
himself that the keepsake cannot harm him: "'It would be a joke, if
hair could rise from the dead!'" Yet the narrator warns that the joke is
at Legree's expense: "Ah, Legree! that golden tress *was* charmed; each
hair had in it a spell of terror and remorse for thee." As an epigraph for
the chapter, Stowe uses lines from canto 4 of *Childe Harold's Pilgrimage,* in which Byron describes how slight things, "tokens," may bring
back on the heart the heavy weight of grief, striking the "electric chain"
of memory. Sensation and memory produce emotion. Stowe's curls and
Fern's shoes do rise from the dead. They are sentimental tokens that
ignite a circuit of personal and cultural associations. They are symbols
of loss that fill the present, emblems of the writer's authority and
authenticity.[34]

In her display of sentimental fetishes, Fern acknowledges a debt to
Stowe. She reveals to the reader that Ruth has kept not only Daisy's shoe
but also one of her golden curls. Daisy's curls gather affect from Eva's.
Fern need only gesture with the shoe or toward the curls in part because
Stowe has invested them with emotion. Yet Fern's curls are not Stowe's.
They teach the reader an unnerving lesson. The narrator reveals that
Ruth's second child Katy has been admiring her mother's regard for the
vestiges of Daisy: "'I should like to die, and have you love *my* curls
as you do Daisy's, mother'" (49). Ruth complies with her wishes and
severs one of Katy's brown curls. Then the child volunteers one of her
own little shoes, and her mother places the tokens of the living and dead
daughters in a box: "the little sister shoes lay with the twin ringlets,
lovingly side by side" (49). Rather than giving her comfort that she will
rejoin her lost daughter after death, Fern gives Ruth the immediate
satisfaction of preserving her sentimental attachments through a liv-

ing daughter who transforms herself into a collection of relics for her mother.

Like Mitchell, who in *Reveries of a Bachelor* exhibits his dead son and wife to his readers despite their lack of "material type" or "objective form," Fern holds out the little shoe in the faith that her readers will recognize and respond. Like the familiar narratives sketched in *Reveries*, Fern's little shoe comes to the reader already occupied. Thus Fern's apparent hyperbole in describing the shoe—"no artist could trace such vivid pictures; no harp of sweetest sounds could so fill the ear with music"—accurately conveys the magnitude of sentimental endowments. For Fern, convention is not the inert, vacant container that many modern critics would describe, with their preference for irony and subversion. Instead, it is a set of forms saturated with affect and rife with possibilities. Roland Barthes captures the kind of force Fern draws upon in his notion of "écriture" as outlined in his early *Writing Degree Zero*: the historically inflected patterns of syntax, diction, and logic that elicit recognition with but an allusion or a gesture. Fern's display of the little shoe is such a gesture, producing a response out of proportion to its specific referent, tapping into the codes shared between writer and many of her readers. Fern's familiar tune literally produced a popular song in the 1850s entitled "Little Daisy," based on the short-lived character from *Ruth Hall*. The remarkable thing about Fern's little shoe is that she dangles it in front of her readers and, despite the fact that only a stylized child ever set an insubstantial foot in it and despite the fact that Fern is clearly using a cliché to contrive a reaction, it works.[35]

A similar effect is on display in Fern's essay "A Little Bunker Hill," first published in the Boston *Olive Branch* in 1852 and reprinted in *Fern Leaves*. Fern counsels her female readers "to pursue the 'Uriah Heep' policy" in their struggle with men to gain their rights: "look 'umble, and be desperate cunning. Bait them with submission, and then throw the noose over the will." This covert tactic is emblazoned on the pages of a newspaper. Yet Fern is not revealing any secrets in "A Little Bunker Hill." She assumes that men will find their women's submission so familiar and so satisfying that they will still yield. The husbands know that they are being manipulated by the practiced docility of their wives. Instead of terminating the play, this knowledge heightens its pleasures. The confidence Fern shares in public with her female readers involves a complicated mixture of understatement and overplaying. In *Ruth Hall*, authority is augmented, not dispelled, by exposure.[36]

Fern flaunts her power in *Ruth Hall* but also strategically wields it. She not only elicits feeling from her readers, she also channels it in unexpected directions. If the narrator begins by dangling a familiar possession, she ends by exhibiting a very different property: a copy of a certificate from the Seton Bank proclaiming that Ruth Hall owns one hundred shares, ten thousand dollars' worth, of its capital stock. In a potent visual moment in the text, the certificate is pictured on the page, held out to the reader. All of Fern's formidable literary devices—the draining of affect from other characters to Ruth, the shifts in tone that validate Ruth's interior state, the analogies between maternal and literary urgencies, the satire of the male literary marketplace—are geared toward this display. Fern invests the stock certificate, the emblem of male success, with female significance. She validates female speculation and extends its terms and contexts. The narrative of *Ruth Hall* justifies her claims. Fern seeks to alter the structures of feeling that define female and male achievement in mid-nineteenth-century America. She wishes to train her audience to respond to the stock certificate as automatically and fully as she knows they will respond to that little half-worn shoe. She seeks to make a stock certificate a stock sentimental object, a capitalistic fetish for women as well as men, inscribed with Ruth's name and with her own.[37]

In "My Old Inkstand and I; or, The First Article in a New House," an essay written after the success of *Ruth Hall* to celebrate Parton's 1856 move to Brooklyn, Fern adds to her new investments. Addressing her inkstand as a friend and partner, she urges it to become a "talisman" for her daughter. She praises its ability to transmute tears into ink and insults into profit. Like Mitchell, whose *Reveries of a Bachelor* could be retitled "I and My Cigar," and Melville in "I and My Chimney," both of whose male personae defend themselves with sentimentalized phallic objects, Fern brandishes her literary weapon against the world in "My Old Inkstand and I." Despite the gender stereotypes, it is Fern whose aggression is more overt and Mitchell and Melville whose narrators retreat behind their domestic barricades. The men of feeling are steeped in nostalgia over lost youth and power, while the woman of feeling seizes the opportunities presented by economic and social change. Sentimentalism makes possible such literary gender turns: Ik. Marvel withdraws to his fireside and feints with his cigar, while Fanny Fern, with her inkstand at her side, relishes the sight of her victims littering the marketplace.[38]

Like Mitchell and Melville, Fern presents a scene of reading in which she meditates on her own audience and practice. Ruth has begun to attract a great deal of notice and conjecture for her articles written under the pseudonym "Floy." Late one night, she reads two letters. The first is from a Mr. John Stokes, who praises her trenchancy and substance and suggests she collect her essays in a book. Ruth is grateful for the encouragement, but it is the second letter that moves her: "It was in a delicate, beautiful, female hand; just such a one as you, dear Reader, might trace, whose sweet, soft eyes, and long, drooping tresses, are now bending over this page" (136). "Mary R." appreciates the "ministrations" and "serious moods" of "Floy" (136). Writer and reader don't know each other's faces, but they recognize each other's hearts. Fern endorses the sentimental communion that takes place as the result of representing the depths of human feeling on the printed page. Her "ministrations" often involve an Emersonian urging to self-aggrandizement and a sense that female as well as male hearts vibrate to iron strings. Later, Fern describes different types of letters that "Floy" receives after her book *Life Sketches* is published. These are communications mostly from men who seek to satisfy their own needs at her expense (153–55, 164–65, 181–82, 188). Each of these readers wants a piece of Ruth. Through these letters, Fern indicates the double edge of sentimental publication. When a writer exposes herself, she initiates emotional exchange but also makes herself vulnerable to the desires of a hungry audience.[39]

In "A Chapter on Literary Women," collected in *Fern Leaves,* Fern suggests some of the risks involved in sentimental display, when she has a character named the Colonel express his reservations about female writers: "Just fancy my wife's heart turned inside-out to thousands of eyes beside mine, for dissection." The Colonel is eventually bested in debate by his opponent, Minnie, who insists that hearts are not private male property, but are public, and that women writers must use their God-granted "power of expressing the same tide of emotions that sweep, perchance, over the soul of another."[40] Yet Fern's clinical metaphors and her anxieties about vulnerability carry forward to *Ruth Hall.* The persistent images of cardiac probing in Mitchell and Fern represent the object and techniques of sentimental discourse and also suggest the studied artificiality and fundamental strangeness of the sentimental project. The exposures of Mitchell and Fern help us to understand the studied strangeness of Melville's *Pierre.*

BLOOD, INK, AND TEARS: THE STRANGLING DIASTOLE AND SYSTOLE OF *PIERRE*

Shocked by the apparent discovery of an illegitimate sister sired and hidden by his father and casting about for a course of action that will both preserve the family honor and acknowledge his sibling, Pierre Glendinning dedicates himself to the "heart": "well may my heart knock at my ribs,—prisoner impatient of his iron bars. . . . The heart! the heart! 'tis God's anointed; let me pursue the heart!" (91). In *Pierre,* Melville details the disastrous results of that quest. Pierre discovers that his heart is empty and graven. Neither God nor a benevolent human nature has anointed its motions. The faster it beats, the more tightly he becomes bound in its cage. In analyzing the character of Pierre's feelings, and particularly the motives and effects of his grand resolution to announce that he and his "sister" Isabel have been secretly married, Melville shows how truth becomes lies, how virtue dovetails into vice, how protecting your "sister" is also lusting after her, and how preserving the family honor results in the deaths of your mother, your fiancée, your cousin, and yourself. Pierre's heart labors under the burdens of history, family, society, and literature.

Melville's cardiology contradicts the claims of Shaftesbury's moral philosophy, evoked by many sentimental writers. Pierre's feelings are revealed to be neither spontaneous nor benevolent. Melville's contorted, insinuating prose indicates that feelings are a treacherous ground for moral action. From Pierre's first glimpse of her, Isabel elicits an unstable mixture of emotion: "the face somehow mystically appealing to his own private and individual affections; and by a silent and tyrannic call, challenging him in his deepest moral being, and summoning Truth, Love, Pity, Conscience, to the stand" (49). In the double gesture that characterizes *Pierre*'s rhetoric, the narrator asserts that everything is fine and suggests that everything is dreadfully awry. The moral imperative here is a "tyrannic" call. Pierre's "own private and individual affections" will be shown to be the product of centuries of training. "His deepest moral being" will contain chambers of horror. Truth, Love, Pity, and Conscience will be summoned to witness, but so will Guilt, Rage, Inadequacy, and Lust. In her letter to him revealing her "identity," Isabel urges Pierre to come to her and yield to "that heavenly impulse" (64), and later she assures him that "the impulse in me called thee, not poor Bell" (159); yet Melville from the start questions Pierre's impulses and raises doubts about the motives behind Isabel's call. In the world represented in *Pierre,* contrary to the *Reveries* of Donald Grant Mitchell, feeling is not simply feeling and sentiments are not self-validating. Unlike the spaces between the lines in Fern's *Ruth Hall,* the interstices in *Pierre* are murky and troubling, filled not with the comforts of irony or sympathy but with the choking "ambiguities" named in the subtitle of the book and relentlessly personified: the "ineffable hints and ambiguities" (84), the "ever-creeping and condensing haze of ambiguities" (151), the "roguish ambiguities" (220).[41]

When Pierre first receives Isabel's letter informing him that they share the same father, he speculates that she might be an impostor who has set out to manipulate his feelings like the "brisk novelist" who will "steal gushing tears from his reader's eyes" (69–70). Yet he immediately feels that the letter is true, based on a memory that his delirious, dying father cried out for his daughter, on the innuendoes he detects in a secretly painted portrait of his youthful father, and on the similarities he sees between this image and Isabel's features. In explaining Pierre's response, the narrator describes the different standards of public and private evidence: "In the cold courts of justice the dull head demands oaths, and holy writ proofs; but in the warm halls of the heart one single, untestified memory's spark shall suffice to enkindle such a blaze of evidence, that all the corners of conviction are as suddenly lighted up as a midnight city by a burning building, which on every side whirls its reddened brands" (71). The narrator here undermines, while he elevates, such intimate proof. It is "untestified," implying that memory might not be a reliable witness. Pierre's spark threatens not only to illuminate the case of Isabel but also to incinerate it and to consume the very edifice of conviction.

Late in the book, Pierre again questions his belief in Isabel's identity and the sequence of actions prompted by this belief. In a picture gallery in lower Manhattan, he sees a portrait, a "Stranger's Head by the Unknown Hand," whose resemblance to the secretly painted portrait of his father makes him doubt the train of associations which had confirmed his kinship with Isabel (351). When he sees a similarity between Isabel and this anonymous, and possibly imaginary, portrait, he realizes his impulsiveness. He regains his confidence, however, when Isabel, on a ferry in New York harbor, feels the motion of the waves and links it with the memory of her voyage to America from France, where she had been born after the liaison between her mother and Pierre's father. Pierre "cannot resist the force of this striking corroboration" of her story (355). Yet Isabel could be enacting her responses for strategic effect, just as brisk novelists elicit gushing tears. Melville suggests, but does not confirm, that Isabel is a virtuoso manipulator of Pierre's feelings in the tableau of Isabel, her head illuminated and her body framed in an altar of double-casement windows, playing the scintillating strings of her mother's guitar and also the heartstrings of the rapt Pierre (149–52; see also 126–27). Isabel's performance may be genuine or it may be calculated, or it may be both. By the end of *Pierre,* the sentimental equation has come unraveled. The narrator raises suspicions about the qualities of sensation and memory that produce emotion.

Pierre is represented as both victim and victimizer of Isabel. Early in the book, as he waits for Isabel to resume telling the obscure story of her early life, the narrator tells us that Pierre's sympathetic gaze is fixed upon one of Isabel's precious charms: her "wonderfully beautiful ear, which chancing to peep forth from among her abundant tresses, nestled in that blackness like a transparent sea-shell of pearl" (119). Although the narrator, Pierre-like, assures his readers that Pierre feels nothing but brotherly love for Isabel, his self-canceling prose implies that this brother's love has no bounds: "And Pierre felt that never, never would he be able to embrace Isabel with the mere brotherly embrace; while the thought of any other caress, which took hold of any domesticness, was entirely vacant from his uncontaminated soul, for it had never consciously intruded there" (142). The narrator clearly protests too much. He will show that Pierre's soul is indeed marred by unconscious intrusions. The convoluted negatives, the reluctance to settle for the "mere brotherly," and the hastily withdrawn glimpse of "any other caress" all suggest that in Pierre's mind and heart there are unruly forces. Denial becomes avowal in this elaborate occultatio, as the narrator prepares the reader to understand Pierre's casting of himself as "the grand self-renouncing victim" (173).

The forces compelling Pierre are so knotted and so disfiguring that Pierre cannot confront their sources or consequences and the narrator can barely contain himself. After he declares his "marriage" to Isabel in the presence of his one-time fiancée Lucy and his mother, and just before that "marriage" is consummated in what seems to be a sexual encounter between Pierre and Isabel, delivered in a twisted euphemism ("Then they changed; they coiled together; and entangledly stood mute" [192]—some kind of serpent sex, with more than a nod to the "Laocoon" [184]), Pierre has an insight: "Over the face of Pierre there shot a terrible self-revelation" (192). Pierre glimpses and then avoids. The nar-

rator details how Pierre's belabored sentiments lead him to the moral de-
termination to have sex, or something, with his sister, but he cannot
name the act Pierre commits, or seems to commit. (It is difficult to describe *Pierre* without one's own language writhing and buckling.) The
narrator refrains because the word "incest" itself would not begin to
convey the substance of Pierre's acts and responses. When the narrator
describes Pierre's attraction to Isabel as "the nameless awfulness of his
still imperfectly conscious, incipient, new-mingled emotion toward this
mysterious being" (206), he alerts his readers that they have the privilege of witnessing the formation of new feelings. "New-mingled" is a
peculiar neologism, evoking the mingling, fangling, and mangling of
Pierre's emotions.[42]

In one of the many passages of subtle psychology, during which the
narrator seeks to "steal yet further into Pierre" (107), he describes the
split stage of Pierre's consciousness:

> Strange wild work, and awfully symmetrical and reciprocal, was that now
> going on within the self-apparently chaotic breast of Pierre. As in his own
> conscious determinations, the mournful Isabel was being snatched from her
> captivity of world-wide abandonment; so, deeper down in the more secret
> chambers of his unsuspecting soul, the smiling Lucy, now as dead and ashy
> pale, was being bound a ransom for Isabel's salvation. (105)

Pierre imagines himself performing a role worthy of his Revolutionary
War grandfathers and rescuing a maiden from the plight into which she
has been cast by her (and his) father's betrayal. Yet beneath the boards
another drama is being enacted, one in which Pierre binds Lucy in order
to free Isabel. In the cruel emotional calculus outlined by the narrator,
Isabel is purchased at the cost of Lucy. As in the sentimental theater of
Adam Smith, there are two Pierres. Here, though, the internal spectator
has abdicated his post. In *Pierre*, the scrutinizing self does not offer a social mirror in which the acting self can measure its conduct. Instead the
second self undermines the self's intentions and executes dark deeds in
the gothic chambers of the heart. Rather than serving as an audience for
the self's portrayal of sympathy, this second self enacts a companion
melodrama of cruelty. Neither grounded in Shaftesbury's moral sense
nor governed by Smith's internal monitor, the sentimental spectacles
in *Pierre* are "Strange wild work." Later in the book, when Pierre has
learned to doubt his disinterestedness and has come to fear that his obscure and restive feelings may be scripting his behavior, he tells Isabel,
quoting *Hamlet,* that "Virtue and Vice" are "two shadows cast from

one nothing." He torments himself because it is "the law" that "a nothing should torment a nothing": "for I am a nothing. It is all a dream—
we dream that we dreamed we dream" (274). *Pierre* represents not the
reveries but the vertiginous nightmares of a bachelor.

Although the narrator is steeped in nostalgia, he also acknowledges
its illusory qualities. Saddle Meadows, as we have seen, is not the kind
of home to which a young man should wish to return. When Pierre in
New York City yearns for the "innocence and joy" (286) of his youth
after hearing that his mother has died, this tender feeling is a sign of his
unbalanced mind. Although the narrator repeatedly invokes "the most
direful blasts of Fate" (104) to explain the disastrous turns in the narrative, his allusions, insinuations, and inventories provide a more material
account of Pierre's downward spiral. Sharing many of Melville's own
family and writerly obsessions, in many senses Melville's self-projection,
Pierre is described sympathetically, but this sympathy is mixed with
unsparing scrutiny. The narrator cautions his readers: "But I shall follow the endless, winding way,—the flowing river in the cave of man;
careless whither I be led, reckless where I land" (107). Despite the effort
of some critics to divide *Pierre*'s narrative voices into separate perspectives, such as naive and ironic, the power of the book seems to me to
derive from a volatile blend of sentimental absorption and searing self-
consciousness.[43]

Between the intention and the act in *Pierre* falls the shadow of the
feelings. The represented world is charged with feeling, as Melville
makes vivid in his repeated electrical analogies:

> In their precise tracings-out and subtile causations, the strongest and fieriest
> emotions of life defy all analytical insight. We see the cloud, and feel its
> bolt; but meteorology only idly essays a critical scrutiny as to how that
> cloud became charged, and how this bolt so stuns. The metaphysical writers
> confess, that the most impressive, sudden, and overwhelming event, as well
> as the minutest, is but the product of an infinite series of infinitely involved
> and untraceable foregoing occurrences. Just so with every motion of the
> heart. (67)

Pierre's heart is "charged to overflowing" (110), and Isabel is "charged
. . . with . . . immense longings" (158). Pierre and Isabel are bound
by a "physical electricness" (151). *Pierre* tells a story of overheating
and burning out. Melville embarks on the complex and, as he acknowledges, infinite task of attempting to analyze the motions of the heart.
This exhausting, excruciating sentimental anatomy is conducted in su-

percharged rhetoric. As Fitz-James O'Brien put it delicately in 1853: "Thought staggers through each page like one poisoned. Language is drunken and reeling. Style is antipodical and marches on its head."[44]

Melville's style in *Pierre* has been the subject of much critical concern. Some read Melville's tortuous prose as the result of biographical pressures, indicating his strained temperament (Mumford, Matthiessen, and Murray). Others interpret Melville as trying but failing to write a popular sentimental novel (Howard and Parker). Others argue that Melville sought to parody the evasions of sentimental culture (Braswell and Douglas). Recently, Sacvan Bercovitch has described *Pierre* as a "parody turned against itself, a satire of the comic *pretensions* of the parodic mode." Bercovitch's remarks about involuted parody seem apt. Across the chapters of this book, I have been arguing against a surface and depth model of interpreting Melville's prose, in which the critic with an aptitude for irony can peel the popular from the profound and the disturbing from the exhilarating. In this chapter on antebellum sentiment, I have argued that the hierarchical divisions between sentiment and satire are the result of twentieth-century reflection rather than mid-nineteenth-century literary practice. In the texts of Mitchell, Melville, and Fern, rhetorical excess aids the satiric and sentimental strategies of exposure, not exposure of depth beneath surface but exposure of the texture and effects of discourse. Mitchell and Fern seek depth of feeling in the weave of the written page. In *Pierre,* Melville strains and tears the fabric.[45]

Melville traces Pierre's palpitations in an exhaustive series of references to Pierre's personal and national genealogies and to gendered accounts of feeling from Plato's *Symposium* to Byron's *Manfred.* He delineates the heightening and thwarting of male desire for women, for other men, for heroic achievement, and for self-dominion. *Pierre* unfolds in linked discursive registers, in which types of feeling are fused with the bodies of characters. The book begins with the allure of the "Sentimental" Lucy, moves through the "Gothic" mysteries of Isabel, and climaxes in the striving, mutilated torso of the "Romantic" Pierre. In this movement from "Sentimental" to "Gothic" to "Romantic," Melville recapitulates the previous century of British and American literary history. The emotional excess in *Pierre* is not the result of a self-referential system like Mitchell's in *Reveries of a Bachelor. Pierre's* excess is produced not by a lack of referents but by an infinitely involved series of referents.[46]

Pierre is filled with structures that entice and recede. In book 2, the narrator describes Pierre, whom Lucy has sent up to her room to retrieve her artist's portfolio, standing transfixed before her bed:

> Now, crossing the magic silence of the empty chamber, he caught the snow-white bed reflected in the toilet-glass. . . . So he advanced, and with a fond and gentle joyfulness, his eye now fell upon the spotless bed itself, and fastened on a snow-white roll that lay beside the pillow. Now he started; Lucy seemed coming in upon him; but no—'tis only the foot of one of her little slippers, just peeping into view from under the narrow nether curtains of the bed. Then again his glance fixed itself upon the slender, snow-white, ruffled roll; and he stood as one enchanted. Never precious parchment of the Greek was half so precious in his eyes. Never trembling scholar longed more to unroll the mystic vellum, than Pierre longed to unroll the sacred secrets of that snow-white, ruffled thing. But his hands touched not any object in that chamber, except the one he had gone thither for. (39)

Lucy's "little slipper" and her "snow-white roll" are fraught with desire. The little slipper advances and peeps. Like Fern's little shoe, it seems to have a life of its own. Her roll is described as beyond value and representation—and beyond Pierre's access. Melville links text and sex in the image of Lucy's "mystic vellum," whose "sacred secrets" the trembling scholar Pierre longs to unfold. " 'Open it!' " says Lucy, a few lines later, referring in part to her portfolio, " 'why, yes, Pierre, yes; what secret thing keep I from thee? Read me through and through. I am entirely thine. See!' " (40).

Like Queequeg's living parchment, Lucy's vellum invites and impedes. A strong sense of sentimental prescription informs the narrator's account of Pierre's responses to Lucy. The narrator himself seems bound and burdened by the received diction and syntax of heterosexual desire. The language here is not, as is often said of sentimental language, deformed in order to evade the sexual or bodily realities of life. The euphemism, periphrasis, projection, and displacement frustrate but also shape Pierre's desire. As Pierre writes to Lucy in book 5, elliptically accounting for his mysterious absence from her aunt's cottage the previous night: "But where one can not reveal the thing itself, it only makes it more mysterious to write round it this way" (94). Writing round it, circling the object of desire, defining it asymptotically—*Pierre* explores such intensifying effects.[47]

It is not only Pierre's prescribed feelings, it is also his proscribed feelings that are conveyed in a heavy verbal hand. Pierre's possibly incestuous attraction to Isabel is rendered in sentences of sexualized circumlocution. The bond between Pierre and his cousin Glen is elevated into a stratosphere not devoid of earthly incitements: "the empyrean of a love which only comes short, by one degree, of the sweetest sentiment enter- tained between the sexes. Nor is this boy-love without the occasional fillips and spicinesses, which at times, by an apparent abatement, en- hance the permanent delights of those more advanced lovers who love beneath the cestus of Venus" (216–17). The one small degree that sep- arates Pierre and Glen heightens the allure. The abatements of "boy- love" are only apparent and the "permanence" of heterosexual delight is undermined. Yet Pierre and Glen inevitably engage in a ritual contest over Lucy. In the duel staged at the end of the book, an enraged Pierre kills his cousin. The manly desire represented in *Pierre* is tense, resem- bling more the unsettling den of "Aladdin's Palace" in *Redburn* than the sensuous avowals of "A Bosom Friend" or "A Squeeze of the Hand" in *Moby-Dick*. In his portrayals of Pierre's feelings about Lucy, Isabel, Glen, and himself, Melville articulates a paralyzing, inscribed intimacy.[48]

In the sections of *Pierre* dealing with Isabel, the pressures of gothic modes in general and of Poe's language and images in particular are felt strongly. Isabel narrates a gothic childhood for herself: elusive origins, secluded and crumbling houses, sealed rooms, unsolved riddles. The narrator dwells on Isabel's mortuary charms, especially her veil of black hair (112, 140, 147). Earlier he had catalogued Lucy's sentimental fea- tures: spangled hair, tinted cheeks, heavenly orbs (24–25). Neither face quite coheres. Describing Isabel, Melville's prose seems to take on the obsessive, incantatory qualities of Poe's late poetry. When Lucy asks Pierre to tell her about his vision of Isabel's mysterious face, she re- marks: "Some nameless sadness, faintness, strangely comes to me. Fore- taste I feel of endless dreariness" (37). The narrator writes of Isabel: "Was not the face—though mutely mournful—beautiful, bewitch- ingly?" (107). The alliteration and rhyme and the emphasis on sound and meter threaten here, as they do in Poe's late poetry, to disrupt the syntax. In describing Isabel, Melville seems to have been drawn to Poe's gothic tales of the heart, his poetic search for "the Rhythmical Creation of Beauty," and his fascination with the embodiments and dissolutions of female form. Both Lucy and Isabel, emblems of the sentimental and the gothic, hang like "pendants" within Pierre's heart (41).[49]

When Isabel describes her responses to "the beautiful infant" she en- countered when she was a girl, Melville out-Poes Poe, transmuting his poetical experiments into passages of compellingly awful prose:

> this beautiful infant first brought me to my own mind, as it were; first made me sensible that I was something different from stones, trees, cats; first undid

in me the fancy that all people were as stones, trees, cats; first filled me with
the sweet idea of humanness; first made me aware of the infinite mercifulness,
and tenderness, and beautifulness of humanness; and this beautiful infant
first filled me with the dim thought of Beauty; and equally, and at the same
time, with the feeling of the Sadness; of the immortalness and universalness
of the Sadness.... Now I first began to reflect in my mind; to endeavor after
the recalling past things; but try as I would, little could I recall, but the bewilderingness;—and the stupor, and the torpor, and the blankness, and the
dimness, and the vacant whirlingness of the bewilderingness. Let me be still
again. (122)

Yes, Isabel, please—be still. The heartstrings are played most peculiarly
in this scene, in which Poe's unearthly music is used to represent the sentimental tableau of "mother" and "beautiful infant" (portions of this
passage could be lines from "The Raven" or "Ulalume"). Melville seems
to take pleasure in crossing the sentimental wires here. Isabel is not the
mother of this beautiful infant. She perceives "the sweet idea of humanness" and secures her identity in inhuman and deranged prose. In this
passage, the force of habit is blunted. Isabel's eerie responsiveness con-
founds the reader. Unlike Fern, who will dangle her little shoe confident
of eliciting sympathy, Melville displays the preeminent sentimental
tableau—woman and child—and unravels the guarantee of spontaneous, shared response.

The "Romantic" language of masculine isolation and defiance per-
meates many of the narrator's descriptions of Pierre's inner state. A
Saddle Meadows Manfred, Pierre calls upon the Terror Stone to crush
him if Virtue and Truth have no meaning in a duplicitous world (134).
On the verge of his departure to New York City, after burning the secretly painted portrait of his father and bundles of family documents,
Pierre addresses the flames and declares his independence: "'Hence-
forth, cast-out Pierre hath no paternity, and no past; and since the Future is one blank to all; therefore, twice-disinherited Pierre stands un-
trammeledly his ever-present self!—free to do his own self-will and
present fancy to whatever end!'" (199). Yet this declaration has a price,
which is exacted over the course of the narrative. Pierre's dream of freedom is fulfilled at the end of the book in his vision of the shattered, recalcitrant terrain of the Mount of Titans. The narrator reports that his
body is in a state of internal revolt. Pierre's blood "had in vain rebelled
against his Titanic soul" and his eyes "did also turn downright traitors
to him, and with more success than the rebellious blood.... The pupils
of his eyes rolled away from him in their own orbits" (341).

Pierre's vertigo leads to the vision of himself as Enceladus, the mythological Titan thwarted in his effort to regain his divine birthright. Through the disordered movement of his eyes, the image of a local rock formation comes to life. With "distorted features, scarred and broken" (345), it reminds him of the mutilated rebel. Pierre imagines that this figure turns to face him:

> he saw a moss-turbaned, armless giant, who despairing of any other mode of wreaking his immitigable hate, turned his vast trunk into a battering-ram, and hurled his own arched-out ribs again and yet again against the invulnerable steep.
> "Enceladus! it is Enceladus!"—Pierre cried out in his sleep. That moment the phantom faced him; and Pierre saw Enceladus no more; but on the Titan's armless trunk, his own duplicate face and features magnifiedly gleamed upon him with prophetic discomfiture and woe. (346)

This is Melville's most emphatic and self-reflexive moment of the self seeing itself in the image of another, the culmination of a series of recognitions that began with Tommo confronting the tattooed visages of the Marquesans in *Typee*. Against a desolate backdrop, Pierre visibly personifies himself in the classic example of impractical assault. Enceladus mirrors to Pierre his own position as an "American Enceladus" (346), not an "ever-present self . . . free to do his own self-will" (199), but a self trammeled by his past; not the possessor of a white jacket that can be cast off and regenerated, but a prisoner encased in a cage of stone. Pierre sees his own heritage in the Titan's nightmare genealogy, both the son and grandson of an incest, held down by his earthly mother and seeking to overcome his divine father. The search for integrity climaxes not in the seamless proportions of the *Apollo Belvedere*, the promise held out in *Typee,* but in the shivered features of Enceladus. Amputated and impotent, Enceladus completes the series of emotionally ravaged bodies in *Pierre*.[50]

Although Pierre, like Ik. Marvel and Fanny Fern, receives letters from his readers, these are the readers of his immature work, and they consist mostly of letters from publishers who wish to dress up and market his meager output of sonnets, meditative poems, and moral essays (246–48). Isabel's letter produces the most moving effects on Pierre. She describes her Glendinning parentage and her plight, and she asks him to come to her. "'Here I freeze in the wide, wide world,'" she writes, echoing the predicament of Susan Warner's orphaned Ellen (64). Then Melville opens the sentimental valves:

> This letter, inscribed in a feminine, but irregular hand, and in some places almost illegible, plainly attesting the state of mind which had dictated it;—stained, too, here and there, with spots of tears, which chemically acted

upon by the ink, assumed a strange and reddish hue—as if blood and not tears had dropped upon the sheet;—and so completely torn in two by Pierre's own hand, that it indeed seemed the fit scroll of a torn, as well as bleeding heart;—this amazing letter, deprived Pierre for the time of all lucid and definite thought or feeling. He hung half-lifeless in his chair; his hand, clutching the letter, was pressed against his heart, as if some assassin had stabbed him and fled; and Pierre was now holding the dagger in the wound, to stanch the outgushing of the blood. (64–65)

Tears mingle with the ink on the paper and assume the appearance of blood. Words, like tears and like blood, become bodily secretions. Isabel's heart thus becomes legible. Unlike the tears and ink in Mitchell and Fern, which bind writer, character, and reader, the mixture in *Pierre* is corrosive. After Pierre's mother dies, his tears do not cinch or cleanse but "like acid burned and scorched" (285). Like Whitman in "Calamus," who joins words and wounds ("O drops of me! trickle slow drops,/Candid, from me falling—drip, bleeding drops,/From wounds made to free you when you were prisoned"), Melville metaphorically exposes how intimate translations can mutilate and drain. Like a dagger, Isabel's letter pierces Pierre's heart. Like a poultice, it prevents his wound from weeping. The letter elicits yet blocks the flow. Such is the sentimental bind that defines the story and discourse of *Pierre,* in which feeling surges and strangles. Violence and liquidity are emphasized in this heart-to-heart encounter between Pierre and Isabel.[51]

Throughout *Pierre,* letters are not tokens of sentiment that minister to the soul, as they are in Mitchell and Fern. Instead, Melville associates letters with misunderstanding and injury. In the first part of the book, Isabel's letter outlining her obscure past "stabs" Pierre (65). At the end of the book, Pierre receives two communications that ignite his fatal gestures. One is from his publishers Steel, Flint, and Asbestos (obviously not a sympathetic lot), who accuse him of trying to swindle them by pretending that the vile satire he has submitted is a popular novel. The other is from his cousin Glen and Lucy's brother Frederic, branding him a hypocrite who pretends to be an honorable man but who lives with both his wife and his fiancée. Pierre grinds the two letters beneath his heels, declaring that he is "hate-shod" (357). Then he tears Glen and Frederic's letter and uses it as wadding for his pistols. These loaded guns are Pierre's letters to the world.

Although Isabel's disruptive feminine hand may indicate Melville's discomfort with female authorship, in *Pierre* he figures neither popular writers and readers nor sentimental violence exclusively as female. In his satire of "Young America in Literature," Melville, as Fern will do in

Ruth Hall, criticizes the fraternally corrupt and commodified New York literary world. Pierre's own mature male authorship is portrayed as more crippling than Isabel's blade-like words. Again, ink and blood are conjoined:

> Two books are being writ; of which the world shall only see one, and that the bungled one. The larger book, and the infinitely better, is for Pierre's own private shelf. That it is, whose unfathomable cravings drink his blood; the other only demands his ink. But circumstances have so decreed, that the one can not be composed on the paper, but only as the other is writ down in his soul. And the one of the soul is elephantinely sluggish, and will not budge at a breath. Thus Pierre is fastened on by two leeches;—how then can the life of Pierre last? Lo! he is fitting himself for the highest life, by thinning his blood and collapsing his heart. He is learning how to live, by rehearsing the part of death. (304–305)

Ink draws on blood, as the soul is translated to paper. For ink to lie thick, the blood must be thinned. Sentiment becomes a kind of lethal transfusion. Writing is represented as a parasitic activity, books as bloodsuckers. The self does not stand apart from itself and evaluate its behavior; instead, the self feeds upon itself.[52]

Melville's sentimental exposures resemble the bodily displays of antebellum sensationalism, the extruded eyeballs and decanted brains of George Lippard. In Melville's treatise concerning the sentimental affections, ardent responses not only produce material effects on the body, they rupture it. Isabel's shriek "seemed to split its way clean through [Pierre's] heart, and leave a yawning gap there" (45). The sight of Pierre causes Isabel's chest to expand and contract, "as though some choked, violent thing were risen up there within from the teeming region of her heart" (46). Melville stages his scenes of reading and writing as cardiac episodes. He calls attention to the "strange alloy" of ink and tears (159) that forms the substance of Isabel's letter and the texture of his own prose. The splittings and enmeshings of "I" and "you" that generate feeling in Mitchell and Fern become literal gashes and snares in *Pierre.* Melville so overplays his rhetorical and narrative hands that he violates the expectations of an audience accustomed to the pleasures of contrivance, an audience ready to be seduced by the writer's histrionic intimacies. Melville botches the calculations for popularity. He alienates his readers from their affections.[53]

In metaphor after metaphor, the narrator seeks to delineate the interior spaces of the self: "the infernal catacombs of thought" (51), "the warm halls of the heart" (71), "the flowing river in the cave of man"

(107), the "awfulness of amplitude" in "the Switzerland of his soul" (284), and "a spiral stair in a shaft, without any end" (289). When the narrator describes the insights withheld from Pierre, he mixes geology, architecture, and necrology:

> Ten million things were as yet uncovered to Pierre. The old mummy lies buried in cloth on cloth; it takes time to unwrap this Egyptian king. Yet now, forsooth, because Pierre began to see through the first superficiality of the world, he fondly weens he has come to the unlayered substance. But, far as any geologist has yet gone down into the world, it is found to consist of nothing but surface stratified on surface. To its axis, the world being nothing but superinduced superficies. By vast pains we mine into the pyramid; by horrible gropings we come to the central room; with joy we espy the sarcophagus; but we lift the lid—and no body is there!—appallingly vacant as vast is the soul of a man! (284–85)

Here is the central ideological recognition in *Pierre*. The geologist delves into the strata of rock, the archaeologist mines into the pyramid and lifts the lid on the sarcophagus, the narrator lays open Pierre—and they find an eloquent, layered emptiness. Although Pierre's heart lacks depth, its surface is belabored, crossed and re-crossed with lines of feeling. Pierre is presented as a victim of sentiments that *Pierre* illuminates but also perpetuates, resists but also reinforces, understands but cannot elude.[54]

Pierre's story is familiar: the parental competitions and humiliations, the gender polarities, the sexual repressions and sublimations, the quest for secrets, the desire for potency, the pathos of failed ambition. It is familiar not only because Melville reminds us of its literary and philosophical heritage, and not only because he recycles plots, characters, and phrases, but also because this story is in many ways Melville's own. As Melville tells his story, he is amused, horrified, moved, disgusted, disgusted that he is moved. He seems transfixed by the persistence of ideology, the compulsions of feeling and thought. In *Moby-Dick,* Ishmael acknowledges these compulsions with a sense of absurdity and disbelief. The narrator of *Pierre* is more embroiled. Melville seems to lose the faith of his previous books, with their restorative excess, that individual expression can alter inherited forms. In *Pierre,* Melville offers vehement introspection rather than the exuberant exchanges with his readers that characterized his earlier works. The narrator journeys not to the Marquesas nor around Cape Horn nor to the whaling grounds of the Pacific, nor does he explore behind the faces or inside the skin or beneath the crania of others. Instead, he dissects the heart of his own character. *Pierre* is the tale of going down into oneself and finding occupied territory.

In Mitchell and Fern, Poe and Stowe, the display of sentiment augments its effects, as writer, characters, and readers enjoy the pleasures of shared lines, scenes, and responses. In *Pierre,* Melville rails at the script of feelings. In this twisted theater, characters play shifting parts: mothers become sisters, sisters become wives, fiancées become cousins, cousins become lovers, heroes become villains. Characters strike poses and stumble over lines. They often seem to be speaking parts from other productions. The plots are stale and explosive. In the final act, Pierre thrusts his two pistols in the breast pockets of his coat, stalks down the avenue, confronts his cousin Glen in the triangular space of City Hall Park—"the very proscenium of the town" (359)—and, before a panicked audience, shoots Glen dead. Within the space of the next few pages, Pierre is arrested, Lucy dies of shock, Pierre takes poison from Isabel, and Isabel herself swallows poison and collapses with a flourish over her "brother's" body. In *Pierre,* the performances of characters and narrator are fixed and out of control. The book falls apart into melodrama.

The story and the discourse of *Pierre* are saturated with a sense of insidious structural contradiction. Melville acknowledges that the discourses of the heart produce forceful and yet constricting responses. As the book progresses, the constriction increases in direct proportion to the force. The more deeply Pierre feels, the more banal his sentiments become. The more Pierre strives to do good, the worse he does. The more Pierre struggles, the more tightly he becomes bound. Such is the drastic diastole and systole of *Pierre.* This is the keen pathos of the book. Melville figures the contradictions in the "central conceit" (209) of the pamphlet "Chronometricals and Horologicals," pages of which Pierre finds crumpled on the seat cushion of his coach to New York City. Written by the philosopher Plotinus Plinlimmon, "Chronometricals and Horologicals" analyzes the predicament of the "enthusiast youth" who attempts "to reconcile this world with his own soul" (208). The pamphlet pivots on the disparities between heavenly and earthly measures and cautions against the dangers of attempting to join the two realms. Plinlimmon hints that "by their very contradictions they are made to correspond" (212). Although he counsels "virtuous expediency" (214), this advice is endorsed neither by the narrator's comments nor by Pierre's subsequent actions.[55]

"Chronometricals and Horologicals" describes a problem that fascinated Melville throughout his career: how contradictions are made
to correspond. Delivered in the pamphlet in the registers of Christian
paradox and idealist dilemma, the problem is also an ideological one.
The discrepancy between world and soul in *Pierre* is also a contradiction within world and within soul. The narrator describes how the pamphlet works its way through a tear in his coat pocket, down into the
skirt, and deep into the padding. He unknowingly carries it around with
him for years. It becomes incorporated into the texture of his character.
In *Pierre*, Melville perfects a disfigured prose whose simultaneous assertions of coherence and revelations of disorder convey the ways in
which contradictions are made, barely, to correspond. Hackneyed and
compelling, this prose is both the achievement and the downfall of
Pierre.

In an attempt to free himself from his legacy, Pierre is continually destroying texts. At Saddle Meadows, he rips Isabel's letter and shreds his
copies of the *Inferno* and *Hamlet*. At the Black Swan Inn, he commits to
the fire his youthful literary efforts, the secretly painted portrait of his
father, and family documents, including his correspondence with his
cousin Glen. In New York City, he burns the letter he receives from
Lucy. Pierre is frequently found beside a fireplace, not inducing reveries
but attempting to incinerate his relations. Yet these attempts are futile.
Toward the end of the book, laboring over his own book, Pierre seems
to understand his impasse: "Yet that knowing his fatal condition does
not one whit enable him to change or better his condition" (303). The
narrator and author also seem to suffer from this fateful insight. In
Pierre, the texts that are torn turn out to be lining the internal surfaces
of the self.

Over the course of *Pierre*, Melville dangles before the reader not a
little half-worn shoe but the thoroughly worn heart of Pierre—the ultimate sentimental fetish. The pumping, strangling heart is not the kind
of keepsake the reader will wish to preserve on the parlor table. The
stage properties in *Pierre* possess lives of their own: the inscribed hearts;
father Glendinning's portrait, which whispers, smiles, and stares; Isabel's guitar, which sings to her and knows her history; Lucy's little slip-
pers, which peep out from under the curtains of her bed; and the restless, eerie gift book on display during the narrator's "hymn to Love" in
book 2: "Love is both Creator's and Saviour's gospel to mankind; a
volume bound in rose-leaves, clasped with violets, and by the beaks of

humming-birds printed with peach-juice on the leaves of lilies" (34). Popular between 1825 and 1865, gift books were published annually as presents for Christmas and New Year. They contained sketches, short stories, poems, and illustrations, and printed works by writers such as Sigourney, Stowe, Child, Willis, T. S. Arthur, Longfellow, Hawthorne, Emerson, and Poe. Lavishly bound, these repositories of antebellum literary and visual culture were on conspicuous display in many middle-class households. Melville's elaborate book of Love (one shudders to think about how many hummingbirds sacrificed their beaks) is the gift book to end all gift books.[56]

The narrator's "hymn to Love" in general and the florid gift book in particular have been attacked by twentieth-century critics who decry Melville's style in *Pierre,* especially in the opening sections, as insufferably mawkish. Lewis Mumford, F. O. Matthiessen, and Newton Arvin all adduce the gift book as evidence of Melville's loss of artistic control. Mumford laments the absence of "both taste and discretion": "In *Pierre* he was no longer the cool rider of words, but the flayed and foaming horse, running away." Matthiessen describes how "confused insecurity of intention could reduce [Melville's] voice to an impotent echo of the *Lady's Book.*" Murray is moved to metaphorical violence: "More than anything it is the language—not so much the long neologisms and convoluted sentences, but the idiom of fervent passion—which at too frequent points through sheer inanity, if not falsity, makes one wince and squirm, until a hand automatically reaches out for some object, anything, with which to oust 'Love's sweet bird from her nest.'" Yes, as I have been arguing, it *is* the language: vibrant, volatile, ornate, tenacious, implicating. The reflections and recognitions in *Pierre* seem to produce extreme responses in its readers, who wish to throw the book across the room or to clasp it to their breast. Such visceral responses seem appropriate for Melville's most intimate anatomy.[57]

Nineteenth-century reviewers of American literature often selected edifying passages with which to instruct their readers in the lessons of sensibility. These textual "beauties" were self-evidently to represent the proper forms of expression. Style was implicitly acknowledged as a vehicle for ideological training and sentimental consent. Faced with the prose of Melville's *Pierre,* however, with its immoderate, involuted lessons and its lack of a clear match between intention and effect, most nineteenth-century reviewers and many twentieth-century critics resorted to printing admonitory "uglies." Rather than illustrate Melville's elegance or purity, these passages revealed his deviance.[58] Melville's prose, in *Pierre* most emphatically but also in the books preceding it, is full of such overwrought passages, many of which I have sought to highlight in this study. Instead of executing decorous turns, Melville twists open his rhetoric. Like the gift book in *Pierre*, Melville's anatomies are alive with clichés and teeming with figures.

Post Mortem

After the Anatomies

Concluding is hard to do. This is particularly true in writing about Melville because he vexes the elegant figure, the usual form, and the finishing touch. Although it seems that Melville's literary career must have ended with the ashes of *Pierre*, it did not. Still to come were the point-of-view experiments in the short fiction (1853–1856), the insinuating studies of character, form, and reform in *The Confidence-Man* (1857), the aspects of Civil War victory examined through various poetic genres in *Battle-Pieces* (1866), the exacting lines of *Clarel*'s spiritual, scientific, and sexual quest (1876), and Melville's ultimate, unfinished reflection on "measured forms" and "ragged edges": the painstaking inquiry into the mysteries of desire, narrative, and authorship in *Billy Budd* (1888?–1891).[1]

Yet *Pierre* does mark a turn. In the sections describing Pierre's literary efforts, Melville takes stock of his own literary experience. He contemplates the cage of expectations he created for himself by relying in *Typee* and *Omoo* on the "rich and peculiar experience" of his South Pacific journeys to establish a persona and attract an audience, and he weighs the cost of premature success (259). He ponders the critics who, valuing "Perfect Taste," complained about his lack of "smoothness" and "genteelness" and reprimanded him for his "vulgarity" and "vigor" (245–46). He voices frustration at what he perceives as the inverse relationship between merit and success, since the books he considered his best earned the least notice and profit (262, 339). He describes the grueling work schedule, practical impediments, and personal inadequacies that weighed on him during the writing of *Moby-Dick* (282–85, 340–42). He confesses his weariness with extravagant literary performances: "only hired to appear on the stage, not voluntarily claiming the public attention; their utmost life-redness and glow is but rouge, washed off in private with bitterest tears; their laugh only rings because it is hollow; and the answering laugh is no laughter to them" (258). Characteristically, he then distances himself from such melancholy, suggesting that it, too, is part of a sentimental script: "There is nothing so slipperily alluring as sadness" (258–59). He evaluates his compositional methods, in which he combustibly mixed autobiography, reading, and imagination in his "frenzied ink" and "directly plagiarized from his own experiences" (302).

The phrase "plagiarized from his own experiences" nicely captures the self-incorporation and appropriation in Melville's early works and the sense in which Melville's experiences were only partly his own. The phrase also conveys Melville's uneasiness with exposure. He describes the author's dilemma, in a digression from his account of Pierre's juvenalia, thus: "It is impossible to talk or to write without apparently throwing oneself helplessly open" (259). His narrator muses on the disquieting revelations experienced by anyone who has "gone down into himself" (176). In a summer 1851 letter to Hawthorne, Melville describes how he has "unfolded within" himself with alarming speed during the first phase of his writing career: "But I feel that I am now come to the inmost leaf of the bulb, and that shortly the flower must fall to the mould." Both narrator and correspondent suggest that Melville has reached a limit. Exposures—discursive, ideological, and inevitably personal—make Melville's anatomies vital and risky undertakings. In *Pierre,* Melville, like Pierre before Lucy's easel, sees his own anatomy: "The floor was scattered with the bread-crumbs and charcoal-dust; he looked behind the easel, and saw his own portrait, in the skeleton" (357). In Pierre, Melville watches himself feel, and recoils.[2]

From *Typee* through *Pierre,* Melville examines the overwrought surfaces—bodies, landscapes, and pages—and the inscribed interiors—eyes, minds, and hearts—of mid-nineteenth-century America. Until *Pierre,* he retains the hope, however tenuous it becomes as the books progress, that he as observer is not bound and marked as are the Typee, the Africans and African Americans both slave and "free," Queequeg, Tashtego, and Daggoo, Lucy and Isabel. His critiques imply that he can be both inside and comparatively unimpaired. In *Pierre,* the sense of confinement and damage is overpowering. The outward journeys in the earlier books in search of exotic bodies and the inward journeys of *Pierre* all end in the figure of the crisscrossed heart, the token of subjectivity, removed from its sheltering cavity. Thus, in *Pierre,* Melville offers the ultimate scene of writing and reading in the series that began with the tattooed faces in *Typee.*

Melville's metaphors in *Pierre* epitomize his anatomy project and resonate with the images employed by twentieth-century theorists of ideology. The "surface stratified on surface" (285) excavated by Melville's geologist is reminiscent of the tectonics of personality outlined by Antonio Gramsci in *The Prison Notebooks:*

> The personality is strangely composite. . . . The starting-point of critical elaboration is the consciousness of what one really is, and is "knowing thyself" as a product of the historical process to date which has deposited in you an infinity of traces, without leaving an inventory. . . . It is not enough to know the *ensemble* of relations as they exist at any given time as a given system. They must be known genetically, in the movement of their formation. For each individual is the synthesis not only of existing relations, but of the history of these relations. He is a précis of all the past.[3]

Melville makes material the Delphic injunction to "know thyself." He represents his narrators and protagonists as composites, whose characters have been historically formed and fractured, in texts that are themselves layered and seamed. Seeking to provide an inventory of the infinite, he restages scenes, amplifies figures, unfolds conceits, and alludes without end. Knowledge is reflexive and extensive in Melville's anatomies. To go down into oneself is to expose shared deposits. Melville's deeply mined narrators and protagonists are representative men.

The intricate spaces of the heart in *Pierre,* the "catacombs," "halls," "windings," "spiral stairs," "pyramid," "room," and "sarcophagus," suggest an architecture of personality similar to the "structures of feeling" described by Raymond Williams in *Marxism and Literature:*

> We are talking about characteristic elements of impulse, restraint, and tone; specifically affective elements of consciousness and relationships: not feeling against thought, but thought as felt and feeling as thought: practical consciousness of a present kind, in a living and interrelating continuity. We are then defining these elements as a "structure": as a set, with specific internal relations, at once interlocking and in tension.[4]

Melville examines the articulations of private and public and thought and feeling. He shows how feelings have become fixed to the parts of the human body and represents these structures in relation and extraordinary tension. In *Keywords*, Williams provides a historical inventory of concepts such as literature, nature, privacy, and society. Melville presents a similar inventory for the "keywords" of nineteenth-century selfhood—face, skin, head, eyes, heart—and their compounds: human, man, race, nation. In *Marxism and Literature*, Williams urges that the affective and cognitive landscape be charted so that readers can learn to maneuver strategically and to discern new formations. The difficulty of achieving such a perspective is evident in the apprehensions of *Typee* and *White-Jacket*, the overwhelming bodies of *Moby-Dick*, and the enthralling visions of *Pierre*.

By the end of *Pierre*, Melville seems to have reached not a Williams-like appreciation of process and practical consciousness, but an Althusserian insight about the confinements of subjectivity.[5] Yet for Melville, structure is never destiny. What ends with *Pierre* is not Melville's belief in human agency or multiple subjectivities or his career-long effort to catalogue the encounter between inherited forms and individual response; what ends is his experiment with exuberant, inside critique. *Pierre* marks the rupture of Melville's anatomies. There are many reasons for Melville's shift in literary practice: the uncomfortable disclosures about family history, the sexual confusions and allures, the devastating political judgments, Melville's intellectual and formal restlessness, the utter financial and critical failure of *Pierre*. All of these alter the shape of Melville's career. Yet I am pointing to the fundamental importance of the ideological recognitions in *Pierre*.

With *Pierre*, which critics have long interpreted as a turning point, Melville did not conclude his "quarrel with fiction," since from the start he was interested not in "fiction" but in forms that mixed fiction, autobiography, travel narratives, sailor narratives, ethnology texts, and aesthetic treatises (to name only the genres I have highlighted in the preceding chapters). Nor did he reject convention, since he continued to be fascinated by the ways in which ideas were produced and received. Nor did he repudiate literature or lose faith in the communicative power of art, since after *Pierre* he continued to write, turning his energies to other genres, particularly the short story and the poetic sequence.[6]

Nor did Melville revolt against the assumptions of his middle-class readers, as critics such as William Charvat and Ann Douglas have forcefully argued. Clearly he expressed ambivalence about his perceived audience in his letters and his books. Yet figured in *Pierre* is not an author, narrator, or character that is split from the public, but a self that finds the public inside. *Pierre* unfolds a confounding insight about the forces that move the writer to speak. If Melville revolts—and certainly there is retreat in *Typee* and disgust in *Pierre*—he revolts against assumptions that he has displayed as a shared cultural inheritance. Rather than keeping distant from his audience's horizon of expectations, he journeys to its edge. In *Pierre*, Melville acknowledges an intimate complicity with his readers that disrupts his faith in the revelatory, transformative possibilities of the hearty transactions and interior critiques he had practiced since *Typee*. This unsettling of confidence is represented in the choreographed reversals of syntax and position in *The Confidence-Man* (1857), and particularly in the shared narratives of Indian-hating. Described as ingested and incorporated into the sinews, these narratives bind backwoodsman, judge, and cosmopolitan, Southerner, Westerner, and Easterner.[7]

Pierre represents the maturing of Melville's skepticism about the feasibility and benefits of gaining a thorough "consciousness of what one really is." The kind of catalogue of consciousness undertaken in the earlier anatomies is represented as a balked effort to account for an infinity of traces. The awareness gained is described as an accumulating burden, a series of insights that incarcerates. Melville's expansive, incorporative sentences collapse under the weight of their discoveries.

Throughout his career, Melville's ideological inquiries are linked with his verbal practice. He locates ideology in the substance of nineteenth-century discourse: the constitution of subjects, the relationships between subjects and objects, the conjugation of verbs, the structures of metaphor, analogy, personification, allusion, and elision. Melville's rhetoric and forms shift with his emphases. After the overwritten hearts of *Pierre*, he engages in a phase of underwriting in the meticulous short stories and the slippery pitches of *The Confidence-Man*. He continues his encyclopedic attention to nineteenth-century ideas in works such as *The Confidence-Man* and *Clarel*, but his techniques are different.

Melville's last work of fiction, *Billy Budd, Sailor (An Inside Narrative)*, begins with a figure from Melville's past: a handsome African whose symmetrical form, ebony chest, and shapely head make him the center of attention and object of desire for his companions and for the narrator. *Billy Budd* is Melville's final meditation on the body and its secrets. The narrator begins by examining the features of one handsome sailor and then studies another, the title character, Billy Budd, an Adam before the serpent. The young Budd is executed on the order of his judicious, paternal captain, Edward Vere, for killing the malicious master-at-arms, John Claggart, with an involuntary blow to the head. Once again, the desire to know bodies and characters generates an extended inquiry. Yet there is a difference. In *Billy Budd,* it is as though Melville sought to shape a verbal equivalent to the caresses in *Moby-Dick.* Melville fashions a remarkable instrument for touching upon character, a subtle, scrupulous prose that again and again announces the limits of its reach, the recesses it cannot know. Insistently allegorical and emblematic, precise and ambiguous, this prose continually tempts readers to take its story and its characters too simply. This transparent opacity insulates the objects of study from interpretive violence. It is a prose that pursues character but refrains from penetrating, fixing, or ranking. Rather than judging Vere or opening Budd to view, the narrator seeks to imagine and understand their actions, as far as he can, while preserving their "inviolable" "privacy."[8] *Billy Budd* is an "inside narrative" about the inability of a narrator to get inside, to read surface in depth, to gain full access to the character of his characters.

In "The Attic Landscape," part of *Timoleon* (1891), Melville's last, privately printed volume of poems, he describes the desire for formal clarity and discipline. "The Attic Landscape" appears in the section of *Timoleon* entitled "Fruit of Travel of Long Ago," whose poems were first written in the late 1850s, after Melville had returned from a therapeutic trip to Europe and the Near East. He reworked these poems at the end of his life. "Fruit of Travel" inaugurates and closes his poetic career. In "The Attic Landscape," Melville imagines a terrain very different from that with which he began in *Typee, White-Jacket, Moby-Dick,* and *Pierre:*

> Tourist, spare the avid glance
>   That greedy roves the sight to see:
> Little here of "Old Romance,"
>   Or Picturesque of Tivoli.
>
> No flushful tint the sense to warm—
> Pure outline pale, a linear charm.
> The clear-cut hills carved temples face,
> Respond, and share their sculptural grace.
>
> 'Tis Art and Nature lodged together,
>   Sister by sister, cheek to cheek;
> Such Art, such Nature, and such weather
>   The All-in-All seems here a Greek.

Melville qualifies his Attic desires with an equivocating "seems" in "The Attic Landscape" (God "seems" a Greek), with an unsettling comparison between Parthenon and courtesan in "The Parthenon," and with an end-rhymed association between symmetry and rigidity in the poem "Greek Masonry." He precedes the Grecian poems with a cluster of poems describing the enticements of ornament and obscurity in Italian scenes. He follows them with two poems describing the blinding incandescence of the Egyptian desert and the sterile, enduring form of the Great Pyramid. In "Fruit of Travel of Long Ago," Melville reflects upon his shift away from "magnitude," "lavishness," and "innovating willfulness," the terms cast off in the poem "Greek Architecture." [9]

In Melville's prose works of the 1840s and early 1850s, there is nothing like the abstract yearnings and classic lines of "The Attic Landscape" and the Greek sequence in *Timoleon*. In his anatomies, Melville does not spare, but indulges the "avid glance." He examines the impurities, as well as the purities, of outline. He carves human faces, assays the tints of flesh, lays open the head, uproots the landscape, and holds out his heart in his hand. He draws out the allure and the risks of exorbitance. "Art" and "Nature," lodged together in nineteenth-century discourse about race, gender, sentiment, and nation, are pulled apart in Melville's anatomies, their ligaments exposed.

In his influential 1851 letter to Hawthorne, Melville writes: "What I feel most moved to write, that is banned,—it will not pay. Yet, altogether, write the *other* way I cannot. So the product is a final hash, and all my books are botches." [10] Despite his affecting self-dramatizations here, Melville's anatomies suggest that the deepest obstacles to his expression at the climax of the first part of his career lay not in a recalcitrant and unrewarding market but in what and how the "I" feels. From *Typee* through *Pierre*, Melville probes the structures and impulses of feeling and shows that one's own way of feeling and writing is inseparable from the "other ways." He demonstrates the salience of hashes and the profit of botches. Melville's hashes and botches, his anatomies, are the remarkable product of a sustained, exuberant critique that reaches its intimate limits in *Pierre*.

Notes

INTRODUCTION: INTIMATE EXCESS

1. Melville, *Moby-Dick*, 344. Subsequent references to the Northwestern-Newberry edition (see bibliography) are made in parentheses in the body of this chapter.

2. *Queequeg Rescues Tashtego* (1986) is one of six pastels interpreting scenes from *Moby-Dick* that Milloff produced in the mid-1980s. The others are *The Chase—Third Day* (1985), *Stripping the Whale* (1985), *Attacking the Pod, or the Living Wall* (1986), *How Ahab Lost His Leg* (1986), and *The Dying Whale* (1986). In each picture, Milloff meditates on violence, flesh, race, and labor. At the center of the carnage in *Stripping the Whale*, human and whale flesh intersect. Queequeg's angled body is crossed by a long, thick strip of blubber, sliced and hooked. Milloff gives Queequeg's skin a gray cast, covered with tiny geometric tattoos. Elizabeth A. Schultz reproduces and analyzes the series in *Unpainted to the Last*, plates 53–56, figures 8.62 and 8.63; pp. 240–56.

3. On Melville, discourse, and ideology, see Rogin, *Subversive Genealogy;* Bercovitch and Jehlen, *Ideology and Classic American Literature;* and Dimock, *Empire For Liberty*. For ironic readings, see Duban, *Melville's Major Fiction* and "Chipping with a Chisel"; and Samson, *White Lies*. On Melville's ambivalences, see Bell, *Development of the American Romance*, 231–35; and Emery, "Topicality of Depravity in 'Benito Cereno'" and "'Benito Cereno' and Manifest Destiny." Andrew Delbanco has described the diminishing returns of the two-choice approach to Melville studies, either celebrating the writer's transcendence or indicting him for his complicity, in "Melville in the '80s," 710. Several critics have discussed Melville's prose ability to inhabit and analyze perspectives; see especially Berthoff, *The Example of Melville*, 204–11; and also Abrams, "*Typee* and *Omoo*," 33–34; Herbert, *Marquesan Encounters*, 158–59;

Samson, *White Lies*, 8, 133; and Levine, *Conspiracy and Romance*, 186–88, 215, 223. Stephen Greenblatt describes similar qualities in Shakespeare, achieved through "a peculiarly intense submission," in *Renaissance Self-Fashioning*, 252–54. My own study is particularly indebted to Sacvan Bercovitch, who describes the mutual shapings of history, rhetoric, and ideology; to Michael Paul Rogin, who intertwines Melville's biography, family history, and nineteenth-century politics; and to Wai-chee Dimock, who argues for analogies between Melville's rhetoric and antebellum social practices. I also have learned a great deal from Carolyn L. Karcher on Melville's urgent interests in nineteenth-century racial theory, in *Shadow over the Promised Land;* and from Sharon Cameron on flesh and philosophy, in *The Corporeal Self.*

4. O'Brien, "Our Authors and Authorship," 389–90. O'Brien also wrote an early assessment of Melville's career, "Our Young Authors—Melville" (1853).

5. Northrop Frye, *Anatomy of Criticism*, 308–14; see also Philip Stevick, "Novel and Anatomy." For historical background on the anatomy, or Menippean satire, see Kirk, *Menippean Satire*, ix–xxxiii. Critics who connect Melville to the literary anatomy include Donald Deidrich Schultz, in *Herman Melville and the Tradition of the Anatomy;* McCarthy, "Elements of Anatomy in Melville's Fiction"; Kern, "Melville's *The Confidence-Man*"; Mushabac, *Melville's Humor;* and Lee, "*Moby-Dick* as Anatomy." Although Frye refocused modern attention on the anatomy, the Russian critic Bakhtin, whose work was not available in English translation until the late 1960s and early 1970s, had analyzed the relationships between the genre and the works of Rabelais and Dostoevsky thirty years earlier. See Bakhtin, *Rabelais and His World* and *Problems of Dostoevsky's Poetics.* Bakhtin outlines his proposals for stylistic analysis in "Discourse Typology in Prose."

6. Gramsci, *Selections from the Prison Notebooks*, 324, 333; Raymond Williams, *Marxism and Literature*, 128–35; Foucault, *The Order of Things*, 132. The phrase "nomination of the visible" occurs (in translation) during Foucault's discussion of European natural history and refers to his argument that scientific observation sought to reduce its objects to clear, finite, linear structures. Melville covers much of the same conceptual ground as his contemporary, Karl Marx. Despite the differences in their political commitments, authorial stances, and forms of expression and despite Melville's doubts about social revolution, both Marx and Melville perform nineteenth-century anatomies of consciousness. Both analyze how contradictions are made to correspond and how alienation and violence are naturalized. Rogin links Melville and Marx as critics of bourgeois split subjectivity, unmaskers of social division, and analysts of failed rebellion, in *Subversive Genealogy*, 17–20, 102–220. H. Bruce Franklin associates Melville and Marx in terms of their concerns with working-class consciousness and the formation of subjectivity, in *Prison Literature in America*, 38–49. Recent critics who use the term "anatomy" to describe their ideological inquiries include Lauren Berlant, in *The Anatomy of National Fantasy* (on Hawthorne and nationalism); David Theo Goldberg, in *Anatomy of Racism* (on contemporary racial discourse); and Robyn Wiegman, in *American Anatomies.* Wiegman translates Foucault's *Order of Things* to the United States, placing race at the center of his account. I take the notion of an "American grammar

book" from Hortense Spillers' analysis of the enduring diction, syntax, and metaphors of African slavery in "Mama's Baby, Papa's Maybe." The strange materiality of Melville's figures and concerns have been remarked upon by two of his sharpest writer-critics—D. H. Lawrence, in *Studies in Classic American Literature*, 154–55, and Charles Olson, in *Call Me Ishmael*, 81–105.

7. Eagleton, *Ideology*, 106. For a twentieth-century attempt to anatomize America, see William Carlos Williams, *In the American Grain*. On anatomy and history, see Kirk, *Menippean Satire*, ix–xxxiii; Bakhtin, "Discourse Typology in Prose," 183–84; and Donald Deidrich Schultz, *Herman Melville and the Tradition of the Anatomy*, 53–56.

8. The separation between figurative and historical registers is apparent in Babbalanja's revealing tropes of "perverse bodies" in chapter 155 and in the flat allegory of United States expansionist and slavery politics in chapters 157–62. Several critics have interpreted *Mardi* as a key text in Melville's creative development; see Merrell R. Davis, *Melville's "Mardi,"* and Richard H. Brodhead, "*Mardi*: Creating the Creative." In *Empire for Liberty*, Wai-chee Dimock analyzes the logics of individualism and Manifest Destiny in *Mardi*, in which sovereignty dovetails with subjection (42–75). The influence on *Mardi* of the literary anatomists, particularly Rabelais and Burton, is described by Merrell R. Davis in *Melville's "Mardi,"* 62–78, and by F. O. Matthiessen in *American Renaissance*, 122–24.

9. Melville, *Correspondence*, 191. Traditionally, the letter has been dated around June 1, 1851. Recently, Parker has argued for a date in early May; see Parker, *Herman Melville: A Biography*, 1:840–44. Other self-representations Melville offers in his letter include a Pittsfield farmer tinkering with his corn and potatoes; a raconteur in Heaven with Hawthorne; a neglected prophet ("Though I wrote the Gospels in this century, I should die in the gutter"); a victim of the mass-market and popular taste ("To go down to posterity is bad enough, any way; but to go down as a 'man who lived among the cannibals'!"); a searcher for Truth and a brooder on Fame; and a spontaneously generated intellect ("Until I was twenty-five, I had no development at all"). The personal and financial pressures under which Melville labored during the writing of *Moby-Dick* are described by Leon Howard in *Herman Melville: A Biography*, 150–79, and by Hershel Parker in his historical note to the Northwestern-Newberry *Moby-Dick*, 618–35, 659–84, and his *Herman Melville: A Biography*, 1:702–865 passim. For examples of critics who use Melville's compelling phrases from the letter to Hawthorne as defining terms, see Vincent, *The Trying-Out of "Moby-Dick,"* 25–35; Baym, "Melville's Quarrel with Fiction"; Bell, *The Development of the American Romance*, 36; Yannella, "Writing the 'Other Way'"; and Brodhead, *School of Hawthorne*, 17–47. For influential founding images of Melville, see the three early biographies: Weaver, *Herman Melville: Mariner and Mystic*; Freeman, *Herman Melville*; and Mumford, *Herman Melville*. Some critics recently have begun to question the oppositions between Melville and the marketplace; see Wald, *Constituting Americans*, 122–56; and Post-Lauria, *Correspondent Colorings*.

10. In "Herman-Neutics," Philip Weis describes the inordinate identifications of Melville scholars with their object of study.

CHAPTER ONE: LOSING FACE IN *TYPEE*

1. The Lawrence quotations are from his *Studies in Classic American Literature*, 141, 146–47. The inquiry into the reasons for the flight from "paradise" dates back to the earliest reviews in 1846. See, for example, John Sullivan Dwight's review from the Brook Farm *Harbinger* and the anonymous review in *Douglas Jerrold's Shilling Magazine,* both reprinted in Milton Stern, *Critical Essays on Herman Melville's "Typee,"* 22–27 and 35–37. For the line of *Typee* criticism that extends from Lawrence, see the essays by William Ellery Sedgwick, Newton Arvin, Milton R. Stern, James E. Miller, Jr., Richard Ruland, and Robert E. Abrams, reprinted in Stern,*Critical Essays.* See also Dillingham, *An Artist in the Rigging,* 9–30. In "False Sympathy in Melville's *Typee,*" Mitchell Breitwieser revises this traditional line, arguing that the flaws lie in the observing consciousness rather than in the culture observed. Other critics who analyze the narrator's flawed perceptions include Thomas J. Scorza, in Stern, *Critical Essays,* and John Samson, in *White Lies,* 22–56. In *Marquesan Encounters* T. Walter Herbert suggests—accurately, it seems to me—that the boundary between narrator and writer in *Typee* is not consistent, clean, or neat (149–92).

2. The quotations on cannibalism are from a letter written in 1850 by Sophia Hawthorne to her mother (reprinted in Metcalf, *Herman Melville: Cycle and Epicycle,* 91) and James E. Miller's *Reader's Guide to Herman Melville,* 33. Critics who focus on cannibalism as *the* trouble in Tommo's paradise include Richard Chase, Newton Arvin, Milton R. Stern, Richard Ruland, John Seelye, and Robert E. Abrams, in Milton Stern, *Critical Essays on "Typee."* Caleb Crain argues for the congruences between cannibalism and homosexuality across Melville's fiction, both being represented as "unspeakable" and both inducing "panic." I also will chart a pattern of cannibalism representations, but will evaluate that pattern differently and in relation to a complementary set of tattooing representations. See Crain, "Lovers of Human Flesh." Among the critics who attend to both threats but do not distinguish between cannibalism and tattooing are Richard Chase, Edgar A. Dryden, Richard Ruland, and Thomas J. Scorza, in Milton Stern, *Critical Essays.* See also Pullin, "Melville's *Typee:* The Failure of Eden," and Giltrow, "Speaking Out." Recently, in *Strike through the Mask,* Elizabeth Renker has argued that tattooing represents the deeper fear (19–23). See also Schueller, "Colonialism and Melville's South Sea Journeys," 13.

3. In considering the prospect of bodily, and especially facial, marking in *Typee* and in antebellum culture, I have found two theoretical works to be especially useful: Michel Foucault's *Discipline and Punish* and Michael Fried's *Realism, Writing, and Disfiguration.* For the purposes of this chapter, I am less interested in Foucault's intoxication with incarceration, especially toward the end of the book, or in his startling account of the "military dream" of a disciplinary society (although this does seem to me the concern of Melville's 1850 *White-Jacket; or, The World in a Man-of-War*). In discussing *Typee,* I am more interested in Foucault's analysis of visual "examination" as combining hierarchical observation and normalizing judgment: "It is a normalizing gaze, a surveillance that makes it possible to qualify, to classify and to punish. It establishes over in-

dividuals a visibility through which one differentiates them and judges them" (184). As will become clear in my discussion of tattooing, ethnology, and racial identity, I argue for the persistence of spectacle and the significance of vivid corporeal marking, which Foucault minimizes in his analysis of nineteenth-century inspection. Fried brilliantly analyzes Stephen Crane's obsession with the "scene of writing" and the threat that the materiality of writing posed to his attempt to represent "reality." According to Fried, this obsession was revealed in Crane's fascinating images of upturned and disfigured faces. My account of Melville's *Typee* deals with some of the same issues and images, in a less thematic and self-referential way. That is, I try to specify the historical and racial dimensions of the fear of writing; to detail the ways in which late-eighteenth- and nineteenth-century bodies were written upon; and to analyze the mid-nineteenth-century investments in the human face.

4. I discuss the following narratives: G. H. von Langsdorff's *Voyages and Travels in Various Parts of the World* (1813–1814); A. J. von Krusenstern's *Voyage round the World* (1813); David Porter's *Journal of a Cruise Made to the Pacific Ocean* (1815); William Ellis's *Polynesian Researches* (1833); Charles S. Stewart's *A Visit to the South Seas* (1831); James F. O'Connell's *A Residence of Eleven Years in New Holland and the Caroline Islands,* which was edited from his verbal narration ([1836] 1972); Frederick Debell Bennett's *Narrative of a Whaling Voyage round the Globe* (1840); and John Coulter's *Adventures in the Pacific* (1845). Langsdorff, Porter, Ellis, and Stewart have been identified by scholars as sources used by Melville in writing *Typee.* Page references to the above editions (see bibliography) will be made in parentheses in the body of the text.

5. Charles Roberts Anderson describes the differences between Melville's actual four-week stay and his narrator Tommo's fictional four-month visit. Melville deserted the whaler *Acushnet* with his companion Richard Tobias Greene and remained on Nukuheva from July 9–August 9, 1842. See Anderson, *Melville in the South Seas,* 69–195. Anderson emphasizes Melville's use of Langsdorff's *Voyages and Travels* (1813–1814), Porter's *Journal of a Cruise* (1815), and Stewart's *Visit to the South Seas* (1831). In *Marquesan Encounters,* T. Walter Herbert deepens the investigation of sources, juxtaposing the interpretive perspectives of Melville (the Romantic), David Porter (the spokesman for the Enlightenment), and Charles S. Stewart (the Calvinist). Leon Howard describes the excisions and revisions in the three versions of *Typee* published in 1846: English (February), Original American (March), and Revised American (July). See his historical note in the Northwestern-Newberry edition of *Typee,* pp. 277–301. All quotations from *Typee* are taken from this edition and given in parentheses in the body of the chapter.

6. In *Colonial Encounters,* Peter Hulme examines the Carib/Arawak distinction and analyzes cannibalism as the "defining feature" (3) and the "central regulating mechanism" (85) of colonial discourse (1–87). Despite the passage of three hundred years and the shift in location from the Atlantic to the Pacific, the founding trope still resonates in *Typee* and in other narratives of Marquesan encounter. In *The Man-Eating Myth,* William Arens emphasizes the ideological functions of the accusation of cannibalism and argues that the charge—naming

the most profane act imaginable—is "an aspect of cultural-boundary construction and maintenance" (145) found across cultures and periods (139–62).
Arens points out that the Arawaks accused the Caribs, too. Scholarly debate
about the facts and the discourse surrounding cannibalism has been fierce; see,
for example, Jehlen, "History before the Fact," Hulme, "Making No Bones: A
Response to Myra Jehlen," and Jehlen, "Response to Peter Hulme."

7. Arens, *Man-Eating Myth*, 89. On Cook and his voyages, see Beaglehole,
The Life of Captain James Cook, and Withey, *Voyages of Discovery*. W. Patrick
Strauss describes Cook's popularity in America in *Americans in Polynesia*,
148–53.

8. The evidence for cannibalism encountered during Cook's voyages is considered by Withey in *Voyages of Discovery*, 132–43, 217–18, 243–44, 282–
83, and 299–300. The likelihood of Marquesan cannibalism is discussed by
E. S. Craighill Handy in *The Native Culture in the Marquesas*, 218–21, and by
Charles Roberts Anderson in *Melville in the South Seas*, 100–10. Focusing
on Cook's second voyage (1772–1775), Gananath Obeyesekere analyzes in
"'British Cannibals'" how the discourse and practice of cannibalism were constructed in a complex dialogue between Europeans and Polynesians. Cook and
his astronomer William Wales tell the story of cannibalism on board the *Resolution*. The journals of both men are collected in the second volume of Beaglehole's *Journals of Captain James Cook on His Voyages of Discovery*. In his textual introduction, and in the sections entitled "Subordinate Ms. Sources" and
"Printed Sources," Beaglehole describes the histories and publications of the
various texts. For Cook's version of the events, see Beaglehole, *Journals of Cook*,
2:292–95; for the account given by Wales, see Beaglehole, *Journals of Cook*,
2:818–19. Subsequent references to the Cook and Wales journals are given in
parentheses in the body of the text. Beaglehole, in *Life of Cook*, 358–59, and
Withey, in *Voyages of Discovery*, 243–44, discuss the events on board the *Resolution*. Captain Brown's story is told by Francis Allyn Olmsted in *Incidents of
a Whaling Voyage*, 197–98, reprinted in Anderson, *Melville in the South Seas*,
92–93. Peter Hulme analyzes Smith's versions of his captivity and the role of
Pocahontas in *Colonial Encounters*, 137–73. John Samson notes Melville's
"Pocahontas" invention in *White Lies*, 29–30.

9. See "Burney's Log," collected in Beaglehole, *Journals of Cook*, 2:749–52.
Subsequent references to this log are given in parentheses in the body of the text.

10. Melville parodies the conventions of cannibal exposure in the encounter
between Ishmael and Queequeg in "The Spouter-Inn" chapter of *Moby-Dick*. I
discuss this scene in detail in chapter 3.

11. On "addiction," see David Porter, *Journal of a Cruise*, 2:45, and Langsdorff, *Voyages and Travels*, 1:142–43, 148. In *Torrey's Narrative*, 127–30,
William Torrey plays upon the clichés, not only lifting the veil from the cannibal feast but also inviting his readers to the table. He claims that he participated
in a human repast following a Marquesan battle. In apparently invented detail,
he describes the preparation, cooking, and disjointing of enemy bodies and the
surfeited stupor of the diners. He implies that he developed a taste for the "nicely
prepared" "delicious morsel[s]," which, he assures his readers, they would have
shared if they had been in his place.

12. Like Krusenstern, Cook expresses horror at the gap between savage and civilized man; unlike Krusenstern, he argues that this gap will close with time and with education. In the paragraph following the description of cannibalism on the *Resolution,* he meditates on cultural evolution, seeking to understand, if not quite excuse, the New Zealanders' behavior. Cannibalism, Cook reasons, is an ancient, customary practice, a vestige of savage life that is difficult to shed but that eventually will be discarded as the islanders continue to evolve (Beaglehole, *Journals of Cook,* 2:294–95).

13. E. S. Craighill Handy, in *Native Culture in the Marquesas,* 218–220, and Charles Roberts Anderson, in *Melville in the South Seas,* 100–110, discuss the distorting lenses of language and cultural perspective and the roles played by unreliable Polynesian and European informants who provided many travelers with their evidence. William Arens evaluates classic and contemporary stories of flesh eating in *Man-Eating Myth,* 43–116.

14. Edward Belcher, *Narrative of a Voyage round the World,* 2:317.

15. Geoffrey Sanborn analyzes Melville's strategic, defamiliarizing invocations of cannibalism in "Benito Cereno." See Sanborn, "Where's the Rest of Me?"

16. In "'The Thrice Mysterious Taboo,'" Alex Calder analyzes the "teasingly scrupulous sentences" in which Melville presents the circumstantial evidence for cannibalism. Comparing Melville's accounts with those in Charles S. Stewart and David Porter, Calder suggests that the vessel whose lid is raised by Tommo may be a coffin and the human remains he glimpses may be the product of Marquesan burial practices. According to Calder, Melville refuses to back an explanation for what Tommo sees; instead, he explores the continuum between interpretation and conviction.

17. In *Narrative of a Whaling Voyage,* Bennett writes that the distress associated with facial tattooing led to its being considered "an essential manly characteristic" among Marquesans and that "those who are destitute of such distinction are looked upon as effeminate" (1:307). O'Connell claimed that he had been tattooed by women, which seems unlikely but adds a female threat to the ordeal; see James F. O'Connell, *A Residence of Eleven Years,* 113–16. Later in the century, P. T. Barnum magnified the violence in his advertisement for the tattooed Captain Costentenus. An advertisement in an 1879 issue of *P. T. Barnum's Illustrated News* proclaims Costentenus as the survivor of "OVER 7,000,000 BLOOD-PRODUCING PUNCTURES"; see Barnum, *Selected Letters,* 201. According to Barnum, Costentenus's tattooing was performed by Asian captors as a torture for his complicity in an uprising of Chinese mine workers. On Costentenus, see Bogdan, *Freak Show,* 243–49. In the early twentieth century, the anthropologist Willowdean C. Handy reported that male Marquesans in the northwest islands, which include Nukuheva, stressed the pain endured in obtaining their elaborate designs; see Handy, *Tattooing in the Marquesas,* 23. A member of the Bayard Dominick Expedition to the Marquesas in 1920–1921, Handy offers a vivid portrait of Marquesan tattooing.

18. On the structure of human skin, see Samuel Stanhope Smith, *An Essay on the Causes of the Variety of Complexion and Figure in the Human Species,* 35; and White, *An Account of the Regular Gradation in Man,* 101–102. In

plate 4 of his book, White graphically represents the "cutis vera, or True Skin."
In an engraving of a "square portion of the skin of a Negro," the darker upper
layers, the cuticle and the rete mucosum, are peeled to the left in order to reveal
the "white" foundation. Langsdorff, in *Voyages and Travels,* 1:117, 122–23,
Krusenstern, in *Voyage round the World,* 1:155, and Charles S. Stewart, in *Visit
to the South Seas,* 1:228, all speak of their aesthetic appreciation of tattooing.
James F. O'Connell refers to his Marquesan persecutors as "savage printers"
(115). The anthropologist W. C. Handy (1922) takes a formal approach to tattooing in *Tattooing in the Marquesas,* casting her effort as one of preservation
and appreciation for an art of "pure design" (3, 24). She evaluates tattooing in
art historical terms, describing the body of conventions from which the artists
drew, the similarities between tattooing motifs and adzing and carving patterns,
and the division of labor in the imprinting process—the master tattooist who
outlines the designs and the disciples who fill them in (9–15).

19. For discussions of Marquesan beauty, see Krusenstern, *Voyage round the
World,* 1:151; Langsdorff, *Voyages and Travels,* 1:112–14; David Porter, *Journal of a Cruise,* 2:62, 86; Charles S. Stewart, *Visit to the South Seas,* 1:228,
255; Bennett, *Narrative of a Whaling Voyage,* 1:308–309, 312; and Melville,
Typee, 180–84. Krusenstern and Langsdorff praise Nukuhevan men more than
they praise the women. In *Melville in the South Seas* (121–26), Anderson traces
Melville's descriptions of the Nukuhevans to his various sources; on pp. 190–91
he considers possible reasons for Melville's dependence on these sources. For
Figueroa on Mendaña, see chapter 3 of the anonymously written *An Historical
Account of the Circumnavigation of the Globe,* which excerpts translated pas-
sages from Figueroa's *Hechos de Don Garcia Hurtado de Mendoza Quarto
Marques de Canete* (1613). Melville mentions both Figueroa and *Circumnavi-
gation of the Globe* in *Typee* (183).

20. G. H. von Langsdorff outlines the goals of the Krusenstern voyage and
the role of Counsellor Tilesius in his introduction (1:v–xi). On Blumenbach, see
Jordan, *White over Black,* 222–23; Horsman, *Race and Manifest Destiny,* 47,
54–55; and Bieder, *Science Encounters the Indian, 1820–1880,* 61–63. In *Visit
to the South Seas* (1832), Charles S. Stewart describes Piaroro, a Happar chief,
as being "of admirable proportions, with a general contour of figure, and round-
ness and polish of limb, that would do grace to an Apollo" (1:228). In *Journal
of a Cruise* (1815), David Porter also compares the proportions of Nukuhevan
men to statuary (2:62). In *Typee,* Melville describes the formal perfection of the
islanders: "nearly every individual of their number might have been taken for a
sculptor's model. . . . Many of their faces present a profile classically beautiful,
and in the valley of Typee, I saw several who, like the stranger Marnoo, were in
every respect models of beauty" (180, 184). In celebrated stanzas, Byron praises
the "ideal Beauty" of the marble *Apollo* in the Belvedere court of the Vatican;
see canto 4, stanzas 161–63, of *Childe Harold's Pilgrimage,* 194–95. At the
beginning of the twentieth century, Pauline Hopkins, writing in the *Colored
American Magazine,* plays the *Apollo Belvedere* game but unsettles the rules.
Hopkins argues that the *Apollo* (and the *Venus de Milo*) were chiseled from
Ethiopian slave models, and she champions a mulatto named Thomas E. White
as "the finest known living example of symmetrical physical development in a

human being." White surpasses even the *Apollo* because his "arms are of the proper length according to the standard of the Caucasian race"; see Hopkins, "Venus and the Apollo Modeled from Ethiopians," 465. On the links between ethnology and aesthetics, see Honour, *The Image of the Black in Western Art,* vol. 4, part 1, 11–27, and part 2, 12–21; and Stafford, *Body Criticism,* 1–45 ff.

21. Both of the passages quoted were removed before publication of the American editions of *Typee.* In the historical note to the Northwestern-Newberry edition of *Typee,* Howard speculates that these bowdlerizations of the English edition were performed under the direction of Melville's American publisher, John Wiley (283–84). In "Melville and Marquesan Eroticism," William Heath discusses the attractions of Marquesan women for Melville and for other Western travelers.

22. White, *Account of the Regular Gradation in Man,* 135.

23. On the elaborateness of Marquesan male tattooing, see Langsdorff, *Voyages and Travels,* 1:119–21; Ellis, *Polynesian Researches,* 1:205–09; Bennett, *Narrative of a Whaling Voyage,* 1:306–10; and also W. C. Handy, *Tattooing in the Marquesas,* 14. The process is described in Coulter, *Adventures in the Pacific,* 209–13; Ellis, *Polynesian Researches,* 1:205–06; James F. O'Connell, *Residence of Eleven Years,* 112–16; and Langsdorff, *Voyages and Travels,* 1:116–22. The analogy between tattoos and clothing is made by Ellis in *Polynesian Researches,* 1:207, and by Langsdorff in *Voyages and Travels,* 1:117–18. W. C. Handy describes "a complete suit of tattooing for the men" as "including the eyelids, often the inside of the nostrils, tongue, palms and back of the hand, arms, legs, and the entire trunk but not the penis, which all save one of our modern informants deny ever to have been tattooed" (*Tattooing in the Marquesas,* 14). Margaret Mead also comments on the extent of traditional tattooing in the Marquesas, in *An Inquiry into the Question of Cultural Stability in Polynesia,* 72–74, 81.

24. It is not surprising that Melville would have been attracted to Langsdorff's narrative. Of all the contemporary travel writers, Langsdorff seems closest to Melville. In resonant language, both writers describe Marquesan culture with a relatively open eye and mind, with a comparative minimum of insistence that the society conform to a priori expectations. Melville's uncle John D'Wolf had voyaged with Langsdorff to Russia in 1805, an event to which Melville's narrator alludes in chapter 7 of *Redburn.* Melville quotes Langsdorff's *Voyages and Travels* in chapter 45 of *Moby-Dick,* "The Affidavit." On the Langsdorff-Melville connection, see Parker, *Herman Melville: A Biography,* 1:356–57.

25. Cabri and an Englishman named Roberts were European residents of Nukuheva whom several early Western travelers encountered. These two confidence men served as somewhat unreliable interlocutors between the islanders and the visitors. Krusenstern relied heavily on Roberts for his information, Langsdorff somewhat more skeptically on Cabri. Reading Krusenstern, one suspects that Roberts played the captain like a virtuoso, heightening his fears of savagery in an effort to establish himself as the leading European intermediary and to secure a new supply of guns and ammunition (*Voyage round the World,* 1:174–83). Roberts's "eye-witness" tales of cannibalism served as Krusenstern's sole evidence for his belief in Marquesan flesh-eating. One also

suspects, reading Krusenstern, that Roberts and Cabri may have exaggerated their rivalry so that their joint corroboration of Marquesan cannibalism would be especially persuasive. Roberts and Cabri weave in and out of Krusenstern's and Langsdorff's accounts of the Marquesas, two elusive presences who shape the textures of these early narratives. In *Typee,* Melville questions the depth of knowledge possessed by the European or American who "officiates as showman of the island on which he has settled" (170). In *Melville in the South Seas,* Charles Roberts Anderson suggests that Cabri was a model for Melville's renegade sailor Lem Hardy in *Omoo* (154). On the nineteenth-century exhibition of tattooed people—Polynesian, European, and American—see Bogdan, *Freak Show,* 241–56. Krusenstern (*Voyage round the World,* 1:156) and Ellis (*Polynesian Researches,* 1:266) claim that sailors eagerly sought to undergo the process of ornamental tattooing. Saul H. Riesenberg describes contemporary reaction to O'Connell in "The Tattooed Irishman," 15. In *Freak Show,* Bogdan suggests that audiences found O'Connell's story even more engrossing than his tattoos (242). In "'Made in the Marquesas,'" John Evelev links the positions and predicaments of Melville, O'Connell, and Cabri as "exotic objects" or "freak performers" in their own cultures (29–36).

26. In *Freak Show,* Bogdan discusses nineteenth-century American exhibitions of South Pacific "cannibals," including shows in New York City in the 1830s and Barnum's "Cannibal Chief" in 1842 and his famous, and fictitious, "Figi Cannibals," first presented in 1872 (178–87). Arens raises the question of "evidence" throughout *The Man-Eating Myth.*

27. Benjamin Rush discusses Moss and the two discolored white women in his address delivered before the American Philosophical Society on July 14, 1792 (see Rush, "Observations"). Samuel Stanhope Smith considers Moss in *Essay on the Causes of the Variety of Complexion,* 52, 58–59. Winthrop D. Jordan describes Rush's interest in Moss and Rush's arguments about skin color as "disease," in *White over Black,* 517–525. See also William Stanton, *The Leopard's Spots,* 5–7. In *Body Criticism,* Stafford discusses the scientific study of the "white Negro" (319–29).

28. Melville, *Moby-Dick,* 198. Subsequent page references to the Northwestern-Newberry edition (see bibliography) are given in parentheses in the body of the text. John D. Davies discusses the history of phrenology, its significance in nineteenth-century American culture, and the popularizing role of the Fowler brothers, in *Phrenology: Fad and Science.* According to Charles Colbert, antebellum portrait painters relied upon phrenology as a philosophical foundation for articulating the meanings of the human head; see Colbert, "'Each Little Hillock hath a Tongue,'" 298.

29. See Camper, *The Works of the Late Professor Camper;* Lavater, *Essays on Physiognomy;* Morton, *Crania Americana;* Nott and Gliddon, *Types of Mankind.*

30. Squier, "American Ethnology," 386. In "Memoir of the Life and Scientific Labors of Samuel George Morton," published as part of Nott and Gliddon's compendium *Types of Mankind* (1854), Dr. Henry S. Patterson makes explicit the most important reason why "Ethnology should be eminently a science for American culture": "It is manifest that our relation to and management of

these people [the Red American, the Negro, the Asian laborer] must depend, in a great measure, upon their intrinsic race-character" (xxxii–xxxiii). In *White over Black,* Jordan describes the long foreground to Enlightenment racial anatomy. In *The Leopard's Spots,* William Stanton defines the contributions of the "American school" of ethnology in the middle of the nineteenth century, particularly the work of Samuel Morton, Josiah Nott, and George Gliddon. I discuss these three figures and the "American school" more fully in chapter 3. George M. Frederickson, in *The Black Image in the White Mind,* and Reginald Horsman, in *Race and Manifest Destiny,* argue that the 1830s and 1840s in America marked a turning point in racial thinking, a pervasive acceptance of inherent racial inferiority fueled by the demonstrations of the "American school." They dispute Stanton's conclusion that these ethnologists had only a marginal effect on history and politics. Horsman places American efforts in the vanguard of Western scientific racism (157). In *Science Encounters the Indian,* Robert E. Bieder suggests that Horsman overstates the acceptance of the polygenetic doctrines of the "American school" at mid-century. Bieder acknowledges that polygenism posed a "serious threat" to traditional beliefs in scriptural authority and human equality. Yet he insists that the debate between polygenists, who argued for separate (and implicitly unequal) creations, and monogenists, who believed in a singular (and potentially equal) creation, was still hotly contested among scientists in the two decades before the Civil War (187). Robyn Wiegman applies Foucault's analysis of the movement from natural history to comparative anatomy in *The Order of Things* (1966) to nineteenth-century U.S. racial science; see Wiegman, *American Anatomies,* 21–42.

31. Barbara Stafford reproduces Camper's *Ape to Apollo Belvedere* illustration in *Body Criticism,* 111. Plate 2 of Charles White's *Account of the Regular Gradation in Man* is a pull-out chart detailing the progress in facial angle and skull shape from the "Negro" head to the ideal form of the "Grecian Antique." Honour juxtaposes late-eighteenth- and nineteenth-century aesthetics and racial theories, although he retreats from asserting a symbiotic relationship, insisting on the artist's relative lack of contamination; see *Image of the Black in Western Art,* vol. 4, part 2, 12–21. In *Body Criticism,* Stafford gives a stronger version of the mutual shapings of science and art: science "set the example and provided the technical images and tropes" for the artistic sphere (21). She also analyzes the visualization of knowledge in Enlightenment art and science (1–45). In *The Order of Things,* Foucault describes how vision became the privileged sensory vehicle for modern knowledge (125–65). In *The Leopard's Spots,* William Stanton discusses the replacement of aesthetics by calipers in anthropology beginning in the late eighteenth century (3–44). Colbert considers the shared perceptions of the phrenologist and artist in the work of Combe, Caldwell, Quidor, Powers, and Cole; see Colbert, " 'Each Little Hillock hath a Tongue' " and "Dreaming up 'The Architect's Dream.' " Stepan, in "Race and Gender," and Stafford, in *Body Criticism,* analyze the role played by metaphor in shaping scientific and aesthetic thinking about the human body.

32. Thomas Sewall, *An Examination of Phrenology; in Two Lectures,* 44. In his first lecture, Sewall explains the history and principles of phrenology; in his second, he demonstrates that phrenology is scientifically inaccurate,

misrepresenting the structure of the brain and cranium. Reginald Horsman argues that phrenologists in the 1820s and 1830s led the scientific quest for evidence of inherent physical differences among the races; see Horsman, *Race and Manifest Destiny*, 56–59, 116–28, 142–45. See also Bieder, *Science Encounters the Indian*, 59–64, 70–80; Stepan, "Race and Gender," 45–47; and Colbert, *A Measure of Perfection*, 212–81. In "'Each Little Hillock,'" Colbert reproduces Sewall's frontispiece and discusses the phrenological importance of the measurement from ear to mental "organ" (291–93). Although the craniometer may strike the late-twentieth-century viewer as a curiosity, the device is no less peculiar in its operation or its embodiment of cognitive desire than the array of anthropometrical instruments employed by nineteenth-century scientists; see Topinard, *Anthropology*, 193–314. And the craniometer is not a relic of the early nineteenth century. The instrument reappears ominously in one of Roman Vishniac's photographs of Berlin in 1933. It lurks in a store window behind the figure of his daughter Mara, beneath an advertisement offering to measure skulls and authenticate Aryan identity; see Vishniac, *A Vanished World*, photograph 15.

33. In his "Explanation of the Plates," Langsdorff describes the *young Nukahiwan* as holding the skull of a slain enemy (*Voyages and Travels*, 1:xiv). On Marquesan use of skulls of the enemy, see ibid., 1:150–51, Porter, *Journal of a Cruise*, 2:50, and Bennett, *Narrative of a Whaling Voyage*, 1:312.

34. In his lecture "Statues in Rome," delivered in 1857 and 1858, reconstructed by Merton M. Sealts in *Melville as Lecturer*, Melville celebrates the *Apollo Belvedere* as the "crowning glory" (136) of the Vatican museum, displaying the "incorruption" of "pure marble" (150): "it gives a kind of visible response to that class of human aspirations of beauty and perfection that, according to Faith, cannot be truly gratified except in another world" (136–37). Sealts describes both contemporary enthusiasm for the *Apollo* as the model of perfect manhood and Melville's longstanding interest in the statue (136 n. 14). Sealts's reconstruction is reprinted, with revisions, in *The Piazza Tales and Other Prose Pieces*, 398–409. Melville alludes to the *Apollo Belvedere* in "On the Slain Collegians" (*Battle Pieces* [1866], 157) and in "The 'Gees" ([1856], *in The Piazza Tales and Other Prose Pieces*, 350). Gail Coffler argues that the *Apollo Belvedere* was the key image in Melville's aesthetic theory; see Coffler, "Classical Iconography in the Aesthetics of *Billy Budd, Sailor.*"

35. Exceptions to these agitated accounts of tattooing occur in the first, framing chapter of *Typee*. Here a more detached Tommo describes the ludicrous tattoo "goggles" worn by the King of Nukuheva and tells an anecdote about the Queen of Nukuheva, who enthusiastically compares her own designs with those of an old sailor (8). In a twist on Marquesan classicism, Tommo describes the spiral tattoos on her legs as resembling "two miniature Trajan's columns." This anecdote climaxes in an off-color joke about the queen exposing her tattooed buttocks. The story has the flavor of a recycled sailors' tale, rather than an actual reminiscence.

36. Charles Roberts Anderson, *Melville in the South Seas*, 453.

37. Interpretations of tattooing as conversion are offered by Stern and Dryden, in Milton Stern, *Critical Essays on "Typee"*; Spengemann, *The Adventur-*

ous Muse, 178–88; and Pullin, "The Failure of Eden." The personal, but not racial, cost of Tommo's threatened loss of face is discussed by Abrams and Wenke, in Stern, *Critical Essays,* and Ziff, *Literary Democracy,* 1–12. Stern and Ruland, in Stern, *Critical Essays,* read facial tattooing as a physical analogue for the mental confinement that endangers the Westerner in unconscious Polynesia. In "'Made in the Marquesas,'" John Evelev links Melville's response to tattooing to his ambivalence about writing. Evelev argues that Melville's first book exposed him to the distorting demands of a literary marketplace in which South Pacific displays were a valuable commodity. Elizabeth Renker also associates tattooing and writing anxieties, suggesting that the tattooed faces in *Typee* register what she takes to be Melville's discomfort with his own disfigured pages on which he appropriated and mutilated his source texts; see Renker, *Strike through the Mask,* 1–23.

38. In describing his horror of tattooing, Tommo echoes the language of his captain, who, early in the narrative, warns the sailors against the machinations of the Marquesans. Captain Vang describes the fate of a sailor on shore leave who had his "face damaged for life, for the cursed heathens tattooed a broad patch clean across his figure-head" (34).

39. Melville, *Omoo,* 27.

40. For examples of flesh that "creeps" and "crawls" in contemporary texts, see Leech, *Thirty Years from Home,* 50, and Northup, *Twelve Years a Slave,* 243. Melville used Leech's book as a source in writing *White-Jacket.*

41. Melville seems to have echoed Ellis's description of tattooing as an "index of character" in the language of his lecture "The South Seas," as reconstructed by Merton M. Sealts in *Melville as Lecturer* (178). In "The South Seas," delivered in 1858 and 1859, Melville reflects humorously on tattooing: "Many of the natives think it necessary for their eternal welfare, and, unless a man submits to being tattooed, he is looked upon as damned. In their opinion I may now be in peril, for I stoutly resisted the importunities of the native artists to be naturalized by marks on my face as from a gridiron" (177). At the limits of adaptation, Melville links tattooing and the broiling of flesh. Sealts's reconstruction is reprinted, with revisions, in *The Piazza Tales and Other Prose Pieces,* 410–20.

42. Hawthorne, *The Scarlet Letter,* 96.

43. Although W. C. Handy's illustrations date from 1922—eighty years after Melville's visit to the Marquesas—mid-nineteenth-century observers confirm the traditional aspect of the face patterns. In *Narrative of a Whaling Voyage* (1840), Bennett describes typical markings: "His entire person was very curiously tattooed, including the three broad bands passing across the face, in the situation of the forehead, eyes, and mouth, so peculiar to the Marquesan men" (1:284). Regrettably, *Typee* was not as successful as Melville had hoped it would be and so it was not published in a more expensive illustrated edition, as his contract with the Harpers permitted (Howard, historical note to Northwestern-Newberry *Typee,* 294–95). It would be interesting to have a set of tattooing prints from *Typee* to compare with Melville's descriptions and with the pictures in Langsdorff's and W. C. Handy's volumes.

44. Mitchell Breitwieser analyzes the "fear of reversed parts" that haunts the

last section of *Typee*—the fear that the eater will be eaten and the writer written upon; see "False Sympathy in Melville's *Typee*," 411–14. In *Marquesan Encounters,* Herbert interprets the texts of Porter, Charles S. Stewart, and Melville as dramas of Western self-definition that unfold on the Nukuhevan stage. He analyzes moments of crisis, when the cultural identities of the narrators are tested and vindicated (128–35, 142–48, 192–96 ff.).

45. In "Melville and Marquesan Eroticism," Heath observes that Tommo's use of a boat hook as a weapon is "aptly ironic" in its resemblance to the sharp implements of the tattooist (61). The two English words "Home" and "Mother" seem to have been too much for one of the parties involved in revising the original American edition of *Typee*. The revised American edition reads "one expressive English word I had taught him—'Home.'" See Howard, historical note to Northwestern-Newberry *Typee*, 291.

46. For Child's catalogue, see "An Appeal for the Indians," 220–24. Melville's passage on civilized sadism, and several paragraphs that precede and follow it, were removed in the revised American edition of *Typee*. Such an excision indicates that although the gesture had become customary by the nineteenth century, it still retained the power to disturb. For an African American version of the comparative critique, see David Walker's *Appeal*, 23–29.

The entire Montaigne passage from "Of Cannibals" (which Melville certainly had in mind while crafting his own statements on cannibalism) reads, in Donald M. Frame's translation: "I think there is more barbarity in eating a man alive than in eating him dead, and in tearing by tortures and the rack a body still full of feeling, in roasting a man bit by bit, in having him bitten and mangled by dogs and swine (as we have not only read but seen within fresh memory, not among ancient enemies, but among neighbors and fellow citizens, and what is worse, on the pretext of piety and religion), than in roasting and eating him after he is dead." See *The Complete Essays of Montaigne*, 155. The 16th-century French has been quoted from *Essais de Michel de Montaigne*, 2:175. In "Montaigne, Melville, and the Cannibals," Gorman Beauchamp aligns the positions of Montaigne and Melville, focusing on their defenses of cannibalism and arguing that Melville novelistically expands on Montaigne's earlier expository claims. Thomas J. Scorza links Melville's *Typee* to Montaigne's "Of Cannibals," Shakespeare's *The Tempest,* and Rousseau's *First and Second Discourses,* as part of a Western utopic tradition, in Stern, *Critical Essays*, 232–37.

CHAPTER TWO: JUMPING OUT OF ONE'S SKIN IN *WHITE-JACKET*

1. Robert S. Levine calls the analogy between seaman and slave "central to all of [Melville's] sea fiction," in *Conspiracy and Romance*, 197. See also Zirker, "Evidence of the Slavery Dilemma in *White-Jacket*." Myra C. Glenn discusses the resonances between the anti-flogging and anti-slavery debates, particularly during the Congressional session of 1848–1850; see "The Naval Reform Campaign Against Flogging," and *Campaigns Against Corporal Punishment,* 112–21. *White-Jacket* was published at the climax of the overlapping debates about the extension of chattel slavery into the territories conquered in the war with

Mexico and the abolition of flogging in the American navy. Northerners argued for "free labor" and moral persuasion and southerners argued for slave labor and the necessity of corporal punishment to maintain social order. See Glenn, "Naval Reform Campaign," 418–23, and Charles Roberts Anderson, *Melville in the South Seas,* 429–31. Richard H. Brodhead argues that scenes of corporal punishment, depicted across antebellum culture in texts ranging from popular fiction to pedagogical treatises, helped to authorize new forms of intimate discipline; see *Cultures of Letters,* 13–47. In *The Wages of Whiteness* David R. Roediger analyzes the analogy between white workers and black slaves made by labor activists between 1830 and 1860, arguing that the comparison "takes us to the heart of the process by which the white worker was made,"(65–92 ff.).

In *White-Jacket,* sailors are flogged in chapter 33 (in which the young white sailors Mark, Antone, John, and Peter are punished for fighting on the gun deck), chapter 67 (in which the mulatto Rose-Water is beaten for fighting with a black sailor without the captain's permission and the narrator White-Jacket barely escapes punishment after he is falsely accused of shirking his duties), and chapter 87 (in which the aged white sailor Ushant is given twelve strokes for refusing to shave his beard). I will argue that the final, fantastic twist on this series is offered in chapter 92, in which the narrator flogs himself. All citations to *White-Jacket* in this chapter will be taken from the Northwestern-Newberry edition (see bibliography) and given in parentheses in the body of the text.

2. Reprinted in Douglass, *My Bondage and My Freedom,* 414.

3. H. Bruce Franklin compares the concerns with class antagonism and the objective formation of subjective consciousness in Melville and in Marx, although he tends to collapse Melville into Marx; see *Prison Literature in America,* 38–49. Michael Paul Rogin links both writers' analyses of revolutionary failure in 1848; see *Subversive Genealogy,* 155–220 ff. Mitchell Breitwieser compares Marx and Melville's analyses of divided selfhood, in "False Sympathy in Melville's *Typee,*" 401–02.

4. Describing Melville as a democratic idealist and an anti-democratic realist, Larry J. Reynolds criticizes the aristocratic posturings of Melville's first-person narrator in *White-Jacket;* see "Anti-Democratic Emphasis in *White-Jacket.*" Melville's point-of-view dilemmas are similar to those of Richard Henry Dana, Jr., in *Two Years Before the Mast* (1840), an influential source for *White-Jacket.* See Philbrick, introduction to *Two Years Before the Mast,* 24–29, and Lucid, "The Influence of *Two Years Before the Mast* on Herman Melville."

5. In *Melville in the South Seas* (349–434), Charles Roberts Anderson outlines Melville's experience of spending fourteen months on board the frigate *United States* between August 1843 and October 1844, and details Melville's transmutations of this experience and of his source materials into the voyage of the *Neversink* in *White-Jacket.* See also Vincent, *The Tailoring of Melville's "White-Jacket."* Melville must have appreciated the allegorical redundancy of a United States frigate named the *United States.* On the belatedness of Melville's naval-reform rhetoric in *White-Jacket,* see Anderson, *Melville in the South Seas,* 420–31, and Dimock, *Empire for Liberty,* 99–104. Melville was not the only American author to walk the decks of the *United States.* In 1833, Nathaniel Parker Willis, the journalist and editor who helped to shape antebellum middle-

class literary culture, was invited by the officers of the frigate to join them on a six-month cruise around the Mediterranean. Willis describes his trip in *Pencillings by the Way*, 1:229, 232, 251; 2:45, 365–68. Unlike Melville, Willis attended a ball on the *United States* (2:45) and extolled "the wonders of sea-discipline" and the "beautiful . . . results of order!" (1:232–33). Melville became acquainted with Willis in the late 1840s. See Parker, *Herman Melville: A Biography*, 1:471–72, 398–400, 566–67, 718–20. Willis will be referred to again in the fourth and fifth chapters of this book.

6. While Zirker, in "Evidence of the Slavery Dilemma," interprets the tonal mixture of the chapters on the "Massacre of the Beards" as evidence of Melville's ambivalence about the egalitarian import of his narrative (488–90), my sense is that the narrator's humor, the sense of jocular distance and of insulated position, sharpens the violence even as it blunts his rebuke. It is also important to remember that the jolly chapters on the beards climax in the scourging of old Ushant (chapter 87) and in the denunciation of "Flogging through the Fleet" (chapter 88).

7. See Foucault, *Discipline and Punish*. As a regulating institution, Melville's *Neversink* employs the three ways of organizing the power to punish outlined by Foucault: the sovereign and his force, the social body, and the administrative apparatus (130–31). Myra C. Glenn links the narratives of punishment written by sailors with those written by prisoners, in *Campaigns Against Corporal Punishment*, 85–101. Contemporary reviewers of *White-Jacket* commented on the relentless brutality of the system Melville described. See, for example, the reviews collected in Watson G. Branch, *Melville: The Critical Heritage* (229–35)—specifically, those in *Saroni's Musical Times* (March 30, 1850), the *New York Tribune* (April 2, 1850), and the *Boston Post* (April 10, 1850).

8. In an unpublished essay, "Cover for a Docile Body: Discipline, Strategy, and the Tactics of Everyday Life in Melville's *White-Jacket*," Phillip Kiekhaefer analyzes the sailors' forms of resistance, using Michel de Certeau's notions of "practices" and "tactics."

9. On the analogy between state and ship made repeatedly in political and literary texts in the turbulent decades before the Civil War, see Heimert, "*Moby-Dick* and American Political Symbolism," 499–500, and Levine, *Conspiracy and Romance*, 191–92. Levine discusses the antebellum sea narrative as part of a wider representation of "total institutions" in the North and South, including asylums, prisons, and slave plantations (168–82). Philbrick, in his introduction to *Two Years Before the Mast*, 21–23, and Lucid, in "Influence of *Two Years Before the Mast*," 243, describe the market for factual voyage narratives written from the point of view of the common sailor, stimulated in the 1840s by the success of *Two Years Before the Mast*. In his review of Browne's *Etchings of a Whaling Cruise*, Melville comments on the disenchanting effects of sailors' narratives; see *The Piazza Tales and Other Prose Pieces*, 205–11. Contemporary reviewers of *White-Jacket* praised Melville's revealing "forecastle point of sight," the sense they received of being admitted behind the scenes and below the decks. See the comments in *Atlas* (February 9, 1850) and *Saroni's Musical Times* (March 30, 1850), collected in Watson G. Branch, *Melville: The Critical Heritage*, 224–26, 229–31. Melville's analysis of shipboard regulation is distinguished by his ex-

haustive attention to detail. He takes the conventional chapter outlining maritime order (the focus of Dana's chapter 3 or Leech's chapter 2) and dilates such scrutiny to form the substance of his entire narrative.

10. Calhoun, "Compromise Speech of 1850," 45. Too ill to deliver the speech, Calhoun arranged for it to be read by James Mason, his senatorial colleague from Virginia.

11. Fitzhugh, *Cannibals All!*, 22, 260. Eugene D. Genovese analyzes Fitzhugh's social thought in *The World the Slaveholders Made*, 118–244. In *Alternative Americas*, Anne Norton describes Southern concepts of labor upon which Fitzhugh drew in formulating his attack on wage labor and defense of slavery (234–39). We might read the work of Martin Delany as a pointed response to Fitzhugh's calls to abandon the critical presumptions of the anatomist in favor of organic acceptance; see Delany, *The Condition, Elevation, Emigration, and Destiny of the Colored People of the United States*, particularly the call to "the colored people of the United States" "to understand our true position, to realise our actual condition, and determine for ourselves what is best to be done" (15), and the analysis of the social body in Delany's *Blake; or, the Huts of America*. In *The Condition, Elevation, Emigration, and Destiny of the Colored People of the United States*, Delany shifts the terms of the comparison between southern and northern slaves. Instead of arguing for wage or white slavery, Delany equates the degradation of enslaved blacks in the South and "free" blacks in the North (14–30).

12. Fitzhugh, *Cannibals All!*, 7–20 ff.; Grimké, "Letter VIII: The Condition of Women in the United States," 59–60; Fuller, *Woman in the Nineteenth Century*, 19–22; Elizabeth Cady Stanton, "Declaration of Sentiments and Resolutions," 79–80; Fisk, "Capital Against Labor," 199–204; Walsh, "Facts for the Millions" and "Workingmen"; R. T. H., "White and Black Slavery"; Douglass, *My Bondage and My Freedom*, 309–11, 433–34; William Wells Brown, *Clotel; or, The President's Daughter*, 145. Karen Sánchez-Eppler examines the dangers of cross-racial identifications in *Touching Liberty*, 14–49. In *Women and Sisters*, Jean Fagan Yellin discusses how Angelina Grimké and Lydia Maria Child juxtaposed the circumstances of free and enslaved women and how writers such as Sojourner Truth and Harriet Jacobs questioned such comparisons (3–96). Sean Wilentz discusses the labor radicals Evans and Walsh, in *Chants Democratic* (326–59). David R. Roediger examines the anxious comparisons between workers and slaves made by antebellum labor activists, in *Wages of Whiteness*, 65–92. He argues that "white slavery" was the frequently used term in the decades before the Civil War, preferred to either "slavery of wages" or "wage slavery." According to Roediger, the term "white slavery" avoided specifically attacking the capitalist wage system or challenging the idea of slavery itself. Jonathan Glickstein and Eric Foner analyze the different assumptions about ownership (self-ownership versus ownership of productive property) that separated the abolitionist movement and the labor movement and made the analogy between workers and slaves a figure of contention between the two groups of reformers. See Glickstein, "'Poverty Is Not Slavery,'" and Foner, "Workers and Slavery." Marcus Cunliffe describes the jeremiads of Cobden, Carey, and others against British wage slavery and anti-U.S. propaganda, in *Chattel Slavery and*

Wage Slavery, 32–68. He explains the ways in which the analogy between black chattel slavery and white wage slavery was exchanged across the Atlantic in the fierce debates between Great Britain and the United States about abolition, economics, and national character. Catherine Gallagher writes about the worker/ slave analogy in British political discourse of the 1830s and 1840s; see *The Industrial Reformation of English Fiction,* 3–35.

13. See Sánchez-Eppler, *Touching Liberty,* 14.

14. Melville, *White-Jacket,* 53–56, 89–91, 134–51, 225–29. Douglass, *Narrative of the Life of Frederick Douglass,* 114–16, 118–19, and *My Bondage and My Freedom,* 250–56, 259–61, 441–45.

15. Northup, *Twelve Years a Slave;* Prince, *The History of Mary Prince;* Jacobs, *Incidents in the Life of A Slave Girl;* Mattison, *Louisa Picquet, The Octoroon.* In *Prison Literature in America,* Franklin compares the narratives of antebellum slaves, sailors, and prisoners (124–37). In *Conspiracy and Romance,* Levine discusses how seaman narrators compare maritime discipline to other forms of antebellum social regulation, including the plantation and the asylum (168–85).

16. Douglass, *Narrative,* 106; Dana, *Two Years Before the Mast,* 335. William L. Andrews analyzes the dynamics between writer and implied reader in fugitive slave narratives, arguing that after 1840, rather than catering to expectations, writers became more concerned with enlarging the free white reader's imagination through rhetorical means; see *To Tell a Free Story,* 29–30, 64–66, 95–96, 137–138, 212–13, 247–54 ff.

17. Bourne, *Picture of Slavery in the United States of America;* Weld, *American Slavery As It Is,* 62–72 ff.

18. Douglass, *Narrative,* 51, and *My Bondage and My Freedom,* 177, 359; Spillers, "Mama's Baby, Papa's Maybe." For scenes of flogging in slave narratives written by men, see William Wells Brown, *Narrative of William W. Brown,* 15, 18, 23–25, 38–39, 44, 53–58; Bibb, *Narrative of the Life and Adventures of Henry Bibb,* 130, 139; Pennington, *The Fugitive Blacksmith,* 6–11; Northup, *Twelve Years a Slave,* 241–43, 322–23, 365; and Douglass, *My Bondage and My Freedom,* 87, 92, 113, 148, 201, 208, 257, 313, 414, 430.

Many female narrators direct their readers' attention to the less melodramatic and more mundane, but equally disturbing, ways in which bodies are marked. In *Incidents in the Life of a Slave Girl* (1861), Harriet A. Jacobs writes that Linda's tormentor, Dr. Flint, never allowed anyone to whip her because the marks would be visible to his family and friends and would lay him open to censure in the small North Carolina town in which they lived. Instead, he applied the lash of his gaze, pursuing with his eyes and leaving her no space unexposed (27–36). See also *Louisa Picquet, the Octoroon* (1861), by the abolitionist minister H. Mattison, which describes his efforts to get Picquet to divulge the intimate details of her floggings and reveals his obsession with establishing and grading skin color. Of course, the difference between male and female representations of corporal punishment is a matter of emphasis, strategy, or decorum and does not reflect a difference in treatment of male and female slaves, as *The History of Mary Prince* (1831) reminds us. Her narrative offers an unrelenting catalogue of physical cruelty inflicted on slaves in the British West Indies.

Douglass's depiction of whipped female bodies has become the focus of critical debate. Jenny Franchot and Deborah E. McDowell argue that Douglass constructs his male identity over the exposed bodies of female victims, adopting dominant bourgeois ideas about masculinity and repeating gestures that repress and objectify women. See Franchot, "The Punishment of Esther," and McDowell, "In the First Place." Douglass participates in and is limited by antebellum ideologies of manhood, according to Valerie Smith, in *Self-Discovery and Authority in Afro-American Narrative*, 20–28; David Leverenz, in *Manhood and the American Renaissance*, 108–34; and Richard Yarborough, in "Race, Violence, and Manhood." In *To Tell a Free Story*, William L. Andrews argues that Douglass's rhetorical skill in his whipping set-pieces signifies a reversal of power dynamics, in which he calls attention to himself as wielder of words (132–35). Eric J. Sundquist describes Douglass's strategic use of the master's rhetorical and ideological tools, in *To Wake the Nations*, 83–134.

19. The signature whip also appears in other illustrations in Bourne; see engravings 4 (*A Slave Plantation*) and 10 (*Kidnapping*). According to the accompanying text, the figure on the incline in *Flogging American Women* is a carpenter who forced the slave driver to stop scourging the woman.

20. Northup, *Twelve Years a Slave*, 243, 365. Like Captain Thompson's rope in the famous flogging scene in chapter 15 of Dana's *Two Years Before the Mast* (1840), the master Epps's lash in *Twelve Years a Slave* (1853) inscribes his authority. Franchot argues that the whip authorizes Douglass's words in his *Narrative* and *My Bondage and My Freedom* ("The Punishment of Esther," 154–55). Sundquist describes the rumors that Nat Turner's body had been skinned and tanned after his execution, in *To Wake the Nations*, 82.

21. Douglass, *My Bondage and My Freedom*, 316–17; Delany, *Blake*, 117. In the epigraph to *The Anti-Slavery Harp* (1848), William Wells Brown quotes Thomas Campbell's poem on the "two emblems" of the United States flag—the stars of "white man's liberty" and the stripes, signifying "Negro scars." The engraving above the epigraph depicts a shirtless African American man bound to a flagpole, his back scored with lines. Campbell's complete poem, "Epigram to the United States of North America (written in 1838)," can be found, with some differences in wording, in *The Complete Poetical Works of Thomas Campbell*, 340.

22. Pennington, *Fugitive Blacksmith*, 6–11.

23. Northup, *Twelve Years a Slave*, 349, 350. Later in the narrative, under the watchful eye of Epps, Northup is forced to actually whip the slave Patsey. The flogging takes place before Epps's wife and children assembled on their piazza and before Patsey's fellow slaves huddled at a distance. She is broken in both body and mind by the experience. In *Beloved* (1987), Toni Morrison artistically appropriates the lash, refiguring the welts on Sethe's back as a sculpted chokecherry tree, literalizing and cultivating "the roots of her sorrow" (16–18, 79, 93).

24. Chandler, "Mental Metempsychosis," 13.

25. New York *Daily Tribune*, September 30, 1850; quoted in Abbott, "*White-Jacket* and the Campaign Against Flogging in the Navy," 25.

26. Leech, *Thirty Years from Home*, 50–51, 61–62, 240.

27. Meyers's sketches and excerpts from his journal were not published until the twentieth century. His *Punishment* is said to be the first picture of flogging in the U.S. Navy made by an eyewitness. See Meyers, *Journal of a Cruise to California and the Sandwich Islands,* and *Sketches of California and Hawaii.* Meyers's naval service paralleled Melville's time at sea. While Meyers's ship, the *Cyane,* was in Honolulu in August 1843, Melville shipped home from the same port on the frigate *United States.*

28. Leech, *Thirty Years,* 237.

29. Browne, *Etchings of a Whaling Cruise,* 505; Franklin, *Prison Literature,* 32–33; Leech, *Thirty Years,* 59.

30. McNally, *Evils and Abuses in the Naval and Merchant Service Exposed,* 128–29.

31. Many northern labor reformers used the analogy with slavery to delineate a racial choice, arguing that wage slavery was a more oppressive system than chattel slavery. See, for example, Brownson, *The Laboring Classes,* 10–11, and Walsh, "Facts for the Millions." Southern supporters of slavery agreed. See R.T.H, "White and Black Slavery," and Fitzhugh, *Cannibals All!* Stowe resists making a choice between oppressions, when she has the southerner St. Clare explain to his northern cousin Ophelia that both chattel slavery and wage capitalism "appropriat[e] one set of human beings to the use and improvement of another, without any regard to their own." See Stowe, *Uncle Tom's Cabin,* 269–70. In *Chattel Slavery and Wage Slavery,* Cunliffe describes how northern workers elevated their oppression over that of southern black slaves. He suggests a variety of explanations: the tendency for a group to give priority to its own problems, the fear of competition from free black labor, racial prejudice, and the alignment of workers' movements with the southern-influenced Democratic Party (20–31). In *Wages of Whiteness,* Roediger emphasizes the role of racial ideology and particularly the evolution of a white working-class consciousness: "Chattel slavery provided white workers with a touchstone against which to weigh their fears and a yardstick to measure their reassurance" (66). Roediger also describes the northerners' retreat from the analogy and its degrading associations in the late 1840s and 1850s (80–87).

32. McNally's elision of the slave trade and "middle passage" is in the grand tradition of Thomas Jefferson, who explained in "Query XIV" of *Notes on the State of Virginia* that "Many millions of them [blacks] have been brought to, and born in America" (266). For further examples of the effort to bind sailors to the white community at the expense of slaves, see John A. Lockwood's articles on "Flogging in the Navy" (1849), 103, 237–41, 321, 542. Frederickson employs Pierre L. van den Berghe's concept of "Herrenvolk democracies" in his analysis of antebellum white democracy, in *The Black Image in the White Mind,* 61–62, 89–95 ff. Roediger argues that "Herrenvolk republicanism" would be a more accurate term (*Wages of Whiteness,* 59–60). Zirker places *White-Jacket* in the context of debates over white egalitarian Democratic party politics in the late 1840s ("Evidence of the Slavery Dilemma," 478–82). Larry Reynolds associates Melville's stance not with the Democratic egalitarians but with James Fenimore Cooper's "valid aristocracy," in "Anti-Democratic Emphasis in *White-Jacket,*" 17.

33. McNally, *Evils and Abuses*, 130. Edmund S. Morgan magisterially explicates the master/slave dialectic on American soil, in *American Slavery/ American Freedom*.

34. Browne, *Etchings of a Whaling Cruise*, 489–90, 490, 491.

35. Morrison, "Unspeakable Things Unspoken," 11–14ff., with responses by Hazel Carby (35–43) and Eric Foner (44–49). See also Morrison, *Playing in the Dark*.

36. Dana, *Two Years Before the Mast*, 152.

37. Ibid., 156.

38. Ibid., 184–85.

39. In "Twenty-Four Years After," the retrospective essay that Dana substituted for the last chapter in revised editions of *Two Years Before the Mast* after 1869, Dana recounts the subsequent experience of his shipmates and attempts to rehabilitate the shattered Sam: "Sam seemed to have got funny again" (525). Yet the tentative verb and ambivalent adjective raise doubts about his recovery. In "Benito Cereno" (1855), Melville's Spanish captain Cereno, like Dana's sailor Sam, suffers internal collapse after occupying the position of a slave—a fate uncomprehended by the American captain Amasa Delano, whose obliviousness is his salvation.

40. Dana, *Two Years Before the Mast*, 40, 524, 157. On the biographical Dana and for a comparison of the sailor narratives of Dana and Melville, see Ferguson, *Law and Letters in American Culture*, 257–72. In *Manhood and the American Renaissance*, Leverenz analyzes Dana's "patrician detachment" and his achievement of manhood (205–16).

41. Charles Roberts Anderson, *Melville in the South Seas*, 429–31; Dimock, *Empire for Liberty*, 99–101. In Chapter 29 of *Omoo* (1847), Melville's narrator reluctantly admits that flogging on board men-of-war is sometimes necessary.

42. In chapter 26 of *Moby-Dick*—"Knights and Squires"—Melville also suggests a virile hemorrhaging: "That immaculate manliness we feel within ourselves, so far within us, that it remains intact though all the outer character seem gone; bleeds with keenest anguish at the undraped spectacle of a valor-ruined man" (117).

43. According to Charles Roberts Anderson, no person like Dr. Cuticle ever set foot on board the *United States* and no amputation like the one depicted in chapter 63 ever took place; see *Melville in the South Seas*, 401–405. Anderson argues for a source in Smollett's *Roderick Random*. Vincent suggests that Melville was parodying G. J. Guthrie's 1820 *Treatise on Gun-Shot Wounds*, in *Tailoring of "White-Jacket*," 140–44. In "Lovers of Human Flesh," Caleb Crain discusses Cuticle's operation as a "cannibal feast" (37–38). Cindy Weinstein reads Cuticle's amputations as Melville's comment on the widening divisions of literary labor, in *The Literature of Labor and the Labors of Literature*, 33–36. Dr. Cuticle's operation echoes the grisly scene of dismemberment in Poe's *Narrative of Arthur Gordon Pym* (155). Instead of the "extremity of horror" experienced by Poe's narrator at the sight of his shipmate Augustus's putrefied leg coming off in the hands of Dirk Peters, Melville's narrator represents Dr. Cuticle's satisfaction with a job nicely done.

44. As Richard Dean Smith explains, alacrity in amputation was necessary

because of the pain experienced by patients before the introduction of general anesthesia in the mid-nineteenth century. See Smith, *Melville's Complaint*, 47, 52. Yet Melville represents Dr. Cuticle's dispatch as a result of technical pride, rather than of compassion.

45. For examples of the kinds of abolitionist polemics Melville invokes in *White-Jacket*, see Pease and Pease, *The Anti-Slavery Argument*, especially chapters 3–6 ("Immediate Emancipation," "Sentiment," "Religion," "Economics") and 8–9 ("Natural Rights and Natural Law," "Civil Liberties"). Rogin describes Melville's condemnation of the whip in 1850 during the heated debate over slavery as "politically provocative"; see *Subversive Genealogy*, 90. Zirker interprets Melville's veiled references to chattel slavery as a sign of his "ambivalence and his implicitly apologist stance," in "Evidence of the Slavery Dilemma," 485. She suggests that Melville's caution stemmed from his fears about the breakup of the national Union, and she sees it as "the symptom of an ideological contradiction which he had yet to resolve" but would settle in his next book, *Moby-Dick* (486). In *Melville's Major Fiction*, Duban argues for a conscious and successful anti-slavery allegory in *White-Jacket* (64–67, 73–75).

46. In Melville's *Confidence-Man* (1857), the character Black Guinea shares Guinea's African origins and his designation as a coin of the realm. The white passengers on board the "Fidèle" scrutinize him and debate his value (see chapter 3). Guinea in *White-Jacket* is based on the slave Robert Lucas, who served on the *United States* with Melville and was granted his freedom in Massachusetts on October 11, 1844, in a ruling delivered by Lemuel Shaw, Chief Justice of the state supreme court and Melville's father-in-law after his marriage to Elizabeth Shaw in 1847. See Charles Roberts Anderson, *Melville in the South Seas*, 432–33; Zirker, "Evidence of the Slavery Dilemma," 482–83; and Levy, *The Law of the Commonwealth and Chief Justice Shaw*, 68–71.

47. Stessel, "Melville's *White-Jacket*: A Case Against the 'Cat,'" 40; Karcher, *Shadow over the Promised Land*, 39–55; Zirker, "Evidence of the Slavery Dilemma," 482–84. Zirker discusses the egalitarian racism of seamen's narratives (484–88).

48. Critics have often noticed the analogy between sailor and slave in *White-Jacket*, arguing either that it is politically progressive (Franklin, *Prison Literature in America*; Rogin, *Subversive Genealogy*) or that it is politically regressive (Zirker, "Evidence of the Slavery Dilemma"). Karcher, one of the few critics to not only notice but also analyze the analogy, suggests that it forms part of Melville's larger literary strategy of "breaking down racial barriers and inculcating color blindness in human relations." Karcher has doubts about the effectiveness of this tactic; see *Shadow over the Promised Land*, 39–55.

49. Michael Paul Rogin describes how Melville arranges the flogging scenes "to break down the voyeuristic distance," in *Subversive Genealogy*, 93–94.

50. For Douglass's anecdote about the literary slave in *The Columbian Orator*, see *Narrative*, 83–84, and *My Bondage and My Freedom*, 157–58. In *Melville in the South Seas*, Charles Roberts Anderson discusses Melville's invention of the near-flogging incident (409–412). According to Anderson, Melville witnessed 163 floggings in his fourteen months on board the *United States* (425). Zirker calls Captain Claret's change of mind a "pleasant wish-

fulfillment," arguing that Melville avoided the fatal ending that occurred in his main source for the incident at the gangway, William Leggett's "Brought to the Gangway." In this 1834 story, the seaman enacts his imagined revenge on the captain who threatens to flog him. See Zirker, "Evidence of the Slavery Dilemma," 486–87, and also Leggett, *Naval Stories*, 153–79. Samuel Leech, however, offers a precedent for the reprieve. In *Thirty Years from Home* (1843), he describes a first lieutenant's successful pleading for a sailor condemned to flogging, as well as several of his own close calls (52, 78, 86, 258). At the end of his life and his writing career, Melville retold the story of the escape from flogging in the nostalgic musings of the old sailor, Bridegroom Dick. Dick tells his wife how the magnanimous captain of his frigate taught a drunken and disorderly Finnish sailor a lesson of submission by mustering the crew, lashing him to the gratings, and ordering the boatswain's mates to their positions, but then commanding that he be released at the last moment. See "Bridegroom Dick" in *Collected Poems of Herman Melville*, 175–78.

51. Dickinson, "A Weight with Needles on the pounds—," #264 in *The Poems of Emily Dickinson*, 1:189; Loeffelholz, *Dickinson and the Boundaries of Feminist Theory*, 105–6. In *Billy Budd*, Melville meditates on the penetrations of naval authority, focusing on the English Mutiny Act, the model for the United States Articles of War. In the pivotal chapter 21, Captain Vere explains to a reluctant shipboard court that they would not be condemning Billy; rather "it would be martial law operating through us." See *Billy Budd, Sailor*, 110.

52. Howard P. Vincent suggests sources for the white jacket in Thomas Carlyle, *Sartor Resartus* (1833–34); Dana, *Two Years Before the Mast* (1840); and Henry James Mercier and William Gallop's 1841 *Life in a Man of War*; see Vincent, *Tailoring of "White-Jacket,"* 12–15. For interpretations of the jacket, see James E. Miller, *A Reader's Guide to Herman Melville*, 70–74; Vincent, *Tailoring of "White-Jacket,"* 15–25, 225–229; Larry J. Reynolds, "Anti-Democratic Emphasis," 21–28; and Dimock, *Empire for Liberty*, 96–97. Miller sees the difference represented by the jacket as erased in an act of democratic rebirth at the end of the book; Reynolds see the persistence of privilege. In *Redburn* (1849), published immediately before *White-Jacket*, the protagonist's long, large-buttoned moleskin shooting-jacket alienates him from the sailors below and above his station on the trading ship *Highlander*. See *Redburn*, 3, 19, 72–76, 201, 221–22. Although Wellingborough Redburn's shooting-jacket shrinks in the rain, rather than swells like White-Jacket's garment, it, too, divulges the interior: "until at last I thought it would completely exhale, and leave nothing but the bare seams, by way of a skeleton, on my back" (74).

53. Melville, *Pierre*, 284–85, 288–89.

54. James Duban briefly describes the reversals in color perspective in *White-Jacket*, in *Melville's Major Fiction*, 66.

55. In *Empire for Liberty*, Dimock argues that the jacket renders the character socially legible: "That he should be named after his attire is only too fitting, for that is indeed what he is: not a person but a jacket, an outer garment, all surface and all visibility" (96).

56. On the clothing records of the *United States*, see Charles Roberts Anderson, *Melville in the South Seas*, 417–18. Vincent discusses Melville's use of

Life on Board a Man-of-War, by a British Seaman (1829) in *Tailoring of "White-Jacket,"* 221–25.

57. In *The Confidence-Man* (1857), Melville plays variations on the theme of the encounter between subjects. A meditation on the challenge of being confronted with characters who cannot be read and questions that cannot be answered, *The Confidence-Man* consists of a series of encounters between confidence men and their marks on a Mississippi steamboat, during which positions are reversed and partners are changed and language is twisted with abandon.

58. Webb, *The Garies and Their Friends,* 2, 188, 191, 193.

59. Melville, *Moby-Dick,* 414.

60. Melville himself never experienced the fall from the yard that he ascribes to his semi-autobiographical narrator, as Charles Roberts Anderson demonstrates in *Melville in the South Seas,* 412–17. Thomas O. Selfridge, at the time a recruiting officer in Boston for the United States Navy and later commissioned as a rear-admiral, castigated Melville's story of his fall in a manuscript written in July 1850, but not published until 1935. Calling the fall "tenfold more preposterous" than the "absurd" anecdote of White-Jacket being mistaken for a ghost by his shipmates in chapter 19, Selfridge attacked Melville's veracity. See Charles Roberts Anderson, "A Reply to Herman Melville's *White-Jacket* by Rear-Admiral Thomas O. Selfridge, Sr.," 130–31. Melville's source for the fall episode in Nathaniel Ames, *A Mariner's Sketches* (1831), is discussed by Anderson in *Melville in the South Seas,* 415–17, and by Vincent in *Tailoring of "White-Jacket,"* 202–16. Vincent argues for a final three-act drama of "Fall, Submersion, and Salvation" and suggests that Melville may have gotten the idea for the garment filling with water from the 1829 *Life on Board a Man-of-War* (213–29). The search for specific sources seems beside the point in taking account of this powerful, phantasmal scene. The source for the narrator's using his knife to lay open his jacket and himself has not been "found." It is located, I am arguing, in Melville's response to the vibrant and unsettling presence of the analogy with slavery across antebellum political discourse.

61. This dream of purification is shared by Aylmer and projected onto the body of Georgiana in Hawthorne's "The Birthmark" (1843). Unlike Aylmer, White-Jacket experiments on his own body and, in Melville's version, the patient survives.

62. *Moby-Dick,* 488.

63. Dana, *Two Years Before the Mast,* 152; Browne, *Etchings of a Whaling Cruise,* 496.

64. David R. Roediger outlines a similar logic to blackface minstrelsy, in which the mutability and mobility of white performers depended on the presumed fixity of their black objects; see *Wages of Whiteness,* 122–27. In a strange passage in "Self-Reliance" (1841), Ralph Waldo Emerson laments the loss of white resilience. Using the New Zealander as a foil for the effete North American in his skeptical analysis of civilized progress, Emerson imagines delivering a blow and watching the native flesh renew itself: "But compare the health of the two men, and you shall see that the white man has lost his aboriginal strength. If the traveller tell us truly, strike the savage with a broad axe, and

in a day or two the flesh shall unite and heal as if you struck the blow into soft pitch, and the same blow shall send the white to the grave." See *Essays and Lectures,* 279. In "Self-Reliance," his most astringent account of individuality, Emerson longs for flesh that is yielding and insensate.

65. Again and again, Melville's *Confidence-Man* (1857) cautions the reader about the insecurities of analogy. See especially the dispute in chapter 22 between Pitch and the Philosophical Intelligence Officer over the character of boys. As the Philosophical Intelligence Officer proceeds "by analogy from the physical to the moral" (121), attempting to prove progressive development, his analogies, riddled with puns, raise the possibility of discontinuous, unpredictable change. Promising the clarity of stable relations between terms, his analogies unfold into ambiguity.

66. In Melville's later fiction, the freedom offered by changing one's clothes is severely qualified. In *Israel Potter* (1855), the title character, trapped on board a British privateer and fearing that his jacket will expose him as an American sailor, drops the telltale garment overboard. Rather than ensuring his safety, his act leads to a prolonged and agitated effort to find a proper station. Jacketless, unclassifiable, Israel wanders the decks in search of acceptance among any class of sailors. See *Israel Potter: His Fifty Years of Exile,* 133–41. Unlike the redeeming divestment in *White-Jacket,* the repeated putting on and off of disguises in *Israel Potter* signifies the protagonist's increasing dislocation and entrapment. For the title character or characters in Melville's *Confidence-Man* (1857), identity is unmoored rather than secured by a succession of costumes. White-Jacket's paring is reminiscent of the illustrated men in Renaissance anatomies who slice off their skin to reveal their internal structures. See, for example, the figure who displays his muscles (all of them), while he holds his skin in one hand and a knife in the other, in Juan de Valverde's *Anatomia del corpo umano* (1560), reproduced in Laqueur, *Making Sex,* 76. White-Jacket, however, peels his skin in order to evade, rather than invite, the reader's inspection.

67. Melville, *Moby-Dick,* 304, 305, 307, 420.

68. Ibid., 480–81; *Pierre,* 294. In *Mardi* (1849), Babbalanja entices King Media with the philosophy contained in physiology: "how many millions there are who live from day to day by the incessant operation of subtle processes in them, of which they know nothing. . . . A soul . . . is lodged in a frame, whose minutest action is full of unsearchable wisdom." See Melville, *Mardi; and a Voyage Thither,* 505.

69. Gerlach, "Messianic Nationalism in the Early Works of Herman Melville," 12, 22. See the unsigned review "*White Jacket; or The World in a Man-of-War,*" in the *Southern Literary Messenger* 16 (1850), 251–52. Although the choice between ironic and literal readings seems false, the critical debate is revealing. It is a debate about the reach and limits of the author, interpretive practices, and the social functions of literature. In the party of irony are Gerlach; Duban ("Chipping with a Chisel" and *Melville's Major Fiction,* 63–65); and Samson (*White Lies,* 139–48, 161–62). In the party of complicity is Zirker ("Evidence of the Slavery Dilemma," 491–92). Recently there has been a productive revaluation of irony in Melville's work, in which the intricacy and

intimacy of Melville's positions have been acknowledged. In *Empire for Liberty*, Dimock analyzes the paean as "represented discourse." She portrays a Melville on the inside pushing out: "the deadpan incisiveness at once summarizes and cuts through everything that has gone on before. *White-Jacket* abounds with such local puncturing efforts, efforts aimed not so much at 'ripping open' the textual fabric as at showing its strain" (103). In an introduction to a recent paperback edition of *Moby-Dick*, Edward Said describes the uncanny accuracy of Melville's expansionist discourse: "Melville's contribution is that he delivers the salutary effect as well as the destructiveness of the American world presence, and he also demonstrates its self-mesmerizing assumptions about its providential significance." See Said, introduction to *Moby-Dick*, xxi. See also Levine, *Conspiracy and Romance*, 165–67, 215–16, and Martin and Snead, "Reading Through Blackness." This revaluation began with Barbara Johnson's lapidary "Melville's Fist: The Execution of Billy Budd" (1979), reprinted in Johnson, *The Critical Difference*, 79–109. Johnson argues that Melville embodies ironic (Claggart) and literal (Budd) perspectives. Instead of asking readers to choose, he shows through the character of Captain Vere how readings take place in historical contexts that define the relations between irony and belief.

70. Melville, *Pierre*, 141. Melville manipulates sermonic form and content throughout his extended fiction, testing claims and tracing links between theology, politics, and personality. See the anti-American jeremiad delivered in the anonymous scroll in chapter 161 of *Mardi* (1849); Father Mapple's "two-stranded lesson" dividing his audience into sailors who obey and captains who command, in chapter 9 of *Moby-Dick;* the cook Fleece preaching self-restraint to the sharks in chapter 64 of *Moby-Dick;* and the mystic Plotinus Plinlimmon's lecture on failure and structural contradiction in book 14, section 3, of *Pierre* (1852).

71. Sidney Kaplan describes a pattern, not only in *White-Jacket* but also in *Mardi* and *Redburn*, of trenchant social criticism followed by a counsel of patience. See Kaplan, "Herman Melville and the American National Sin," 316–25.

72. For discussions of Cole's *Voyage of Life*, see Powell, *Thomas Cole*, 84–97, and Wallach, "Thomas Cole: Landscape and the Course of American Empire," in Truettner and Wallach, *Thomas Cole*, 98–101. In 1847, Melville saw paintings by Cole at the New-York Gallery of the Fine Arts and the American Art Union. Melville alludes to the obscure staircases, plunging spaces, infinite regresses, and ring-bolts and chains in Piranesi's etchings *Le Carceri [The Prisons]*, in *Clarel*, part 2, canto 35 (1876); he also may refer to Piranesi in "The Blanket" chapter of *Moby-Dick* (1851) and in books 21 and 26 of *Pierre* (1852). See Gretchko, "Melville at the New-York Gallery of the Fine Arts"; Leyda, *The Melville Log*, 1:261–62; Furrow, "The Terrible Made Visible," 249–51; and Moore, *That Cunning Alphabet*, 148–49. Moore suggests that Cole's *Voyage of Life* lies behind the inspirational painting in Father Mapple's chapel in chapter 8 of *Moby-Dick* (123). In chapter 4 of this book, I argue that Melville may have Cole in mind when he uproots the landscape of *Pierre*.

CHAPTER THREE: GETTING INSIDE HEADS IN *MOBY-DICK*

1. Patterson, "Memoir of the Life and Scientific Labors of Samuel George Morton," xxxviii. Shakespeare, *Hamlet, Prince of Denmark*, 220 (act 5, scene 1, lines 159–64).

2. Morton describes his methods in *Crania Americana*, 249–68, and the more accurate measurements made with lead shot in *Crania Ægyptiaca*, 20. He sounds the customary vanitas note in a poem on the recent death of his son, written a year before his own death in 1851. Patterson reprints the poem at the end of his memoir; see Nott and Gliddon, *Types of Mankind*, lvii. Morton received his second medical degree in 1823 from Edinburgh University, where he was influenced by Scottish faculty psychology. Terence Martin describes the authority of Scottish philosophy in the early United States, in *The Instructed Vision*.

3. For a discussion and reproductions of vanitas paintings, see Haak, *The Golden Age*, 125–29. Roland Mushat Frye describes European memento mori images in the fifteenth century and "Young Man with a Skull" portraits in the sixteenth century, visual traditions that Shakespeare translated to the London stage in the graveyard scene of *Hamlet*. See Frye, *The Renaissance Hamlet*, 205–220. Frye reproduces the Lucas print (215) and the Hals oil painting (208). For copies of Dürer's St. Jerome, see Walter L. Strauss, *The Complete Engravings, Etchings, and Drypoints of Albrecht Dürer*, 163; and Wölfflin, *Drawings of Albrecht Dürer*, plate 56. For Zurbarán's St. Francis, see Gállego and Gudiol, *Zurbarán: 1598–1664*, plates 82, 193, 249, 372. The Belgian anatomist Andreas Vesalius included a nice twist on convention—a skull contemplated by a skeleton—in his *De Humani Corporis Fabrica* (1543) and his *Epitome* (1543). See Saunders and O'Malley, *The Illustrations from the Works of Andreas Vesalius of Brussels*, plates 22 and 79.

4. For descriptions of the facial goniometer, see Morton, *Crania Americana*, 250–53, 255–56.

5. Draper, *Human Physiology, Statical and Dynamical*, 581–86. Draper elaborates and endorses Prichard's front view, linking facial shape (prognathous, pyramidal, and elliptical) with social state (savage, pastoral, civilized) and racial group (Negro, Asiatic, European) in a geometry of progress.

6. Morton, *Crania Ægyptiaca*, 27; Nott and Gliddon, *Types of Mankind*, 414; Draper, *Human Physiology*, 563–602. For an example of the shift from reliance on cutaneous differences to cranial ones, see White, *An Account of the Regular Gradation in Man*. In this 1799 work, Charles White, the English surgeon and comparative anatomist, laments the scientific ignorance of the brain and nerves and describes color as "the principal and most characteristic distinction" (64, 99); see also Cartwright, "Diseases and Peculiarities of the Negro Race." In this article, written in 1851, the Louisiana doctor and popularizer Samuel A. Cartwright argues that there are "more indelible and durable differences than color" (65). The Horsman quote is from *Race and Manifest Destiny*, 58. In *Science Encounters the Indian, 1820–1880*, Robert E. Bieder describes the sweep of Morton's anatomy lessons: "he was a teacher who taught Americans that by viewing the Indian's skull . . . one could both discern the Indian's

past and predict his future" (101). Charles Colbert discusses the ways in which phrenology envisioned the human head as a landscape of meaning, in "'Each Little Hillock hath a Tongue'—Phrenology and the Art of Hiram Powers," 296–98.

7. On Morton's ideas and career, see Patterson, "Memoir of the Life and Scientific Labors of Samuel George Morton," xvii–lvii; William Stanton, *The Leopard's Spots*, 24–53, 113–21; Frederickson, *The Black Image in the White Mind*, 74–77; Horsman, *Race and Manifest Destiny*, 125–35; and Bieder, *Science Encounters the Indian*, 55–103. In "The Haunting of White Manhood," Nelson discusses Morton's role at the center of a fraternity of ethnologists. Bieder describes American collectors' zeal for Native American crania, the grave-robbing it inspired, and contemporary Native American fury at the practice (64–67). At the beginning of *Crania Americana*, Morton "respectfully solicits the further aid of gentlemen interested in the cause of science, in procuring the *skulls of all nations*, and forwarding them to his address in this city" (v). In the sections describing specific skulls, Morton often acknowledges the procurer and provides a thumbnail history of the skull. He poses the Egyptian question in *Crania Ægyptiaca*, 1.

8. Morton, *Crania Americana*, 5–7. In *Crania Ægyptiaca*, Morton argues against the validity of paintings that represented ancient Egyptian rulers as dark-skinned, claiming that such portrayals were merely conventional and did not reflect actual appearances. Yet in the last section of his book, he bases his argument for the permanence of Caucasian dominance and Negro slavery on physiognomic evidence in Egyptian bas-reliefs and paintings. If color is conventional, why not physiognomy? If physiognomy is credible, why not color? Stephen Jay Gould analyzes Morton's scientific methods, in particular the ways in which prejudice distorts the selection of evidence and tabulation of data, in *The Mismeasure of Man*, 50–72.

9. Morton tentatively states his findings at the beginning of *Crania Americana* (3). He makes his declaration at the end of *Crania Ægyptiaca* (66). I have taken the three external causes from Samuel Stanhope Smith's Enlightenment *Essay on the Causes of the Variety of Complexion and Figure in the Human Species* (1787, 1810). Smith argued for the mutability of human appearance.

10. Soemmerring's catalogue was excerpted by the pioneering British comparative anatomist Charles White in his *Account of the Regular Gradation in Man* (1799) and by the emigré Frenchman J. H. Guenebault, who translated into English the chapters on blacks in the second volume of J. J. Virey's influential *Histoire naturelle du genre humain* (1824) and published them in South Carolina along with extracts from White and Soemmerring as *Natural History of the Negro Race* (1837). Hugh Honour discusses Virey's racial aesthetics in *The Image of the Black in Western Art*, vol. 4, part 2, 18.

11. Whitman, [untitled fifth poem], in *Leaves of Grass: The First (1855) Edition*, 116–23; "I Sing The Body Electric," in *Leaves of Grass: A Textual Variorum*, 1:121–32. The poem appears numbered "3" in the "Enfans d'Adam" section of the 1860 edition of *Leaves of Grass* and is entitled "I Sing the Body Electric" in the 1867 edition. Whitman's revisions of the poem after 1856 are minor. In a chapter evaluating Whitman's complicated gestures of mediation and

identification, Karen Sánchez-Eppler describes the poet as "dismembering" the slave's body and repeating "the bloody, physical differentiations of plantation life"; see *Touching Liberty*, 56–57. I have a different sense of the poet as auctioneer, based on Whitman's insistence that he is treating not only black but also white and red bodies, on an examination of Whitman's own second thoughts about the noun "slave" in 1856, and on a reading of the poem as revising, not simply repeating, historical acts of violence.

12. Whitman, "I Sing the Body Electric," lines 133–37, 148–49, in *Leaves of Grass: A Textual Variorum*, 1:131–32.

13. For Whitman's catalogues of trees and rivers, see his preface to the 1855 edition of *Leaves of Grass*, in *Leaves of Grass: The First (1855) Edition*, 7; for the catalogue of American characters and activities, see the poem that came to be titled "Song of Myself," lines 257–352, in ibid., 37–41.

14. Morton refers to Collins's lithographs in his preface (iv); Combe describes his delight at their correctness and beauty (269); and Collins himself discusses them in the advertisement inserted at the end of the volume.

15. For other exquisite lithographs, see particularly plate 4 (*Peruvian of the Ancient Race, from Arica*), plate 11c (*Peruvian from the Temple of the Sun*), and plate 34 (*Potowatomie*). The lithographs in *Crania Ægyptiaca*, most of which were done by T. Sinclair from the drawings of M. S. Weaver, are much inferior to the illustrations in *Crania Americana*. They are more coarsely executed, without the passion for texture, shadow, and contour; diminished (none is life-size); and grouped in rows, sometimes nine to a page, rather than held out individually to the viewer. *Crania Ægyptiaca* is a pale version of its predecessor, shorter (67 pages of text and 13 pages of plates compared with 294 pages of text and 76 pages of plates), and smaller (nine-and-three-quarters by twelve-and-a-quarter inches compared with eleven by fifteen-and-one-half inches).

16. In producing the lithographs for plates 20 and 21, Collins did not have the skulls in front of him, as he did for most of the other plates in *Crania Americana*. Morton did not own the Natchez skulls; he had been sent drawings by an enthusiastic colleague. Morton describes Native American practices of cranial shaping and discusses the Natchez skulls in particular (159–62). For other portrayals of manipulated crania, see plates 45 (*Killemook Chief*) and 46 (*Clatsap from Columbia River*).

17. Ibid., 82.

18. Nott and Gliddon, *Types of Mankind*, ix. On the theoretical contributions of the "American school," see William Stanton, *Leopard's Spots*; Frederickson, *Black Image in the White Mind*, 74–82; and Horsman, *Race and Manifest Destiny*, 122–38. Robert J. C. Young traces the influence of Morton, Nott, and Gliddon on the debate about race in Britain. See *Colonial Desire*, 118–41. Insisting on separate creations, the proponents of the "American school" combined the objects and arguments of earlier thinkers such as Lord Kaims, who focused on North American Indians as the test case for the diversity of origins on the basis of historical evidence and moral causes, and Charles White and J. A. Smith, who focused on Negroes as the test case for diversity on the basis of anatomical comparisons. For another racist summary of the 1850s, see John Campbell's ethnology anthology, *Negro-Mania* (1851).

19. William Stanton excerpts the acknowledgment of debt to Morton from the *Charleston Medical Journal,* in *The Leopard's Spots,* 144. Patterson quotes the *London Medico-Chirurgical Review* appraisal of Morton's work in his "Memoir of the Life and Scientific Labors of Samuel George Morton," xxxiv.

20. Nott and Gliddon, *Types of Mankind,* 79, 414. Nott is the polemicist and redactor; Gliddon is the biblical pedant. When Nott offers his "own" scientific findings, they are amateurish and arrogant, and include a survey of hat dealers to determine the circumference of the heads of the white population of the United States (452) and a series of caricatures to "demonstrate the truth" of the likeness between Negroes, apes, and chimpanzees (458–59). He bluntly challenges the reader to produce any evidence of Negro or Indian cultural achievement (59, 461). Reginald Horsman describes the publication history of *Types of Mankind,* in *Josiah Nott of Mobile,* 171–200.

21. Cartwright, "Diseases and Peculiarities of the Negro Race," 332. Nott quotes *Ezekiel* 37:2–3 on "dry bones" in Nott and Gliddon, *Types of Mankind,* 267. Morton evokes the valley full of bones waiting for their resuscitator when he describes Peruvian gravesites in *Crania Americana,* 109, and Egyptian tombs in *Crania Ægyptiaca,* 1.

22. Nott and Gliddon, *Types of Mankind,* 80, 412. The elaborate pun on "types" is deepened when one considers that compositors since the late eighteenth century have described metal relief type in bodily terms: face, neck, shoulder, belly, feet. "Permanence" is the refrain that runs through Nott's "legitimate deductions" about racial types at the end of part I (465). Samuel Stanhope Smith's *Essay on the Causes of the Variety of Complexion and Figure in the Human Species* was published in 1787 and revised and expanded in 1810. In tracing the shift from "Varieties" to "Types," I do not mean to suggest a golden age of ethnology in which observers celebrated a happy human relativity; rather, my intention is to describe a constriction of sympathy and imagination. Both Smith and Nott seek to establish racial standards, yet in Smith's *Essay,* characteristics are not immutable and thus not the enduring sign of character. The shift from one to many races paralleled the growing interest in the fundamental differences between the male and female sexes. See Laqueur, *Making Sex,* 1–24, 149–92.

23. After "Your head is the type of your mentality," the second epigraph in the Fowlers' *Illustrated Self-Instructor* reads, "Self-knowledge is the essence of all knowledge." In the logic of the Fowlers, self-knowledge is head knowledge. On the careers of Orson and Lorenzo Fowler and the extraordinary popularity of phrenology, see Madeleine B. Stern, *Heads and Headlines,* Davies, *Phrenology,* and Colbert, *Measure of Perfection.* On phrenology and ethnology, see Horsman, *Race and Manifest Destiny,* 56–59, 116–28, 142–45, Stepan, "Race and Gender," 45–47, and Colbert, *Measure of Perfection,* xii, 212–81.

24. Fowler and Fowler, *Illustrated Self-Instructor,* 132, 134, 133. The visual epitome of the Fowlers' incarnation of mental faculties can be found in their famous profile of the *Symbolical Head,* in which the cranium is laid out in tracts and populated (see figure 4 of this book, which is a reproduction of this diagram). The *Symbolical Head* numbers the regions, keys the numbers to a list, and illustrates each faculty with a cranial vignette. Organ number six, "Combativeness," is represented by two young men engaging in fisticuffs just to the

left of the ear. At organ number thirty-six, "Causality," an Isaac Newton-like figure watches a piece of fruit drop from a tree on the forehead. Criticizing phrenology, Thomas Sewall writes keenly about the satisfactions it appears to offer; see Sewall, *An Examination of Phrenology; in Two Lectures,* 62–63.

25. Poems by Dickinson with ethnological resonance would include Johnson numbers 263 ("A single Screw of Flesh"), 264 ("A Weight with Needles on the pounds—"), 292 ("If your Nerve, deny you—"), 451 ("The Outer—from the Inner/Derives its Magnitude—"), 479 ("She dealt her pretty words like Blades—"), 578 ("The Body grows without—"), and 1138 ("A Spider sewed at Night"). Divided into lines and stanzas, the passage from the Fowlers on "Locating Spirituality" looks and sounds like a Dickinson poem. Another Fowler passage that shares Dickinson's sense of jaunty, eerie bodily meter is the description of how to find the organs of Time, Tune, and Mirthfulness: "Time and Tune join each other, while Time, Tune, and Mirthfulness occupy the three angles of a triangle, nearly equilateral, the shortest side being Time and Tune" (*Self-Instructor,* 134). In *Touching Liberty,* Sánchez-Eppler analyzes Dickinson's embodiments in political terms (126–31, 140–41).

26. Fowler and Fowler, *Illustrated Self-Instructor,* 133.

27. Cartwright, "Slavery in the Light of Ethnology," 697; "Diseases and Peculiarities of the Negro Race," 68–69, 212, 505. Thomas Jefferson, *Notes on the State of Virginia,* 269–70. Cartwright takes his image of the "Anatomical knife" from Jefferson. Yet in Jefferson's "Query XIV," the knife is only one of many tools of analysis, and Jefferson makes a distinction, elided by Cartwright and his medical contemporaries, between human substance and human faculties. Jefferson's devastating speculations about racial inequality, "hazarded with great diffidence" in "Query XIV," were invoked by generations of ethnologists, including Charles White, J. J. Virey, and Josiah Nott. They were also attacked by generations of African American intellectuals, such as Benjamin Banneker, David Walker, William Wells Brown, and James McCune Smith. On Cartwright, see Frederickson, *Black Image in the White Mind,* 55–60 passim, and Horsman, *Race and Manifest Destiny,* 153–54.

28. Guenebault, *Natural History of the Negro Race,* 23, 53; Cartwright, "Slavery in the Light of Ethnology," 711; Van Evrie, "Negroes and Negro Slavery," 2. On Van Evrie, see Frederickson, *Black Image in the White Mind,* 60–70, 91–96, and Horsman, *Race and Manifest Destiny,* 135, 280. The experiments performed on Brown are detailed in Chamerovzow, *Slave Life in Georgia,* 40–43. In "The Monster" (1898), written at the end of the ethnological century, Stephen Crane captures the disfiguring effects of racial science in his story of the African American Henry Johnson, who becomes a "monster" in Dr. Trescott's laboratory.

29. Hawthorne, *Scarlet Letter,* 174, 172; "The Birthmark," in *Tales and Sketches,* 766; "Egotism; or, the Bosom Serpent," in ibid., 793. In another portrayal of the body's involuntary disclosures, the Fowlers describe the shaping propulsion of the "Language" organ: "When it is large, it pushes the eyes downward and outward, and of course shoves them forward, which gives them a full and swollen appearance, as if they were standing partly out of their sockets, and causes both the upper and under eyelids to be wide and broad. When the eyes

are sunken, and their lids narrow, Language will be found small" (*Illustrated Self-Instructor,* 134).

30. On Puritan desires to discern holiness, see Morgan, *Visible Saints,* and Colacurcio, "Visible Sanctity and Specter Evidence." On the bosom serpent, see Arner, "Of Snakes and Those Who Swallow Them." In a subplot about racial passing in *The Garies and Their Friends* (1857), Frank J. Webb spins an African American bosom serpent tale. As the character Clarence explains, "I must shut this secret [that he is black] in my bosom, where it gnaws, gnaws, gnaws, until it has almost eaten my heart away"; see *The Garies and Their Friends,* 324-25.

31. Wilbur, "Edgar Allan Poe," 378; Poe, "The Man of the Crowd," in *The Short Fiction of Edgar Allan Poe,* 287, 283.

32. Poe, "Berenice," in *The Short Fiction of Edgar Allan Poe,* 72-74. Dana D. Nelson argues that Poe explores the affective bonds of ethnologists such as Morton, Nott, and Gliddon in his short story "Some Words with a Mummy" (1845). See Nelson, "The Haunting of White Manhood."

33. On the well-documented interest of Poe and Whitman in phrenology, see Hungerford, "Poe and Phrenology" and "Walt Whitman and his Chart of Bumps"; also Aspiz, *Walt Whitman and the Body Beautiful,* 109-41; Erkkila, *Whitman the Political Poet,* 176-83; and Davies, *Phrenology,* 118-25.

34. Squier, "American Ethnology, 398; Bachman, *The Doctrine of the Unity of the Human Race,* 147-51. *Putnam's* published two assessments of ethnology, one accepting Nott and Gliddon's proof of permanent racial diversity but also insisting on spiritual unity, and the other supporting a single creation; see "Is Man One or Many?" and "Are All Men Descended From Adam?" On Squier, see William Stanton, *Leopard's Spots,* 82-88, and Bieder, *Science Encounters the Indian,* 104-45. On Bachman, see Stanton, *Leopard's Spots,* 123-36. Horsman describes the cultural triumph of the new theories of innate racial difference, in *Race and Manifest Destiny,* 157ff., and *Josiah Nott,* 183ff.

35. Lowell, "The Prejudice of Color," 16, 18-19. Lydia Maria Child rejects racial craniology in her *Anti-Slavery Catechism,* 28-29.

36. Douglass, "The Claims of the Negro Ethnologically Considered," address delivered before the literary societies at Western Reserve College, July 12, 1854, 291, 296, 304. Although Douglass names *Crania Americana* as the target of his attack on Morton's Egyptological sleight-of-hand, he must be referring to *Crania Ægyptiaca.*

37. Douglass, "Claims of the Negro," 297, 298. Recently, Henry Louis Gates, Jr., reprinted an excerpt from Douglass's section entitled "The Bearings of the Question" as a striking and sad comment on the persistence of scientific racialism. Gates was responding to Murray and Hernnstein's IQ manifesto, *The Bell Curve.* See Gates, "Why Now?"

38. Douglass, "Claims of the Negro," 304-05. Waldo S. Martin, Jr., discusses Douglass's challenge to the ethnological consensus and the ways in which his critique was limited by his own ambivalence toward the various races and his endorsements of Americanism and assimilation; see Martin, *The Mind of Frederick Douglass,* 197-250. For other contemporary African American anti-ethnologies, see James McCune Smith, "Civilization: Its Dependence on Physical Circumstances" and "On the Fourteenth Query of Thomas Jefferson's *Notes*

on Virginia" (both published in 1859); for a later response, see Delany, *Principia of Ethnology* (1879).

39. William Wells Brown, *Clotel*, 123; Weld, *American Slavery As It Is*, 171, 169. Farrison identifies Weld as Brown's source in his notes to *Clotel*, 250–51. Brown's documentary design, heterogeneous form, and critical aims in *Clotel* share affinities with such abolitionist anatomies as Weld's *American Slavery As It Is*.

40. Brown, *Clotel*, 122–25.

41. The *Life of Okah Tubbee* plays striking variations on the theme of "removal," not only in the geographical sense of forced resettlement (Tubbee discusses the Choctaw "removal"), but also in a psychic sense. The text represents Tubbee's struggle to define his racial and masculine identity through acts of dissociation. Littlefield outlines the complicated publishing history of the *Life* in his introduction, xxiii–xxv, xxxiii–xxxiv ff.

42. Apess's "An Indian's Looking Glass for the White Man" appeared in the first edition of his narratives of religious conversion and Native American identity formation, *The Experiences of Five Christian Indians of the Pequot Tribe* (1833). It was removed in 1837. See Apess, *On Our Own Ground: The Complete Writings of William Apess*, lxvi–lxvii, 99–100, 155–61. There are several affinities between the discursive projects of Apess and those of Melville. Compare, for example, the turning of expectations about "whiteness" in *A Son of the Forest* (1831) and *Indian Nullification* (1835) with the "Whiteness of the Whale" chapter in *Moby-Dick* (1851), and compare the undoing of American myths in the "Eulogy on King Philip" (1836) with the Saddle Meadows sections of *Pierre* (1852). Barry O'Connell analyzes Apess's literary techniques in his introduction to *On Our Own Ground*.

43. Apess, *On Our Own Ground*, 158, 157.

44. Ibid., 157. At the end of "Eulogy on King Philip" (1836), Apess insists that the crimes of the fathers need not stigmatize the sons. See ibid., 310.

45. Apess, ibid., 160.

46. White describes his debt to Hunter in *An Account of the Regular Gradation in Man*, 41; Beale describes his debt in *Natural History of the Sperm Whale*, 70. For resonances between whale and human anatomy in Melville's sources, see Beale, ibid., 9–32, 70–135, 185–87, and Bennett, *Narrative of a Whaling Voyage round the Globe*, 2:145–228. Melville alludes several times to Hunter and to Owen; see *Moby-Dick*, 135, 263, 457. All subsequent citations will be to the Northwestern-Newberry edition (see bibliography) and given in parentheses in the body of the text.

47. Beale discusses the debate over whale classification, in *Natural History of the Sperm Whale*, 9–12; Vincent describes Melville's contribution, in *The Trying-Out of "Moby-Dick,"* 135–42. Melville refers to the discrepancy between whale skeleton and shape in *Moby-Dick*, 263, 453, 457; see also Beale quoting Hunter, in *Natural History*, 72. The discrepancy is illustrated in the text and plates in Frank's *Herman Melville's Picture Gallery*, 48–53.

48. Vincent, *Trying-Out of "Moby-Dick,"* 121, 125; Zoellner, *Salt-Sea Mastodon*, 154; Melville's letter to Richard Henry Dana, Jr., May 1, 1850, in *Correspondence*, 162. Scholars identify as "cetological" the chapters dealing

with whaling and whale anatomy that cluster between chapters 32 and 105, and especially between chapters 68 and 86. In *Trying-Out of "Moby-Dick,"* Vincent broadly includes 45 chapters; in "The Composition of Moby-Dick," James Barbour more narrowly lists 20 chapters. I will focus on the sequences of chapters treating the whale's body. For discussions of Melville's reliance on sources for his cetology chapters, especially Beale's *Natural History of the Sperm Whale* (1839), but also Bennett's *Narrative of a Whaling Voyage* (1840), Scoresby's *Account of the Arctic Regions* (1820), and Cheever's *The Whale and His Captors* (1850), see Vincent's invaluable *Trying-Out of "Moby-Dick";* Barbour, "The Writing of *Moby-Dick*"; and Parker's section on sources in the historical note to the Northwestern-Newberry edition of *Moby-Dick,* 635–46.

The whale chapters have been interpreted as documentary base by Matthiessen (*American Renaissance: Art and Expression in the Age of Emerson and Whitman,* 416–17), Arvin (*Herman Melville,* 158–59, 167–69), and Vincent (*Trying-Out of "Moby-Dick,"* 121–26); they have been interpreted as a critique of empiricism by Hirsch (*Reality and Idea in the Early American Novel,* 194–99), Ward ("The Function of the Cetological Chapters in *Moby-Dick*"), Moore (*That Cunning Alphabet: Melville's Aesthetics of Nature,* 59–176), and Spanos (*Errant Art of Moby-Dick,* 190–203); as a reflection on literary practice by Dryden (*Melville's Thematics of Form,* 83–113); as a treatise on relativism by Brodtkorb (*Ishmael's White World,* 25–27, 142–48) and Greenberg ("Cetology: Center of Multiplicity and Discord in *Moby-Dick*"); and as a demythification of Leviathan and acceptance of a naturalistic other by Zoellner (*The Salt-Sea Mastodon,* 146–90).

Since Melville's acquisition of sources during the writing of *Moby-Dick* can be pinpointed (he borrowed Scoresby's *Account of the Arctic Regions* from the New York Society Library on April 29, 1850, and received Beale's *Natural History of the Sperm Whale* from England via George P. Putnam on July 10, 1850), the cetological chapters have served as evidence in scholarly hypotheses about the book's composition and its supposed transformation from factual whaling voyage to work of art. For critics who theorize two phases of composition, see Howard, "Melville's Struggle with the Angel" and *Herman Melville: A Biography,* 150–79; Hayford, "Two New Letters of Herman Melville"; Vincent, *Trying-Out of "Moby-Dick,"* 22–52; George R. Stewart, "The Two *Moby-Dicks*"; and Hayford, "Unnecessary Duplicates: A Key to the Writing of *Moby-Dick.*" Three stages are proposed by Barbour in "The Writing of *Moby-Dick,*" "The Composition of *Moby-Dick,*" and "'All My Books Are Botches'"; and by Howard in *The Unfolding of Moby-Dick.* Harrison Hayford reviews the theories in section 5 of the historical note to the Northwestern-Newberry *Moby-Dick,* 648–59. Peter Shillingsburg and Julian Markels criticize the surmises about composition presented as fact. See Shillingsburg, "The Three *Moby-Dicks*"; Markels, "The *Moby-Dick* White Elephant"; and also Bercaw, *Melville's Sources,* 24–27. I share Robert Milder's belief in the "stubborn meaningfulness" of the cetology chapters in the published text of *Moby-Dick* and his skepticism about considering them as vestiges of a more elementary book. See Milder's "The Composition of *Moby-Dick.*" While the debate over textual genesis might seem arcane to all but ardent Melvilleans, it raises larger interpretive questions and its terms strangely echo nineteenth-century ethnological debates about creation and character. Is there one *Moby-Dick* or are there multiple, hierarchical *Moby-Dicks*? Can we fix the internal character of the text on the basis of external evidence?

49. See Jon. 1.2; Job 41.

50. Critics who structure the cetology chapters include Vincent, who, in *Trying-Out of "Moby-Dick,"* 237–69 ff., clusters chapters on whale skin and blubber (chapters 66–72) and whale heads (chapters 73–80); Zoellner, who, in *Salt-Sea Mastodon*, 146–75, identifies "Stubb Kills a Whale" (chapter 61) as the boundary between Ishmael's "conceptual" and "perceptual" views of the whale and "Cistern and Buckets" (chapter 78) as the turning point at which he accepts mortality; and Greenberg, who distinguishes a pattern in which a living object resists being categorized in empirical and rational terms, in "Cetology: Center of Multiplicity and Discord." Taking issue with Zoellner, Greenberg argues for an "aesthetics of heterogeneity" (9) and against a "linear meaningfulness" for the cetology chapters, and he criticizes efforts to locate them in the "story-time of the *Pequod*'s voyage" (13). Although my reading of the cetology chapters differs from Zoellner's narrative of naturalistic acceptance, I too argue for a meaningful sequence, one that takes its terms, logic, and trajectory from nineteenth-century ethnology.

51. See Beale, *Natural History of the Sperm Whale*, 1–13, and Vincent, *Trying-Out of "Moby-Dick,"* 135–42.

52. Melville conjoins whales, books, and men in other writings of the early 1850s. In two summer 1851 letters to Hawthorne, Melville puns on his working title, describing the characteristics of the "Whale" that he is writing. See *Correspondence*, 190–96. Melville's "A Thought on Book-Binding" (1850), a review of Cooper's *Red Rover*, is an extended joke about books as "a species of men." According to Melville, the sober muslin binding of his edition of *Red Rover* does not reliably express its contents. Both books and men, circulating in society, "should be appropriately apparelled. Their bindings should indicate and distinguish their various characters." See Melville, *Piazza Tales and Other Prose Pieces*, 237–38. In the cetology chapters of *Moby-Dick*, Melville further extends this joke about the propriety of judging a book by its cover.

53. Spillers, "Mama's Baby, Papa's Maybe," 68. Scoresby describes how commodities were extracted from the whale, in *An Account of the Arctic Regions*, 2:397–437. Bennett reports that whalers defined sperm whales according to the quantity of oil they would produce, in *Narrative of a Whaling Voyage*, 2:155.

54. On the dark color of the whale, see Beale, *Natural History of the Sperm Whale*, 31–32, and Bennett, *Narrative of a Whaling Voyage*, 2:155, 165. In *Moby-Dick*, Melville notes the black color of whales (141), and of sperm whales in particular, describing the large whale killed by Stubb as "of an Ethiopian hue" (283). As scholars have long recognized, in representing Moby Dick Melville drew on tales of the "White Whale of the Pacific." For an example, see J. N. Reynolds, "Mocha Dick" (1839). Vincent discusses these tales in *Trying-Out of "Moby-Dick,"* 168–77.

55. Winthrop D. Jordan traces the charged genealogy of antitheses between

"black" and "white," in *White over Black*, 4–11, 512–41. David Brion Davis discusses the negative connotations of "blackness" for Europeans, but also its ambiguities, in *The Problem of Slavery in Western Culture*, 447–50. Recently, critics have turned their attention to the meanings of "whiteness." See, for example, Michaels, "The Souls of White Folk" and *Our America*; Saxton, *The Rise and Fall of the White Republic*; Roediger, *The Wages of Whiteness*; Lott, *Love and Theft*; Ignatiev, *How the Irish Became White*; and Rogin, *Blackface, White Noise*.

56. Khalil Husni surveys critical views on the "whiteness" of the whale, most of which deal with philosophy to the exclusion of flesh; see Husni, "The Whiteness of the Whale." Toni Morrison powerfully suggests that "the white whale is the ideology of race" and that in *Moby-Dick* Melville examines "the moment in America when whiteness became ideology," in "Unspeakable Things Unspoken," 15–16. D. H. Lawrence proclaims that Moby-Dick is "the deepest blood-being of the white race," in *Studies in Classic American Literature*, 169. For analyses of how Melville's text is enmeshed in the debates about slavery, freedom, and union that raged during the political crisis of 1850, see Heimert, "*Moby-Dick* and American Political Symbolism," Duban, *Melville's Major Fiction*, 82–148, and Rogin, *Subversive Genealogy*, 102–51. C. L. R. James remarkably reads *Moby-Dick* as a book about United States and world politics in the 1950s, as well as the 1850s. See *Mariners, Renegades and Castaways* (1953). Emerson puns on "appalling" with a self-revelatory effect similar to Melville's, when he writes in the "Race" chapter of *English Traits* (1856) that "Race in the negro is of appalling importance." See *English Traits*, in *Essays and Lectures*, 792. In *The Narrative of Arthur Gordon Pym* (1838), Poe also presents a vision of whiteness, in the milky cascade and snowy figure encountered by the narrator at the climax. Yet Poe offers an apotheosis rather than a specter, reinforcing rather than agitating racial orders; see *The Narrative of Arthur Gordon Pym of Nantucket*, 236–42. In an appendix to *Pym*, Beaver compares the white revelations of Poe and Melville (280–81).

57. David H. Hirsch charts Melville's use of Locke, in *Reality and Idea*, 197–99. Locke distinguishes between primary and secondary qualities, between the qualities in bodies and the ideas produced by them in the mind, in book 2, chapter 8, of *An Essay Concerning Human Understanding* (1690), 132–43. James McCune Smith analyzes "whiteness" in terms similar to Melville's, in "On the Fourteenth Query of Jefferson's *Notes* on *Virginia*," 233.

58. G. J. Barker-Benfield details the rise of gynecology and obstetrics in *The Horrors of the Half-Known Life*—a title that is taken from chapter 58 of *Moby-Dick*. See also Russett, *Sexual Science*. Nancy Leys Stepan draws out the analogies, in "Race and Gender." Robyn Wiegman analyzes the ways in which nineteenth-century studies of racial and sexual differences sustained and clarified one another, in *American Anatomies*, 43–78. Londa Schiebinger suggests that male comparative anatomists often assumed that the racial subject was male. She discusses the eighteenth-century European context in *Nature's Body*, 145–60. Melville invokes sexual science in his disturbing, prolonged examination of female reproductive labor in "The Tartarus of Maids"; see *Piazza Tales and Other Prose Pieces*, 323–35.

59. Stuart M. Frank has gathered the sources and types for Melville's references in these three chapters, in *Herman Melville's Picture Gallery*, 1–55. The twisting of image by expectation in these whale pictures is as entertaining and eye-opening as Melville implies.

60. The Reverend Henry T. Cheever describes a similar visceral eruption: "Before the blubber was all off, the huge entrails of the whale burst out like barrels, at the wounds made by the spades and lances" (59); see *The Whale and His Captors*, which Melville used as a cetological source.

61. Dickinson's poem was first published in Mabel Loomis Todd's Dickinson collection, *Poems: Third Series*, 80. Todd placed it in the "Love" section and gave it the bizarre title "Loyalty." Thomas Johnson numbers the poem 861 and dates it about 1864, in *The Poems of Emily Dickinson*, 2:644. The original poem in Dickinson's own handwriting appears with different line breaks and slightly different punctuation from Johnson's printed version. See R. W. Franklin's facsimile edition of *The Manuscript Books of Emily Dickinson*, 2:1038. I have tried to approximate the appearance of the manuscript poem. According to the *Oxford English Dictionary*, the "sk" spelling for "skeptic" was the ordinary form in the nineteenth-century United States, while "sc" was standard in England and France. In France, unlike England, the "sc" in "sceptic" is pronounced softly, as in "sceptre." In Johnson #1059, "Sang from the Heart, Sire," the singer mutilates herself by piercing her heart with her own beak; her tune drips red. The phrase "Thomas' faith in anatomy" appears in the "Master" letter that begins "If you saw a bullet hit a Bird." Although Dickinson scholars number and date this letter differently, they agree that it was written in the early 1860s. For a facsimile, transcript, and manuscript history, see *The Master Letters of Emily Dickinson*, 5–10, 31–46. The flood of gore was also a feature of abolitionist flogging scenes; see, for example, the accounts of whipping in which "it appeared just as if it had rained blood" and in which "blood ran down and filled [the victim's] shoes," collected in Weld, *American Slavery As It Is*, 62–72.

62. Krusenstern, *Voyage round the World*, 1:180.

63. Knox, *Races of Men*, 7.

64. Melville expands on the remarks of Beale and Bennett on the villous characteristics of the whale's skin. See Beale, *Natural History of the Sperm Whale*, 90; Bennett, *Narrative of a Whaling Voyage*, 2:166. Scoresby explains the flensing process, in *Account of the Arctic Regions*, 2:298–304. Frank reprints illustrations, in *Herman Melville's Picture Gallery*, 65, 73. Readers with fleshly tastes may wish to consult the photographs in Hall, *Sperm Whaling from New Bedford*, 135–51.

65. Melville probably takes his chapter title, "The Blanket," from Beale, *Natural History of the Sperm Whale*, 32. Separate treatments of the skin, head, and skeleton are found in both cetological and ethnological texts. See Beale, *Natural History of the Sperm Whale*; Bennett, *Narrative of a Whaling Voyage*; White, *Account of the Regular Gradation in Man*; and Draper, *Human Physiology*.

66. For cetological and ethnological discussions of skin color and structure, see Beale, *Natural History of the Sperm Whale*, 31–32, 90–92, and Bennett, *Narrative of a Whaling Voyage*, 2:164–66, both of which emphasize the black-

ness of the whale's skin; and White, *Account of the Regular Gradation in Man,* 99–124, Samuel Stanhope Smith, *Essay on the Causes of the Variety of Complexion and Figure in the Human Species,* 23–93, J. A. Smith, "Lecture Introductory," 43–48, and Draper, *Human Physiology,* 233–42. Bennett describes the sperm whale's delicate, transparent epidermis, detachable after death, in *Narrative of a Whaling Voyage,* 2:165. Ethnologists shared an interest in lucid skin. See, for example, Samuel Stanhope Smith on "the external, or scarf-skin, which is an extremely fine netting, and perfectly transparent in the darkest coloured nations," in *Essay on the Causes of the Variety of Complexion,* 35.

67. Beale identifies the blubber as the "true skin" of the whale, in *Natural History of the Sperm Whale,* 31, 92. Bennett catalogues the yield of the whale in terms of commercial products, in *Narrative of a Whaling Voyage,* 2:153–55, 223–28.

68. Beale sketches the "linear impressions" in *Natural History of the Sperm Whale,* 31; Bennett, on the other hand, portrays the whale's skin as "smooth and naked," in *Narrative of a Whaling Voyage,* 2:164. Samuel Stanhope Smith imagines that human skin, like the features and form of the human countenance, encodes "habits of the body," accumulated impressions of personal and national history; see Smith, *Essay on the Causes of the Variety of Complexion,* 28–29. Both cetologists and ethnologists described the saturated structures of the skin. See Beale, who quotes a Professor Jacob on the interlaced fibers of cetacean skin in which oil is deposited, in *Natural History of the Sperm Whale,* 91–92, and Samuel Stanhope Smith, who compares the intermediate layers of human skin to a "honeycomb," "filled with a delicate mucous, or viscid liquor," in *Essay on the Causes of the Variety of Complexion,* 35.

69. Mansfield and Vincent link Ahab's address to the whale's head and the graveyard scene in *Hamlet;* see Mansfield and Vincent, notes to *Moby-Dick,* 761.

70. Melville takes his domestic analogies for the roof and Venetian blinds of the whale's mouth from Cheever, *The Whale and his Captors,* 57, 83. See Mansfield and Vincent's notes to their edition of *Moby-Dick,* 769. Cheever also compares the features of right and sperm whales (66–69).

71. Melville's metaphor, the "battering-ram," is again taken from Cheever, *The Whale and His Captors,* 155–56. Ishmael more fully joins the debate over which whale is best, sperm or right, in the "Cetology" chapter (135). Mansfield and Vincent describe the views of Beale and Scoresby in notes to *Moby-Dick,* 674.

72. Vincent discusses the Schiller poem in *Trying-Out of "Moby-Dick,"* 260–61.

73. Vincent identifies a source for Melville's knowledge of the Heidelburgh Tun in a passage and a print from a 1748 edition of John Harriss's *Navigantium atque Itinerantium Bibliotheca* (rev. ed., 1748). See *Trying-Out of "Moby-Dick,"* 262–63, and the illustration facing page 304. Melville gleans information about the structure of the sperm whale's head from both Beale, *Natural History of the Sperm Whale,* 73–79, and Bennett, *Narrative of a Whaling Voyage,* 2:160–61.

74. Although I have been unable to locate any record of Melville's having read Morton's *Crania Americana* or *Crania Ægyptiaca*, much circumstantial evidence suggests that he had Morton in mind in this chapter: the craniometrical dynamics and racial types in "Cistern and Buckets"; the references to physiognomy and phrenology in "The Prairie" and "The Nut," which form the second and third panels in the triptych; his later satire of ethnology in "The 'Gees'" (1856); and the currency of Morton's ideas in antebellum culture. In describing Tashtego's misfortune, Melville has reworked passages from Scoresby, who remarks on the dangers of sailors falling into the mouths of whales and being drowned during flensing. Scoresby tells the story of a harpooner who became attached by a boat hook to the carcass of a whale. Holding onto the whaleboat, his foot fastened to the sinking jawbone, the harpooner risked being "drawn asunder," but was saved when his companions grappled the carcass, drew it back to the surface, and detached the harpooner. See Scoresby, *Account of the Arctic Regions,* 2:302–303. In "Cistern and Buckets," Melville ethnologizes Scoresby's account of the accident. He emphasizes the reversal in which the manipulator becomes the victim of his carcass. In moving the stage from the skin to the head and altering the action from flensing to baling, Melville embodies the procedures of craniometry.

75. In an 1849 review of Francis Parkman's *California and Oregon Trail,* dissenting from Parkman's racialism, Melville similarly mingles Greek mythology and U.S. ethnology: "We are all of us—Anglo-Saxons, Dyaks and Indians—sprung from one head and made in one image." See "Mr. Parkman's Tour," in *Piazza Tales and Other Prose Pieces,* 231.

76. Cheever, *The Whale and His Captors,* 156. As Vincent points out, Melville corrects Cheever, who probably meant to refer to the domed Pantheon rather than to the Parthenon; see *Trying-Out of "Moby-Dick,"* 266–67. Although Vincent argues that Melville's use of Cheever is another example of his "particularization of the general," Cheever's phrenological fantasy is itself notably specific and concrete. The whale seems resistant to traditional medical science also. Ishmael outlines the difficulties faced by whale surgeons (310) and whale dentists (332).

77. Mansfield and Vincent discuss Melville's interest in Lavater, Gall, and Spurzheim, in the notes to their edition of *Moby-Dick,* 773–74. Brodtkorb reads the incoherence of the whale's face as Melville's insistence that "process can wear no fixed forms," in *Ishmael's White World,* 25, 27, 144. According to Ward, in "The Function of the Cetology Chapters," and Greenberg, in "Cetology: Center of Multiplicity and Discord," Melville argues that the whale is greater than the scientific sum of its parts. Despite Ishmael's composure in "The Prairie" about the loss of face, in chapter 59 he is amazed by the "vast pulpy mass" of a giant squid with "no perceptible face or front" (276)—a physiognomical and phrenological nightmare.

78. Quoting Hunter, Beale describes the difficulty in locating the small brain cavity of the sperm whale, which often could be identified only by tracing its juncture with the spinal canal, in *Natural History of the Sperm Whale,* 73–79. Melville's critique of physiognomy and phrenology is reminiscent of Hegel's

assessment in *Phenomenology of Mind* (1807), 338–72. In his reading of *Moby-Dick,* John T. Irwin distinguishes between the two cranial approaches; see *American Hieroglyphics,* 304–306.

79. For analyses of the two chapters as mockeries of cranial science, see Vincent, *Trying-Out of "Moby-Dick,"* 265–67; Ward, "Function of the Cetology Chapters," 176–83; Aspiz, "Phrenologizing the Whale"; and Moore, *That Cunning Alphabet,* 143–54. Tyrus Hillway acknowledges Melville's interest, in "Melville's Use of Two Pseudo-Sciences." Irwin argues that the "essential ambiguity" in *Pierre* is the "undecipherability of the hieroglyphics of the human face," in *American Hieroglyphics,* 311–12. William B. Dillingham links Melville's Pierre and Johann Kaspar Lavater, in *Melville's Later Novels,* 147–72. Pierre's father owned a copy of Lavater's "wonderful work on Physiognomy" (*Pierre,* 79). Christopher Rivers analyzes Lavater's narratives of the face, in *Face Value,* 66–103. Melville appears categorically to reject physiognomy and phrenology in his defense of the natural inconsistency of fictional characters in chapter 14 of *The Confidence-Man* (1857); yet in *Clarel* (1876), Melville's young student protagonist is still "scanning" faces, hoping that he can read the character of his fellow pilgrim Vine, "a face indeed quite overlaid/With tremulous meanings, which evade/Or shun regard." See *Clarel,* part 1, canto 33, lines 69–77.

80. Leslie Katz links the tactile gaze with the erasure of female flesh in *Moby-Dick,* in "Flesh of His Flesh," 8–9.

81. On scientific perplexity over the nature of the whale's spout, see Vincent, *Trying-Out of "Moby-Dick,"* 286–94. In giving his opinion that the spout was respirated vapor rather than ejected water, Melville was closely following Beale and Bennett.

82. Mansfield and Vincent unfold Melville's allusions to Exodus 33.23 and Browne's *Religio Medici* part 1, sec. 13, in notes to *Moby-Dick,* 786.

83. Vincent points out that the island of Tranque is off the coast of Chile and not among the Arsacides; see *Trying-Out of "Moby-Dick,"* 356–57.

84. Beale describes his debt to Constable for the use of his specimen, in *Natural History of the Sperm Whale,* 72, 77–88.

85. Robert K. Martin provides the fullest analysis of the tactile, homosexual, radically democratic alternative offered by "A Squeeze of the Hand" and the Ishmael-Queequeg couple, in *Hero, Captain, and Stranger,* 77–83. Melville may have received literary inspiration for his sperm-bath reverie from the "grand washes" in chapters 30 and 33 of Dana's *Two Years Before the Mast* (1840), in which the sailors soap and scrub one another. See Dana, *Two Years Before the Mast,* 372–73, 424–25.

86. Later, more positively, Ishmael compares Queequeg's arm to the "patchwork quilt" of the counterpane on the bed in the Spouter-Inn (25). He also describes Queequeg's cheek not as marked by the shade of a single latitude but as a geographical microcosm, whose various tints seem to "show forth in one array, contrasting climates, zone by zone" (30). Carolyn L. Karcher analyzes Ishmael's evolving perceptions in his encounter with Queequeg, in *Shadow over the Promised Land,* 64–73. I see Ishmael and Queequeg's "egalitarian marriage" as less stable and the "cultural relativism" as less comfortable for Melville. In em-

phasizing Queequeg's "purple" hue, Melville again reverses expectations, giving the Polynesian a royal cast. Melville critics continue, strangely, to deliberate whether Queequeg is black. See Simpson, "Melville and the Negro," 28–29; Widmer, *The Ways of Nihilism*, 69–70, n. 11; Gredja, *Common Continent of Men*, 86–97; and most recently, Rampersad, "Melville and Race," 170. Karcher describes Queequeg as one of Melville's "composite racial figures," in *Shadow over the Promised Land*, 65; see also Robert K. Martin, *Hero, Captain, and Stranger*, 79.

87. There are similar tactile moments in Whitman. For examples from the "Enfans d'Adam" sequence in the 1860 edition of *Leaves of Grass,* see the third poem, where "the body itself balks account" and touch stimulates a "curious sympathy"; and the last poem, where the speaker asks the reader to "Touch me," a desire explored in the subsequent "Calamus" cluster of poems. See *Leaves of Grass: Facsimile Edition of the 1860 Text,* 291, 301, 314.

88. In *Woman in the Nineteenth Century* (1845), Margaret Fuller reforms her syntax with a similar aim, insisting that gender is not circumscribed by stable characteristics: "Male and female represent the two sides of the great radical dualism. But, in fact, they are perpetually passing into one another. Fluid hardens to solid, solid rushes to fluid. There is no wholly masculine man, no purely feminine woman." See Fuller, *Woman in the Nineteenth Century,* 103.

89. For the declarations of identification, see Beverly, *History and Present State of Virginia* (1705), 9; and Walt Whitman, ["Song of Myself"], line 834, in *Leaves of Grass: The First (1855) Edition,* 62.

90. In "Benito Cereno" (1855), Melville's narrator also keeps a respectful or strategic or tantalizing or anxious distance from his racialized figure, in this case the "hive of subtlety" that is the head of the enslaved rebel Babo. See *Piazza Tales and Other Prose Pieces,* 116 ff.

91. Sketches for Queequeg's "mystical treatise" can be found in *Typee,* where Kory-Kory's tattoos suggest "the idea of a pictorial museum of natural history, or an illustrated copy of 'Goldsmith's Animated Nature'" (83) and *Omoo,* where Marbonna's tattooed face "was as good as a picture-book" (307). The view of Queequeg by his coffin also resembles in some ways the view of Langsdorff's *young Nukahiwan,* plate 7 in *Voyages and Travels* (reproduced as figure 6 in this book and discussed in chapter 1).

92. Like Ishmael, John Paul Jones in Melville's *Israel Potter* (1855) has tattoos confined to his right arm. Unlike Ishmael, Jones's markings are mysterious, covering the whole inside of his arm: "a sort of tattooing such as is seen only on thorough-bred savages—deep blue, elaborate, labyrinthine, cabalistic" (62). Jones relishes the emblems of his secret savagery. In a scene that echoes the Spouter-Inn scene in *Moby-Dick,* Israel, like Ishmael, watches from under the covers as the "savage" bares his skin.

93. Child, "Letter XXXVI ['The Indians']," *Letters from New York,* 260–69. Carolyn L. Karcher includes the letter and briefly discusses Child's refutation of Morton, in her edition of Child's *Hobomok and Other Writings on Indians,* 181–90. In August 1843, Child selected for book publication forty of the fifty-eight "Letters" that she had written for the New York *National Anti-Slavery Standard* between August 1841 and May 1843. This collection was a

popular and financial success, as was a second series of *Letters from New York* (1845) that reprinted material published in the Boston *Courier*. The *Letters* helped to restore Child's literary career, which had been eclipsed by hostility to her argument for immediate emancipation in *An Appeal in Favor of That Class of Americans Called Africans* (1833). See Clifford, *Crusader for Freedom*, 169–81; and Karcher, "Censorship, American Style" and *The First Woman in the Republic*, 295–319.

94. Child, *Letters from New York*, 265–66. The "intense desire" is also present in Thomas Gray's "Confessions of Nat Turner" (1831). Although Gray explains that he recorded Turner's "confession" in order to expose his criminality and to protect southern society from further assaults, his "interest in the operations of a mind like his" (15) also involves curiosity about the motives and means of Turner's rebellion and a grudging respect. Eric J. Sundquist analyzes the complicated narrative dynamics, in *To Wake the Nations*, 36–83.

95. Douglass, *My Bondage and My Freedom*, 281. In "The Heroic Slave" (1853), a fictional account of the slave revolt on board the Virginia cargo ship *Creole*, Douglass's overtures take surprising turns. He begins his story by giving his white character Listwell, along with his readers, an opportunity to overhear the thoughts on liberty of the enslaved Madison Washington, who will become the leader of the revolt. A northern traveler in Virginia, Listwell "had long desired to sound the mysterious depths of the thoughts and feelings of the slave" (28). Douglass satisfies but also deflects such desires. He climaxes "The Heroic Slave" not with another soliloquy by Washington or with a stirring recital of violence on board the ship, but with a version of the events told by an anxious white southerner, Tom Grant. The first mate on the *Creole*, Grant is torn between acknowledging the justice and dignity of Washington's revolt and adhering to his own preconceptions about African American savagery. Thus Douglass ends his story by sounding the mysterious depths of the thoughts and feelings of a free white man. Access, suggests Douglass, goes both ways.

96. Appiah, *In My Father's House*, 45–46.

97. For representative examples, see William Ellery Sedgwick, *Herman Melville*: "The object is indifferent, the subject is all that is needed because the subject always sees himself. This is Pip's version of the solipsism of consciousness, a theme Melville continually broaches in *Moby-Dick*" (111); and Wenke, *Melville's Muse*: "This interpretive tableau reinforces the relativistic hermeneutical activity" (152).

CHAPTER FOUR: PENETRATING EYES IN *PIERRE*

1. Melville, *Pierre*, 3. Subsequent references to *Pierre* will be made to the Northwestern-Newberry edition (see bibliography) and given in parentheses in the text.

2. In chapters 1 and 3, we have seen how the body was compared to a landscape. In this chapter, we will see how the comparison worked both ways. The famous German naturalist Alexander von Humboldt refers to the "physiognomy of nature," in *Cosmos*, 2:97. Melville connects landscape and face in chapter 79 of *Moby-Dick*.

3. For the *Boston Post* review (August 4, 1852), see Higgins and Parker, *Critical Essays on Herman Melville's "Pierre,"* 32–33. The remainder of the plot summary reads: "All at once, Pierre learns that his father has left an illegitimate daughter, who is in poverty and obscurity. His conscience calls upon him to befriend and acknowledge her—although, by the way, his proof of the fact that the girl is his father's offspring is just nothing at all. On the other hand, he will not discover to the world or to his mother the error of his (supposed) sainted father, and he adopts the novel expedient of carrying off the girl, and giving out that he has married her. His mother discards him and soon dies of wounded love and pride, and his betrothed is brought to the brink of the grave. She finally recovers somewhat, and strange to say, invites herself to reside with Pierre and his sister, who, as far as the world and herself were concerned, are living as husband and wife. The relatives of Lucy, as a matter of course, try to regain her, and brand Pierre with every bad name possible. The latter finally shoots his cousin who had become the possessor of the family estate and a pretender to the hand of Lucy—is arrested and taken to prison. There he is visited by the two ladies, the sister and the betrothed. Lucy falls dead of a broken heart and Pierre and his sister take poison and also give up the ghost." *Godey's Magazine and Lady's Book* (October 1852) published one of the few reviews of *Pierre* to suggest that Melville might in some interesting way be manipulating contemporary narrative and stylistic conventions. See Higgins and Parker, *Critical Essays,* 54–55.

4. For modern views of Saddle Meadows as untroubled Eden, see Murray, introduction to *Pierre,* xxxiii–xliv; Lewis, *The American Adam,* 148–49; and Jehlen, *American Incarnation,* 186, 198–99, 206. Richard H. Brodhead suggests that Saddle Meadows is "overripe, its very lushness a symptom of unresolved and unrecognized problems." See Brodhead, *Hawthorne, Melville, and the Novel,* 167.

5. At the end of book 4, when the narrator describes Pierre's resistance to the innuendo of his father's portrait, he repeats and extends the "thought-channels" metaphor, with an emphasis on fluid mechanics: "Nor did the streams of these reveries seem to leave any conscious sediment in his mind; they were so light and so rapid, that they rolled their own alluvial along; and seemed to leave all Pierre's thought-channels as clean and dry as though never any alluvial stream had rolled there at all" (85).

6. Dieter Groh and Rolf-Peter Sieferle argue that representations of nature became strained—more literal and less metaphorical and allegorical—through a kind of bourgeois compensatory urgency, as the natural world became the object of increasing exploitation under the pressures of advancing capitalism; see "Experience of Nature in Bourgeois Society and Economic Theory."

7. Gombrich, "The Renaissance Theory of Art and the Rise of Landscape," 121; Groh and Sieferle, "Experience of Nature," 573; Willis, *American Scenery,* 3. Subsequent references to the Imprint Society edition of *American Scenery* (see bibliography) will be made in parentheses. Gombrich describes the institutional changes signified by the rise of landscape painting in seventeenth-century Europe, particularly the developing commercial relations in the "modern" art world, in which labor was divided among specialists and images began to be produced for anonymous consumers in a competitive market. Kenneth

Myers describes the American context for the production of landscapes in the rapidly expanding post-1812 economy, in *The Catskills*, 31–76. Over the past two decades, critics of British culture have delineated a politics of the pastoral and the picturesque, exploring the relations between landscape and ideology. See Barrell, *The Idea of Landscape* and *The Dark Side of the Landscape*; and Bermingham, *Landscape and Ideology*. See also Raymond Williams's pathbreaking *The Country and the City*. On the ideology of the American landscape, see Kolodny, *The Lay of the Land*; Jehlen, *American Incarnation*; and Angela Miller, *The Empire of the Eye*. Attending to the symbolic content of nineteenth-century United States landscape painting, Miller analyzes the complex relationships between the dilemmas of representation and those of nation building, and she describes how New York writers and artists consolidated a specifically Northern nationalism. Like Miller, Lawrence Buell cautions against critical reductions; see *The Environmental Imagination*, 31–52ff.

8. Knight, *An Analytical Inquiry into the Principles of Taste*, 151. On the foundations of associationist psychology, see Kallich, "The Association of Ideas and Critical Theory." Walter John Hipple outlines the ideas of William Gilpin, Uvedale Price, Humphrey Repton, Richard Payne Knight, and Dugald Stewart, the theorists of the picturesque, in *The Beautiful, the Sublime, and the Picturesque in Eighteenth-Century British Aesthetic Theory*, 185–302. Christopher Hussey discusses the picturesque link between emotion and vision, in *The Picturesque*, 1–17. In "Nine Revisionist Theses on the Picturesque," Kim Ian Michasiw challenges beliefs about the ties between discourse and action and argues for differences within the picturesque tradition. According to Michasiw, Gilpin, representing the first phase of the picturesque, argued for a contingent relation between subject and object, an anti-aesthetic alternative to the imperialist eye of Price and Knight, who presided over the second phase.

9. On the associationist debate in the early United States, see Streeter, "Association Psychology and Literary Nationalism in the *North American Review*, 1815–1825." Washington Irving opens his *Sketch Book* (1819–1820) with an influential comparison between European and American landscapes; see *The Sketch Book of Geoffrey Crayon, Gent.*, 744. The phrase "fanciful associations" is from Irving's essay on "The Catskill Mountains" in the anonymously edited *Home Book of the Picturesque* (72), but could also apply to the contributions of Bayard Taylor, Henry Tuckerman, Mary Field, or William Cullen Bryant. Analyzing mid-nineteenth-century fascinations with images of miasma and infection, David C. Miller describes "associationism gone crazy," in *Dark Eden*, 185. Callow discusses the New York City artists and writers who molded American views, in *Kindred Spirits*, 3–38. The sights of the Hudson River Valley were at the center of interest for antebellum painters, tourists, and aesthetic theorists. See the exhibition catalogues and accompanying essays in Myers, *The Catskills*; Howat, *American Paradise*; and Patricia Anderson, *The Course of Empire*. On the "American picturesque," see Powell, "Thomas Cole and the American Landscape Tradition: The Picturesque" and "Thomas Cole and the American Landscape Tradition: Associationism"; Moore, *That Cunning Alphabet*, 1–58; Berthold, "Charles Brockden Brown, *Edgar Huntly*, and the Origins of the American Picturesque"; and Sweet, *Traces of War*, 79–106, 138–64.

10. Melville is concerned with the picturesque across his writings, from the sightseeing traumas of the young American protagonist in *Redburn* (1849) through *Pierre* (1852), whose aesthetic scrutiny seems to have set in motion the meticulous construction of frame, manipulation of perspective, and density of allusion in the sketches of the mid-1850s: the walled views of "Bartleby" (1853); the cindered prospects and ocular illusions seen from Rock Rodondo in the fourth sketch of "The Encantadas" (1854) and, in the eighth sketch, the oval frame of branches that renders the stranded Hunilla a helpless witness to the beautiful deaths upon the water of her husband and brother; the orientations and disorientations of perspective in "Benito Cereno" (1855); the overlapping borders of the diptychs—"Poor Man's Pudding and Rich Man's Crumbs" (1854), "The Paradise of Bachelors and the Tartarus of Maids" (1855), and the unpublished "The Two Temples"—that associatively implicate America with England, male with female, and rich with poor; the disturbing, sexually charged landscape of "The Tartarus of Maids"; and the disenchantments of "The Piazza" (1856), in which the narrator enters the magical view he has framed and returns haunted, like Pierre, by the face and the story of a strange, distressed woman he encounters. Moore makes "The Piazza" the centerpiece in his analysis of Melville's picturesque critique, in *That Cunning Alphabet,* 43–58. Memories saturate the landscapes of Melville's poetry: the aftermaths and epitaphs of "Shiloh" and "Malvern Hill" in *Battle-Pieces* (1866) and the melancholy, barren scenes of "Jerusalem" and "The Wilderness" in *Clarel* (1876). In "At the Hostelry," part of the unfinished *Burgundy Club,* Melville pens a dialogue about the meaning of the term "picturesque" among famous painters; see the *Collected Poems of Herman Melville,* 313–38. For an anthology of essays examining Melville's interest in the visual arts, see Sten, *Savage Eye,* and especially John Bryant's "Toning Down the Green: Melville's Picturesque" (145–161). Bryant continues his analysis of the fusions and mediations of Melville's "picturesque" in *Melville and Repose,* 16–19, 139–40, 200–204.

11. Cole, "Essay on American Scenery," 98, 109, 108. Subsequent references to the Prentice-Hall edition (see bibliography) will be made in parentheses in the text. Cole's "Essay" was first delivered as a lecture in 1835 before the New-York Lyceum and published the following year. For discussions of the essay, see Powell, "Cole: The Picturesque," 116, and "Cole: Associationism," 115–16; and Moore, *That Cunning Alphabet,* 29–31.

12. For histories and descriptions of the mounds, see Silverberg, *Mound Builders of Ancient America;* on the debate about degeneration versus supplantation, see Bieder, *Science Encounters the Indian,* 108–19; on mounds adduced as evidence of American antiquity, see William Stanton, *The Leopard's Spots,* 82–89. Thomas Jefferson describes his own excavation of a burial mound, in search of answers about ancient Indian culture; see Jefferson, *Notes on the State of Virginia,* 223–26.

13. The quotations from "The Prairie" can be found in William Cullen Bryant, *Poetical Works,* 186, 188. Among those who subscribed to the theory that the mound builders were members of an "unknown race" was President Andrew Jackson; see Jackson, "Second Annual Message" (December 6, 1830), 520–21. Washington Irving comments on the function of Native American

associations in the "Traits of Indian Character" essay in *The Sketch Book* (1002–1012).

14. For reproductions, see Powell, *Thomas Cole,* 54–55, 76, 82–83, 114–15. Cole's friend William Cullen Bryant represents "veiling" as the primum mobile of Cole's art in his famous "Funeral Oration on the Death of Thomas Cole" (1848): "He carried to his painting room the impressions received by the eye and there gave them to the canvas; he even complained of the distinctness with which they haunted him. 'Have you not found,' said he, writing to a distinguished friend—'I have—that you never succeed in painting scenes, however beautiful, immediately on returning from them? I must wait for time to draw a veil over the common details, the unessential parts, which shall leave the great features, whether the beautiful or the sublime, dominant in the mind'" (97).

15. For reproductions and analyses of *The Course of Empire* and *The Past and The Present,* see Truettner and Wallach, *Thomas Cole: Landscape into History,* 85–98; see also Angela Miller, *Empire of the Eye,* 21–39, and "Thomas Cole and Jacksonian America."

16. For other American versions of the picturesque catalogue, see Roque, "The Exaltation of American Landscape Painting," 22 (quoting New York Governor Clinton), and E. L. Magoon, in *The Home Book of the Picturesque,* 25–44.

17. William Gilmore Simms gives an exhortatory version of the territorial imperative, with an emphasis on the shaping power of American natural features, in *Views and Reviews in American Literature, History and Fiction,* 16–17. Although a southerner, Simms in the 1840s was closely associated with the New York City writers known as "Young America," a group which Melville satirizes in *Pierre,* particularly in book 17. In *Seeing and Being,* Carolyn Porter describes the scandal that arises in American literary texts when the reified observer is exposed as a participant in the construction of the world. In the antebellum instances I am discussing here, a different kind of transaction is taking place. The relationship between subject and object is not characterized by fantasies of detachment and disclosures of relation; instead, the connection might be described as an urgent, destructive embrace. Cole was of two minds about America as nature's nation, attracted to the transformative potential of the landscape, but cautious about American exceptionalism and distrustful of American democracy. He decried the devastation of nature that came with "progress." See Angela Miller, *Empire of the Eye,* 21–64.

18. Cole's catalogue of "absences" is reminiscent of Crèvecoeur's famous list in the third letter of his *Letters from an American Farmer* (1782).

19. See Howat, *American Paradise,* 125–27, for a description of the divine characters and for an account of the development of *The Oxbow* through a series of sketches, including a direct tracing of a plate in Captain Hall's *Forty Etchings Made with a Camera Lucida in North America in 1827 and 1828,* a book harshly critical of things American. Richard S. Moore interprets *The Oxbow* as an embodiment of Cole's "Essay on American Scenery," in *That Cunning Alphabet,* 29–32. Bryan Jay Wolf outlines the psychic drama of oppression and release in many of Cole's early paintings, in *Romantic Re-Vision,* 177–236. Nygren dis-

cusses Cole's important role in the transformation of American landscapes from pastoral "views" to wilderness "visions," in *Views and Visions*, 3–76.

20. Angela Miller analyzes the tension between nature and culture in *The Oxbow* and the treatment of Cole's legacy after his death in 1848, in *Empire of the Eye*, 39–49, 65–105, 137–65; see also Wallach's "Thomas Cole: Landscape and the Course of American Empire,"76–77.

21. For biographical information on Willis, see Auser, "Nathaniel Parker Willis," 373–76. Willis was the target of Poe's satire in "The Duc De L'Omelette" (1832) and the (scandalous) model for the pretentious dilettante Hyacinth in *Ruth Hall*, the 1855 novel written by his sister Sara Willis Parton ("Fanny Fern"). He also was friendly with Melville's brother Gansevoort and promoted Herman's career. See Parker, *Herman Melville: A Biography*, 1:397–400, 566–67, 718–20).

22. See also "Descent into the Valley of Wyoming (Pennsylvania)," in which the text interprets eighteenth-century Shawnee fury against whites as a justified response to the atrocious murder of the orator Cornstalk, while the engraving depicts leisured perambulations and a gracefully cultivated contemporary valley (77–80).

23. Bartlett engraves a sunnier, domesticated *Oxbow* in his version of the famous *View from Mount Holyoke*, in Willis, *American Scenery*, 14–16.

24. Washington Irving offers a satiric image of the "devouring mind's eye" in "The Legend of Sleepy Hollow" (1820), in which the lanky Ichabod Crane imagines the livestock on Van Tassel's Hudson Valley farm dressed up as his dinner. As Crane "rolled his great green eyes over the fat meadow lands," his "imagination expanded with the idea" of converting the rich fields of the farm into cash (*Sketch Book*, 1067). Brian Saunders discusses sentimental "appetite" in Irving's *Sketch Book* and Melville's *Redburn*, in "Melville's Sea Change." Edward Everett celebrates the "complementary" American political and industrial revolutions, in his oration on "Fourth of July at Lowell" (1830). For Everett, the development of Lowell from empty acreage to industrial community within a decade was economic magic, a sign of the wonder-working American difference (65–66). Melville expresses skepticism about such commercial transformations. In "The Paradise of Bachelors and the Tartarus of Maids" (1855), he represents a Lowell-like factory as hell for the mill girls. In "The Happy Failure: A Story of the River Hudson" (1854), his narrator recounts the shortcomings of his uncle's invention: the "Great Hydraulic-Hydrostatic Apparatus for draining swamps and marshes, and converting them, at the rate of one acre the hour, into fields more fertile than those of the Genessee." In "Report of the Committee on Agriculture" (1850), which Melville may have helped his cousin Robert Melvill write, the author makes fun of "material improvement." See *The Piazza Tales and Other Prose Pieces*, 316–35, 254–61, 449–51; on the attribution of the "Report" to Melville, see 788–91.

25. Bryant, *Poetical Works*, 4, 7, 19; Willis reprints Bryant's stanza in *American Scenery*, 5. Bryant wrote "The Ages" for delivery before the Harvard Phi Beta Kappa Society on the occasion of its 1821 commencement.

26. "Disembowered" appears to have been Bryant's invention. The first, and last, usage cited in the *Oxford English Dictionary* comes from "The Ages."

27. In the penultimate section of *American Scenery*, "View from the Mountain House, Catskill," Willis does provide a conventional climax (356–59). Accompanying an engraving of the prospect from the landmark hotel, he offers a long passage excerpted from Harriet Martineau, in which she describes the lessons of visual limitation and spiritual humility she learned while contemplating the fields of the Lord. Yet Willis's heart is not in these lessons. After dutifully presenting and dispensing with Mrs. Martineau, he gets down to business.

28. *The Home Book of the Picturesque*, 72. Further page references to the Scholars' Facsimiles edition (see bibliography) will be given in parentheses in the text. In his introduction to this edition, Motley F. Deakin discusses the picturesque gift book in general and the *Home Book* in particular. Timothy Sweet analyzes Susan Cooper's essay, in *Traces of War*, 89–92. J. F. Cooper and Irving both died in the 1850s. Bryant lived until 1878, his poetry writing largely behind him. Toward the end of his career, he edited the lavish two-volume gift book, *Picturesque America; or, the Land We Live In* (1872–1874), in which American prospects extend to the Pacific coast.

29. James Fenimore Cooper, *The Pioneers*, 44, 283.

30. Durand's painting commemorates the death of Cole in February 1848. Commissioned by Durand's patron, Jonathan Sturges, *Kindred Spirits* was presented to Bryant in appreciation for his "Funeral Oration on the Death of Thomas Cole," delivered before the National Academy of Design on May 4, 1848. See Howat, *American Paradise*, 108–110.

31. In the July 23 entry of her literary daybook *Rural Hours* (1850), Cooper reorients the viewer, granting prominence to a group of venerable pine trees who witness with gravity the vicissitudes of the land. Discussing this passage and others, Buell calls attention to Cooper as a careful observer and an advocate for the "ecocentric" perspective. I have been suggesting that Cooper's position is less stable and that such instability is the concern of "A Dissolving View." See Buell, *Environmental Imagination*, 47–48, 265–66, 409–12.

32. For parallels between Melville's family history and his fictional representations in *Pierre*, see Murray, notes to *Pierre*, 429–40; and Rogin, *Subversive Genealogy*, 159–86. See also Parker, "Melville and Politics."

33. There is a similar effect when the narrator justifies his aside on surnames, asserting "the great genealogical and real-estate dignity of some families in America" (12). The phrase looks fine at first glance, when the emphasis falls on the eminently acceptable "genealogical dignity," but the innuendoes of "real-estate dignity" are more difficult to assimilate. John Carlos Rowe analyzes Melville's conversions of democracy and aristocracy in "Romancing the Stone," 212–17.

34. Melville visited Indian mounds at St. Louis in 1840 on a western trip with his friend Eli Fly. See Robertson-Lorant, *Melville: A Biography*, 83.

35. On Melville's allusions to the Anti-Renter struggles, see Murray, notes to *Pierre*, 435–36; Otter, "Eden of Saddle Meadows," 68–72; Fredericks, *Melville's Art of Democracy*, 106–10; and Nixon, "Compromising Politics and Herman Melville's *Pierre*," 722–25. Henry Christman describes the history in *Tin Horns and Calico*. See also the "Anti-Renter's Declaration of Independence" (July 4, 1839). James Fenimore Cooper referred to the conflict in the 1840s as

"the great American question of the day" (see Cooper, *Letters and Journals,* 5:52). Cooper justified the class and economic structure in the Hudson River Valley in a trilogy of historical novels, beginning with colonial times in *Satanstoe* (1845), continuing through the Revolution in *The Chainbearers* (1845), and concluding with *The Redskins* (1846) and its contemptuous portrayal of the tenant rebels. For an autobiographical account of poverty in the midst of New York State plenty in the 1830s and 1840s, see Henry Conklin's autobiographical *Through "Poverty's Vale."*

36. Paul Royster argues that in the "Mount of Titan" scenes, Melville represents the "mythically disguised social landscape" of Saddle Meadows, in which unequal class structure is depicted as part of the natural order. See Royster, "Melville's Economy of Language," 329–34. Mark Z. Slouka reads the "Mount of Titans" as an apocalyptic undoing of American ideas about the regenerative perception of nature, in "Demonic History: Geography and Genealogy in *Pierre.*"

37. On Melville and the Van Rensselaers, see Parker, *Herman Melville: A Biography,* 1:134–36, 155–57. Thomas Cole painted *The Gardens of the Van Rensselaer Manor House* (1840) and *The Van Rensselaer Manor House* (1841). For reproductions, see Truettner and Wallach, *Thomas Cole: Landscape into History,* 175.

38. Richard B. Morris describes the context, evolution, and aftermath of Shays' Rebellion, in "Insurrection in Massachusetts." I am grateful to Jeanne C. Howe for suggesting the significance in *Pierre* of the analogy between Shays' Rebellion and the Anti-Renter conflicts.

39. Murray discusses the correspondences in *Pierre* between autobiography, topography, and fiction, in his notes to *Pierre,* 429–32, 462. See also Vincent, *Melville and Hawthorne in the Berkshires,* and Parker, "Melville and the Berkshires." In *Herman Melville: A Biography,* Parker quotes an October 17, 1850, letter from Melville's sister Augusta to her friend Mary Blatchford, in which she discusses Melville's naming of "Arrow-head" (1:785). On picturesque interest in the Berkshires, see Hickey and Oedel, *A Return to Arcadia.* Church's *View Near Stockbridge* is reproduced on page 36 and discussed on pages 31 and 35.

40. For Jackson's "Message," see Remini, *Andrew Jackson:* "Say to [the Creeks] where they now are, they and my white children are too near to each other to live in harmony and peace. Their game is destroyed, & many of their people will not work, & till the earth. Beyond the great river Mississippi where a part of their nation have gone, their father has provided a country, large enough for them all, and he advises them to remove to it. There, their white brethren will not trouble them . . . and they can live upon it, they and all their children as long as grass grows or water runs in peace and plenty. It will be theirs forever" (128). Michael Paul Rogin analyzes Jackson as national patriarch, in *Fathers and Children.* For Thoreau's allusion, see *Week on the Concord and Merrimack Rivers,* 7; for Melville's allusion, see *Typee,* 202. The quotation from Speckled Snake is in Virginia Irving Armstrong, *I Have Spoken,* 57. For representative examples of Native American argument about contrasting land claims, as transcribed by European interpreters, see the speeches by the Shawnee chief Tecumseh (1810) in Armstrong, *I Have Spoken,* 43–44; by the Suquamish and

Duwamish chief Seattle (1854) in Swann and Krupat, *Recovering the Word,*
518–21; and by the Sioux leader Sitting Bull (1877), in Turner, *Portable North
American Indian Reader,* 254–55. For an attack on American duplicity, see the
speech of the Flathead chief Charlot to his people in 1876, when they were being pressured to leave their lands in Montana, in Armstrong, *I Have Spoken,* 99.

41. Irving, *Sketch Book,* 744. At the end of his career, in the conjuring of
"Rip Van Winkle's Lilac" and the nostalgia of "A Dutch Christmas up the Hudson in the Time of the Patroons," both part of the unpublished *Weeds and Wild-
ings,* Melville turns back to Washington Irving with affection, rather than with
the criticism of *Pierre* or *Redburn* or much of the short fiction. In "Dutch Christmas up the Hudson," he revisits the associative landscape of *Pierre,* portraying
the manor as a nostalgic, organic retreat, not as the pathological ground of
Saddle Meadows. See Melville, *Collected Poems,* 271–72, 281–94.

42. Melville's "Love," clapping its brass-plate hands and blowing its horned
mouth, resembles Christopher Pearce Cranch's caricature of a passage from
"The American Scholar"—"This is my music. This is myself"—in which an
Emersonian creature is represented fingering a nose that has elongated into a
clarinet. The drawing is reproduced as figure 7 in F. DeWolfe Miller, *Christopher Pearce Cranch and His Caricatures of New England Transcendentalism.*

43. Emerson, *Essays and Lectures,* 9–11. "Nature" was published in the
same year as Cole's "Essay on American Scenery." In *American Incarnation,*
Jehlen argues that the "axis" of the American landscape is pivoted in *Pierre.* Instead of the characteristic horizontal and open-ended perspective found most famously in Jefferson's expanding Blue Ridge horizons in *Notes on the State of
Virginia,* the view in *Pierre* is vertically blocked by the mountains surrounding
Saddle Meadows and the walls of New York City (219–225).

44. Thoreau, *A Week on the Concord and Merrimack Rivers; Walden, or
Life in the Woods; The Maine Woods; Cape Cod,* 470–71. In another extraordinary scene, Dickinson frames a face-to-face encounter in landscape terms in
her poem "Like Eyes that looked on Wastes—." Unlike the loving acknowledgment in "The Ponds" or the swarming impact in *Pierre,* when eyes look into eyes
in this Dickinson poem they see nothing: "Just Infinites of Nought—." Thomas
H. Johnson gives this poem number 458 and dates it circa 1862 in *The Poems
of Emily Dickinson,* 1:353.

CHAPTER FIVE: INSCRIBED HEARTS IN *PIERRE*

1. Melville, *Pierre,* 86. All citations to *Pierre* are taken from the
Northwestern-Newberry edition (see bibliography) and given in the text.

2. Ann Douglas describes her verbal "test" in *The Feminization of American
Culture,* 308. Alison M. Jaggar critiques the split between cognition and affect
and gives a feminist analysis of the emotions, in "Love and Knowledge: Emotion
in Feminist Epistemology." For critics on sentiment, see E. Douglas Branch, *The
Sentimental Years, 1836–1860;* Pattee, *The Feminine Fifties;* Papashvily, *All the
Happy Endings;* Herbert Ross Brown, *The Sentimental Novel in America,
1789–1860;* Douglas, *The Feminization of American Culture;* Tompkins, *Sensational Designs;* Fisher, *Hard Facts;* Nancy Armstrong, *Desire and Domes-*

tic Fiction; Berlant, "The Female Woman"; Brodhead, *Cultures of Letters*, 13–46; and Samuels, *The Culture of Sentiment*. Susan K. Harris surveys critics on nineteenth-century women's novels, many of whom automatically associate sentimentalism with women's fiction; see *19th-Century Women's Novels*, 1–12.

3. Baym, *Woman's Fiction* and *American Women Writers and the Work of History, 1790–1860*; Kelley, *Private Woman, Public Stage*; Davidson, *Revolution and the Word*. The division into competing critical camps, following either Douglas or Tompkins, has been noted by Nancy Schnog, in "Inside the Sentimental," 23 n. 4; by G. M. Goshgarian, in *To Kiss the Chastening Rod*, 9–12; and by Laura Wexler, Lauren Berlant, and Shirley Samuels, in Samuels, *The Culture of Sentiment*, 9–12, 270, 283–84 n. 6.

4. David S. Reynolds, *Beneath the American Renaissance*, 337–67; and Romero, "Domesticity and Fiction," 110–18, and "Vanishing Americans," 115–27.

5. Melville, *Moby-Dick*, 563. Poe, "Twice-Told Tales. By Nathaniel Hawthorne" (1842), in *Essays and Reviews*, 572; see also Poe's obsessive, ironic account of how he constructed "The Raven" in order to dictate his readers' responses, in "The Philosophy of Composition" (1846), in ibid., 13–25. Stowe, *Uncle Tom's Cabin* (1852), 515. I have quoted phrases from the second poem in Whitman's "Calamus" cluster in the 1860 *Leaves of Grass*; see *Leaves of Grass: Facsimile Edition of the 1860 Text*, 342. Ann Douglas describes American sentimental literature as having been produced under the "intense self-consciousness characteristic of a new mass medium: the transactions between cultural buyer and seller, producer and consumer shaped both the content and the form"; see Douglas, *Feminization of American Culture*, 8–9. Janet Todd similarly characterizes British literary production in the second half of the eighteenth century, in *Sensibility*, 12.

6. Sánchez-Eppler, *Touching Liberty*, 26. Shirley Samuels usefully defines "sentiment" in nineteenth-century America as "not so much a genre as an operation or a set of actions within discursive models of affect and identification," in her introduction to *The Culture of Sentiment*, 6.

7. Both Richard H. Brodhead, in the American context, and Nancy Armstrong, in the British, interpret scenes of reading in nineteenth-century sentimental texts as emblematic of the procedures through which authority was internalized, emotions were regulated, and a middle-class subject was formed. See Brodhead, *Cultures of Letters*, 42–47, and Armstrong, *Desire and Domestic Fiction*, 203–50. Recent critics writing on British and European literature have analyzed the theatricality of sentimentalism. See Fred Kaplan, *Sacred Tears*, 18–20, 52–56; Markley, "Sentiment as Performance"; and especially Marshall, *The Figure of Theater* and *The Surprising Effects of Sympathy*, 1–8ff.

8. On the women and men of feeling in the British tradition, see Todd, *Sensibility*, 4, 88–128. Recent criticism on Mitchell and Curtis has been sparse. See Douglas, *Feminization of American Culture*, 282–93, and Barker-Benfield, *The Horrors of the Half-Known Life*, 10–13. On Mitchell, see Kime, *Donald G. Mitchell*; Tew and Peskin, "The Disappearance of Ik. Marvel"; and Bertolini, "Fireside Chastity." Judging by the number of panels dealing with mid-

nineteenth-century male sentimentalism at literary conferences, renewed attention is being directed at these figures, and at Mitchell in particular. Although Nathaniel Parker Willis is sometimes grouped with Mitchell and Curtis (Douglas does so), his writing is not sentimental in the sense that I am developing. In the collections *Pencillings by the Way* (1835) and *Hurrygraphs* (1853), for example, Willis sketches scenery, celebrity, and society on the continent and in Britain and New York, rather than examining the display of feelings. Willis is primarily interested in molding American manners and consolidating middle-class culture. He luxuriates in the dinners, drawing rooms, and castles in the London and Scotland sections of *Pencillings,* and he describes the necessity for cultivating American "style" in his essay "Society and Manners in New York," in *Hurrygraphs,* 283–89. Mitchell's debt to Irving is explicit: he dedicates his second book, *Dream Life* (1851), to him, expanding his praise in the preface to the 1863 edition. Remarks on the influence of Sterne and Irving on Mitchell are made by Fitz-James O'Brien in his 1853 essay, "Our Young Authors: Mitchell," 75, and by Ann Douglas in *Feminization of American Culture,* 282–89. Since the reputation of Mackenzie's *Man of Feeling* (1771) was in eclipse by the middle of the nineteenth century, it is hard to gauge his possible influence on Mitchell and Curtis. Mackenzie's fragmentary tale of a young Englishman whose feelings were "too tender to be suffered by the world" would seem to have had resonance for the two American writers; see *Man of Feeling,* 91. Although Mitchell and Curtis were the most prominent male sketch sentimentalists of the 1850s, they were not the only ones; see also Henry Tuckerman, *Leaves from the Diary of a Dreamer* (1853).

9. Irving genders male and female spheres of activity in the "The Broken Heart" chapter of *The Sketch Book,* 802–03. The two most famous American stories in the book, "Rip Van Winkle" and "The Legend of Sleepy Hollow," portray the insular, antiquated, enchanted spaces of the Catskills and Tarry Town. Irving reflects on his practice in chapters such as "The Art of Book Making," "The Mutability of Literature," and "The Angler." He describes the powers of the imagination in "A Royal Poet" and "Stratford-on-Avon." Mitchell's retreats were imaginative and literal. In 1855, he purchased a farm near New Haven, Connecticut, which became his home for the rest of his long life. From the experiences at his farm, he produced two books defending and celebrating the vanishing rural life, *My Farm At Edgewood* (1863) and *Wet Days at Edgewood* (1865).

10. On Adam Smith's theatrical self, see *The Theory of Moral Sentiments* (1759; ed. E. G. West, 1976), 47–53, 161–62, 204–05, 227–29, 234–35, 247; see also West's introduction, 31–43. For discussions of Smith and sentimentality, see Todd, *Sensibility,* 23–28; Marshall, *Figure of Theater,* 167–92, and *Surprising Effects of Sympathy,* 4–5; and Fred Kaplan, *Sacred Tears,* 18–20. On Smith's rewriting of the metaphors of theater and mirror, taken from David Hume, see Mullan, *Sentiment and Sociability,* 43–56. In emphasizing the free flow of feelings and the endless reflections of sentiment between subject and object, Mitchell may be said to be following a sentimental tradition that descends from Hume rather than from Smith.

11. Todd discusses the different formal and philosophical problems confronted by female and male writers in their sentimental narratives in eighteenth-century Britain, in *Sensibility*, 88–109. The quotes are from Fitz-James O'Brien's two-part discussion "Our Young Authors: Mitchell," 74–75, and "Our Young Authors: Melville," 157. O'Brien makes a contrast, which I will dispute, between Mitchell as an author of the inner heart and Melville as the observer of external forms. Tellingly, O'Brien cannot endure *Pierre*.

12. Tocqueville, *Democracy in America* (1835, 1840), 2:219. David Leverenz discusses masculine ideologies and literary exchanges in *Manhood and the American Renaissance*, 9–41, 72–107.

13. The ambivalences felt by male "American Renaissance" writers toward their audiences have been charted by a long line of scholars, including William Charvat *(Profession of Authorship in America, 1800–1870)*; Ann Douglas *(Feminization of American Culture)*; Michael Gilmore *(American Romanticism and the Marketplace)*; Kenneth Dauber *(Idea of Authorship in America)*; and Stephen Railton *(Authorship and Audience)*. On Mitchell's career, see Kime, *Donald G. Mitchell*; on Curtis, see Milne, *George William Curtis and the Genteel Tradition*. Tew and Peskin discuss the popularity of *Reveries of a Bachelor*, in "Disappearance of Ik. Marvel." Richard B. Sewall reports that *Reveries* was one of Emily Dickinson's favorite books, and he analyzes themes and sensibilities shared between the two writers; see Sewall, *The Life of Emily Dickinson*, 678–83.

14. For Curtis's narrator's invitation to Coverdale, see *Prue and I*, 58. The narrator admires Coverdale as a builder of imaginary castles, but seems uninterested in Hawthorne's repeated warnings about the unsoundness of such structures. "Titbottom's Spectacles," one of the interpolated stories in *Prue and I*, describes the effects on a bookkeeper of wonderful eyeglasses that reveal the characters of the people he views; it is a gentle version of such Hawthorne tales as "The Minister's Black Veil" (1836) and "Egotism; or, the Bosom-Serpent" (1843). Other champions of reverie proclaimed their affection for Hawthorne. In *Leaves from the Diary of a Dreamer* (1853), Henry Tuckerman sketched Hawthorne as elusive and attractive, possessed of "a peculiar and rare mental alchemy which can transmute the dross of the common and the immediate into gold" (153). Tuckerman's narrator explains that he prefers Hawthorne's heartfelt fancies to his cold allegories. Whitford compares the illusory bachelor narrators of Mitchell and Hawthorne in "*The Blithedale Romance*: Hawthorne's Reveries of a Bachelor." We might add the names of Curtis, Tuckerman, and Mitchell to those writers enrolled in Richard H. Brodhead's *School of Hawthorne*.

15. Hawthorne, *The Blithedale Romance*, 91, 90, 156, 64–65, 94, 135.

16. Melville, "Bartleby, the Scrivener," in *Piazza Tales and Other Prose Pieces*, 14, 27; "I and My Chimney," in ibid., 360. Merton M. Sealts tells the story of Melville's magazine publications in his historical note to *The Piazza Tales and Other Prose Pieces*, 476–514. The "superficial skimmer" phrase, used by many critics to validate ironic readings of Melville's short fiction, is taken from Melville's remark that Hawthorne often gave his darkest tales de-

ceptively simple and innocent titles. See Melville's review, "Hawthorne and His Mosses" (1850), in *Piazza Tales and Other Prose Pieces*, 251. R. Bruce Bickley compares the descriptions of the Temple Bar in the "London Antiquities" chapter of Irving's *Sketch Book* and Melville's "Paradise of Bachelors," in *The Method of Melville's Short Fiction*, 87–90. On Melville's sketches as parodies of Mitchell and Curtis, see Douglas, *Feminization of American Culture*, 379–88, and Pancost, "Donald Grant Mitchell's *Reveries of a Bachelor* and Herman Melville's 'I and My Chimney.'" A recent exception is Vincent J. Bertolini, who reads Melville, in "I and My Chimney" and "The Lightning-Rod Man," as making active and public the resistance to "heteroerotic and procreative norms" suggested by Mitchell in *Reveries;* see Bertolini, "Fireside Chastity," 722–27. Male sentimentalists such as Mitchell and Curtis were drawn to aspects of Melville's sensibility, as they also were to Hawthorne. In *Reveries of a Bachelor,* Mitchell praises the exotic visions in *Typee* (21). Curtis enthusiastically recommended "I and My Chimney" for publication at *Putnam's,* calling the story "capital, genial, humorous," although he had some doubts about the form of "Benito Cereno" and the style of "The Bell Tower." See Leyda, *The Melville Log,* 2:507, 500–502. In *Prue and I,* Curtis's narrator affectionately alludes to Melville's short fiction, reporting that Titbottom the bookkeeper had been seen in the company of Bartleby the scrivener (85). The narrator also mentions "The Encantadas" (171).

17. Donald Grant Mitchell ["Ik. Marvel"], *Reveries of a Bachelor,* 141–45. All subsequent citations are made to the Scribner edition (see bibliography) and given in parentheses in the text. For a discussion of Irving's influence, see Hedges, introduction to *The Sketch Book of Geoffrey Crayon, Gent.,* xix–xxi.

18. Douglas, *Feminization of American Culture,* 284–89.

19. Mitchell, *Dream Life,* 11. Subsequent citations are made to the Scribner edition (see bibliography) in parentheses in the text. Although well received on its publication in 1851, *Dream Life* is a less satisfying book than *Reveries of a Bachelor.* Mitchell tells the story of "Clarence," in effect expanding "Paul's" story from *Reveries* to fill an entire volume. *Dream Life* lacks the eccentricity, intensity, intricacy, and violence of its predecessor.

20. Kime, *Donald G. Mitchell,* 140, 13, 48, 60. Tew and Peskin discuss Mitchell's popularity among young male and female readers in the 1850s and describe his verbal maneuverings, in "The Disappearance of Ik. Marvel." Leverenz analyzes the rhetorical strategies through which Thoreau, Melville, Whitman, Hawthorne, and Emerson sought to refashion their own senses of masculinity and to alter the stances of their implied male readers. See "'I' and 'You' in the American Renaissance," in Leverenz, *Manhood and the American Renaissance,* 9–41.

21. G. J. Barker-Benfield discusses Todd and links the masturbatory reveries of Mitchell and Melville, in *The Horrors of the Half-Known Life,* 11–13, 163–74. Robert K. Martin analyzes the masturbatory aspects of Carlo's organ-grinding in *Redburn* and the sperm-squeezing in *Moby-Dick;* see Martin, *Hero, Captain, and Stranger,* 54–57, 79–83. James Creech speculates on ways of reading "homosexual" writing in nineteenth-century literature in general and in Melville in particular, in *Closet Writing/Gay Reading.* For other examples of the

smoking habits of male literary figures in the 1850s, see Miles Coverdale's private enjoyment of his cigar in *The Blithedale Romance* (1852), and the narrator of Melville's "I and My Chimney" (1856), who is deeply attached both to his pipe and to his embattled, unsightly chimney.

22. Mitchell represents epistolary exchanges not only in the frame to his second chapter but also within the reveries themselves; see *Reveries of a Bachelor*, 242, 267, and *Dream Life*, 161.

23. See Edwards, *A Treatise Concerning the Religious Affections*, 127–35 ff. Trained at Yale, Mitchell admired Edwards and included a biographical chapter on him in his *American Lands and Letters*, 58–67. On Mitchell's Yale days, see Dunn, *The Life of Donald G. Mitchell (Ik Marvel)*, 42–73.

24. On anxieties about representation and authenticity, see Haltunnen, *Confidence Men and Painted Women*.

25. Mary Kelley describes the parallels between the lives of Ruth Hall and Sara Parton, in *Private Woman, Public Stage*, 152–58; see also Warren, *Fanny Fern: An Independent Woman*, 66–73 ff. Many of the articles collected in the two *Fern Leaves* anthologies served as sketches for the characters, situations, and stances in *Ruth Hall*. See, for example, "The Widow's Trials," "Self-Conquest," "Thorns for the Rose," and "Dark Days," in *Fern Leaves from Fanny's Portfolio*, 17–33, 49–58, 182–85; and "Shadows and Sunbeams" and "Summer Friends," in *Fern Leaves from Fanny's Portfolio: Second Series*, 13–35, 91.

26. For Fern's strategic advice to her female readers, see "The Weaker Vessel" and "A Little Bunker Hill," in *Fern Leaves*, 337–38, 346–47. On Fern's rhetoric, see Douglas [Wood], "The 'Scribbling Women' and Fanny Fern," 18; Nancy Walker, "Wit, Sentimentality and the Image of Women in the Nineteenth Century," 9; Dresner, "Sentiment and Humor"; Warren, *Fanny Fern*, 4, 121–22, 135–39; and Susan K. Harris, *19th-Century American Women's Novels*, 114, 127. Attempting to avoid the critical equation of narrative endings with ideological closure, Harris offers the category of the "subversive middle," the space in many mid-nineteenth-century American women's novels where the writer eludes formal pressures to begin or end and, instead, represents alternative possibilities for female action (20–23). David S. Reynolds describes Fern's shifting personae in *Fern Leaves* and *Ruth Hall*, in *Beneath the American Renaissance*, 402–407. In "The Female Woman," Lauren Berlant avoids the Scylla and Charybdis of sentiment and satire. She analyzes the ways in which Fern's journalistic sketches, part of the female culture industry, helped publicly to produce a generic private woman.

27. Fern [Parton], *Ruth Hall: A Domestic Tale of the Present Time*, 167. Subsequent citations are made to the Rutgers edition (see bibliography) in parentheses in the text.

28. In discussing British sentimentalism and Thackeray in particular, Fred Kaplan makes similar points about the need to distinguish among varieties of sentiment and the possibility that irony can elevate, as well as deflate, sentiment; see Kaplan, *Sacred Tears*, 71–74, 95–105. Philip Fisher argues that the modern critical premium placed on irony distorts our understanding of the sentimental project in England and America, in *Hard Facts*, 91–99. Nina Baym, in *Woman's*

Fiction, and Jane Tompkins, in *Sensational Designs,* both argue for the need to recover a sense of the significance of sentimental convention for nineteenth-century women readers. In "Sentiment and Humor," Zita Z. Dresner shows that many mid-nineteenth-century female writers, such as Ann Stephens, Frances Whitcher, and Fanny Fern, produced both sentimental and satiric sketches. As I have noted in my discussions of Curtis and Mitchell, the same was true for male writers. The popularity in the mid-nineteenth-century United States of the works of Charles Dickens, the master of sentiment and satire, should give pause to those critics who argue for hierarchy or discontinuity.

29. Fern specifies and critiques gendered words of wisdom in *Fern Leaves,* 380–81, and *Fern Leaves: Second Series,* 257–58, 261, 291, 386–87. Margaret Fuller engages in a similar practice of watching words, in *Woman in the Nineteenth Century* (1845), 30–31 ff.

30. For other examples of how Fern creates a "space between," see the movement from Ruth's vigil at Harry's deathbed to Mrs. Hall's distress at the inconvenience and expense of making the trip to see her dying son (54); from Harry's death to Hyacinth's aesthetic distress at Ruth's anguish (58–59); and from the elder Halls' surrender before the Lord's will in the death of their son to their interest in the arrival of Mrs. Hall's dressmaker (61). Fern often bends sentimental apostrophes and odes in *Ruth Hall.* See her apostrophe to the "silken reins" of love (23) and her two odes on Ruth's first-born child, which mix metaphors of maternal reflection and inscription (24, 29).

31. *Fern Leaves,* 327. In *Fern Leaves,* Fern has fun with the manly puns relished by such male sentimentalists as Mitchell. She fixes on mid-nineteenth-century men's obsessions with their dickeys, treating them as absurd emblems of simulated manhood and wondering why "Men's Dickeys Never Fit Exactly" (327). Fern targets the New York male periodical culture in *Fern Leaves,* 326–28, 357–58; *Fern Leaves: Second Series,* 87–88, 92–94, 381–83; and *Ruth Hall,* 158–161 ff. New York City's importance in the development of a national publishing industry is discussed by Susan Geary in "The Domestic Novel as a Commercial Commodity" and by Mary Kelley in *Private Woman, Public Stage.* Perry Miller details the rivalries among male literary figures in New York in the 1840s and 1850s, in *The Raven and the Whale.*

32. Geary, "Domestic Novel as a Commercial Commodity," 383–90.

33. For Daisy's fleeting appearances, see *Ruth Hall,* 24–25, 29–30, 36–37, 44–45. Barton Levi St. Armand describes sentimental deathbed rituals, in *Emily Dickinson and Her Culture,* 52–65.

34. Stowe, *Uncle Tom's Cabin,* 432, 436, 430. Stowe takes her chapter title and her epigraph from stanza 23 in canto 4 of *Childe Harold's Pilgrimage,* 155. In *Pierre,* Melville appears to invoke Byron's meteorological and electrical analogies from the 23rd and 24th stanzas of canto 4, when he has his narrator describe the impossibility of tracing the charge of the cloud and the stun of the lightning bolt that produce Pierre's memories and emotions (*Pierre,* 67). Gillian Brown analyzes Stowe's sentimental fetishes, comparing them to Marx's commodity fetishes and discussing Eva's curls in particular, in *Domestic Individualism,* 39–60. Lynn Wardley suggests an affinity between sentimental fetishism and African American animism, in "Relic, Fetish, Femmage." St. Armand dis-

cusses Eva's distribution of her golden curls in the context of Victorian keepsake customs; see *Emily Dickinson and Her Culture*, 60–62.

35. Barthes, *Writing Degree Zero*, 1–6, 44–49 ff. On "écriture," see Culler, *Structuralist Poetics*, 131–60, and *Roland Barthes*, 28–31, 58–59. Susan K. Harris links Barthes's ideas about "écriture" to nineteenth-century women's fiction, in *19th-Century American Women's Novels*, 32–33. Joyce W. Warren reports on the success of the song "Little Daisy," written by G. F. Wurzel and published by Frith, Pond and Co., in *Fanny Fern*, 124.

36. "A Little Bunker Hill," *Fern Leaves*, 346. Discussing P. T. Barnum's popular strategies of self-exposure, Neil Harris analyzes audience interest in being manipulated again and again. See his chapter "The Operational Aesthetic" in *Humbug: The Art of P. T. Barnum*, 59–89. Of course, not all readers were swayed by Fern's performance in *Ruth Hall*. Some reviewers, male and female, saw her as overstepping the boundaries of female decorum. On the harsh professional reviews and the popular success of *Ruth Hall*, see Warren, *Fanny Fern*, 124–30.

37. Philip Fisher describes how popular literary forms can "mass small patterns of feeling in entirely new directions," in *Hard Facts*, 19. In "The Female Woman" (448), Lauren Berlant compares the different achievements represented by Ruth's stock certificate in *Ruth Hall* and Linda Brent's bill of sale in *Incidents in the Life of a Slave Girl* (1861); see Berlant, "The Female Woman," 448.

38. Fern, *Fresh Leaves*, 103–105.

39. "Trust thyself: every heart vibrates to that iron string," is the text whose severe doctrine is preached in "Self-Reliance" (1841). See Emerson, *Essays and Lectures*, 260.

40. Fern, *Fern Leaves*, 176, 177.

41. Shaftesbury discusses the moral sense in book 1, part 3, of *An Inquiry Concerning Virtue, or Merit*, 23–47. On moral philosophy and sentimentalism, see Todd, *Sensibility*, 23–28; Fred Kaplan, *Sacred Tears*, 3–38; and Camfield, "The Moral Aesthetics of Sentimentality: A Missing Key to *Uncle Tom's Cabin*." In a characterization applicable to the narrators of Mitchell and Curtis, Todd describes how the British man of feeling was often represented as "a compassionate, sensitive Shaftesburian soul" in conflict with "a materialistic, callous and Hobbesian world"; see *Sensibility*, 90.

42. Contemporary reviewers seemed particularly disturbed by Pierre's resolve to make Isabel his wife and by the hints of incest. See, for example, the review printed in the New York *Albion* (August 21, 1852), which itself "shrinks from naming" the crime. The review is reprinted in Higgins and Parker, *Critical Essays on Herman Melville's "Pierre,"* 37–40. Recently, G. M. Goshgarian has analyzed incest (in *Chastening the Rod*) and James Creech has suggested homosexuality (in *Closet Writing/Gay Reading*) as the scandalous secrets that contort Melville's prose in *Pierre*. Yet, as we have seen in earlier texts and shall see in *Pierre*, Melville is skeptical about the revelatory language of secrets.

43. On Melville and his autobiographical Pierre, see Weaver, *Herman Melville*, 334–44; Murray, introduction to *Pierre*; Parker, "Why *Pierre* Went Wrong"; Higgins and Parker, "The Flawed Grandeur of Melville's *Pierre*";

Rogin, *Subversive Genealogy*, 155–86; Tolchin, *Mourning, Gender, and Creativity*, 138–61; Creech, *Closet Writing/Gay Reading*, 93–179; and Renker, *Strike Through The Mask*, 24–41. Analyzing the points of view in *Pierre*, Sacvan Bercovitch identifies not only naive and sardonic voices, but also a third "self-aware" voice—that of the author who recognizes but cannot solve the text's contradictions. Still, such a separation seems too tidy for the reckless, explosive *Pierre*. See Bercovitch, *The Rites of Assent*, 254–55 ff.

44. Fitz-James O'Brien, "Our Young Authors: Melville," 163. See also the complaint against style in the *American Whig Review*, November 1852, reprinted in Higgins and Parker, *Critical Essays on "Pierre*," 63.

45. Bercovitch, *Rites of Assent*, 253. Bercovitch interprets the verbal excess in *Pierre* as delivered in "the voice of the betrayed idealist" (294). For psychobiographical accounts of Melville's style in *Pierre*, see Mumford, *Herman Melville*, 196–222; Matthiessen, *American Renaissance*, 471–87; and Murray, introduction to *Pierre*, xlii–xliv. The *New York Day Book* put this case more succinctly in the headline to its brief, dismissive review of September 7, 1852: "Herman Melville Crazy." See Higgins and Parker, *Critical Essays on "Pierre*," 50. Neal L. Tolchin sees Melville's style as performing "a complex grief work," in which he retaliates against a culture that produced his father's fall and blocked his expression of feelings over his loss; see Tolchin, *Mourning, Gender, and Creativity*, 138–62. For *Pierre* as a failed effort to write a popular novel, see Howard, *Herman Melville: A Biography*, 180–95, and historical note to *Pierre*, 365–79. Those who interpret *Pierre* as parody include William Braswell, in "The Satirical Temper of Melville's *Pierre*" and "The Early Love Scenes in Melville's *Pierre*"; Robert Milder, in "Melville's Intentions in *Pierre*"; and Ann Douglas, in *Feminization of American Culture*, 349–95. Douglas argues that Melville turned "decisively and openly against the middle-class sentimental-minded feminized reading public he had essentially tried to evade or educate in his previous work" (373). Gillian Brown interprets Melville as attacking sentimentalism but revises the received view, criticizing rather than endorsing such an attack. She argues that in *Pierre* Melville sought to define and defend a self-contained male literary economy and to appropriate female authority; see Brown, *Domestic Individualism*, 135–69. Other critics describe the phenomenological lessons taught by Melville's rhetoric. Michael S. Kearns argues that the "single controlling intent is to force readers to experience ambiguity," in "Interpreting Intentional Incoherence," 50. Brian Higgins and Hershel Parker maintain that "Under the delusion that he was appealing simultaneously to superficial and eagle-eyed readers . . . Melville devised elaborate strategies for disguising his themes," shaping a "complex strategy of following baffling ambiguities with dazzling clarification," in "Reading *Pierre*," 229–30. Attending to the rhetorical context of nineteenth-century popular fiction, Charlene Avallone suggests that *Pierre*'s style was not as aberrant as it might seem to twentieth-century readers, in "Calculations for Popularity." Avallone's point is well-taken, yet *Pierre* still seems, well, aberrant.

46. For an inventory of Melville's references to the philosophy and literature of emotion, see Henry A. Murray's grandly annotated edition of *Pierre*. Janet Todd discusses the literary aftermath of sentimentalism in Gothic and Roman-

tic productions; see Todd, *Sensibility*, 9, 141–46. Although James Creech argues in *Closet Writing/Gay Reading* that Melville invoked the sentimental and the gothic as "alibis" to disguise homoerotic passion (156–65), Melville's attention to these modes seems to me to form the substance of his intellectual effort in *Pierre*. I do not mean my description of the broad movement from "Sentimental" to "Gothic" to "Romantic" to be exhaustive. In the New York City sections, for example, Melville examines the ideas of antebellum reform: the ascetic manicheanism of health reformers such as Sylvester Graham (in Melville's account of the "Apostles") and the repressive and liberating practices of the communitarians, particularly the celibate Shakers and the complexly married Oneida Community members (in his portrayal of the relations between Pierre, Isabel, Delly, and Lucy in their shared apartment). Sheila Post-Lauria links *Pierre* to French sensational fiction, in *Correspondent Colorings*, 123–47. Departing from an earlier sense of *Pierre* as incoherent, recent critics have described the text as a comprehensive critique of interpretation itself. Edgar A. Dryden argues that Melville undermined "the notion of writing as original creation and reading as an authentic act of discovery"; see "The Entangled Text," 171. Priscilla Wald argues that Melville challenged fundamental assumptions about narrativity and about the "national script of identity," in "Hearing Narrative Voices in Melville's *Pierre*," 132. In *The Rites of Assent*, Bercovitch argues that Melville analyzed two centuries of American hermeneutics based on a faith in "the concentricity of self, text, and interpretation" (270). According to Bercovitch, Melville moves in *Pierre* from Christian faith to Romantic doubt to the decentering shock of modernism (275–85).

47. Wai-chee Dimock describes how both knowledge and individuals are produced in *Pierre* through the uncovering of secrets, in *Empire for Liberty*, 140–75. On sex as "*the* secret" of modern societies, see Foucault, *The History of Sexuality*, vol. 1, 33–35, 53–73. For a representative complaint against the "evasions" of sentimental language, see Herbert Ross Brown, *The Sentimental Novel*, 122–23. Richard H. Brodhead describes the "sexual logic" of *Pierre*, in which desires are repressed and then extravagantly sublimated, in *Hawthorne, Melville, and the Novel*, 179. In the euphemistic, oblique qualities of Melville's prose, James Creech sees an effort to give utterance to interdicted homosexual desires, in *Closet Writing/Gay Reading*, 44–61.

48. Recently, critics have begun to examine Pierre's desires for Glen; see Lackey, "The Despotic Victim," 72, and Creech, *Closet Writing/Gay Reading*, 172–79. On "Aladdin's Palace," see chapter 46 of *Redburn*.

49. In the early diptych, "Fragments from A Writing Desk" (1839), Melville links sentimental and gothic quests for female beauty; see *Piazza Tales and Other Prose Pieces*, 191–204. The presence of Poe recurs in the later chapters of *Pierre*, when Pierre the author, laboring on his masterwork alone in his cold room, neither eating nor sleeping, takes on the burden of the male and the pathos and promise of the female Poe figure. Pierre decays and becomes spiritualized even as we stare, and his disintegration is also his enlightenment. Melville seems to evoke Poe's death in the streets of Baltimore in book 25, when Pierre collapses on the deserted pavements of New York City (341). Burton R. Pollin reviews Melville's many allusions to Poe in "Traces of Poe in Melville." Poe

describes his poetics in his 1842 review of Longfellow's *Ballads and Other Poems*, in *Essays and Reviews*, 683–96 (the phrase "Rhythmical Creation of Beauty" is on page 688); in "The Philosophy of Composition" (1846), in ibid., 13–25; and in *Eureka: A Prose Poem*, in *Poetry and Tales*, 1257–1359.

50. Henry A. Murray unfolds Melville's allusions to Enceladus in his notes to the Hendricks House edition of *Pierre*, 501–2. Recent criticism of *Pierre* has focused on Melville's images of radical masculine self-possession. See Jehlen, *American Incarnation*, 185–226; Dimock, *Empire for Liberty*, 140–75; and Gillian Brown, *Domestic Individualism*, 135–70. Yet in *Pierre*, the self-made man—and Melville's cognate, the original author, "solitary as at the Pole" (338)—are acknowledged as figures of fantasy, and the self-in-relation is frequently represented. See, for example, Pierre's speech to Isabel about "the infinite entanglements of all social things" (191) and the narrator's caution to the reader: "The world is forever babbling of originality" (259).

51. Walt Whitman, "Calamus" number 15, in *Leaves of Grass: Facsimile Edition of the 1860 Text*, 361. David Marshall analyzes Rousseau's "ink of sympathy," in *Surprising Effects of Sympathy*, 171–77.

52. For the "Young America in Literature" satires, see books 17 and 18 of *Pierre*. Gillian Brown compares the literary satires of Melville and Fern, emphasizing passages in which Melville figures his readers as female, in *Domestic Individualism*, 139–43. In chapter 180 of *Mardi* (1849), Melville describes the creative process in healthier terms. The "imaginary beings" inside the writer have a genial, rather than glutting, relationship with their host. Introspection is rewarded, rather than punished. In this chapter, Melville predicts the kinds of formal criticisms that will be leveled not only at *Mardi* but also at *Pierre*. See Melville, *Mardi*, 591–602.

53. In an April 16, 1852, letter to Richard Bentley, the prospective British publisher of *Pierre*, Melville perversely insisted that his book was "very much more calculated for popularity than anything you have yet published of mine— being a regular romance, with a mysterious plot to it, & stirring passions at work, and withall, representing a new & elevated aspect of American life." See Melville, *Correspondence*, 226. Melville does not seem to have considered actual letters to be vehicles of truth any more than fictional ones. *Pierre* may be many things, but "regular" it is not. Nor does it ever seem to have been, despite Hershel Parker's recent "reconstruction" of the "original" *Pierre*; see Parker, *Pierre; or, The Ambiguities: The Kraken Edition*, xi–xlvi ff.

54. For recent readings of the "vacant as vast" passage, see John Carlos Rowe, who interprets it as Melville's critique of capitalistic alienation, in "Romancing the Stone," 226–27; and Sacvan Bercovitch, who interprets it as Melville's meditation on the paradoxes of narcissism and the futility of the search for absolute independence, in *Rites of Assent*, 257. In *The Confidence-Man* (1857), in scene after scene describing the encounters between confidence men and "victims," with apparent amusement rather than exasperation, Melville considers how belief can be both empty and sustaining.

55. Trenchant analyses of the ideological constraints in *Pierre* have been offered recently by Priscilla Wald, in "Hearing Narrative Voices in *Pierre*," and by Sacvan Bercovitch, in *Rites of Assent*, 285–306. In his novel *Edgar Huntly*

(1799), Charles Brockden Brown paints a similar portrait of misguided virtue and spontaneous and combustible sentiment.

56. On gift books, see Thompson, *American Literary Annuals & Gift Books, 1825–1865*, 1–48 ff. Some gift books were offered for occasions other than Christmas and New Years—to commemorate birthdays or even "all seasons." Their quality and influence declined after 1845, as they competed with the less expensive monthly magazines. These miscellanies had sources in European literary annuals and in Irving's *Sketch Book* (1819–20). Thompson reports that no works of Melville were reprinted or excerpted in any antebellum gift books (23–24).

57. The quotes are from Mumford, *Herman Melville*, 207–208; Matthiessen, *American Renaissance*, 486; and Murray, introduction to *Pierre*, xlii. See also Arvin, *Herman Melville*, 230–31. The critical history of the "hymn to Love" is surveyed by William Braswell in "Early Love Scenes," 284–85; by Alan Holder in "Style and Tone in Melville's *Pierre*," 76; and by Charlene Avallone in "Calculations for Popularity," 97–99.

58. For contemporary reviews of *Pierre* that displayed Melville's fearsome "beauties," see those from the *American Whig Review* (November 1852) and the London *Athanaeum* (November 20, 1852), in Higgins and Parker, *Critical Essays on "Pierre,"* 63–68, 68–69. Herbert Ross Brown describes the penchant for extracting "beauties," in *The Sentimental Novel*, 166. Nina Baym analyzes reviewers' attention to style, in *Novels, Readers, and Reviewers*, 130–39. See also Terry Eagleton on the uses of textual "beauties," in *Walter Benjamin, or, Towards a Revolutionary Criticism*, 102.

POST MORTEM: AFTER THE ANATOMIES

1. Melville, *Billy Budd, Sailor,* 128. Warner Berthoff describes the exploratory qualities of Melville's mind with great sensitivity to the diction, syntax, and rhythms of his prose; see *The Example of Melville*. On Melville's "non-naildownableness," see also Kopley, "Sendak on Melville: An Interview," 6.

2. Herman Melville to Nathaniel Hawthorne, [June 1?], 1851, in *Correspondence*, 193.

3. Gramsci, *Selections from the Prison Notebooks*, 324, 353.

4. Raymond Williams, *Marxism and Literature*, 132.

5. See Althusser, "Ideology and Ideological State Apparatuses."

6. I allude to arguments by Nina Baym in "Melville's Quarrel with Fiction"; by Stephen Railton in *Authorship and Audience*, 152–201; and by John Carlos Rowe in "Romancing the Stone." Shirley M. Dettlaff reviews the debate about whether or not Melville "lost faith in art" in his later fiction and poetry; see Dettlaff, "Melville's Aesthetics," 644–50.

7. For critics who oppose Melville to his audience, see Charvat, *Profession of Authorship in America*, 204–82, and Douglas, *Feminization of American Culture*, 349–95. Michael T. Gilmore surveys statements about the conflict between American romantic writers and their audiences, in *American Romanticism and the Marketplace*, 5–6. Expanding on a suggestion from Charvat, Stephen Railton argues that Melville projected his own anxieties about author-

ship onto his imagined audience and then internalized this division; see Railton, *Authorship and Audience,* 152–62, 189–201. With the exception of Douglas, who details the sentimental culture she criticizes, it is sometimes difficult in this vein of criticism to discern the specific content of middle-class "convention." Valuable cautions against uncritically accepting claims by antebellum male writers who cast themselves as martyrs are offered by Nina Baym in "Melodramas of Beset Manhood," David Leverenz in *Manhood and the American Renaissance,* 17, and Stephen Railton in *Authorship and Audience,* 200–201. On Melville's narratives of Indian-hating, see *The Confidence-Man,* 139–59.

8. Melville, *Billy Budd,* 115.

9. Melville, "The Attic Landscape," "The Parthenon," "Greek Masonry," and "Greek Architecture," in *Timoleon,* in *Collected Poems of Herman Melville,* 245–46, 246–47, 248. Leon Howard speculates on the composition of *Timoleon,* in *Herman Melville: A Biography,* 263–65, 332–33; William H. Shurr analyzes its structure, in *The Mystery of Iniquity,* 151–80. Shirley M. Dettlaff links the thematic treatments of form in *Timoleon* and *Clarel,* in "Ionian Form and Esau's Waste," 220–21 ff.

10. Herman Melville to Nathaniel Hawthorne, [June 1?], 1851, in *Correspondence,* 191.

Bibliography

Abbott, Collamer M. "*White-Jacket* and the Campaign Against Flogging in the Navy." *Melville Society Extracts* 89 (1992): 24–25.

"About Niggers." *Putnam's Monthly Magazine* 6 (1855): 608–12.

Abrams, Robert E. "*Typee* and *Omoo*: Herman Melville and the Ungraspable Phantom of Identity." *Arizona Quarterly* 31 (1975): 33–50.

Alibert, Jean-Louis. *Clinique de l'Hôpital Saint-Louis, ou traité complet des maladies de la peau, contenant la description de ces maladies et leurs meilleurs modes de traitement.* 2 vols in 1. Paris: Chez B. Cormon et Blanc, 1833.

Althusser, Louis. "Ideology and Ideological State Apparatuses (Notes towards an Investigation) (January–April 1969)." In *Lenin and Philosophy and Other Essays,* translated by Ben Brewster, 123–73. New York: Monthly Review Press, 1972.

Ames, Nathaniel. *A Mariner's Sketches.* Providence, R.I.: Cory, Marshall and Hammond, 1830.

Anderson, Charles Roberts. *Melville in the South Seas.* New York: Columbia University Press, 1967.

———. "A Reply to Herman Melville's *White-Jacket* by Rear-Admiral Thomas O. Selfridge, Sr." *American Literature* 7 (1935): 123–44.

Anderson, Patricia. *The Course of Empire: The Erie Canal and the New York Landscape, 1825–75.* Rochester, N.Y.: Memorial Art Gallery of the University of Rochester, 1984.

Andrews, William L. *To Tell a Free Story: The First Century of Afro-American Autobiography, 1760–1865.* Urbana: University of Illinois Press, 1986.

"Anti-Renter's Declaration of Independence." July 4, 1839. In *We, the Other People: Alternative Declarations of Independence by Labor Groups, Farmers, Woman's Rights Advocates, Socialists, and Blacks, 1829–1975,* edited by

Philip S. Foner, 59–63. Urbana: University of Illinois Press, 1976.

Apess, William. *On Our Own Ground: The Complete Writings of William Apess, a Pequot,* edited by Barry O'Connell. Amherst: University of Massachusetts Press, 1992.

Appiah, Kwame Anthony. *In My Father's House: Africa in the Philosophy of Culture.* New York: Oxford University Press, 1992.

"Are All Men Descended From Adam?" *Putnam's Monthly Magazine* 5 (1855): 79–99.

Arens, William. *The Man-Eating Myth: Anthropology and Anthropophagy.* New York: Oxford University Press, 1979.

Armstrong, Nancy. *Desire and Domestic Fiction: A Political History of the Novel.* New York: Oxford University Press, 1987.

Armstrong, Virginia Irving, ed. *I Have Spoken: American History Through the Voices of the Indians.* Chicago: Swallow Press, 1984.

Arner, Robert D. "Of Snakes and Those Who Swallow Them: Some Folk Analogues for Hawthorne's 'Egotism; or, the Bosom Serpent.'" *Southern Folklore Quarterly* 35 (1971): 336–46.

Arvin, Newton. *Herman Melville.* New York: William Sloane Associates, 1950.

Aspiz, Harold. "Phrenologizing the Whale." *Nineteenth-Century Fiction* 23 (1968): 18–27.

———. *Walt Whitman and the Body Beautiful.* Urbana: University of Illinois Press, 1980.

Auser, Cortland P. "Nathaniel Parker Willis." In *Dictionary of Literary Biography,* vol. 3, edited by Joel Myerson, 373–76. Detroit: Gale Research Co., 1979.

Avallone, Charlene. "Calculations for Popularity: Melville's *Pierre* and *Holden's Dollar Magazine.*" *Nineteenth-Century Literature* 43 (1988): 82–110.

Bachman, John. *The Doctrine of the Unity of the Human Race Examined on the Principles of Science.* Charleston, S.C.: C. Canning, 1850.

Bakhtin, Mikhail. "Discourse Typology in Prose." In *Readings in Russian Poetics: Formalist and Structuralist Views,* edited by Ladislav Matejka and Krystyna Pomorska, 176–96. Cambridge, Mass.: MIT Press, 1971.

———. *Problems of Dostoevsky's Poetics,* edited and translated by Caryl Emerson. Minneapolis: University of Minnesota Press, 1984.

———. *Rabelais and His World,* translated by Hélène Iswolsky. Cambridge, Mass.: MIT Press, 1968.

Barbour, James. "'All My Books Are Botches': Melville's Struggle with *The Whale.*" In *Writing the American Classics,* edited by James Barbour and Tom Quirk, 25–52. Chapel Hill: University of North Carolina Press, 1990.

———. "The Composition of Moby-Dick." *American Literature* 47 (1975): 343–60.

———. "The Writing of Moby-Dick." Ph.D. diss., UCLA, 1970.

Barker-Benfield, G. J. *The Horrors of the Half-Known Life: Male Attitudes Toward Women and Sexuality in Nineteenth-Century America.* New York: Harper and Row, 1976.

Barnum, P. T. *Selected Letters of P. T. Barnum,* edited by A. H. Saxon. New York: Columbia University Press, 1983.

Barrell, John. *The Dark Side of the Landscape: The Rural Poor in English Painting, 1730–1840*. Cambridge: Cambridge University Press, 1980.
———. *The Idea of Landscape and the Sense of Place, 1730–1840*. Cambridge: Cambridge University Press, 1972.
Barthes, Roland. *Writing Degree Zero*, translated by Annette Lavers and Colin Smith. London: Jonathan Cape, 1967.
Baym, Nina. *American Women Writers and the Work of History, 1790–1860*. New Brunswick, N.J.: Rutgers University Press, 1995.
———. "Melodramas of Beset Manhood: How Theories of American Fiction Exclude Women Authors." *American Quarterly* 33 (1981): 123–39.
———. "Melville's Quarrel with Fiction." *PMLA* 94 (1979): 909–23.
———. *Novels, Readers, and Reviewers: Responses to Fiction in Antebellum America*. Ithaca, N.Y.: Cornell University Press, 1984.
———. *Woman's Fiction: A Guide to Novels by and about Women in America, 1820–1870*. Ithaca, N.Y.: Cornell University Press, 1978.
Beaglehole, J. C. *The Journals of Captain James Cook on His Voyages of Discovery*. 4 vols. Cambridge: Published for the Hakluyt Society at the University Press, 1955–1974.
———. *The Life of Captain James Cook*. Stanford, Calif.: Stanford University Press, 1979.
Beale, Thomas. *The Natural History of the Sperm Whale . . . to Which is added a Sketch of a South-Sea Whaling Voyage in Which the Author Was Personally Engaged*. London: John Van Voorst, 1839.
Beauchamp, Gorman. "Montaigne, Melville, and the Cannibals." *Arizona Quarterly* 37 (1981): 293–309.
Beaver, Harold. Appendix to *The Narrative of Arthur Gordon Pym of Nantucket*, by Edgar Allan Poe. New York: Penguin, 1986.
Belcher, Edward. *Narrative of a Voyage round the World, Performed in Her Majesty's Ship Sulphur, During the Years 1836–42*. 2 vols. London: Henry Colburn, 1843.
Bell, Michael Davitt. *The Development of the American Romance: The Sacrifice of Relation*. Chicago: University of Chicago Press, 1980.
Bennett, Frederick Debell. *Narrative of a Whaling Voyage round the Globe, from the Year 1833 to 1836. Comprising Sketches of Polynesia, California, the Indian Archipelago, etc. with an Account of Southern Whales, the Sperm Whale Fishery, and the Natural History of the Climates Visited*. 2 vols. London: Richard Bentley, 1840.
Bercaw, Mary K. *Melville's Sources*. Evanston, Ill.: Northwestern University Press, 1987.
Bercovitch, Sacvan. *The Rites of Assent: Transformations in the Symbolic Construction of America*. New York: Routledge, 1993.
Bercovitch, Sacvan, and Myra Jehlen, eds. *Ideology and Classic American Literature*. New York: Cambridge University Press, 1986.
Berlant, Lauren. *The Anatomy of National Fantasy: Hawthorne, Utopia, and Everyday Life*. Chicago: University of Chicago Press, 1991.
———. "The Female Woman: Fanny Fern and the Form of Sentiment." *American Literary History* 3 (1991): 429–54.

Bermingham, Ann. *Landscape and Ideology: The English Rustic Tradition, 1740–1860.* Berkeley: University of California Press, 1986.

Berthoff, Warner. *The Example of Melville.* Princeton, N.J.: Princeton University Press, 1962.

Berthold, Dennis. "Charles Brockden Brown, *Edgar Huntly,* and the Origins of the American Picturesque." *William and Mary Quarterly* 41 (January 1984): 62–84.

Bertolini, Vincent J. "Fireside Chastity: The Erotics of Sentimental Bachelorhood in the 1850s." *American Literature* 68 (1996): 707–37.

Beverly, Robert. *The History and Present State of Virginia, in Four Parts.* 1705. Edited by Louis B. Wright. Chapel Hill: University of North Carolina Press, 1947.

Bibb, Henry. *Narrative of the Life and Adventures of Henry Bibb, An American Slave, Written by Himself.* 1849. In *Puttin' On Ole Massa,* edited by Gilbert Osofsky, 51–171. New York: Harper Torchbooks, 1969.

Bickley, R. Bruce, Jr. *The Method of Melville's Short Fiction.* Durham: Duke University Press, 1975.

Bieder, Robert E. *Science Encounters the Indian, 1820–1880: The Early Years of American Ethnology.* Norman: University of Oklahoma Press, 1986.

Bogdan, Robert. *Freak Show: Presenting Human Oddities for Fun and Profit.* Chicago: University of Chicago Press, 1988.

Bourne, George. *Picture of Slavery in the United States of America.* Middletown, Conn.: E. Hunt, 1834.

Branch, E. Douglas. *The Sentimental Years, 1836–1860.* New York: D. Appleton-Century Company, 1934.

Branch, Watson G., ed. *Melville: The Critical Heritage.* London and Boston: Routledge and Kegan Paul, 1974.

Braswell, William. "The Early Love Scenes in Melville's *Pierre.*" *American Literature* 22 (1950): 283–89.

———. "The Satirical Temper of Melville's *Pierre.*" *American Literature* 7 (1936): 424–38.

Breitwieser, Mitchell. "False Sympathy in Melville's *Typee.*" *American Quarterly* 34 (1982): 396–417.

Brodhead, Richard H. *Cultures of Letters: Scenes of Reading and Writing in Nineteenth-Century America.* Chicago: University of Chicago Press, 1993.

———. *Hawthorne, Melville, and the Novel.* Chicago: University of Chicago Press, 1976.

———. "*Mardi:* Creating the Creative." In *New Perspectives on Melville,* edited by Faith Pullin, 29–53. Kent, Ohio: Kent State University Press, 1978.

———. *The School of Hawthorne.* New York: Oxford University Press, 1986.

Brodtkorb, Paul, Jr. *Ishmael's White World: A Phenomenological Reading of "Moby-Dick."* New Haven, Conn.: Yale University Press, 1965.

Brown, Gillian. *Domestic Individualism: Imagining Self in Nineteenth-Century America.* Berkeley: University of California Press, 1990.

Brown, Herbert Ross. *The Sentimental Novel in America, 1789–1860.* New York: Pageant Books, 1959.

Brown, William Wells, ed. *The Anti-Slavery Harp: A Collection of Songs for Anti-Slavery Meetings.* Boston: Bela Marsh, 1848.

———. *Clotel; or, The President's Daughter: A Narrative of Slave Life in the United States.* 1853. Reprint, with preface by Jean Fagan Yellin. New York: Arno Press and the *New York Times,* 1969.

———. *Narrative of William W. Brown.* 1847. Reprinted in *Five Slave Narratives,* edited by William Loren Katz. New York: Arno Press and the *New York Times,* 1969.

Browne, J. Ross. *Etchings of a Whaling Cruise, with Notes of a Sojourn on the Island of Zanzibar. To Which Is Appended A Brief History of the Whale Fishery; Its Past and Present Condition.* 1846. Reprint. Cambridge, Mass.: Belknap Press of Harvard University Press, 1968.

Brownson, Orestes A. *The Laboring Classes.* 1840. Reprint. Delmar, N.Y.: Scholars' Facsimiles and Reprints, 1978.

Bryant, John. *Melville and Repose: The Rhetoric of Humor in the American Renaissance.* New York: Oxford University Press, 1993.

———. "Toning Down the Green: Melville's Picturesque." In *Savage Eye: Melville and the Visual Arts,* edited by Christopher Sten, 145–61. Kent, Ohio: Kent State University Press, 1991.

Bryant, William Cullen. "Funeral Oration on the Death of Thomas Cole." Delivered before the National Academy of Design on May 4, 1848. In *American Art, 1700–1960: Sources and Documents,* edited by John W. McCoubrey, 96–97. Englewood Cliffs, N.J.: Prentice-Hall, 1965.

———. *Picturesque America; or, the Land We Live In: A Delineation by Pen and Pencil of the Mountains, Rivers, Lakes, Forests, Water-Falls, Shores, Cañons, Valleys, Cities, and other Picturesque Features of Our Country.* 2 vols. New York: D. Appleton, 1872–1874.

———. *Poetical Works of William Cullen Bryant, Collected and Arranged by the Author.* New York: D. Appleton, 1878.

Buell, Lawrence. *The Environmental Imagination: Thoreau, Nature Writing, and the Formation of American Culture.* Cambridge, Mass.: Belknap Press of Harvard University Press, 1995.

Burke, Emily P. *Reminiscences of Georgia.* Oberlin, Ohio: J. M. Fitch, 1850.

Byron, Lord. *Childe Harold's Pilgrimage.* 1818. In *Byron,* edited by Jerome J. McGann, 19–206. New York: Oxford University Press, 1986.

Calder, Alex. "'The Thrice Mysterious Taboo': Melville's *Typee* and the Perception of Culture." Forthcoming in *Representations.*

Calhoun, John C. "Compromise Speech of 1850." Delivered in the United States Senate on March 4, 1850. In *Selected American Speeches on Basic Issues (1850–1950),* edited by Carl G. Brandt and Edward M. Shafter, Jr., 43–70. Boston: Houghton Mifflin, 1960.

Callow, James T. *Kindred Spirits: Knickerbocker Writers and American Artists, 1807–1855.* Chapel Hill: University of North Carolina Press, 1967.

Cameron, Sharon. *The Corporeal Self: Allegories of the Body in Melville and Hawthorne.* Baltimore: Johns Hopkins University Press, 1981.

Camfield, Gregg. "The Moral Aesthetics of Sentimentality: A Missing Key to *Uncle Tom's Cabin.*" *Nineteenth-Century Literature* 43 (1988): 319–45.

Campbell, John. *Negro-Mania: Being an Examination of the Falsely Assumed Equality of the Various Races of Men.* Philadelphia: Campbell and Power, 1851.

Campbell, Thomas. *The Complete Poetical Works of Thomas Campbell,* edited by J. Logie Robertson. London: Oxford University Press, 1907.

Camper, Petrus. *The Works of the Late Professor Camper, on the Connexion between the Science of Anatomy and the Arts of Drawing, Painting, Statuary, etc. etc. in Two Books. Containing a Treatise on the Natural Difference of Features in Persons of Different Countries and Periods of Life.* 1791. Translated by Thomas Cogan. London: Printed for C. Dilly, 1794.

Cartwright, Samuel A. "Diseases and Peculiarities of the Negro Race." *De Bow's Review* 11 (1851): 64–69, 209–13, 331–36, 504–08.

———. "Slavery in the Light of Ethnology." In *Cotton is King, and Proslavery Arguments,* edited by E. N. Elliott, 691–728. Augusta, Ga.: Pritchard, Abbott, & Loomis, 1860.

Chamerovzow, I. A., ed. *Slave Life in Georgia: A Narrative of the Life, Sufferings, and Escape of John Brown, a Fugitive Slave, Now in England.* 1855. Reprint. Savannah: Beehive Press, 1972.

Chandler, Elizabeth Margaret. "Mental Metempsychosis." *The Genius of Universal Emancipation,* 3d series, 1 (February 1831): 171.

Charvat, William. *The Profession of Authorship in America: 1800–1870,* edited by Matthew J. Bruccoli. New York: Columbia University Press, 1992.

Cheever, Henry T. *The Whale and His Captors; or The Whaleman's Adventures, and the Whale Biography, as Gathered on the Homeward Cruise of the "Commodore Preble."* New York: Harper and Brothers, 1850.

Child, Lydia Maria. *Anti-Slavery Catechism.* Newburyport: Charles Whipple, 1836.

———. "An Appeal for the Indians." 1868. In *Hobomok and Other Writings on Indians,* edited by Carolyn Karcher, 213–32. New Brunswick, N.J.: Rutgers University Press, 1986.

———. *An Appeal in Favor of That Class of Americans Called Africans.* Boston: Allen & Ticknor, 1833.

———. *Hobomok and Other Writings on Indians,* edited by Carolyn L. Karcher. New Brunswick, N.J.: Rutgers University Press, 1986.

———. *Letters from New York.* 1843. Reprint. Freeport, N.Y.: Books for Libraries Press, 1970.

Christman, Henry. *Tin Horns and Calico: A Decisive Episode in the Emergence of Democracy.* New York: Holt, 1945.

Clay, Henry. "Compromise Speech of 1850." Delivered in the United States Senate on February 5 and 6, 1850. In *Selected American Speeches on Basic Issues (1850–1950),* edited by Carl G. Brandt and Edward M. Shafter, Jr., 5–42. Boston: Houghton Mifflin, 1960.

Clifford, Deborah Pickman. *Crusader for Freedom: A Life of Lydia Maria Child.* Boston: Beacon Press, 1992.

Coffler, Gail. "Classical Iconography in the Aesthetics of *Billy Budd, Sailor.*" In *Savage Eye: Melville and the Visual Arts,* edited by Christopher Sten, 257–76. Kent, Ohio: Kent State University Press, 1991.

Colacurcio, Michael J. "Visible Sanctity and Specter Evidence: The Moral World of Hawthorne's 'Young Goodman Brown.'" *Essex Institute Historical Collections* 110 (1974): 259–99.

Colbert, Charles. "Dreaming Up 'The Architect's Dream.'" *American Art* 6, no. 3 (Summer 1992): 79–91.

———. "'Each Little Hillock hath a Tongue'—Phrenology and the Art of Hiram Powers." *Art Bulletin* 68 (1986): 281–300.

———. *A Measure of Perfection: Phrenology and the Fine Arts in America.* Chapel Hill: University of North Carolina Press, 1997.

Cole, Thomas. "Essay on American Scenery." 1836. In *American Art, 1700–1960: Sources and Documents,* edited by John W. McCoubrey, 98–110. Englewood Cliffs, N.J.: Prentice-Hall, 1965.

Conklin, Henry. *Through "Poverty's Vale": A Hardscrabble Boyhood in Upstate New York, 1832–1862,* edited by Wendell Tripp. New York: Syracuse University Press, 1974.

Cooper, James Fenimore. *The Letters and Journals of James Fenimore Cooper,* edited by James Franklin Beard. 6 vols. Cambridge, Mass.: Belknap Press of Harvard University Press, 1960–1968.

———. *The Pioneers, or the Sources of the Susquehanna; A Descriptive Tale.* 1823. In vol. 1 of *The Leatherstocking Tales,* edited by Blake Nevins, 1–465. New York: Library of America, 1985.

Cooper, Susan Fenimore. "A Dissolving View." In *The Home Book of the Picturesque: or American Scenery, Art, and Literature,* 79–94. 1852. Reprint. Gainesville, Fla.: Scholars' Facsimiles & Reprints, 1967.

———. *Rural Hours.* 1850. Reprint. Syracuse, N.Y.: Syracuse University Press, 1995.

Coulter, John. *Adventures in the Pacific; with Observations on the Natural Productions, Manners and Customs of the Natives of the Various Islands, together with Remarks on Missionaries, British and other Residents.* Dublin: William Curry, Jun. and Company, 1845.

Crain, Caleb. "Lovers of Human Flesh: Homosexuality and Cannibalism in Melville's Novels." *American Literature* 66 (1994): 25–53.

Crane, Stephen. "The Monster." 1898. In *Prose and Poetry,* edited by J. C. Levenson, 389–448. New York: Library of America, 1984.

Creech, James. *Closet Writing/Gay Reading: The Case of Melville's "Pierre."* Chicago: University of Chicago Press, 1993.

Crèvecoeur, J. Hector St. John de. *Letters from an American Farmer and Sketches of 18th-Century America,* edited by Albert E. Stone. New York: Penguin, 1981.

Culler, Jonathan. *Roland Barthes.* New York: Oxford University Press, 1983.

———. *Structuralist Poetics: Structuralism, Linguistics, and the Study of Literature.* Ithaca, N.Y.: Cornell University Press, 1975.

Cummins, Maria Susanna. *The Lamplighter.* 1854. Edited by Nina Baym. New Brunswick, N.J.: Rutgers University Press, 1988.

Cunliffe, Marcus. *Chattel Slavery and Wage Slavery: The Anglo-American Context, 1830–1860.* Athens: University of Georgia Press, 1979.

Curtis, George William. *Prue and I.* New York: Dix, Edwards, & Co., 1856.

Dana, Richard Henry, Jr. *Two Years Before the Mast: A Personal Narrative of Life at Sea*. 1840. Edited by Thomas Philbrick. New York: Penguin, 1986.

Dauber, Kenneth. *The Idea of Authorship in America: Democratic Poetics from Franklin to Melville*. Madison: University of Wisconsin Press, 1990.

Davidson, Cathy. *Revolution and the Word: The Rise of the Novel in America*. New York: Oxford University Press, 1986.

Davies, John D. *Phrenology: Fad and Science; A 19th-Century American Crusade*. New Haven: Yale University Press, 1955.

Davis, David Brion. *The Problem of Slavery in Western Culture*. Ithaca, N.Y.: Cornell University Press, 1966.

Davis, Merrell R. *Melville's "Mardi": A Chartless Voyage*. New Haven, Conn.: Yale University Press, 1952.

Deakin, Motley F. Introduction to *The Home Book of the Picturesque*. 1852. Reprint. Gainesville, Fla.: Scholars' Facsimiles & Reprints, 1967.

Delany, Martin R. *Blake; or, the Huts of America*. 1859, 1861–1862. Edited by Floyd J. Miller. Boston: Beacon Press, 1970.

———. *The Condition, Elevation, Emigration, and Destiny of the Colored People of the United States, Politically Considered*. 1852. Reprint. Salem, N.H. : Ayer Company, 1988.

———. *Principia of Ethnology: The Origin of Races and Color, with an Archaeological Compendium of Ethiopian and Egyptian Civilization, from Years of Careful Examination and Enquiry*. 1879. Reprint. Baltimore: Black Classic Press, 1991.

Delbanco, Andrew. "Melville in the '80s." *American Literary History* 4 (1992): 709–25.

Dettlaff, Shirley M. "Ionian Form and Esau's Waste." *American Literature* 54 (1982): 212–28.

———. "Melville's Aesthetics." In *A Companion to Melville Studies*, edited by John Bryant, 625–65. New York: Greenwood Press, 1986.

Dickinson, Emily. *The Manuscript Books of Emily Dickinson*. 2 vols, edited by R. W. Franklin. Cambridge, Mass.: Belknap Press of Harvard University Press, 1981.

———. *The Master Letters of Emily Dickinson*, edited by R. W. Franklin. Amherst: Amherst College Press, 1986.

———. *Poems: Third Series*, edited by Mabel Loomis Todd. Boston: Roberts Brothers, 1896.

———. *The Poems of Emily Dickinson*. 3 vols, edited by Thomas H. Johnson. Cambridge, Mass.: Belknap Press of Harvard University Press, 1951–1955.

Dillingham, William B. *An Artist in the Rigging: The Early Work of Herman Melville*. Athens.: University of Georgia Press, 1972.

———. *Melville's Later Novels*. Athens: University of Georgia Press, 1986.

Dimock, Wai-chee. *Empire For Liberty: Melville and the Poetics of Individualism*. Princeton, N.J.: Princeton University Press, 1989.

Dix, Otto. *Der Krieg*. 1924. In *Bellum: Two Statements on the Nature of War*, plates 1–50. Barre, Mass.: Imprint Society, 1972.

Douglas [Wood], Ann. "The 'Scribbling Women' and Fanny Fern: Why Women Wrote." *American Quarterly* 23 (1971): 3–24.

Douglas, Ann. *The Feminization of American Culture*. New York: Alfred A. Knopf, 1977.

Douglass, Frederick. "The Claims of the Negro Ethnologically Considered." Address delivered at Western Reserve College, July 12, 1854. In *The Life and Writings of Frederick Douglass*, 4 vols., edited by Philip S. Foner. Vol. 2: 289–309. New York: International Publishers, 1950.

———. "The Heroic Slave." 1853. In *Three Classic African-American Novels*, edited by William L. Andrews, 23–69. New York: Mentor, 1990.

———. *My Bondage and My Freedom*. 1855. Reprint. New York: Dover Publications, 1969.

———. *Narrative of the Life of Frederick Douglass*. 1845. In *The Classic Slave Narratives*, edited by Henry Louis Gates, Jr., 243–331. New York: Mentor, 1987.

Draper, John William. *Human Physiology, Statical and Dynamical; or, The Conditions and Course of the Life of Man*. 1856. 2d ed. New York: Harper and Brothers, 1858.

Dresner, Zita Z. "Sentiment and Humor: A Double-Pronged Attack on Women's Place in Nineteenth-Century America." *Studies in American Humor* 4 (1985): 18–29.

Dryden, Edgar A. "The Entangled Text: *Pierre* and the Problem of Reading." *Boundary 2*, vol. 7, no. 3, part 2 (1979): 145–73.

———. *Melville's Thematics of Form: The Great Art of Telling the Truth*. Baltimore: Johns Hopkins University Press, 1968.

Duban, James. "Chipping with a Chisel: The Ideology of Melville's Narrators." *Texas Studies in Literature and Language* 31 (1989): 341–85.

———. *Melville's Major Fiction: Politics, Theology, and Imagination*. DeKalb: Northern Illinois University Press, 1983.

Dunn, Waldo H. *The Life of Donald G. Mitchell (Ik Marvel)*. New York: Charles Scribner's Sons, 1922.

Eagleton, Terry. *Ideology: An Introduction*. New York: Verso, 1991.

———. *Walter Benjamin, or, Towards a Revolutionary Criticism*. London and New York: Verso, 1981.

Edwards, Jonathan. *A Treatise Concerning the Religious Affections*. 1746. Vol. 2 of *The Works of Jonathan Edwards*, edited by John E. Smith. New Haven, Conn.: Yale University Press, 1959.

Ellis, William. *Polynesian Researches, during a Residence of Nearly Eight Years in the Society and Sandwich Islands*. 4 vols. New York: J. & J. Harper, 1833.

Emerson, Ralph Waldo. *Essays and Lectures*, edited by Joel Porte. New York: Library of America, 1983.

Emery, Allan Moore. "'Benito Cereno' and Manifest Destiny." *Nineteenth-Century Literature* 39 (1984): 48–68.

———. "The Topicality of Depravity in 'Benito Cereno.'" *American Literature* 55 (1983): 316–31.

Erkkila, Betsy. *Whitman the Political Poet*. New York: Oxford University Press, 1989.

Evelev, John. "'Made in the Marquesas': *Typee*, Tattooing and Melville's

Critique of the Literary Marketplace." *Arizona Quarterly* 48, no. 4 (Winter 1992): 29–45.

Everett, Edward. "Fourth of July at Lowell." In *Orations and Speeches on Various Occasions.* 9th ed. 4 vols. Vol. 2: 47–68. Boston: Little, Brown, and Company, 1878.

Farrison, William Edward. Notes to *Clotel; or, The President's Daughter,* by William Wells Brown. New York: Carol Publishing Group, 1969.

Ferguson, Robert A. *Law and Letters in American Culture.* Cambridge, Mass.: Harvard University Press, 1984.

Fern, Fanny [Sara Willis Parton]. *Fern Leaves from Fanny's Port-Folio.* Auburn, N.Y.: Derby and Miller, 1853.

———. *Fern Leaves from Fanny's Port-Folio: Second Series.* Auburn and Buffalo, N.Y.: Miller, Orton & Mulligan, 1854.

———. *Fresh Leaves.* New York: Mason Brothers, 1857.

———. *Ruth Hall: A Domestic Tale of the Present Time.* 1855. In *Ruth Hall and Other Writings,* edited by Joyce W. Warren, 1–211. New Brunswick, N.J.: Rutgers University Press, 1986.

Fisher, Philip. *Hard Facts: Setting and Form in the American Novel.* New York: Oxford University Press, 1987.

Fisk, Theophilus. "Capital Against Labor. An Address delivered at Julien Hall before the mechanics of Boston on Wednesday evening, May 20, 1835." In *Social Theories of Jacksonian Democracy: Representative Writings of the Period,* edited by Joseph L. Blau, 199–207. New York: Bobbs-Merrill Company, 1954.

Fitzhugh, George. *Cannibals All! or, Slaves Without Masters.* 1857. Edited by C. Vann Woodward. Cambridge, Mass.: Belknap Press of Harvard University Press, 1960.

Foner, Eric. "Workers and Slavery." In *Working for Democracy: American Workers from the Revolution to the Present,* edited by Paul Buhle and Alan Dawley, 21–28. Urbana and Chicago: University of Illinois Press, 1985.

Foucault, Michel. *Discipline and Punish: The Birth of the Prison,* translated by Alan Sheridan. New York: Vintage Books, 1979.

———. *The History of Sexuality,* vol. 1: *An Introduction,* translated by Robert Hurley. New York: Vintage Books, 1980.

———. *The Order of Things: An Archaeology of the Human Sciences: A translation of "Les Mots et les choses."* New York: Vintage Books, 1973.

Fowler, O. S., and L. N. Fowler. *The Illustrated Self-Instructor in Phrenology and Physiology, with One Hundred Engravings, and a Chart of the Character.* New York: Fowlers and Wells, 1852.

Franchot, Jenny. "The Punishment of Esther: Frederick Douglass and the Construction of the Feminine." In *Frederick Douglass: New Literary and Historical Essays,* edited by Eric J. Sundquist, 141–65. New York: Cambridge University Press, 1990.

Frank, Stuart M. *Herman Melville's Picture Gallery: Sources and Types of the "Pictorial" Chapters of "Moby-Dick."* Fairhaven, Mass.: Edward J. Lefkowicz, 1986.

Franklin, H. Bruce. *Prison Literature in America: The Victim as Criminal and Artist*. New York: Oxford University Press, 1989.

Fredericks, Nancy. *Melville's Art of Democracy*. Athens: University of Georgia Press, 1995.

Frederickson, George M. *The Black Image in the White Mind: The Debate on Afro-American Character and Destiny, 1817–1914*. New York: Harper and Row, 1971.

Freeman, John. *Herman Melville*. London: Macmillan, 1926.

Fried, Michael. *Realism, Writing, and Disfiguration: On Thomas Eakins and Stephen Crane*. Chicago: University of Chicago Press, 1987.

Frye, Northrop. *Anatomy of Criticism: Four Essays*. Princeton, N.J.: Princeton University Press, 1957.

Frye, Roland Mushat. *The Renaissance Hamlet: Issues and Responses in 1600*. Princeton, N.J.: Princeton University Press, 1984.

Fuller, Margaret. *Woman in the Nineteenth Century*. 1845. Reprint, edited by Madeleine B. Stern and Joel Myerson. Columbia: University of South Carolina Press, 1980.

Furrow, Sharon. "The Terrible Made Visible: Melville, Salvator Rosa, and Piranesi." *ESQ* 73 (1973): 237–53.

Gallagher, Catherine. *The Industrial Reformation of English Fiction: Social Discourse and Narrative Form, 1832–1867*. Chicago: University of Chicago Press, 1985.

Gállego, Julián, and José Gudiol. *Zurbarán: 1598–1664*. New York: Rizzoli International Publishers, 1977.

Gates, Henry Louis, Jr. "Why Now?" *New Republic*, 31 October 1994, 10.

Geary, Susan. "The Domestic Novel as a Commercial Commodity: Making a Best Seller in the 1850s." *Papers of the Bibliographic Society of America* 70 (1976): 365–93.

Genovese, Eugene D. *The World the Slaveholders Made: Two Essays in Interpretation*. New York: Pantheon Books, 1969.

Gerlach, John. "Messianic Nationalism in the Early Works of Herman Melville: Against Perry Miller." *Arizona Quarterly* 28 (1972): 5–26.

Gilmore, Michael T. *American Romanticism and the Marketplace*. Chicago: University of Chicago Press, 1985.

Giltrow, Janet. "Speaking Out: Travel and Structure in Herman Melville's Early Narratives." *American Literature* 52 (1980): 18–32.

Glenn, Myra C. *Campaigns Against Corporal Punishment: Prisoners, Sailors, Women, and Children in Antebellum America*. Albany: State University of New York Press, 1984.

———. "The Naval Reform Campaign Against Flogging: A Case Study in Changing Attitudes Toward Corporal Punishment, 1830–50." *American Quarterly* 35 (1983): 408–25.

Glickstein, Jonathan. "'Poverty Is Not Slavery': American Abolitionists and the Competitive Labor Market." In *Antislavery Reconsidered: New Perspectives on the Abolitionists*, edited by Lewis Perry and Michael Fellman, 195–218. Baton Rouge: Louisiana State University Press, 1979.

Goldberg, David Theo, ed. *Anatomy of Racism*. Minneapolis: University of Minnesota Press, 1990.

Gombrich, E. H. "The Renaissance Theory of Art and the Rise of Landscape." In *Norm and Form: Studies in the Art of the Renaissance*, 107–21. London: Phaidon, 1966.

Goshgarian, G. M. *To Kiss the Chastening Rod: Domestic Fiction and Sexual Ideology in the American Renaissance*. Ithaca, N.Y.: Cornell University Press, 1992.

Gould, Stephen Jay. *The Mismeasure of Man*. New York: W. W. Norton, 1981.

Gramsci, Antonio. *Selections from the Prison Notebooks,* translated and edited by Quintin Hoare and Geoffrey Nowell Smith. New York: International Publishers, 1971.

Gray, Thomas. "Confessions of Nat Turner." 1831. In *The Nat Turner Rebellion: The Historical Event and the Modern Controversy*, edited by John B. Duff and Peter M. Mitchell, 11–30. New York: Harper and Row, 1971.

Gredja, Edward S. *The Common Continent of Men: Racial Equality in the Writings of Herman Melville*. Port Washington, N.Y.: Kennikat Press, 1974.

Greenberg, Robert M. "Cetology: Center of Multiplicity and Discord in *Moby-Dick*." *ESQ* 27 (1981): 1–13.

Greenblatt, Stephen. *Renaissance Self-Fashioning: From More to Shakespeare*. Chicago: University of Chicago Press, 1980.

Gretchko. John M. J. "Melville at the New-York Gallery of the Fine Arts." *Melville Society Extracts* 82 (1990): 7–8.

Grimké, Sarah. "Letter VIII: The Condition of Women in the United States." 1838. In *Letters on the Equality of the Sexes and the Condition of Women and Other Essays*, edited by Elizabeth Ann Bartlett, 56–61. New Haven, Conn.: Yale University Press, 1988.

Groh, Dieter, and Rolf-Peter Sieferle. "Experience of Nature in Bourgeois Society and Economic Theory: Outlines of an Interdisciplinary Research Project," translated by Peter Vintilla. *Social Research* 47 (1980): 557–81.

Guenebault, J. H. *Natural History of the Negro Race, Extracted from the French of J. J. Virey*. Charleston, S.C.: D. J. Dowling, 1837.

Haak, Bob. *The Golden Age: Dutch Painters of the Seventeenth Century*. New York: H. N. Abrams, 1984.

Hall, Elton W., ed. *Sperm Whaling from New Bedford: Clifford W. Ashley's photographs of Bark Sunbeam in 1904*. New Bedford: Old Dartmouth Historical Society, 1982.

Haltunnen, Karen. *Confidence Men and Painted Women: A Study of Middle-class Culture in America, 1830–1870*. New Haven, Conn.: Yale University Press, 1982.

Handy, E. S. Craighill. *The Native Culture in the Marquesas*. Honolulu: Bernice P. Bishop Museum, 1923.

Handy, Willowdean C. *Tattooing in the Marquesas*. Honolulu: Bernice P. Bishop Museum, 1922.

Harris, Neil. *Humbug: The Art of P. T. Barnum*. Boston: Little, Brown and Company, 1973.

Harris, Susan K. *19th-Century Women's Novels: Interpretive Strategies.* New York: Cambridge University Press, 1990.

Hawthorne, Nathaniel. *The Blithedale Romance.* 1852. Edited by Seymour Gross and Rosalie Murphy. New York: W. W. Norton, 1978.

———. *The Scarlet Letter.* 1850. Edited by Seymour Gross, Sculley Bradley, Richmond Croom Beatty, and E. Hudson Long. 3d ed. New York: W. W. Norton, 1988.

———. *Tales and Sketches.* Edited by Roy Harvey Pearce. New York: Library of America, 1982.

Hayford, Harrison. Historical Note to *Moby-Dick; or, The Whale,* by Herman Melville. Vol. 6 of *The Writings of Herman Melville,* edited by Harrison Hayford, Hershel Parker, and G. Thomas Tanselle, 581–87, 648–59. Evanston and Chicago: Northwestern University Press and the Newberry Library, 1988.

———. "Two New Letters of Herman Melville." *ELH* 2 (1944): 76–83.

———. "Unnecessary Duplicates: A Key to the Writing of *Moby-Dick.*" In *New Perspectives on Melville,* edited by Faith Pullin, 128–61. Kent, Ohio: Kent State University Press, 1978.

Heath, William. "Melville and Marquesan Eroticism." *Massachusetts Review* 29 (1988): 43–65.

Hedges, William. Introduction to *The Sketch Book of Geoffrey Crayon, Gent.,* by Washington Irving. New York: Penguin, 1988.

Hegel, G. W. F. *The Phenomenology of Mind.* 1807. Translated by J. B. Baillie. Introduction by George Lichtheim. New York: Harper and Row, 1967.

Heimert, Alan. "*Moby-Dick* and American Political Symbolism," *American Quarterly* 15 (1963): 498–534.

Herbert, T. Walter, Jr. *Marquesan Encounters: Melville and the Meaning of Civilization.* Cambridge, Mass.: Harvard University Press, 1980.

Hickey, Maureen Johnson, and William T. Oedel. *A Return to Arcadia: Nineteenth Century Berkshire County Landscapes.* Pittsfield, Mass.: Berkshire Museum, 1990.

Higgins, Brian, and Hershel Parker. eds. *Critical Essays on Herman Melville's "Pierre; or, The Ambiguities."* Boston: G. K. Hall, 1983.

———. "The Flawed Grandeur of Melville's *Pierre.*" In *New Perspectives on Melville,* edited by Faith Pullin, 162–96. Kent, Ohio: Kent State University Press, 1978.

———. "Reading *Pierre.*" In *A Companion to Melville Studies,* edited by John Bryant, 211–39. New York: Greenwood Press, 1986.

Hillway, Tyrus. "Melville's Use of Two Pseudo-Sciences." *Modern Language Notes* 64, no. 3 (1949): 145–50.

Hipple, Walter John, Jr. *The Beautiful, the Sublime, and the Picturesque in Eighteenth-Century British Aesthetic Theory.* Carbondale: Southern Illinois University Press, 1957.

Hirsch, David H. *Reality and Idea in the Early American Novel.* The Hague: Mouton, 1971.

An Historical Account of the Circumnavigation of the Globe, and of the

Progress of Discovery in the Pacific Ocean, from the Voyage of Magellan to the Death of Cook. New York: Harper and Brothers, 1837.

Holder, Alan. "Style and Tone in Melville's *Pierre.*" *ESQ* 60 (1970): 76–86.

The Home Book of the Picturesque: or American Scenery, Art, and Literature. 1852. Reprint, introduction by Motley F. Deakin. Gainesville, Fla.: Scholars' Facsimiles & Reprints, 1967.

Honour, Hugh. *The Image of the Black in Western Art,* vol. 4: *From the American Revolution to World War I.* Part 1: *Slaves and Liberators;* part 2: *Black Models and White Myths.* Houston: Menil Foundation, 1989.

Hopkins, Pauline. "Venus and the Apollo Modeled from Ethiopians." *Colored American Magazine* 6 (1903): 465.

Horsman, Reginald. *Josiah Nott of Mobile: Southerner, Physician, and Racial Theorist.* Baton Rouge: Louisiana State University Press, 1987.

———. *Race and Manifest Destiny: The Origins of American Racial Anglo-Saxonism.* Cambridge, Mass.: Harvard University Press, 1981.

Howard, Leon. *Herman Melville: A Biography.* Berkeley: University of California Press, 1951.

———. Historical Note to *Pierre; or, The Ambiguities,* by Herman Melville. Vol. 7 of *The Writings of Herman Melville,* edited by Harrison Hayford, Hershel Parker, and G. Thomas Tanselle, 365–79. Evanston and Chicago: Northwestern University Press and the Newberry Library, 1987.

———. Historical Note to *Typee: A Peep at Polynesian Life,* by Herman Melville. Vol. 1 of *The Writings of Herman Melville,* edited by Harrison Hayford, Hershel Parker, and G. Thomas Tanselle, 277–302. Evanston and Chicago: Northwestern University Press and the Newberry Library, 1968.

———. "Melville's Struggle with the Angel." *Modern Language Quarterly* 1 (1940): 195–206.

———. *The Unfolding of Moby-Dick: Essays in Evidence (a fragment),* edited by James Barbour and Thomas Quirk. Glassboro, N.J.: Melville Society, 1987.

Howat, John K., ed. *American Paradise: The World of the Hudson River School.* New York: Metropolitan Museum of Art, 1987.

Hulme, Peter. *Colonial Encounters: Europe and the Native Caribbean, 1492–1797.* London: Methuen, 1986.

———. "Making No Bones: A Response to Myra Jehlen." *Critical Inquiry* 20 (1993): 179–86.

Humboldt, Alexander von. *Cosmos: A Sketch of a Physical Description of the Universe.* 2 vols, translated by E. C. Otté. New York: Harper and Brothers, 1851.

Hungerford, Edward. "Poe and Phrenology." *American Literature* 2 (1930): 209–31.

———. "Walt Whitman and his Chart of Bumps." *American Literature* 2 (1931): 350–84.

Husni, Khalil. "The Whiteness of the Whale: A Survey of Interpretations, 1851–1970." *College Language Association Journal* 20 (1976): 210–21.

Hussey, Christopher. *The Picturesque: Studies in a Point of View.* London: Putnam, 1927.

Ignatiev, Noel. *How the Irish Became White*. New York: Routledge, 1995.

Irving, Washington. *The Sketch Book of Geoffrey Crayon, Gent.* 1819–1820. In *History, Tales, and Sketches,* edited by James W. Tuttleton, 731–1091. New York: Library of America, 1983.

Irwin, John T. *American Hieroglyphics: The Symbol of the Egyptian Hieroglyphics in the American Renaissance*. Baltimore: Johns Hopkins University Press, 1980.

"Is Man One or Many?" *Putnam's Monthly Magazine* 4 (1854): 1–14.

Jackson, Andrew. "Second Annual Message." December 6, 1830. In *A Compilation of the Messages and Papers of the Presidents, 1789–1897,* edited by James D. Richardson, vol. 2: 500–529. Washington, D.C.: Government Printing Office, 1899.

Jacobs, Harriet A. *Incidents in the Life of A Slave Girl, Written by Herself.* 1861. Edited by Jean Fagan Yellin. Cambridge, Mass.: Harvard University Press, 1987.

Jaggar, Alison M. "Love and Knowledge: Emotion in Feminist Epistemology." In *Gender/Body/Knowledge: Feminist Reconstructions of Being and Knowing,* edited by Alison M. Jaggar and Susan R. Bordo, 145–71. New Brunswick, N.J.: Rutgers University Press, 1989.

James, C. L. R. *Mariners, Renegades and Castaways: The Story of Herman Melville and the World We Live In.* 1953. Reprint, with deletions and afterword. London and New York: Allison and Busby, 1985.

Jefferson, Thomas. *Notes on the State of Virginia.* 1787. In *Writings,* edited by Merrill D. Peterson, 123–325. New York: Library of America, 1984.

Jehlen, Myra. *American Incarnation: The Individual, the Nation, and the Continent.* Cambridge, Mass.: Harvard University Press, 1986.

———. "History before the Fact; or, Captain John Smith's Unfinished Symphony." *Critical Inquiry* 19 (1993): 677–92.

———. "Response to Peter Hulme." *Critical Inquiry* 20 (1993): 187–91.

Johnson, Barbara. *The Critical Difference: Essays in the Contemporary Rhetoric of Reading.* Baltimore: Johns Hopkins University Press, 1980.

Jordan, Winthrop D. *White over Black: American Attitudes Toward the Negro, 1550–1812.* New York: W. W. Norton, 1977.

Kallich, Martin. "The Association of Ideas and Critical Theory: Hobbes, Locke, and Addison." *ELH* 12 (1945): 290–315.

Kaplan, Fred. *Sacred Tears: Sentimentality in Victorian Literature.* Princeton, N.J.: Princeton University Press, 1987.

Kaplan, Sidney. "Herman Melville and the American National Sin: The Meaning of 'Benito Cereno.'" *Journal of Negro History* 41 (1956): 311–38; and 42 (1957): 11–37.

Karcher, Carolyn L. "Censorship, American Style: The Case of Lydia Maria Child." In *Studies in the American Renaissance* (1986), edited by Joel Myerson, 283–303. Charlottesville: University Press of Virginia, 1986.

———. *The First Woman in the Republic: A Cultural Biography of Lydia Maria Child.* Durham, N.C.: Duke University Press, 1994.

———. *Shadow over the Promised Land: Slavery, Race, and Violence in Melville's America.* Baton Rouge: Louisiana State University Press, 1980.

Katz, Leslie. "Flesh of His Flesh: Amputation in *Moby-Dick* and S. W. Mitchell's Medical Papers." *Genders* 4 (1989): 1–10.

Kearns, Michael S. "Interpreting Intentional Incoherence: Towards a Disambiguation of Melville's *Pierre; or, The Ambiguities.*" *Bulletin of the Midwest Modern Language Association* 16 (1983): 34–54.

Kelley, Mary. *Private Woman, Public Stage: Literary Domesticity in Nineteenth-Century America.* New York: Oxford University Press, 1984.

Kern, Alexander C. "Melville's *The Confidence-Man*: A Structure of Satire." In *American Humor: Essays Presented to John C. Gerber,* edited by O. M. Brack, Jr., 27–41. Scottsdale, Ariz.: Arete Publications, 1977.

Kiekhaefer, Phillip. "Cover for a Docile Body: Discipline, Strategy, and the Tactics of Everyday Life in Melville's *White-Jacket.*" Paper. University of California, Berkeley, 1992.

Kime, Wayne R. *Donald G. Mitchell.* Boston: Twayne Publishers, 1985.

Kirk, Eugene P. *Menippean Satire: An Annotated Catalogue of Texts and Criticism.* New York: Garland Publishing, 1980.

Knight, Richard Payne. *An Analytical Inquiry into the Principles of Taste.* London: T. Payne and J. White, 1805.

Knox, Robert. *The Races of Men: A Fragment.* Philadelphia: Lea and Blanchard, 1850.

Kolodny, Annette. *The Lay of the Land: Metaphor as Experience and History in American Life and Letters.* Chapel Hill: University of North Carolina Press, 1975.

Kopley, Richard. "Sendak on Melville: An Interview." *Melville Society Extracts* 87 (1991): 1–6.

Krusenstern, A. J. von. *Voyage round the World, in the Years 1803, 1804, 1805, and 1806.* 2 vols. London: Printed by C. Roworth for John Murray, 1813.

Lackey, Kris. "The Despotic Victim: Gender and Imagination in *Pierre.*" *American Transcendental Quarterly* New Series 4 (1990): 67–76.

Langsdorff, G. H. von. *Voyages and Travels in Various Parts of the World, during the Years 1803, 1804, 1805, 1806, and 1807.* 2 vols. London: Printed for Henry Colburn, 1813–1814.

Laqueur, Thomas. *Making Sex: Body and Gender from the Greeks to Freud.* Cambridge, Mass.: Harvard University Press, 1990.

Lavater, John Caspar [Johann Kaspar]. *Essays on Physiognomy: Designed to Promote the Knowledge and the Love of Mankind.* 1775–1778. 5th ed. Translated by Thomas Holcroft. London: William Tegg, 1848.

Lawrence, D. H. *Studies in Classic American Literature.* New York: Penguin, 1977.

Lee, A. Robert. "*Moby-Dick* as Anatomy." In *Herman Melville: Reassessments,* edited by A. Robert Lee, 68–89. Totowa, N.J.: Barnes and Noble, 1984.

Leech, Samuel. *Thirty Years from Home, or a Voice from the Main Deck, being the Experience of Samuel Leech, who was for Six Years in the British and American Navies: was captured in the British Frigate Macedonian: afterwards entered the American Navy, and was taken in the United States Brig Syren, by the British Ship Medway.* Boston: Tappan and Dennet, 1843.

Leggett, William. *Naval Stories.* New York: G. & C. & H. Carvill, 1834.

Leverenz, David. *Manhood and the American Renaissance.* Ithaca, N.Y.: Cornell University Press, 1989.

Levine, Robert S. *Conspiracy and Romance: Studies in Brockden Brown, Cooper, Hawthorne, and Melville.* New York: Cambridge University Press, 1989.

―――. "Disturbing Boundaries: Temperance, Black Elevation, and Violence in Frank J. Webb's *The Garies and Their Friends.*" *Prospects* 19 (1994): 349–73.

Levy, Leonard W. *The Law of the Commonwealth and Chief Justice Shaw.* Cambridge, Mass.: Harvard University Press, 1957.

Lewis, R. W. B. *The American Adam: Innocence, Tragedy, and Tradition in the Nineteenth Century.* Chicago: University of Chicago Press, 1955.

Leyda, Jay. *The Melville Log: A Documentary Life of Herman Melville, 1819–1891.* 2 vols. 1951. Reprint with supplement. New York: Gordian Press, 1969.

Lippard, George. *The Quaker City; or, the Monks of Monk Hall: A Romance of Philadelphia Life, Mystery, and Crime.* 1845. Edited by David S. Reynolds. Amherst: University of Massachusetts Press, 1995.

Littlefield, Daniel F., Jr. Introduction to *A Sketch of the Life of Okah Tubbee,* by Laah Ceil Manatoi Elaah Tubbee. Lincoln: University of Nebraska Press, 1988.

Locke, John. *An Essay Concerning Human Understanding.* 1690. Edited by Peter H. Nidditch. Oxford: Oxford University Press, 1975.

Lockwood, John A. "Flogging in the Navy." *The United States Magazine, and Democratic Review* 25 (1849): 97–115, 225–242, 318–38, 417–32, 538–43.

Loeffelholz, Mary. *Dickinson and the Boundaries of Feminist Theory.* Urbana and Chicago: University of Illinois Press, 1989.

Lott, Eric. *Love and Theft: Blackface Minstrelsy and the American Working Class.* New York: Oxford University Press, 1993.

Lowell, James Russell. "The Prejudice of Color." In *The Anti-Slavery Papers of James Russell Lowell.* 2 vols. Vol. 2: 16–22. Boston: Houghton Mifflin, 1902.

Lucid, Robert F. "The Influence of *Two Years Before the Mast* on Herman Melville." *American Literature* 31 (1959): 243–56.

Mackenzie, Henry. *The Man of Feeling.* 1771. Introduction by Kenneth C. Slagle. New York: W. W. Norton, 1958.

Mansfield, Luther S., and Howard P. Vincent. Notes to *Moby-Dick,* by Herman Melville. New York: Hendricks House, 1952.

Markels, Julian. "The *Moby-Dick* White Elephant." *American Literature* 66 (1994): 105–22.

Markley, Robert. "Sentiment as Performance: Shaftesbury, Sterne, and the Theatrics of Virtue." In *The New Eighteenth Century: Theory, Politics, English Literature,* edited by Felicity Nussbaum and Laura Brown, 210–30. New York and London: Methuen, 1987.

Marshall, David. *The Figure of Theater: Shaftesbury, Defoe, Adam Smith, and George Eliot.* New York: Columbia University Press, 1986.

———. *The Surprising Effects of Sympathy: Marivaux, Diderot, Rousseau, and Mary Shelley.* Chicago: University of Chicago Press, 1988.

Martin, Charles, and James Snead. "Reading Through Blackness: Colorless Signifiers in 'Benito Cereno.'" *Yale Journal of Criticism* 4, no. 1 (1990), 231–51.

Martin, Robert K. *Hero, Captain, and Stranger: Male Friendship, Social Critique, and Literary Form in the Sea Novels of Herman Melville.* Chapel Hill: University of North Carolina Press, 1986.

Martin, Terence. *The Instructed Vision: Scottish Common Sense Philosophy and the Origins of American Fiction.* Bloomington: Indiana University Press, 1961.

Martin, Waldo S., Jr. *The Mind of Frederick Douglass.* Chapel Hill: University of North Carolina Press, 1984.

Matthiessen, F. O. *American Renaissance: Art and Expression in the Age of Emerson and Whitman.* New York: Oxford University Press, 1941.

Mattison, H. *Louisa Picquet, The Octoroon: A Tale of Southern Slave Life.* 1861. Reprinted in *Collected Black Women's Narratives.* Introduction by Anthony G. Barthelemy. New York: Oxford University Press, 1988.

McCarthy, Paul. "Elements of Anatomy in Melville's Fiction." *Studies in the Novel* 6 (1974): 38–61.

McCoubrey, John W., ed. *American Art, 1700–1960: Sources and Documents.* Englewood Cliffs, N.J.: Prentice-Hall, 1965.

McDowell, Deborah E. "In the First Place: Making Frederick Douglass and the Afro-American Narrative Tradition." In *African American Autobiography: A Collection of Critical Essays,* edited by William L. Andrews, 36–58. Englewood Cliffs, N.J.: Prentice Hall, 1993.

McNally, William. *Evils and Abuses in the Naval and Merchant Service Exposed: with Proposals for Their Remedy and Redress.* Boston: Cassady and March, 1839.

Mead, Margaret. *An Inquiry Into the Question of Cultural Stability in Polynesia.* New York: Columbia University Press, 1928.

Melville, Herman. *Battle-Pieces and Aspects of the War.* 1866. Reprint, introduction by Sidney Kaplan. Amherst: University of Massachusetts Press, 1972.

———. *Billy Budd, Sailor (An Inside Narrative),* edited by Harrison Hayford and Merton M. Sealts, Jr. Chicago: University of Chicago Press, 1962.

———. *Clarel: A Poem and Pilgrimage in the Holy Land.* 1876. Vol. 12 of *The Writings of Herman Melville,* edited by Harrison Hayford, Alma A. MacDougall, Hershel Parker, and G. Thomas Tanselle. Evanston and Chicago: Northwestern University Press and the Newberry Library, 1991.

———. *Collected Poems of Herman Melville,* edited by Howard P. Vincent. Chicago: Hendricks House, 1947.

———. *The Confidence-Man: His Masquerade.* 1857. Vol. 10 of *The Writings of Herman Melville,* edited by Harrison Hayford, Hershel Parker, and G. Thomas Tanselle. Evanston and Chicago: Northwestern University Press and the Newberry Library, 1984.

———. *Correspondence.* Vol. 14 of *The Writings of Herman Melville,* edited by

Lynn Horth. Evanston and Chicago: Northwestern University Press and the Newberry Library, 1993.

———. *Israel Potter: His Fifty Years of Exile.* 1855. Vol. 8 of *The Writings of Herman Melville,* edited by Harrison Hayford, Hershel Parker, and G. Thomas Tanselle. Evanston and Chicago: Northwestern University Press and the Newberry Library, 1982.

———. *Mardi: and a Voyage Thither.* 1849. Vol. 3 of *The Writings of Herman Melville,* edited by Harrison Hayford, Hershel Parker, and G. Thomas Tanselle. Evanston and Chicago: Northwestern University Press and the Newberry Library, 1970.

———. *Moby-Dick; or, The Whale.* 1851. Vol. 6 of *The Writings of Herman Melville,* edited by Harrison Hayford, Hershel Parker, and G. Thomas Tanselle. Evanston and Chicago: Northwestern University Press and the Newberry Library, 1988.

———. *Omoo: A Narrative of Adventure in the South Seas.* 1847. Vol. 2 of *The Writings of Herman Melville,* edited by Harrison Hayford, Hershel Parker, and G. Thomas Tanselle. Evanston and Chicago: Northwestern University Press and the Newberry Library, 1968.

———. *The Piazza Tales and Other Prose Pieces, 1839–1860.* Vol. 9 of *The Writings of Herman Melville,* edited by Harrison Hayford, Hershel Parker, and G. Thomas Tanselle. Evanston and Chicago: Northwestern University Press and the Newberry Library, 1987.

———. *Pierre; or, The Ambiguities.* 1852. Vol. 7 of *The Writings of Herman Melville,* edited by Harrison Hayford, Hershel Parker, and G. Thomas Tanselle. Evanston and Chicago: Northwestern University Press and The Newberry Library, 1971.

———. *Redburn: His First Voyage.* 1849. Vol. 4 of *The Writings of Herman Melville,* edited by Harrison Hayford, Hershel Parker, and G. Thomas Tanselle. Evanston and Chicago: Northwestern University Press and the Newberry Library, 1969.

———. *Typee: A Peep at Polynesian Life.* 1846. Vol. 1 of *The Writings of Herman Melville,* edited by Harrison Hayford, Hershel Parker, and G. Thomas Tanselle. Evanston and Chicago: Northwestern University Press and the Newberry Library, 1968.

———. *White-Jacket; or The World in a Man-of-War.* 1850. Vol. 5 of *The Writings of Herman Melville,* edited by Harrison Hayford, Hershel Parker, and G. Thomas Tanselle. Evanston and Chicago: Northwestern University Press and the Newberry Library, 1970.

Mercier, Henry James, and William Gallop. *Life in a Man-of-War, or Scenes in "Old Ironsides" during Her Cruise in the Pacific.* Philadelphia: Lydia R. Bailey, 1841.

Metcalf, Eleanor Melville. *Herman Melville: Cycle and Epicycle.* Cambridge, Mass.: Harvard University Press, 1953.

Meyers, William H. *Journal of a Cruise to California and the Sandwich Islands in the United States sloop-of-war "Cyane."* Introduction by John Haskell Kemble. San Francisco: Book Club of California, 1955.

———. *Sketches of California and Hawaii.* San Francisco: Book Club of California, 1970.

Michaels, Walter Benn. *Our America: Nativism, Modernism, and Pluralism.* Durham, N.C.: Duke University Press, 1995.

———. "The Souls of White Folk." In *Literature and the Body: Essays on Populations and Persons,* edited by Elaine Scarry, 185–209. Baltimore: Johns Hopkins University Press, 1988.

Michasiw, Kim Ian. "Nine Revisionist Theses on the Picturesque," *Representations* 38 (1992): 76–100.

Milder, Robert. "The Composition of *Moby-Dick*: A Review and a Prospect." *ESQ* 23 (1977): 203–16.

———. "Melville's Intentions in *Pierre*." *Studies in the Novel* 6 (1974): 186–99.

Miller, Angela. *The Empire of the Eye: Landscape Representation and American Cultural Politics, 1825–1875.* Ithaca, N.Y.: Cornell University Press, 1993.

———. "Thomas Cole and Jacksonian America: *The Course of Empire* as Political Allegory." *Prospects* 14 (1989): 65–92.

Miller, David C. *Dark Eden: The Swamp in Nineteenth-Century American Culture.* New York: Cambridge University Press, 1989.

Miller, F. DeWolfe. *Christopher Pearce Cranch and His Caricatures of New England Transcendentalism.* Cambridge, Mass.: Harvard University Press, 1951.

Miller, James E., Jr. *A Reader's Guide to Herman Melville.* New York: Farrar, Straus and Cudahy, 1962.

Miller, Perry. *The Raven and the Whale: The War of Words and Wits in the Era of Poe and Melville.* New York: Harcourt, Brace & World, 1956.

Milne, Gordon. *George William Curtis and the Genteel Tradition.* Bloomington: Indiana University Press, 1956.

Mitchell, Donald Grant ["Ik. Marvel"]. *American Lands and Letters: The Mayflower to Rip-Van-Winkle.* New York: Charles Scribner's Sons, 1897.

———. *Dream Life: A Fable of the Seasons.* 1851. New York: Charles Scribner, 1852.

———. *Reveries of a Bachelor: or, A Book of the Heart.* 1850. New York: Baker & Scribner, 1851.

Montaigne, Michel. *The Complete Essays of Montaigne.* Translated by Donald M. Frame. Stanford, Calif.: Stanford University Press, 1958.

———. *Essais de Michel de Montaigne: Texte Original de 1580 avec les variantes des éditions de 1582 et 1587.* 2 vols. Bordeaux: Féret et Fils, 1870.

Moore, Richard S. *That Cunning Alphabet: Melville's Aesthetics of Nature.* Amsterdam: Rodopi, 1982.

Morgan, Edmund. *American Slavery/American Freedom: The Ordeal of Colonial Virginia.* New York: W. W. Norton, 1975.

———. *Visible Saints: The History of a Puritan Idea.* New York: New York University Press, 1963.

Morris, Richard B. "Insurrection in Massachusetts." In *America in Crisis: Four-*

teen Crucial Episodes in American History, edited by Daniel Aaron, 21–49. New York: Alfred A. Knopf, 1952.

Morrison, Toni. *Beloved.* New York: Alfred A. Knopf, 1987.

———. *Playing in the Dark: Whiteness and the Literary Imagination.* Cambridge, Mass.: Harvard University Press, 1992.

———. "Unspeakable Things Unspoken: The Afro-American Presence in American Literature." *Michigan Quarterly Review* 28 (1989): 1–34.

Morton, Samuel George. *Crania Ægyptiaca; or, Observations on Egyptian Ethnography, Derived from Anatomy, History and the Monuments.* Philadelphia: John Penington, 1844.

———. *Crania Americana; or, A Comparative View of the Skulls of Various Aboriginal Nations of North and South America: to which is Prefixed an Essay on the Varieties of the Human Species.* Philadelphia: J. Dobson, 1839.

Mullan, John. *Sentiment and Sociability: The Language of Feeling in the Eighteenth Century.* Oxford: Clarendon Press, 1988.

Mumford, Lewis. *Herman Melville.* New York: Harcourt, Brace, 1929.

Murray, Henry. Introduction and notes to *Pierre; or, The Ambiguities*, by Herman Melville. New York: Hendricks House, 1949.

Mushabac, Jane. *Melville's Humor: A Critical Study.* Hamden, Conn.: Archon Books, 1981.

Myers, Kenneth. *The Catskills: Painters, Writers, and Tourists in the Mountains, 1820–95.* Yonkers, N.Y.: Hudson River Museum of Westchester, 1987.

Nelson, Dana D. "The Haunting of White Manhood: Poe, Fraternal Ritual, and Polygenesis." *American Literature* 69 (1997): 515–46.

Nixon, Nicola. "Compromising Politics and Herman Melville's *Pierre.*" *American Literature* 69 (1997): 719–41.

Northup, Solomon. *Twelve Years a Slave: Narrative of Solomon Northup.* 1853. In *Puttin' On Ole Massa*, edited by Gilbert Osofsky, 225–406. New York: Harper Torchbooks, 1969.

Norton, Anne. *Alternative Americas: A Reading of Antebellum Political Culture.* Chicago: University of Chicago Press, 1986.

Nott, J. C., and George R. Gliddon. *Types of Mankind: or, Ethnological Researches, Based upon the Ancient Monuments, Paintings, Sculptures, and Crania of Races, and upon their Natural, Geographical, Philological, and Biblical History.* 1854. Reprint. Miami: Mnemosyne, 1969.

Nygren, Edward J. *Views and Visions: American Landscape Before 1830.* Washington, D.C.: Corcoran Gallery of Art, 1986.

Obeyesekere, Gananath. "'British Cannibals': Contemplation of an Event in the Death and Resurrection of James Cook, Explorer." *Critical Inquiry* 18 (1992): 630–54.

O'Brien, Fitz-James. "Our Authors and Authorship: Melville and Curtis." *Putnam's Monthly Magazine* 9 (1857): 384–93.

———. "Our Young Authors: Melville." *Putnam's Monthly Magazine* 1 (1853): 155–64.

———. "Our Young Authors: Mitchell." *Putnam's Monthly Magazine* 1 (1853): 74–78.

O'Connell, Barry. Introduction to *On Our Own Ground: The Complete Writings of William Apess, a Pequot.* Amherst: University of Massachusetts Press, 1992.

O'Connell, James F. *A Residence of Eleven Years in New Holland and the Caroline Islands. Being the Adventures of James F. O'Connell. Edited from his Verbal Narration.* 1836. Edited by Saul H. Riesenberg. Honolulu: University Press of Hawaii, 1972.

Olmsted, Francis Allyn. *Incidents of a Whaling Voyage, to which are added Observations on the Scenery, Manners and Customs, and Missionary Stations of the Sandwich and Society Islands.* New York: D. Appleton, 1841.

Olson, Charles. *Call Me Ishmael: A Study of Melville.* New York: Reynal & Hitchcock, 1947.

Otter, Samuel. "The Eden of Saddle Meadows: Landscape and Ideology in *Pierre.*" *American Literature* 66 (1994): 55–81.

Pancost, David. "Donald Grant Mitchell's *Reveries of a Bachelor* and Herman Melville's 'I and My Chimney.'" *American Transcendental Quarterly* 42 (1979): 129–36.

Papashvily, Helen Waite. *All the Happy Endings: A Study of the Domestic Novel in America, the Women Who Wrote It, the Women Who Read It, in the Nineteenth Century.* New York: Harper, 1956.

Parker, Hershel. *Herman Melville: A Biography,* vol. 1: *1819–1851.* Baltimore: Johns Hopkins University Press, 1996.

———. Historical Note to *Moby-Dick; or, The Whale,* by Herman Melville. Vol. 6 of *The Writings of Herman Melville,* edited by Harrison Hayford, Hershel Parker, and G. Thomas Tanselle, 587–647, 659–756. Evanston and Chicago: Northwestern University Press and the Newberry Library, 1988.

———. "Melville and the Berkshires: Emotion-Laden Terrain, 'Reckless Sky-Assaulting Mood,' and Encroaching Wordsworthianism." In *American Literature: The New England Heritage,* edited by James Nagel and Richard Astro, 65–80. New York: Garland, 1980.

———. "Melville and Politics: A Scrutiny of the Political Milieux of Herman Melville's Life and Works." Ph.D. diss., Northwestern University, 1963.

———, ed. *Pierre; or, the Ambiguities: The Kraken Edition.* Illustrated by Maurice Sendak. New York: HarperCollins, 1995.

———. "Why *Pierre* Went Wrong." *Studies in the Novel* 8 (1976): 7–23.

Pattee, Fred Lewis. *The Feminine Fifties.* New York: D. Appleton-Century, 1940.

Patterson, Henry S. "Memoir of the Life and Scientific Labors of Samuel George Morton." In *Types of Mankind,* by Josiah C. Nott and George R. Gliddon, xvii–lvii. 1854. Reprint. Miami: Mnemosyne, 1969.

Pease, William H., and Jane H. Pease, eds. *The Anti-Slavery Argument.* Indianapolis: Bobbs-Merrill, 1965.

Pennington, James W. C. *The Fugitive Blacksmith.* 1849. Reprinted in *Five Slave Narratives,* edited by William Loren Katz. New York: Arno Press and the *New York Times,* 1969.

Philbrick, Thomas. Introduction to *Two Years Before the Mast,* by Richard Henry Dana. New York: Penguin, 1986.

Poe, Edgar Allan. *Essays and Reviews,* edited by G. R. Thompson. New York: Library of America, 1984.

———. *Poetry and Tales,* edited by Patrick F. Quinn. New York: Library of America, 1984.

———. *The Narrative of Arthur Gordon Pym of Nantucket.* 1838. Edited by Harold Beaver. New York: Penguin, 1986.

———. *The Short Fiction of Edgar Allan Poe,* edited by Stuart Levine and Susan Levine. Urbana and Chicago: University of Illinois Press, 1990.

Pollin, Burton R. "Traces of Poe in Melville." *Melville Society Extracts* 109 (1997): 1–18.

Porter, Carolyn. *Seeing and Being: The Plight of the Participant Observer in Emerson, James, Adams, and Faulkner.* Middletown, Conn.: Wesleyan University Press, 1981.

Porter, David. *Journal of a Cruise Made to the Pacific Ocean, by Captain David Porter, in the United States Frigate Essex, in the Years 1812, 1813, and 1814.* 2 vols. Philadelphia: Bradford and Inskeep, 1815.

Post-Lauria, Sheila. *Correspondent Colorings: Melville in the Marketplace.* Amherst: University of Massachusetts Press, 1996.

Powell, Earl A., III. *Thomas Cole.* New York: Harry N. Abrams, 1990.

———. "Thomas Cole and the American Landscape Tradition: Associationism." *Arts Magazine* 52, no. 8 (1978): 113–17.

———. "Thomas Cole and the American Landscape Tradition: The Picturesque." *Arts Magazine* 52, no. 7 (1978): 110–17.

Prince, Mary. *The History of Mary Prince, a West Indian Slave. Related By Herself.* 1831. Reprinted in *Six Women's Slave Narratives.* Introduction by William Andrews. New York: Oxford University Press, 1988.

Pullin, Faith. "Melville's *Typee*: The Failure of Eden." In *New Perspectives on Melville,* edited by Faith Pullin, 1–28. Kent, Ohio: Kent State University Press, 1978.

R. T. H. "White and Black Slavery." *Southern Literary Messenger* 6 (1840): 193–200.

Railton, Stephen. *Authorship and Audience: Literary Performance in the American Renaissance.* Princeton, N.J.: Princeton University Press, 1991.

Rampersad, Arnold. "Melville and Race." In *Herman Melville: A Collection of Critical Essays,* edited by Myra Jehlen, 160–73. Englewood Cliffs, N.J.: Prentice-Hall, 1994.

Remini, Robert V. *Andrew Jackson.* New York: Twayne, 1966.

Renker, Elizabeth. *Strike through the Mask: Herman Melville and the Scene of Writing.* Baltimore: Johns Hopkins University Press, 1996.

Reynolds, David S. *Beneath the American Renaissance: The Subversive Imagination in the Age of Emerson and Melville.* New York: Alfred A. Knopf, 1988.

Reynolds, J. N. "Mocha Dick." 1839. In *Moby-Dick,* by Herman Melville, edited by Harrison Hayford and Hershel Parker, 571–90. New York: W. W. Norton, 1967.

Reynolds, Larry J. "Anti-Democratic Emphasis in *White-Jacket*." *American Literature* 48 (1976): 13–28.

Riesenberg, Saul H. "The Tattooed Irishman." *Smithsonian Journal of History* 3, no. 1 (1968): 1–17.

Rivers, Christopher. *Face Value: Physiognomical Thought and the Legible Body in Marivaux, Lavater, Gautier, and Zola*. Madison: University of Wisconsin Press, 1994.

Robertson-Lorant, Laurie. *Melville: A Biography*. New York: Clarkson Potter Publishers, 1996.

Roediger, David R. *The Wages of Whiteness: Race and the Making of the American Working Class*. New York: Verso, 1991.

Rogin, Michael Paul. *Blackface, White Noise: Jewish Immigrants in the Hollywood Melting Pot*. Berkeley: University of California Press, 1996.

———. *Fathers and Children: Andrew Jackson and the Subjugation of the American Indian*. New York: Random House, 1975.

———. *Subversive Genealogy: The Politics and Art of Herman Melville*. New York: Alfred A. Knopf, 1983.

Romero, Lora. "Domesticity and Fiction." In *The Columbia History of the American Novel*, edited by Emory Elliot, 110–29. New York: Columbia University Press, 1991.

———. "Vanishing Americans: Gender, Empire, and New Historicism." In *The Culture of Sentiment*, edited by Shirley Samuels, 115–27. New York: Oxford University Press, 1992.

Roque, Oswaldo Rodriguez. "The Exaltation of American Landscape Painting." In *American Paradise: The World of the Hudson River School*, edited by John K. Howat, 21–48. New York: Metropolitan Museum of Art, 1987.

Rowe, John Carlos. "Romancing the Stone: Melville's Critique of Ideology in *Pierre*." In *Theorizing American Literature: Hegel, the Sign, and History*, edited by Bainard Cowan and Joseph G. Kronick, 195–232. Baton Rouge: Louisiana State University Press, 1991.

Royster, Paul. "Melville's Economy of Language." In *Ideology and Classic American Literature*, edited by Sacvan Bercovitch and Myra Jehlen, 313–36. New York: Cambridge University Press, 1986.

Rush, Benjamin. "Observations Intended to Favour a Supposition That the Black Color (As It is Called) of the Negroes Is Derived from the Leprosy." Address delivered before the American Philosophical Society, July 14, 1792. In *Racial Thought in America: From the Puritans to Abraham Lincoln*, edited by Louis Ruchames, 218–25. New York: Grosset and Dunlap, 1970.

Russett, Cynthia Eagle. *Sexual Science: The Victorian Construction of Womanhood*. Cambridge, Mass.: Harvard University Press, 1989.

Said, Edward. Introduction to *Moby-Dick; or, The Whale*, by Herman Melville. New York: Vintage Books/Library of America, 1991.

Samson, John. *White Lies: Melville's Narrative of Facts*. Ithaca, N.Y.: Cornell University Press, 1989.

Samuels, Shirley, ed. *The Culture of Sentiment: Race, Gender, and Sentimentality in Nineteenth-Century America*. New York: Oxford University Press, 1992.

Sanborn, Geoffrey. "Where's the Rest of Me?: The Melancholy Death of Benito Cereno." *Arizona Quarterly* 52, no. 1 (1996): 59–93.

Sánchez-Eppler, Karen. *Touching Liberty: Abolition, Feminism, and the Politics of the Body.* Berkeley: University of California Press, 1993.

Saunders, Brian. "Melville's Sea Change: From Irving to Emerson." *Studies in the Novel* 20 (1988): 371–88.

Saunders, J. B. deC. M., and Charles D. O'Malley, eds. *The Illustrations from the Works of Andreas Vesalius of Brussels.* 1950. Reprint. New York: Dover Publications, 1970.

Saxton, Alexander. *The Rise and Fall of the White Republic: Class Politics and Mass Culture in Nineteenth-Century America.* New York: Verso, 1990.

Schiebinger, Londa. *Nature's Body: Gender in the Making of Modern Science.* Boston: Beacon Press, 1993.

Schnog, Nancy. "Inside the Sentimental: The Psychological Work of *The Wide Wide World.*" *Genders* 4 (1989): 11–25.

Schueller, Malini Johar. "Colonialism and Melville's South Sea Journeys." *Studies in American Fiction* 22 (1994): 3–18.

Schultz, Donald Deidrich. *Herman Melville and the Tradition of the Anatomy: A Study in Genre.* Ph.D. diss., Vanderbilt University, 1969.

Schultz, Elizabeth A. *Unpainted to the Last: "Moby-Dick" and Twentieth-Century American Art.* Lawrence: University Press of Kansas, 1995.

Scoresby, William, Jr. *An Account of the Arctic Regions, with a History and Description of the Northern Whale-Fishery.* 2 vols. Edinburgh: Archibald Constable, 1820.

Sealts, Merton M., Jr. Historical Note to *The Piazza Tales and Other Prose Pieces, 1839–1860.* Vol. 9 of *The Writings of Herman Melville,* edited by Harrison Hayford, Hershel Parker, and G. Thomas Tanselle, 476–514. Evanston and Chicago: Northwestern University Press and the Newberry Library, 1987.

———. *Melville as Lecturer.* Cambridge, Mass.: Harvard University Press, 1957.

Sedgwick, Catharine Maria. *Hope Leslie; or, Early Times in the Massachusetts.* 1827. Edited by Mary Kelley. New Brunswick, N.J.: Rutgers University Press, 1987.

Sedgwick, William Ellery. *Herman Melville: The Tragedy of Mind.* New York: Russell & Russell, 1944.

Sewall, Richard B. *The Life of Emily Dickinson.* 2 vols in 1. New York: Farrar, Straus and Giroux, 1980.

Sewall, Thomas. *An Examination of Phrenology; in Two Lectures.* Washington, D.C.: B. Homans, 1837.

Shaftesbury, Anthony Ashley Cooper, Earl of. *An Inquiry Concerning Virtue, or Merit.* 1699, 1714. Edited by David Walford. Manchester: Manchester University Press, 1977.

Shakespeare, William. *Hamlet, Prince of Denmark,* edited by Philip Edwards. New York: Cambridge University Press, 1985.

Shillingsburg, Peter. "The Three *Moby-Dicks.*" *American Literary History* 2 (1990): 119–130.

Shurr, William H. *The Mystery of Iniquity: Melville as Poet, 1857–1891.* Lexington: University Press of Kentucky, 1972.

Silverberg, Robert. *Mound Builders of Ancient America: The Archaeology of a Myth*. Greenwich, Conn.: New York Graphic Society, 1968.

Simms, William Gilmore. *Views and Reviews in American Literature, History and Fiction: First Series*. 1845. Edited by C. Hugh Holman. Cambridge, Mass.: Belknap Press of Harvard University Press, 1962.

Simpson, Eleanor E. "Melville and the Negro: From *Typee* to 'Benito Cereno.'" *American Literature* 41 (1969): 19–38.

Slouka, Mark Z. "Demonic History: Geography and Genealogy in *Pierre*." *ESQ* 35 (1989): 147–60.

Smith, Adam. *The Theory of Moral Sentiments*. 1759. Edited by E. G. West. Indianapolis: Liberty Classics, 1976.

Smith, J. A. "A Lecture Introductory to the Second Course of Anatomical Instruction in the College of Physicians and Surgeons for the State of New-York." *New York Medical and Philosophical Journal and Review* 1 (1809): 32–48.

Smith, James McCune. "Civilization: Its Dependence on Physical Circumstances." *Anglo-African Magazine* 1 (1859): 5–17.

———. "On the Fourteenth Query of Thomas Jefferson's *Notes on Virginia*." *Anglo-African Magazine* 1 (1859): 225–38.

Smith, Richard Dean. *Melville's Complaint: Doctors and Medicine in the Art of Herman Melville*. New York: Garland, 1991.

Smith, Samuel Stanhope. *An Essay on the Causes of the Variety of Complexion and Figure in the Human Species*. 1787, 1810. Edited by Winthrop D. Jordan. Cambridge, Mass.: Belknap Press of Harvard University Press, 1965.

Smith, Valerie. *Self-Discovery and Authority in Afro-American Narrative*. Cambridge, Mass.: Harvard University Press, 1987.

Soemmerring, Samuel Thomas von. *Über die Korperliche, Verschiedenheit des Negers von Europaër*. 1784. 2d ed. Frankfurt und Mainz: Varrentrapp, Sohn und Wenner, 1785.

Spanos, William V. *The Errant Art of Moby-Dick: The Canon, the Cold War, and the Struggle for American Studies*. Durham, N.C.: Duke University Press, 1995.

Spengemann, William C. *The Adventurous Muse: The Poetics of American Fiction, 1789–1900*. New Haven, Conn.: Yale University Press, 1977.

Spillers, Hortense J. "Mama's Baby, Papa's Maybe: An American Grammar Book." *Diacritics* 17, no. 2 (Summer 1987): 65–81.

Squier, E. G. "American Ethnology: Being a Summary of Some of the Results Which Have Followed the Investigation of this Subject." *American Review: A Whig Journal* 9 (1849): 385–98.

Stafford, Barbara Maria. *Body Criticism: Imaging the Unseen in Enlightenment Art and Medicine*. Cambridge, Mass.: MIT Press, 1991.

Stanton, Elizabeth Cady. "Declaration of Sentiments and Resolutions, by the Woman's Rights Convention, July, 1848." In *We, the Other People: Alternative Declarations of Independence*, edited by Philip Foner, 77–83. Urbana: University of Illinois Press, 1976.

Stanton, William. *The Leopard's Spots: Scientific Attitudes toward Race in America 1815–59*. Chicago: University of Chicago Press, 1960.

St. Armand, Barton Levi. *Emily Dickinson and Her Culture: The Soul's Society.* New York: Cambridge University Press, 1984.

Sten, Christopher, ed. *Savage Eye: Melville and the Visual Arts.* Kent, Ohio: Kent State University Press, 1991.

Stepan, Nancy Leys. "Race and Gender: The Role of Anatomy in Science." In *Anatomy of Racism,* edited by David Theo Goldberg, 38–57. Minneapolis: University of Minnesota Press, 1990.

Stern, Madeleine B. *Heads and Headlines: The Phrenological Fowlers.* Norman: University of Oklahoma Press, 1971.

Stern, Milton R., ed. *Critical Essays on Herman Melville's "Typee."* Boston: G. K. Hall, 1982.

Stessel, H. Edward. "Melville's *White-Jacket:* A Case Against the 'Cat.'" *Clio* 13 (1983): 37–55.

Stevick, Philip. "Novel and Anatomy: Notes Toward an Amplification of Frye." *Criticism* 10 (1968): 153–65.

Stewart, Charles S. *A Visit to the South Seas, in the U.S. Ship Vincennes, during the Years 1829 and 1830; with Scenes in Brazil, Peru, Manilla, the Cape of Good Hope, and St. Helena.* 2 vols. New York: John P. Haven, 1831.

Stewart, George R. "The Two *Moby-Dicks.*" *American Literature* 25 (1954): 414–48.

Stowe, Harriet Beecher. *Uncle Tom's Cabin; or, Life among the Lowly.* 1852. In *Three Novels,* edited by Kathryn Kish Sklar, 1–519. New York: Library of America, 1982.

Strauss, W. Patrick. *Americans in Polynesia, 1783–1842.* East Lansing: Michigan State University Press, 1963.

Strauss, Walter L., ed. *The Complete Engravings, Etchings, and Drypoints of Albrecht Dürer.* New York: Dover, 1972.

Streeter, Robert E. "Association Psychology and Literary Nationalism in the *North American Review,* 1815–1825." *American Literature* 17 (1945): 243–54.

Sundquist, Eric J. *To Wake the Nations: Race in the Making of American Literature.* Cambridge, Mass.: Belknap Press of Harvard University Press, 1993.

Swann, Brian, and Arnold Krupat, eds. *Recovering the Word: Essays on Native American Literature.* Berkeley: University of California Press, 1987.

Sweet, Timothy. *Traces of War: Poetry, Photography, and the Crisis of the Union.* Baltimore: Johns Hopkins University Press, 1990.

Tew, Arnold G., and Allan Peskin. "The Disappearance of Ik. Marvel." *American Studies* 33, no. 2 (1992): 5–20.

Thompson, Ralph. *American Literary Annuals & Gift Books: 1825–1865.* New York: H. W. Wilson, 1936.

Thoreau, Henry David. *A Week on the Concord and Merrimack Rivers; Walden, or Life in the Woods; The Maine Woods; Cape Cod,* edited by Robert F. Sayre. New York: Library of America, 1985.

Tocqueville, Alexis de. *Democracy in America.* 2 vols. 1835, 1840. Edited by Phillips Bradley. New York: Vintage Books, 1945.

Todd, Janet. *Sensibility: An Introduction.* London & New York: Methuen, 1986.

Tolchin, Neal L. *Mourning, Gender, and Creativity in the Art of Herman Melville.* New Haven, Conn.: Yale University Press, 1988.

Tompkins, Jane. *Sensational Designs: The Cultural Work of American Fiction, 1790–1860.* New York: Oxford University Press, 1985.

Topinard, Paul. *Anthropology,* translated by Robert T. H. Bartley. Philadelphia: J. B. Lippincott, 1878.

Torrey, William. *Torrey's Narrative; or, the Life and Adventures of William Torrey, who for the Space of 25 Months, within the Years 1835, '36, and '37, was Held a Captive by the Cannibals of the Marquesas.* Boston: Press of A. J. Wright, 1848.

Truettner, William H., and Allan Wallach, eds. *Thomas Cole: Landscape into History.* Washington: National Museum of American Art, 1994.

Tubbee, Laah Ceil Manatoi Elaah. *A Sketch of the Life of Okah Tubbee.* 1852. Edited by Daniel F. Littlefield, Jr. Lincoln: University of Nebraska Press, 1988.

Tuckerman, Henry. *Leaves from the Diary of a Dreamer. Found Among his Papers.* London: William Pickering, 1853.

Turner, Frederick W., ed. *The Portable North American Indian Reader.* New York: Penguin, 1980.

Van Evrie, John. "Negroes and Negro Slavery; The First, an Inferior Race—The Latter, Its Normal Condition." Baltimore: J. D. Toy, 1853.

Vesalius, Andreas. *The Illustrations from the Works of Andreas Vesalius of Brussels,* edited by J. B. deC. M. Saunders and Charles D. O'Malley. 1950. Reprint. New York: Dover Publications, 1970.

Vincent, Howard P. *Melville and Hawthorne in the Berkshires.* Kent, Ohio: Kent State University Press, 1968.

———. *The Tailoring of Melville's "White-Jacket."* Evanston, Ill.: Northwestern University Press, 1970.

———. *The Trying-Out of "Moby-Dick."* Boston: Houghton-Mifflin, 1949.

Virey, Julien-Joseph. *Histoire naturelle du genre humain.* 1801. 3 vols. Paris: Crochard, 1824.

Vishniac, Roman. *A Vanished World.* New York: Farrar, Straus & Giroux, 1983.

Wald, Priscilla. *Constituting Americans: Cultural Anxiety and Narrative Form.* Durham, N.C.: Duke University Press, 1995.

———. "Hearing Narrative Voices in Melville's *Pierre.*" *Boundary 2,* vol. 17, no. 1 (1990): 100–132.

Walker, David. *Walker's Appeal, in Four Articles, together with a Preamble, to the Colored Citizens of the World, but in particular, and very expressly to those of the United States of America.* 1829. In *Walker's Appeal and Garnet's Address to the Slaves of the United States of America,* 9–88. Salem, N.H.: Ayer, 1989.

Walker, Nancy. "Wit, Sentimentality and the Image of Women in the Nineteenth Century." *American Studies* 22, no. 2 (1981): 5–22.

Wallach, Alan. "Thomas Cole: Landscape and the Course of American Empire." In *Thomas Cole: Landscape into History,* edited by William H. Truettner and Alan Wallach, 23–111. New Haven, Conn.: Yale University Press, 1994.

Walsh, Mike. "Facts for the Millions." *Subterranean,* 13 September 1845.

———. "Workingmen: Read the Reward of your Many Services and Bitter Sacrifices." *Subterranean,* 25 April 1846.

Ward, J. A. "The Function of the Cetological Chapters in *Moby-Dick." American Literature* 28 (1956): 164–83.

Wardley, Lynn. "Relic, Fetish, Femmage: The Aesthetics of Sentiment in the Work of Stowe." In *The Culture of Sentiment,* edited by Shirley Samuels, 203–220. New York: Oxford University Press, 1992.

Warner, Susan. *The Wide, Wide World.* 1850. Afterword by Jane Tompkins. New York: The Feminist Press, 1987.

Warren, Joyce W. *Fanny Fern: An Independent Woman.* New Brunswick, N.J.: Rutgers University Press, 1992.

Weaver, Raymond M. *Herman Melville: Mariner and Mystic.* New York: George H. Doran, 1921.

Webb, Frank J. *The Garies and Their Friends.* 1857. Reprint. New York: Arno Press and the *New York Times,* 1969.

Webster, Daniel. "Compromise Speech of 1850." Delivered in the United States Senate on March 7, 1850. In *Selected American Speeches on Basic Issues (1850–1950),* edited by Carl G. Brandt and Edward M. Shafter, Jr., 71–111. Boston: Houghton Mifflin, 1960.

Weinstein, Cindy. *The Literature of Labor and the Labors of Literature: Allegory in Nineteenth-Century American Fiction.* New York: Cambridge University Press, 1995.

Weis, Philip. "Herman-Neutics." *New York Times Magazine,* 15 December 1996.

Weld, Theodore Dwight, ed. *American Slavery As It Is: Testimony of a Thousand Witnesses.* 1839. Reprint. New York: Arno Press and the *New York Times,* 1969.

Wenke, John. *Melville's Muse: Literary Creation and the Forms of Philosophical Fiction.* Kent, Ohio: Kent State University Press, 1995.

White, Charles. *An Account of the Regular Gradation in Man, and in Different Animals and Vegetables; and from the Former to the Latter.* London: Printed for C. Dilly, 1799.

"White Jacket; or The World in a Man-of-War." Unsigned review in *Southern Literary Messenger* 16 (1850): 250–52.

Whitford, Kathryn. "*The Blithedale Romance:* Hawthorne's Reveries of a Bachelor." *Thoth* 15 (Winter 1974–1975): 19–28.

Whitman, Walt. *Leaves of Grass: The First (1855) Edition,* edited by Malcolm Cowley. New York: Penguin, 1976.

———. *Leaves of Grass: A Textual Variorum of the Printed Poems, Vol. 1: 1855–1856,* edited by Sculley Bradley, Harold W. Blodgett, Arthur Golden, and William White. New York: New York University Press, 1980.

———. *Leaves of Grass by Walt Whitman: Facsimile Edition of the 1860 Text,* introduction by Roy Harvey Pearce. Ithaca, N.Y.: Cornell University Press, 1961.

Whittier, John Greenleaf. "The Panorama." 1856. In *The Poetical Works of John Greenleaf Whittier,* 175–83. Boston and New York: Houghton, Mifflin and Company, 1888.

Widmer, Kingsley. *The Ways of Nihilism: A Study of Herman Melville's Short Novels*. Los Angeles: Anderson, Ritchie, & Simon, 1970.

Wiegman, Robyn. *American Anatomies: Theorizing Race and Gender*. Durham, N.C.: Duke University Press, 1995.

Wilbur, Richard. "Edgar Allan Poe." In *Major Writers of America*. 2 vols., edited by Perry Miller. Vol. 1: 369–82. New York: Harcourt, Brace & World, 1962.

Wilentz, Sean. *Chants Democratic: New York City & the Rise of the American Working Class, 1788–1850*. New York: Oxford University Press, 1984.

Williams, Raymond. *The Country and the City*. New York: Oxford University Press, 1973.

———. *Keywords: A Vocabulary of Culture and Society*. Rev. ed. New York: Oxford University Press, 1985.

———. *Marxism and Literature*. New York: Oxford University Press, 1977.

Williams, Roger. *A Key into the Language of America*. 1643. Edited by John J. Teunissen and Evelyn J. Hinz. Detroit: Wayne State University Press, 1973.

Williams, William Carlos. *In the American Grain*. New York: New Directions, 1956.

Willis, Nathaniel Parker. *American Scenery; or Land, Lake, and River: Illustrations of Transatlantic Nature*. 2 vols. 1840. Reprint. 2 vols. in 1. Barre, Mass.: Imprint Society, 1971.

———. *Hurrygraphs*. Auburn: N.Y.: Alden, Beardsley, 1853.

———. *Pencillings by the Way*. 3 vols. London: John Macrone, 1835.

Withey, Lynne. *Voyages of Discovery: Captain Cook and the Exploration of the Pacific*. New York: William Morrow, 1987.

Wolf, Bryan Jay. *Romantic Re-Vision: Culture and Consciousness in Nineteenth-Century American Painting*. Chicago: University of Chicago Press, 1982.

Wölfflin, Heinrich, ed. *Drawings of Albrecht Dürer*. 10th ed., 1923. Reprint, translated by Stanley Applebaum. New York: Dover, 1970.

Yannella, Donald. "Writing the 'Other Way': Melville, The Duyckinck Crowd, and Literature for the Masses." In *A Companion To Melville Studies*, edited by John Bryant, 63–81. New York: Greenwood Press, 1986.

Yarborough, Richard. "Race, Violence, and Manhood: The Masculine Ideal in Frederick Douglass's 'The Heroic Slave.'" In *Frederick Douglass: New Literary and Historical Essays*, edited by Eric Sundquist, 166–88. New York: Cambridge University Press, 1990.

Yellin, Jean Fagan. *Women and Sisters: The Antislavery Feminists in American Culture*. New Haven, Conn.: Yale University Press, 1989.

Young, Robert J. C. *Colonial Desire: Hybridity in Theory, Culture and Race*. London and New York: Routledge, 1995.

Ziff, Larzer. *Literary Democracy: The Declaration of Cultural Independence in America*. New York: Viking Press, 1981.

Zirker, Patricia Allen. "Evidence of the Slavery Dilemma in *White-Jacket*." *American Quarterly* 18 (1966): 477–92.

Zoellner, Robert. *The Salt-Sea Mastodon: A Reading of Moby-Dick*. Berkeley: University of California Press, 1973.

Index

Compositor: G&S Typesetters, Inc.
Text: 10/13 Sabon
Display: Sabon
Printer and Binder: Haddon Craftsmen, Inc.